British Shipping and World Competition

British Shipping
and World Competition

BY

S. G. STURMEY

UNIVERSITY OF LONDON
THE ATHLONE PRESS
1962

Published by
THE ATHLONE PRESS
UNIVERSITY OF LONDON
at 2 Gower Street, London WC1
Distributed by Constable & Co. Ltd
12 Orange Street, London WC2

U.S.A.
Oxford University Press Inc
New York

© *S. G. Sturmey*, 1962

Printed in Great Britain by
WESTERN PRINTING SERVICES LTD
BRISTOL

Preface

THE main object of this book is set out in the first sentence of Chapter I. That difficulties would be met in realizing this objective is obvious and it is not surprising that, with an industry so secretive as shipping, realization has been incomplete. In particular, the absence of positive information bearing on the problems considered has often meant that direct assessment has been impossible and a comparative study has had to be made.

During the period covered by this book the industry published three statements of its problems, the first in 1917, the second in 1939 and the third in 1960. Despite this documentation, a further study was necessary for several reasons. First, the 1917 and 1939 reports are not available publicly. Second, the reports are descriptive rather than analytic in content. Third, the reports group important and unimportant factors without discrimination and there are a number of notable omissions. Fourth, there is no hint of self-examination by the industry in the reports. Fifth, the recommendations for action in the reports are recommendations to people outside the industry, not plans for self-help; this follows naturally from the absence of self-criticism.

In the text it will often be found that, in addition to explaining the past, I have offered suggestions for the future and tried, generally, to suggest courses of action by which the industry could secure its position for that future. I hope that those shipowners who feel aggrieved at the critical nature of the work will take the time seriously to consider the many positive proposals which are scattered through the ensuing pages.

In writing this book I have incurred very many debts to people and organizations in America, Britain, Ireland, Italy, the Netherlands, New Zealand and Norway. To all who helped me so generously I am deeply grateful. I owe a considerable debt to the Trustees of the Houblon-Norman Fund for providing the financial support which enabled the work to be undertaken. My greatest debt of all is to Basil Mogridge who for two

v

Preface

years laboured patiently collecting material. He proved a hard-working and highly intelligent colleague, a source of inspiration and enthusiasm and a delightful companion. Apart from his invisible contribution, Mr. Mogridge, at my request, took the whole responsibility for the difficult chapter on labour relations and costs, a subject in which he has a particular interest and competence. Professor G. C. Allen and Mr. Mogridge have both read the entire draft and the book has profited greatly from their comments. I am indebted also to Mrs. B. M. Abel for help with proof reading, and to Mr. Mogridge for compiling the index.

The responsibility for errors, whether of fact or interpretation, is wholly mine.

S.G.S.

University College, London
September 1961

vi

Contents

Figures and Tables

FIGURES

TABLES

Figures and Tables

Figures and Tables

The Problem Defined

THE primary object of this book is to answer a single question, namely, why has the tonnage of ships registered[1] in the United Kingdom declined from over 45 per cent of the world total in 1900 to about 16 per cent of that total in 1960? This period has been chosen and only incidental attention paid to the nineteenth century because it was after 1900 that international competition to British[2] shipping as a whole became more important than competition within British shipping. There is no fixed date at which this change occurred and in some trades —for example, the North Atlantic—competition was international after about 1870; in fact, German competition for mail tenders was the immediate cause of reductions in trans-Atlantic postage rates in the third quarter of the nineteenth century. It is, nevertheless, true to say that from about 1850 until the early years of the twentieth century British shipping faced comparatively little international competition whereas in subsequent years such competition grew in intensity. The question posed above is, therefore, concerned with the nature of the competitive challenge and the response elicited from the British industry;

[1] The criterion of registration rather than ownership is used as it is always clearly definable. To use the criterion of ownership leads to numerous difficulties. Shipping companies resident in the United Kingdom own ships registered in other countries; companies registered in other countries, for example, Bermuda, own ships registered in Britain. Companies resident in Britain may be owned by foreign interests and register their ships in the United Kingdom or in other countries. Wherever the ships are actually owned, the country of registration determines the flag they fly, the rules to which they have to conform, the wage rates paid and the manning scales adopted, and the use of the ships in time of war or other emergency.

[2] 'British' is used here as synonymous with 'United Kingdom'. It is usual in shipping statistics to include in the term 'British' ships which are registered in British countries outside the United Kingdom. This usage is not followed here and the term 'Commonwealth' will be used to denote British shipping outside the United Kingdom. Commonwealth shipping registered outside the United Kingdom is included with non-British shipping unless specifically stated.

the statistical consequence of this process of challenge and response is the relative decline noted.

There are four possible answers to the question posed in the preceding paragraph. First, the answer might be found in changes in the underlying competitive situation arising from changes in the economic factors affecting the operation of shipping. Second, interferences with the competitive process might have caused the relative decline; that is, even if Britain possessed economic advantages in the provision of shipping services, state action in other countries might have prevented these advantages from being effective. Third, the answer might be seen to lie in random factors, such as wars with subsequent repercussions, trade changes, or government policies other than those directed specifically to assisting shipping. Fourth, the answer might be found in the reactions of the British shipping industry as a whole to changing circumstances; that is, there might have been internal constraints on growth which were sufficient to produce the situation outlined in the question.

The four approaches to an answer to the question are quite distinct. It is not possible, however, to divide the book neatly into four independent sections each concerned with one possible answer, partly because of the nature of, and limitations on, the available information, partly because considerable repetition of material and arguments would be required if the four approaches were handled separately.

Although the primary object of the book is to answer a single question by looking at the past, there is a secondary objective, namely, to look into the future and assess the prospects of the industry. This secondary objective scarcely influences the historical discussion of Chapters II–IX, but becomes important in the later chapters. In consequence the theoretical argument of Chapters X and XI, which is chiefly intended to reinforce the weak statistical evidence on wage costs, is taken much further than is necessary for that purpose, in order to show the types of ships in the operation of which the British industry is most likely to succeed in the future. The two themes, the past and the future, will also be present in the chapters on conferences and the structure of the industry.

In Chapter XV the threads are unravelled. The four possible

answers will be considered and, in the light of the material presented, an assessment made of the extent to which each can be regarded as, in fact, answering the question. In this way the past will be served and the primary objective achieved. Then in an Epilogue the material relevant to the secondary objective will be used to consider the future prospects of the industry.

The historical chapters are not history in the sense of telling a whole story and only those aspects which bear upon the main theme and seem to have a part in answering the question being asked or in putting relevant material into context are considered. Many of the things left out are important in themselves but their inclusion would both have clouded the picture and increased unduly the size of the book. The same selection of topics has had to be made in the economic chapters, although there both themes are handled together and the chapters lack the singleness of purpose of the earlier chapters. The question of how much material is needed in each chapter to provide context and perspective is a difficult one and there can be no certainty that the right decisions have always been taken on this question; indeed, there is probably no 'right' decision, no selection which will meet the needs of all readers.

On the other hand, not all the material which is relevant has been included. First, shipping is not an industry which enjoys scrutiny and, having its own answers to the disparity between the growth rates of British and world shipping, has been loth to lift, for an outsider, the traditional veil of secrecy which shrouds so many of its operations. Second, much information is simply not available at all as it has never been collected and cannot now be collected. This is particularly apparent in the case of labour costs upon which little reliable material has ever been published, nothing further is available in the way of unpublished data, either processed or in a crude state, and facilities do not exist to enable an outside research worker to collect such data.

The gaps which exist in the available information have meant that conclusions not supportable by empirical evidence have had to be drawn from theoretical arguments. The alternative would have been to ignore all aspects of the subject on which proper information was not obtainable; that is, in effect, to have abandoned the book.

Before studying the events of this sixty-year period as they have affected British shipping, some statistics relating to the period may be examined.

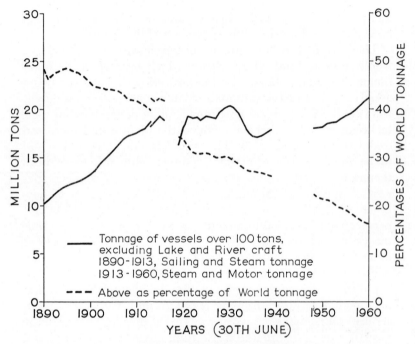

Fig. 1. British shipping tonnage, 1890–1960
Note: U.S. Reserve Fleet included in world total, 1948–60
Source: Lloyd's Register of Shipping

In Figure 1 two lines are shown. One relates to the tonnage of British shipping over the period 1890 to 1960 and shows a rapid growth from just over 10 million tons in 1890 to nearly 18 million tons in 1910, followed by a much smaller growth to a fleet of 21 million tons in 1960. The second line in the figure shows the British-owned tonnage as percentages of world tonnage over the same period. This line shows that even during the period between 1890 and 1910 when the growth of British tonnage was rapid, the share of world tonnage which was British-owned was declining. Since 1910 the fall in the percentage has been

4

continuous and large, from nearly 42 per cent in 1910 to just over 16 per cent in 1960.

It is not enough simply to compare British growth performances with those of the world, as is implicit in Figure 1. The world is not a unified whole but a collection of nations, the shipping of each of which has faced different problems and produced different reactions. In Figure 2, therefore, the tonnages under the flags of the leading maritime countries are shown for the years since 1890. The lines are drawn with a logarithmic vertical scale because it is rates of change, not absolute changes which are important. Further, observations are plotted only at approximately ten year intervals, or at turning points, in order to smooth out minor fluctuations. The figure is presented in two parts for the sake of clarity; the decision to put any country into the lower or the upper section of the figure was taken on purely arbitrary grounds, namely, the desire to reduce congestion in the middle of the figure caused by the number of nations with similarly sized fleets which have grown at about the same rates. Figure 2 shows the American fleet as larger than the British fleet since 1945. This result is achieved only by including the U.S. Reserve Fleet in the figures and when these ships are excluded, which yields the lower American line, the British fleet is shown as remaining, but by a relatively narrow margin, the largest in the world. That the margin has narrowed is no more than is indicated by the percentage figures graphed in Figure 1.

The lines in Figure 2 enable the different character of the growth in different countries to be seen. While the world tonnage has increased in a fairly regular fashion over the whole period, this overall regularity has been obtained by a combination of highly erratic movements in the tonnage of individual countries. Reasonably regular growth curves, such as those of Britain, Norway and the Netherlands can be seen, each displaying a different growth rate but, significantly, each being the curve of a country in which shipping has never been consistently or substantially assisted by the state in the period under consideration. There are countries displaying very rapid growth over limited periods, Japan between 1890 and 1930, Panama since 1930 and, most spectacular of all, Liberia since 1949.

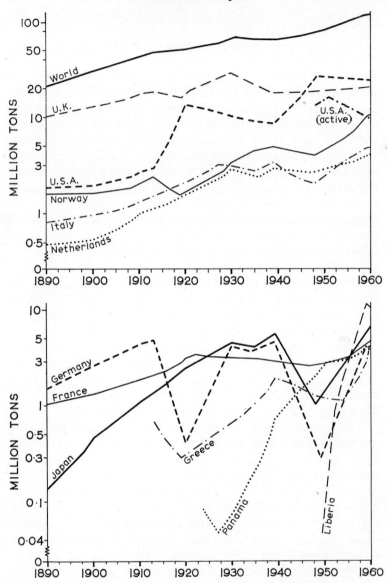

FIG. 2. Tonnages of some important fleets, 1890–1960
Note: U.S. figures include Reserve Fleet
German figures: West Germany only after 1945

There are very jerky patterns, such as that of Germany caused by the loss of her shipping in each of the two world wars, and that of Greece. These different growth achievements have a relevance to the British experience, both through the direct impact which they have had in shaping the competitive conditions in world shipping and through the lessons, if any, which may be learned from the divergent patterns. Within the compass of one book it is not possible to present a detailed picture of the growth experience in each country. However, references will be made throughout the work to these other countries, with closer attention to the Norwegian growth attainment. As can be seen from Figure 2, the Norwegian growth has been very different from that of Britain but, as will be shown, the conditions under which the fleets of the two countries have operated throughout the period have been roughly similar. The combination of similar conditions but divergent experiences in the two countries is of the utmost importance for the explanation of the slow growth of British shipping. Where it is impossible because of a lack of proper information to assess in quantitative terms the effects of any occurrence on the growth of British shipping, it is often possible to determine whether Norwegian shipping was also affected by that occurrence and then, by a comparison between the growths of the two fleets, to see whether a significant rôle in explaining the slow British growth can be attributed to that event.

In Figure 1 it was implicitly assumed that the world outside Britain is homogeneous so far as shipping is concerned. In Figure 2 this fiction was removed and the differing growth experiences of a number of countries were shown. An equally fictitious implicit assumption remains, namely, that ships are homogeneous. For convenience this assumption is retained for much of the work and ships will be considered as an aggregate of identical tons for so long as such a course is possible. The assumption of homogeneity will never be completely dropped, nor the full complexity of a fleet of ships of differing sizes, ages speeds, designs and cost per ton considered. The most that will be done is to relax the assumption sufficiently to recognize classes such as liners, tramps and tankers, or motor ships and steam ships, while the consequences of the higher value per ton

7

of the British liner fleet than of foreign tanker and tramp fleets will also be considered.

Before proceeding, this is a convenient point at which to explain some points of usage and content.

The tonnage figures used throughout the book are gross registered tons, except where otherwise stated. Gross tonnage is a space measurement, one gross ton being equal to 100 cubic feet of permanently enclosed space. There are slight differences in national conventions concerning the definition of permanently enclosed space, but these are of no concern here. The gross ton relates neither to the weight nor to the earning capacity of a ship. Weight is irrelevant here, displacement tonnage being used only for measuring naval combatant vessels. For earning capacity two measures are available, namely, net tonnage and deadweight tonnage. Net tonnage is gross tonnage minus the cubic capacity of non-earning spaces and is a measure of the volume of space available for earning. This measure is customarily employed in calculating the liability of ships to canal and port dues and in compiling statistics of entrances and clearances of ships at ports. Deadweight tonnage is the actual weight in tons of cargo and fuel that a ship can carry when down to her load line, and is generally used in describing tankers and other bulk carriers. It is appropriate for the measurement of such ships, but not for passenger and cargo liners. There is no direct relation between deadweight and gross tonnage and so no way of accurately converting one into the other although this can be done roughly by treating 1,000 gross tons as equivalent to between 1,500 and 1,600 deadweight tons. However, the gross tonnages of ships described in deadweight tons are usually available and in all aggregate figure gross tons will be used.

The restricted meaning given to the word 'British' in this work has already been discussed. British shipping, as defined here, includes ships engaged in a multitude of different trades and covers ships ranging from excursion steamers to Atlantic liners. There is an important division within this range, namely, that between ocean-going ships and coastal and short-sea ships. The study here is only of ocean shipping. The shipping engaged in coastal trades, trading between Britain and the Brest–Elbe range of Continental ports, the Irish Sea trade, fishing and so on faces completely different problems and is best regarded as separate industries. It is not possible, however, always to eliminate such shipping from tonnage statistics; first, the larger short-sea traders are often bigger than the smallest ocean-going ships and, second, the position of the most acceptable dividing line in terms of tonnage has changed over time.

There is, perhaps, a need to comment here on the reasons for omitting any specific discussions of either shipbuilding or ports from this work.

Before the 1914–18 war, the technical lead in ship construction possessed by Britain was a factor assisting shipping and in part accounted for British supremacy as a shipowning nation. However, the shipbuilding industry built ships also for foreign account and the advantage enjoyed by British shipowners from the presence in Britain of an up-to-date shipbuilding industry was initial, not incremental. Since that period, the British shipbuilding industry has been largely surpassed by industries in other countries and except perhaps in the construction of large passenger liners is no longer pre-eminent. If shipowners were tied to building ships in their own countries, the states of the shipbuilding industries in these countries would be important factors accounting for differences in growth rates. This is not the case, however, and at most times shipowners in all countries have had either the freedom to build where they wished or compensation, in the form of construction subsidies, if forced to build at home. Given that British shipowners could build wherever they wished,[1] the failure of the British shipbuilding industry to retain its leadership is not an important factor in explaining the slow growth of British shipping. To argue, as was being argued in the later 1930s, that an important reason for the failure of shipowners in Britain to establish tanker fleets was that British-built tankers cost 15 per cent more than Continental-built tankers was to miss the point completely.

The position is a little more complicated when shipowning and building are parts of an integrated concern under a single ownership. The shipowner may then be torn between damaging

---

[1] The only period of significant length in peace time when British shipowners did not have freedom to contract abroad was from 1945 until about 1951; the restrictions are fully discussed in Chapter VII.

his shipping interests by preserving his building enterprise, or risking the loss of the capital invested in his building enterprise by building outside his own companies. This is a classic weakness of the integrated organization. However, in times of boom the integrated shipping company can presumably get delivery of ships more quickly than the company which must wait in the queues of independent builders and can also avoid the inflation of prices of vessels which occurs when order books are full and delivery dates long. At all times, a go-ahead shipowner associated with a shipbuilding yard, or a go-ahead shipbuilding yard associated with a shipowner can lead to greater progress than would be obtained in a situation where no integration existed; the association between the White Star Line and Harland and Wolff in the years before 1914, and that between the lines of the Kylsant group and the same builder in the construction of a fleet of diesel-engined passenger liners after 1928 are excellent examples. Taking the advantages of integration and the extent of integration into account, it is unlikely that any net adverse effect on the progress of shipping arising from ties between builders and owners can have been large.

There is no discussion in the book of the relative efficiencies of British and other ports. If British ports are old-fashioned and inconvenient, if restrictive practices are common, industrial relations poor and costs high, these factors affect all ships using those ports. Their result would be a diversion of trade from British to other ports wherever possible, a tendency for overseas buyers to purchase from other countries than Britain and for overseas sellers to try to sell in markets in which a smaller part of the total sales proceeds are absorbed in port charges.[1] The effect of these things would be a relative decline in British direct trades and an absolute decline in British entrepôt trades. This would be to the disadvantage of ships serving British trades and to the advantage of those serving other trades. As British shipping grew up largely by serving British trades, the effect of changes in those trades on national shipping is obvious; however, British shipping has always had the freedom to engage

---

[1] This assumes that sellers are price takers, not price makers, when trading in overseas markets. Otherwise the higher port charges would simply be reflected in higher prices.

in non-British trades and hence, if minded towards expansion, to escape any limitations imposed on trade by the condition of British ports. The effect, if any, of British port facilities on the growth of British trade is only one factor among many accounting for changes in the British trading position. Although port facilities may seem to be more intimately related to shipping than, say, general tariff policies or the attitude of British exporters, so far as the growth of shipping is concerned all factors which affect trade are the same. There is, therefore, no reason to single out any one for special mention; either a full analysis of the whole position must be made or the data about British trade must be taken as given. As the interest is in the effects on shipping of changes in trade data, however caused, it seems inappropriate to study the reasons why those data changed.

II

High Water: the pre-1914 Period

CONDITIONS OF SUPREMACY

BRITISH-OWNED shipping dominated the ports and sea-lanes of the world in the years immediately prior to the first world war, the supremacy being based on four factors:

(a) *Colonies*

First and foremost was the British colonial trading policy. The Empire constituted a trading area from which Britain drew imports of raw materials and food and to which she supplied manufactured goods and emigrants. This provided the opportunities for the employment of a shipping fleet, opportunities which, in the days before cables and radio, were more easily grasped by British than by foreign shipowners. The Navigation Acts which, from the close of the sixteenth century to 1849, kept the intra-imperial trade in the hands of British ships and trades from foreign countries in the hands of either British ships or ships of the country of origin of the goods concerned, led to '. . . the early diversion of British shipping to the ocean trades' which '. . . was an important contributory cause to its great expansion after the Napoleonic wars'.[1] Colonial development also affected Britain's ability to build marine steam-engines, the original engine builders being largely the companies which had gained their know-how in producing machinery for crushing sugar-cane in the West Indies.

(b) *Industrialization*

Second, the course of industrialization in Britain provided the developments and knowledge in engineering and metal using which enabled Britain to build iron steamships. During the

[1] *Report of Departmental Committee on Shipping and Shipbuilding*, Cd. 9092, 1918, Final Report, para. 120, p. 71.

earlier part of the nineteenth century, the American merchant fleet, built cheaply from soft woods, was rising in importance. It threatened to eclipse the British fleet built chiefly of hard woods, the indigenous supplies of which were approaching exhaustion. The limitations imposed on the size of ships by the relatively low strength of wood gave an advantage to iron and later steel ships and to the country which could produce those metals. Further, the economic superiority of steamships on an increasing number of trade routes as marine engines were developed enabled Britain to consolidate her lead in world shipbuilding and, as the bulk of the world trade was British trade, in world ship owning also. Industrialization in Britain had led to the extensive development of coalfields and coal provided a high quality indigenous fuel for British steamships and an outward bulk cargo for ships dispatched to bring home food and raw materials. In some respects, coal was the key to the whole situation while the coal trade was an essential element in the economy of the running of tramp ships. The importance of coal will be discussed separately later in this chapter; for the present it is only necessary to note its significance as an aspect of industrialization.

(c) *Population growth*

The third factor was population growth. The population of Britain doubled between 1801 and 1851 and almost doubled again between 1851 and 1901, despite extensive emigration, particularly during the latter period. This population growth outstripped the food producing capacity of Britain and so led to a demand for food imports, provided largely by emigrants from Britain. The food imports were paid for by exports of industrial products and, later in the century, of coal. The emigration, the imports of food and the exports of manufactured goods all provided employment for shipping, and chiefly for British shipping.

The rapidly increasing population also provided for British ships an abundant supply of labour. Wages were low, due to the absence of effective trade union organization among British seamen and the availability of foreign labour which was prepared to accept low wages and the generally poor standard of food and accommodation on ships. Without recourse to cheap foreign and coloured labour, the competitive advantages of the British merchant fleet would have been less due to the necessity to pay wages sufficient to attract all-British crews or, at ruling wage rates, its expansion would have been hindered by labour shortages. In the early twentieth century, as countries such as Norway and Greece began to build up their own shipping fleets on the economic basis of cheap labour, the supplies of foreign labour to British ships were reduced and conditions at sea had to be improved to attract more British labour to the industry. In 1903 Asiatics and foreigners made up about one-third of the labour supply to British ships, but by 1913 this proportion had fallen to one-quarter of a larger total. By 1914, some of the wage rate advantage had been lost, and rising wages became a limiting factor in the expansion of the British merchant fleet although this could be, and was, largely compensated by the operation of ships with lower labour costs per ton than those of rivals paying lower wages. The disadvantage was greatest in the employment of sailing ships and of very slow tramps. In the absence of overall agreed wage rates in the industry, however, the position was different in every port, and owners in Liverpool, which attracted Irish labour, the North-East Coast ports, which attracted Scandinavian labour, and, to a lesser extent, London, were able to continue operating sailing vessels after owners in other ports found them unprofitable.

(d) *Establishment Advantages*

The development and maintenance of liner trades requires an extensive shore organization which, once set up, confers an advantage on the established shipowner which a newcomer has to overcome before he can compete economically. Further, port facilities were frequently privately owned and liner companies established their own wharves and other necessary amenities at ports on their trading routes. The development of rival services was then hindered because the vessels did not enjoy access to existing facilities. Both liners and tramps gain advantages from ready access to ship-repairing facilities in their home ports and from adequate supplies of ships' stores. Initially, of course, these advantages had not been possessed by British ships, but as the leading owner of steamships Britain, during the nineteenth century, had acquired advantages which new competitors did not enjoy. The existence of these advantages was a contributory factor to the maintenance of British domination in liner services.

EXTENT OF SUPREMACY

The extent of the British supremacy can be shown by the statistics relating to the period.

In 1850, the sea-going fleet of the world consisted mainly of sailing ships. Of 6·9 million tons of sailing ships, 3·4 million tons were owned in Britain and 1·5 million tons were owned in the United States. France, with 0·7 million tons, was the only other ocean shipowner of any significance. Of the 250,808 tons of steam tonnage, 168,474 tons were owned in Britain, showing clearly the British lead in steam tonnage. Using the ratio of one ton of steam shipping as being equivalent to four tons of sailing shipping,[1] in 1850 Britain owned 52 per cent of the world steam equivalent sea-going tonnage, while the United States owned 22 per cent. By 1890, the world fleet had risen to 10·2 million tons of sailing ships and 8·6 million tons of steamships, 11·1 million tons of steam equivalent, of which Britain owned almost exactly 50 per cent, while the share of the United States had fallen to under 4 per cent.

The fall in the British proportion between 1850 and 1890 is statistical rather than real and arises from the conversion factor used to reduce sailing tonnage to a steam equivalent. In the early years of the steamship the high percentage of the dead-weight capacity required for bunkers meant that one gross ton of steam tonnage was hardly more effective than one gross ton of sailing tonnage; as steamships improved a more favourable conversion ratio became applicable. This is seen, for example, in the fact that ocean steamship services required subsidies to compete with sailing ships in the earliest years, whereas by 1890 only low-wage countries without indigenous coal supplies or

[1] This is the conversion factor used in *Progress in Merchant Shipping in the United Kingdom and Principal Maritime Countries*, Cd. 6180, 1912, from which source the figures are drawn. The Chamber of Shipping and the Liverpool Steamship Owners' Association in a report in 1917 suggested that a conversion factor of 3·1 was appropriate for converting sailing tonnage to steam equivalent.

countries giving navigation bounties were increasing their sailing fleets. Norway, for example, which owned only 5 per cent of the world steam equivalent tonnage owned the second largest sailing fleet in the world.

During the period between 1890 and 1910 the decline in the British share of steam equivalent tonnage was from 50 per cent to 46 per cent. This relative decline was brought about mainly by the very rapid growth in the fleets of three countries which had become major shipowners, and did not represent a failure of British shipping to maintain its growth in the face of a growing world fleet in general. In terms of effective carrying capacity, it is doubtful if the British share had fallen at all as the British fleet was qualitatively superior to that of the remainder of the world.

The steam equivalent tonnage of the world increased from 11·1 million tons in 1890 to 23·4 million tons in 1910, an increase of 109 per cent. In the same period the three fastest growers among the significant sea-faring nations of the world had overall growth rates as follows:

Germany	180 per cent
Japan	1,161 ,, ,,
Netherlands	168 ,, ,,

The Japanese growth, which started from a very low absolute level in 1890, lifted the country to the position of third maritime nation in 1910. Although the fleets of most other nations also expanded in this period, it is principally to the experiences of Germany and Japan that one must look to explain the slight relative decline in the British share of world tonnage in the period. The important feature of this pre-1910 experience is that the growth in the world fleet was largely, but not entirely, in response to increasing trading opportunities in the world and hardly at all at the expense of actual or potential British growth.

The increase in the German fleet which started in about 1870 occurred alongside increases in German industrialization and foreign trade and the expansion of German dominion into overseas areas. It was aided by the German emigration and trading policies, particularly in the North Atlantic and South American trades.

High Water: the pre-1914 Period

In the nineteenth century and early twentieth century, the migrant trade between Europe and America provided a solid basis for the North Atlantic liner services. In the period 1865–1894 Britain was the greatest source of emigrants to the United States, with an annual average of 119,000 persons,[1] closely rivalled by Germany with 107,000 persons per annum on average over the period. The emigration from Germany was the most important single factor leading Germany to enter the North Atlantic liner trades. After 1895, however, the pattern of emigration changed, with Russia, Austria-Hungary and Italy becoming important. Emigration from Russia averaged 138,000 persons per annum between 1895 and 1914. To reach the Western sea-board these migrants normally crossed Germany and had to pass through cholera-control stations along the Russo-German frontier.[2] These control stations were placed under the management of the leading German shipping companies and were used to secure the traffic to those lines. Even after the cholera epidemic had ended, the control stations were continued and new ones were started. The advantage which German passenger shipping gained from this arrangement was considerable. The Germans did not have it all their own way, however, and in 1906 a Russian line was established in co-operation with the Danish East Asiatic line to take advantage of the opportunities offered by the migrant trades from the Baltic to America.

In the South American trades the German success was an excellent example of the commercial policy of Germany, under which '. . . its commerce and shipping have been so effectively co-ordinated that each contributes directly to the development of the other'.[3] After the South American states had achieved independence, British and Hamburg merchants were prominent in commercial relations with South America and both established business houses in South American ports. The Hamburg business men concerned felt the need for a direct shipping link between South America and continental Europe, in order to

[1] Figures of migration from U.S. Department of Immigration.
[2] See later in this chapter for a further discussion of the control stations.
[3] J. Russell Smith, *Influence of the Great War upon Shipping* (New York, 1919), p. 135.

avoid the trans-shipment of goods in Britain. To secure this, eleven of the most prominent men of the city of Hamburg joined together and established the Hamburg-South America Line in 1871. The direct link between the commercial undertakings and the shipping services thus established was an important factor in securing the success of the venture.

German shipping enjoyed several advantages. First, the German trade through Rotterdam and Antwerp, in which British shipping had largely participated, was diverted to German ports by the grant of concessional railway rates if the ocean part of the carriage occurred in German ships.[1] Second, much of the entrepôt trade through the United Kingdom for Europe went to German ships which could offer direct shipment. Third, German shipowners established an intelligence service which enabled them to discover the identity of consignees of goods shipped in British ships, who could then be canvassed to use German tonnage. Fourth, German lines secured entry to conferences and found the British lines willing to negotiate agreements to allocate territories, the British lines generally agreeing not to expand their services to Continental ports and, in some cases, to abandon calls at such ports altogether in return for a German agreement not to compete in trades to British ports. In this way British liners were excluded from increased participation in the growing trade of Continental ports. Although there is much to criticize in the German trading methods and the support which the Government gave shipping in its fight with the established British lines, it must not be overlooked that in '. . . many respects the severity of that competition was due to the organizing activity of the German steamship companies, to the energy with which they conducted their business, to pains taken in matters of detail. . . .'[2]

Emigration was also a factor influencing the growth of the Italian merchant fleet. The main stream of migration to America from Italy was in the period 1895–1914 when an average of 157,000 persons a year were carried, while in addition there was substantial emigration to South America. Immigration into Argentina and Brazil rose from 109,000 in 1903 to 503,000 in 1912. In the latter year 278,000 of the emigrants were

[1] Cd. 9092, para. 191, p. 86.   [2] Ibid., para. 199, p. 88.

Iberian and 113,000 Italian. The Italian merchant marine received preferences in the carriage of Italian emigrants; the merchant marines of Spain and Portugal were hardly adequate for handling the traffic from Iberia and the Italians were favourably placed to compete for the trade.

The other country with a high growth rate in the period 1890–1910 was Japan. The causes of this growth are to be found in the emergence of Japan as an industrial nation in this period and the willingness of the Japanese to employ skilled European personnel both in shore industries and on board ship. The industrialization was built on a substantial export trade, particularly the new silk trade to the United States and trades to other Eastern countries in which low-priced Japanese goods opened up markets from which British goods had been excluded on price grounds. There was also a significant volume of emigration from the Far East to America in which Japanese shipping was able to participate. The ease with which Japanese lines built up trade in the Pacific and the Far East was partly due to the comparative neglect of the existing opportunities by British lines. American lines were important in the area and remained economically viable until 1915 by the use of Asiatic[1] rather than American labour, but the position did not favour the Americans when they came into competition with ships entirely manned and built by Asiatics.

Japanese shipping enjoyed building and navigation subsidies under a policy dating from 1888. Strictly, such subsidies were unnecessary as Japanese shipping was profitable practically from the start. The subsidies did serve two purposes, however. First, they encouraged shipowners to enter trades where the expectation of profits, whatever the realized profits, were insufficient to justify unsubsidized entry. Second, they added to the resources of ploughed-back profits available to the companies for expansion. In the ten year period 1900 to 1909 inclusive, the net earnings of the leading Japanese shipping companies amounted to 114 million yen, of which 63 million yen were derived from subsidies.[2]

---

[1] The La Follette Act, 1915, which prohibited the employment of Asiatic seamen in American ships would have killed what remained of American ocean shipping immediately had it not been for the high freight rates ruling during the war years.

[2] Jesse E. Saugstad, *Shipping and Shipbuilding Subsidies*, U.S. Department of Commerce (1932), p. 326.

The shipping policy which provided these subsidies must be considered alongside the nature of the Japanese industrialization under which manufacturing, merchanting, banking and shipping facilities were provided by vertically integrated organizations so that without any policy of flag preference or discrimination, exports and imports travelled largely in Japanese ships, while the same ships were able to compete in the market for cargo to fill the space not required by their owners.

WORLD TRADE AND BRITISH SHIPPING

The volume of international sea-borne trade is the most important single factor determining the employment of the world's mercantile marine. Apart from changes in the time taken to complete voyages, the expansion of the world's shipping fleet is ultimately dependent upon the expansion of world trade. The shipping fleet of any one country can expand at a faster rate than the world fleet if that country is able to secure a proportionate share in the faster-growing trades of the world, or if it is able to increase its share in the other trades. On the other hand, the growth of a shipping fleet will be less rapid than that of the world fleet if that fleet is heavily dependent on slower-growing trades or if it fails to secure a share of the faster-growing trades.

It has already been shown that in the quarter century before 1914, British-owned tonnage increased less rapidly than the total of world tonnage. An examination of changes in the composition of world trade in the period will throw some light upon this.

Between 1904 and 1912 world-commodity trade increased by 66 per cent in value terms; the trade of the United Kingdom increased by 46 per cent and that of the remainder of the world increased by 70 per cent. The increase in British trade was an increase in sea-borne trade, whereas part of the increase in non-British trade was land-borne which is of no concern here. The total of world international trade unconnected with Britain was £2,876 million[1] in 1912, made up of £1,976 million sea-borne

---

[1] Figures from *Report of the Committee appointed to advise as to the Measures Requisite for the Maintenance of the British Mercantile Marine,* Chamber of Shipping and Liverpool Steamship Owners' Association, 1917.

trade and £900 million land-borne trade. If it is assumed that these proportions apply in 1904 also, the following result is obtained:

	1904 £m.	1912 £m.
United Kingdom trade	922	1,344
Non-British trade		
Sea-borne	1,115	1,976
Land-borne	500	900
Total international trade	£2,537	£4,220

On this basis, the total sea-borne trade of the world rose from £2,037 million in 1904, of which the British share was 45 per cent, to £3,320 million in 1912 of which the British share was 40 per cent. The increase in total sea-borne trade in value terms is, then, 63 per cent, and in British trade 46 per cent. In value terms, therefore, it is clear that in so far as British shipping was dependent on British trade for its employment, the slower growth of that trade in the period 1904–12 limited the opportunities for expansion open to British shipping.

So far as the employment of shipping is concerned, however, it is trade volume, not trade value, which is important. It is not possible to calculate accurately the total weight of goods moving in the international sea-borne trade of the world in the pre-war years, although a rough calculation suggests a figure of 300 million tons,[1] for 1912. Of this total, about 155 million tons, or about 50 per cent, was British trade made up of imports 58 million tons, exports of coal 77 million tons, and other exports 20 million tons. The volume of trade and the proportion of that trade which was British cannot be calculated for any earlier years. It is clear, however, that both world trade and British trade were considerably larger in 1912 than in 1904. The fall of the British share of trade in value terms between 1904 and 1912 was from 45 per cent to 40 per cent, a fall of 11 per cent of the 1904 share; in volume terms the fall in the British share was probably somewhat smaller because it was the low value, rather than the high value, British trades which increased most in the period. It is clear, however, that the slower growth of British

[1] In Cd. 9092, Third Report, a figure of 250–300 million tons is suggested.

trade than of world trade in general meant that British shipping had to venture to an increasing extent into non-British trades if it was to expand at a rate no lower than that of world shipping.

The share of British shipping in the world was greater than the share of British trade, and in 1912 British ships carried about 52 per cent by value of world trade. They carried 94 per cent of the trade between the United Kingdom and Empire countries, 63 per cent of British trade with foreign countries, and about 30 per cent of the foreign to foreign trades of the world. Of the British fleet, some three-fifths only was employed in British and Empire trades, the balance being employed in indirect trades.[1] The distribution according to trades was 18 per cent in the European and Mediterranean trades and 82 per cent in trades with countries outside Europe, about half of this trade with the American continent, and the other half in trade with South Africa, the Far East and Australasia.

In terms of volume, the percentage of world trade carried in British shipping is less readily determinable, although it was probably lower than the 52 per cent by value which was carried. The difference arises from the smaller British participation in some of the low value bulk trades, in particular, coal and timber, than in the high value trades. British ships carried only about one-third of the world's coal shipments. In the long-haul coal export trade from Britain, British ships carried about 90 per cent of the tonnage shipped, but in the short-haul trades the proportion carried was less than 40 per cent. About 25 per cent of the world's coal trade originated outside Britain; British ships scarcely participated in this trade. In the Scandinavian and Canadian timber trades, the South American nitrate trade, for example, British ships were also unimportant, while the importance of British ships in world grain trades was declining. All of these trades were tramp trades in which the ships of low wage countries, such as Norway and Greece, could operate at rates below those which comparable British ships could accept.

An indication of the share of British shipping in the trades of a number of countries and of the changes between 1890 and 1910

[1] An indirect trade is one carried in a ship of a nationality other than that of the countries at either end of the trading voyage. It is sometimes referred to also as a cross trade.

High Water: the pre-1914 Period

is given by the figures in Table 1. It can be seen that the British share fell substantially in the trades of the European countries listed and less substantially in the other countries shown, except for the trades of Canada, New Zealand, Chile and the Argentine (the 1890 figure for the Argentine was probably not representative). In the long-haul trades of the world, taken as a whole, the extent of the British supremacy was virtually unchanged in the years between 1890 and 1910, the growth of the trade of the world providing the means of employing the enlarged shipping capacity of countries such as the Netherlands, Germany and Japan. It was in the shorter trades that British shipping had begun to feel the challenge to its pre-eminence.

TABLE 1. British share of entrances and clearances at ports
in certain countries, 1890, 1900 and 1910

	Percentages of total tonnage entered and cleared which was British owned		
	1890	1900	1910
	%	%	%
Russia	53	37	33
Germany	35	27	26
Holland	52	42	32
Belgium	53	45	44
France	44	41	36
Italy	49	20	28
United States	53	53	49
Argentine	42	29	34
Chile	47	50	51
Japan	n.a.	39	30
Canada	52	61	70
South Africa	88	90	84
New Zealand	87	92	97
India	88	82	81

n.a. = not available.

Note: Changes in the composition of the statistics make the Italian figures not strictly comparable; the 1900 figure is clearly out of line.
Source: Cd. 9092, Third Report, p. 75.

The size of British trade in relation to world trade and the proportion of world trade carried in British ships are, however,

23

only part of the story. The distribution of British trade is important. The distribution of British exports and imports in 1913 was as follows:

Trade	Percentage of imports: by value	by weight	Percentage of exports: by value	by weight[a]
	%	%	%	%
Europe and Mediterranean	44	60	41	86
Countries outside Europe	56	40	59	14

[a] Relates to coal exports only.
Source: Cd. 9092, Third Report, pp. 76–77.

The first thing to note about these figures is the importance of the European and Mediterranean trades in which only about 45 per cent of the trade was carried in British ships, and which employed only 18 per cent of British ships. British ships were more important in the trade with the Eastern Mediterranean countries in the group, and correspondingly less important in the nearer trades. The second factor of importance is the high proportion of imports from non-European countries which came from the United States of America. To show the real importance of these, further figures are needed, namely:

Imports from	Percentage of total extra-European imports of Britain, 1913: by volume	by value
	%	%
North America	49	40
South America	21	16
Central America	3	3
Africa	2	5
Australasia	7	14
East of Suez	18	22

Source: Cd. 9092, Third Report, p. 81.

Of the imports from North America, two-thirds by volume and four-fifths by value were from the United States of America: 80 per cent of the imports from America travelled in British ships.

Two important features of British trade, which provided the background for the employment of British shipping, emerge from the preceding analysis. These are, first, the decline in the British share of world trade and, second, the importance of the trades with European and Mediterranean countries and the United States of America, that is, trades with countries which already had developing merchant fleets or which, after the war, set out to develop their fleets.

No account of British trade and shipping before 1914 is complete without a discussion of the British coal trade. The use of steamships on the world's trading routes was initially hampered by a shortage of bunker coal along those routes. To serve the needs of British steamers, chains of coaling stations were established along the main trade routes, supplied by coal shipped from Britain. Even when indigenous coal supplies were developed overseas, the high thermal output of British coal gave it precedence for bunkers, and shipowners would rather bunker with Welsh coal in South America, South Africa or the Far East than with the local product. Alongside this export trade to service bunker stations was built up a trade for local markets all over the world.

In 1913, about 85 per cent of the coal exported from Britain was sent to European and Mediterranean areas, of which less than 40 per cent was carried in British ships. The other 15 per cent of the coal was sent further afield, the bulk of it to South America and it was this 15 per cent which was most important for British shipping as it was carried almost entirely in British ships. In 1913, 1·8 million net tons of shipping cleared from the nine principal coal ports for the Argentine, where it could lift grain for the voyage home. Over 1 million net tons of shipping cleared for Brazil and again was in a position to return with grain. British possessions overseas and Egypt were other important markets. The British tramp shipping fleet in these pre-war years was economically dependent on the outward carriage of coal and the inward carriage of bulk cargoes of grain and raw materials, frequently on a triangular or multilateral voyage. By taking coal outwards a long voyage in ballast was avoided and the collier could accept lower freight rates home than a ship which had travelled out in ballast.

25

Foreign ships generally were more important in the export trades of Britain than in the import trades, and in the shorter coal export trades than in the general export trade. For the four years 1910 to 1913 inclusive, the annual average entrances and clearances of ships at British ports with cargo and in ballast respectively were:

	British mil. net tons	Foreign mil. net tons
Entrances:		
with cargo	30·5	14·2
in ballast	12·3	16·5
Clearances:		
with cargo	37·7	23·9
in ballast	5·3	7·0

Source: calculated from Cd. 5480, 6398, 7021, 7616.

It can be seen that although foreign ships provided less than one-third of the entrances with cargo they provided over one-half of the entrances in ballast, the bulk of the foreign ships which entered in ballast taking coal cargoes outwards, chiefly to European and Mediterranean destinations.

NATIONAL SHIPPING POLICIES

The nature of the policy measures adopted for the assistance of national shipping in the years before the 1914–18 war is shown in Table 2.

(a) *Preferences*

With the exception of the reservation of coastal trades to national ships preference legislation was not an important part of the shipping policy of any important maritime nation between the repeal of the British Navigation Laws in 1849 and 1914.

The importance of the Navigation Laws in giving British shipping a start is a matter of debate. Shipping historians, such as Fayle, Lindsay and Thornton and contemporary observers, such as John Ricardo[1] are agreed that the Navigation Laws

[1] His critical *The Anatomy of the Navigation Laws* was published in 1847.

were harmful to British shipping as they encouraged sloth and inefficiency and that it was only when faced with the challenge of world competition after the repeal of the Laws that British shipping found its feet. On the other hand, the Departmental Committee on Shipping and Shipbuilding which reported in 1918 was in no doubt that the Navigation Laws had been an important factor in the development of British shipping by securing to that shipping a monopoly of the long-haul routes in the intra-Empire trade.

TABLE 2. Aid to shipping before 1914 (excluding reservation of coastal trades)

Country	Types of assistance				
	Postal subventions	Operating subsidies	Construction subsidies	Indirect subsidies	Preferences
Austria-Hungary	X	X	X	X	
Brazil	X	X		X	
Denmark	X				X
Egypt	X				
France	X	X	X	X	X
Germany	X				X
Greece	X				
Italy	X	X	X		
Japan	X	X	X		
Mexico		X			
Netherlands	X				
Portugal	X				
Russia	X	X	X	X	X
Spain	X	X	X		
Sweden	X	X			X
United Kingdom	X	X			
United States	X				X

Sources: Report on Bounties and Subsidies in respect of Shipbuilding, Shipping and Navigation in Foreign Countries, Cd. 6899, 1913; Report by G. M. Jones, 119 Special Agent Series, Bureau of Finance and Domestic Commerce, Washington, 1916.

The full pros and cons of the case will not be argued here. It may be noted, however, that the argument of the historians is of the *post hoc ergo propter hoc* variety. During the period before the repeal of the Laws the opportunities for expansion by the British industry were somewhat limited and the only ocean trades of importance were those to America and the East. The period after the repeal of the Navigation Laws, when British shipping grew, was the period in which long-distance trades in wheat, wool, meat, coal and manufactured goods were developed and when the steamship became technically and economically a practicable proposition. In such a situation it is impossible to say what the consequences would have been had the Navigation Laws not been repealed. However, if a distinction is drawn between competition within a national industry and competition between national industries there is no reason to think that, so long as internal competition is a reality, external competition is necessary to secure either efficiency or the growth of the industry. This is not an advocacy of legislation similar to the Navigation Laws, but simply an argument that the fashionable conclusion, that as the repeal of the Navigation Laws was followed by the growth of the British mercantile fleet the former was the cause of the latter, is not necessarily valid.

If the conclusion of the historians is not fully acceptable, neither is that of the Departmental Committee. When the Navigation Laws were repealed, the British Empire trades to Canada and India were important, but the other Empire trades were relatively minor affairs. The British trade with America was also important and between the repeal of the American Navigation Laws in 1815 and the repeal of the British Laws, British shipping was able to secure a place in that trade which was retained. Only in the long-haul trades to Canada, India and America is it historically possible for the continuing success to have been due to the foothold established before 1849, but even in these trades the position was maintained because of the comparative advantages which early industrialization gave to Britain in the domain of steam shipping.

It is important today that in other countries the interpretation placed on the effects of the Navigation Laws often accords with that of the Departmental Committee rather than with that of the historians. This interpretation is that the Navigation Laws, together with postal subventions, enabled Britain to obtain virtual mastery of the shipping business and that it was only when mastery had been secured that politicians and economists preached the virtues of free trade and fastened the idea on dependent territories. Protection and bounties became odious in others when the '. . . bounties and subsidies she had given . . . and the effective monopoly of the carrying trade to and from her colonies and more helpless Asian and American countries had done their work'.[1] This interpretation, which would gain in strength if it referred specifically to the position of British shipping in American trades between 1815 and 1849, has been taken to justify the use of similar means by other countries to develop their own mercantile marines. If preferential legislation was ineffective in securing the growth of the British fleet, then the great concern within the British industry at the spread of discriminatory legislation since 1945 would be completely misplaced. What is clear, however, is that without a closer analysis than the matter has ever been given, the British industry cannot, at one and the same time, claim that the Navigation Laws were a hindrance, not a help to British shipping, but that similar legislation in other countries is a help, not a hindrance, to the fleets of those countries and so is unfair.

The discrimination by Germany in the emigrant trades was noted earlier. The German control stations under the management of the German shipping companies were reinforced by a system under which emigrants from Germany could not be carried without a licence from the German Government and although licenses were issued to non-German lines, the conditions of issue made it difficult for British lines to compete. The German lines, through their management of the control stations, were able to intimidate emigrants and prevent their using British ships, unofficial action which, while not expressly condoned, was not eliminated by the German Government. German control of the shipping companies in Austria-Hungary, and their strong influence over Italian lines served to extend similar attitudes to those countries.[2]

---

[1] 'How other countries develop their shipping,' *Indian Shipping*, I, no. 6 (1949), p. 21.
[2] See *Report on the German Control Stations and the Atlantic Emigrant Traffic* (November 1916), Cd. 9092, 1918.

German shipping was helped by the establishment of preferential railway rates which directly diverted trade to German ships, or acted less directly by diverting trade to German ports at which British competition was limited by the conference territory-sharing agreements. The other preferences noted in Table 2 consisted of the refund by the Swedish, Danish, Russian and Austro-Hungarian Governments of canal dues paid by national ships, special rates for agricultural exports to England carried from Denmark in Danish ships and preferential railway rates in France for goods shipped in French ships to French West Africa, South America, New York, the Levant and the Far East.

(b) *Postal Subventions*

During the nineteenth century, aid to shipping predominantly took the form of postal subventions and in this Britain took the lead. As Thornton points out, in 1837 '. . . there was little to be proud of in the British mercantile marine'. The decision then to put the carriage of mails out to contract was one the commercial importance of which '. . . cannot be too strongly emphasised. . . . The . . . new mail policy of the British Government . . . gave British ocean shipping a start it never lost.'[1] Although the policy was a naval policy, intended to expedite the mails and reduce the cost of carrying them by replacing the alarmingly inefficient naval service, the '. . . mail subventions were of profound consequence in bridging the gap between the known high costs of steamship operation and the commercial revenue obtainable.'[2]

As Table 2 shows, the majority of maritime nations followed the British lead. These early postal subventions may be considered as examples of infant industry subsidies which succeeded in their aim precisely because they were working with, not against, the economic tide. In their other aim, that of providing ships as reserves of the navies of the countries concerned, the policy was less successful. The large express ships of the North Atlantic in particular were extremely useful in the 1914–18 war in the unsuspected rôles of troopships and hospital ships, but early in the war the navies of both Britain and Germany

[1] R. H. Thornton, *British Shipping* (Cambridge, 1959), pp. 21–22.
[2] Ibid., p. 26.

became convinced that they had made a mistake in subsidizing fast mail ships for use as auxiliary cruisers. This realization virtually ended the use of mail subventions as subsidies for this purpose.

(c) *Direct Subsidies*

Direct subsidies, not linked specifically to postal services, appear to have been initiated by France in 1881, followed by Italy, Japan and Austria-Hungary.

The bounties paid by the French and Italian Governments had a limited usefulness. French shipowners claimed that the shipbuilders absorbed the construction subsidy by raising prices, a consequence which a theoretical analysis would suggest as likely. As to the navigation bounties, it has been commented that they encouraged '. . . an excess production of sailing ships and these literally sailed around on the ocean earning their shipping bounties'.[1] In fact, when the sailing fleets of other maritime nations were declining and being replaced by steamships, that of France increased from 444,092 net tons in 1890 to 676,193 net tons in 1905. French steamer tonnage increased from 277,759 net tons in 1880 to 815,567 net tons in 1910, an increase of 194 per cent, while the world ocean-going steam tonnage increased by 346 per cent. In so far as state assistance helped the French merchant marine towards a stronger competitive position, it was the mail subventions which '. . . are regarded as having contributed more . . . than the large sums expended in bounties and subsidies since 1881'.[2] In the case of Italy, the decline in sailing tonnage was retarded, but not halted, by the subsidies, while the tonnage of steamships increased by 761 per cent between 1880 and 1910. This increase cannot be entirely attributed to the subsidy policy since Italian emigration to North and South America was increasing in the period and in other countries, such as Germany and Scandinavia, emigration formed a sound commercial basis for a shipping fleet. The subsidies themselves were relatively modest.

In Japan the position was somewhat different. In 1880 the entire Japanese fleet consisted of 41,215 net tons of sailing

---

[1] F. Eversheim, *Effects of Shipping Subsidisation*, (Bremen, 1958), p. 15.
[2] Russell Smith, *Influence of the Great War upon Shipping*, p. 136.

vessels;[1] in 1910 the fleet comprised 412,859 net tons of sailing vessels and 1,233,785 net tons of steamships. This growth was aided by the subsidies, but not caused by them. Most of the subsidy expenditure was to cover the extension of steamship routes and each subsidy when given contained a provision for its annual reduction. The most important route in terms of subsidies was that to Europe, although from 1910 the services to America absorbed annually nearly one-half of the route subsidies granted. As in the case of the postal subventions previously noted, the Japanese subsidies were clearly infant industry subsidies which had the effect, whatever the intention, of enabling shipping to get started earlier, and to expand faster, than if subsidies had not been paid. The increase in Japanese shipping occurred alongside, and facilitated, an increase in Japanese trade. In 1901, 7·9 million tons of Japanese, and 14·2 million tons of foreign, ships were entered and cleared at Japanese ports; in 1911 the figures were 18·9 million and 21·3 million tons respectively, indicative of a large increase in trade in which foreign lines shared. The increase in Japanese shipping was, therefore, justified by the growth in Japanese trade and was clearly not at the expense of foreign shipping: the extension of trade depended on an increase in the shipping services to and from Japan which it is doubtful if non-Japanese shipping would have provided. Had subsidies not been given, the expansion of the Japanese fleet would have been slower, but the eventual size would not necessarily have been smaller.

Austria-Hungary needs little attention. There was an increase in the steam fleet during the subsidy period, but this was supported by emigration and depended on the migrant trades for its economic success. Between 1901 and 1910, the volume of tonnage entered and cleared at Austrian ports increased by 63 per cent, while the Austrian share of that tonnage increased by 75 per cent, an unexciting return for the subsidy payments.

[1] Figures from Cd. 6180, 1912. G. C. Allen in *A Short Economic History of Modern Japan* (London, 1946), gives figures for the tonnage of ships, excluding sailing ships, of 20 tons and over registered in Japan Proper derived from official Japanese sources. The figure for 1880 is 66,000 tons (table xx, p. 178).

(d) *Summary*

In summary it can be said that before 1914 state interference with shipping was largely effective in giving economically viable organizations a start in their uneconomic infancies, for example the British mail services, Italian and Austro-Hungarian emigrant services, Japanese shipping generally. Where the subsidies attempted to run counter to economic considerations they produced little worth-while result for the expenditure of a lot of money: for example, the French case, and the poor quality of much Italian and Austro-Hungarian tonnage. As Fayle put it, '. . . it was not . . . the ships in receipt of large direct subsidies that proved the most formidable competitors of British shipping'.[1]

In this pre-war period German shipping provided the most formidable competition to British liner services. The German Government viewed sympathetically the growth of national trade and shipping and supported shipping in gaining admission to conferences with territory-sharing agreements with the other lines in those conferences. Apart from the postal subventions, the only direct assistance which German shipping enjoyed was preferential railway rates for goods shipped in German ships. Where the preferential rates were granted for goods travelling in ships in receipt of postal subventions, a substantial advantage was created: this applied for example in the trade to East Africa.[2] The main competitive element, however, was '. . . the efficiency of the German mercantile marine . . .'[3] the effects of which were accentuated by 'unfair' methods.

The subsidy policies of the countries not specifically discussed were of little importance in the period and had little effect on British shipping. In most cases in return for the subsidies granted, the shipping companies concerned had to accept substantial liabilities towards their governments in respect of the training of seamen and holding their ships in readiness for use by their governments in wartime, which did much to reduce the value of the subsidies paid.

[1] C. E. Fayle, *A Short History of the World's Shipping Industry*, p. 274.
[2] See Cd. 9092, pp. 90–105, for a careful analysis of German competition.
[3] Ibid., p. 105.

Conclusion

In the years before the first world war British ships dominated the liner trades of the world, although in the Pacific the competition from Japan, and in the North Atlantic and South American trades the competition from Germany, was making, or threatened, serious inroads into the British share of the trade. The competition from German and Japanese shipping was felt mainly in liner trades. Few other foreign shipping enterprises, however, attempted to overcome the established advantages of British liners. Where attempts were made to enter existing trades, the newcomers were generally repulsed by the combined forces of the lines already in possession of those trades. Entry was easier to trading routes to which the conference system had not extended; this was the case in most of the Pacific trades in which Japanese ships engaged.

The British practice of selling exports on c.i.f. terms and buying imports on f.o.b. terms aided British shipping as it meant that exporters nominated the ships for outward cargoes and importers nominated the ships for inward cargoes. The adoption of this practice in other countries which developed shipping fleets secured to those ships an immediate share of the national trades and the trading methods adopted in Britain which had helped British shipping eventually had a boomerang effect. This effect was important precisely because British trade grew more slowly than world trade so that the widespread adoption of the British trading conventions hindered British shipping in increasing its share of foreign trades. However, the fleets of other countries, such as Denmark, Greece and Norway, which were net suppliers of shipping services were equally affected.

British tramp ships were in a less happy position and were already feeling the effects of competition from Greek and Scandinavian tonnage. It is generally believed that about 60 per cent of British tonnage was tramp tonnage at the outbreak of war and that the proportion of tramp tonnage in the fleets of the remainder of the world was considerably higher, exceeding 90 per cent for countries such as Greece and Norway. The fleets of these other countries were largely composed of older ships, mainly sailing ships and older and less efficient steamers sold out of the British fleet. Although reliable information is completely lacking, it is apparent that wage costs in countries such as Norway, Greece and Japan and navigation bounties based on distance travelled by French and Italian ships, gave to the ships owned in those countries an advantage over British ships in tramp trades although the higher maintenance costs of old ships countered some of the wage cost advantage. Sailing ships had already largely become unprofitable under the British flag because, with longer passages under sail than under steam, voyage costs in sailing ships exceeded those in steamers. In countries in which wage rates were much lower than in Britain, however, sailing ships and slow steamers could operate economically in the tramp trades of the world at freight rates at which similar British ships could not survive. The survival of the British tramp fleet depended on the readiness of British tramp owners to keep at least one step ahead of owners in lower wage countries in the adoption of larger and faster vessels. This they had done, although there were signs that by 1914 the advance had practically stopped with the acceptance of a static concept of the ideal tramp.

III

War and Reconstruction

WAR

THE 1914–18 war had a lasting effect on the position of British shipping. The consequences of the war to shipping '. . . were more direct, more extensive, more lasting and possibly more significant than on any other branch of economic activity'.[1] It is no part of the present work to present a summary history of British shipping in the war; 'on that subject one must write either a volume or nothing at all'.[2] All that is intended is to note those aspects of the war which apparently had a significant effect on the future of the industry.

Britain entered the war with 19·26 million tons of sail and steam ships of over 100 tons, 39·4 per cent of the world total; by June 1919 the fleet had been reduced to 16·56 million tons, 32·5 per cent of world tonnage.[3] The difference between the 1914 and 1919 figures represents war losses not made good. During the war, world shipping losses amounted to 15 million tons, about 2 million tons of which were lost by ordinary marine risks (from 1910–13 marine losses had averaged 605,000 tons per annum). British losses were 9 million tons and foreign losses 6 million tons. The total world fleet increased in the period by about 4 million tons, so that while the British fleet decreased by 3 million tons, the foreign fleet increased by 7 million tons.

The experiences, in terms of tonnage losses, of a number of leading maritime countries are shown in Table 3. Tonnage figures are shown for 1914, 1919 and 1920, the 1920 figures being included to show the effects of the post-war distribution of enemy fleets among the Allied nations.

The shipping of America, Japan, France and Italy seems to

[1] C. E. Fayle, *The War and the Shipping Industry* (London, 1927), p. xiii.
[2] Thornton, *British Shipping*, p. 82.
[3] Tonnage figures from *Brassey's Naval and Shipping Annual*, 1925.

36

have profited most from the war. These four countries will be considered first, followed by the neutral countries, then the enemy countries and finally Great Britain.

TABLE 3. Shipping tonnages, 1914, 1919, 1920. Sea-going steam and motor ships only. Million gross tons

Country	1914	1919	Change 1914–19	1920	Change 1914–20
Austria-Hungary	1·1	0·9	−0·2	0·0	−1·1
Belgium	0·3	0·3	—	0·4	+0·1
Brazil	0·3	0·5	+0·2	0·5	+0·2
British Empire	1·6	1·9	+0·3	2·0	+0·4
Denmark	0·8	0·6	−0·2	0·7	−0·1
France	1·9	1·9	—	2·9	+1·0
Germany	5·1	3·2	−1·9	0·4	−4·7
Greece	0·8	0·3	−0·5	0·5	−0·3
Italy	1·4	1·2	−0·2	2·1	+0·7
Japan	1·7	2·3	+0·6	3·0	+1·3
Netherlands	1·5	1·6	+0·1	1·8	+0·3
Norway	2·0	1·6	−0·4	2·0	—
Russia	1·0	0·5	−0·5	0·5	−0·5
Spain	0·9	0·7	−0·2	0·9	—
Sweden	1·0	0·9	−0·1	1·0	—
United Kingdom	18·9	16·3	−2·6	18·1	−0·8
United States	2·0	9·8	+7·8	12·4	+10·4
World	45·4	47·9	+2·5	53·9	+8·5

Sources: Brassey, 1925; Weltschiffahrts-Archiv, *Facts and Figures* (Bremen, 1959).

(a) *American Shipping*

The fleet which secured the most spectacular wartime growth was that registered under the American flag. By 1914, the American sea-going fleet had decreased to the point where it carried only 10 per cent of the American sea-borne international trade. This was a situation which some Americans viewed with disquiet, but the economic justification was sufficiently strong for the pressure for a greater American share of the trade to be largely ignored. With the outbreak of war, however, American trade was seriously disturbed by the withdrawal of foreign tonnage, which led to an intensification of the demand for an American merchant marine. Later, the demand for merchant ships to replace war losses in the belligerent countries and then the American entry into the war, incited a tremendous ship-building activity in the country. In 1913, American shipbuilding yards had produced only 230,000 tons of ocean shipping; in 1919, 3 million tons of ocean shipping were produced. The American sea-going fleet increased from 2 million tons in 1914, one-half of which was used in coastal services, to 9·8 million tons in 1919. Much of this shipping never saw service; a high proportion, however, was used to secure American entry into the trades of the world. This entry occurred both during the war, for example in the trade between North and South America from which British lines had, perforce, withdrawn, and in the post-war period.

The ships built in America during the war were owned by the Government through the agency of the United States Shipping Board, but it was never intended that these ships should remain in public ownership. On the other hand, having established a mercantile fleet of impressive size, the American Government had no intention of reverting to the pre-war situation as regards shipping. Consequently, the Merchant Marine Act, 1920, was passed 'to provide for the promotion and maintenance of the American Merchant Marine'.[1] Under the Act a reconstituted Shipping Board was directed to sell the vessels built during the war to American citizens, the sales to take place as soon as was practicable. Any vessels not required for the promotion and maintenance of the American Merchant Marine or for which no American purchasers could be found, could be sold to foriegn buyers.

In addition to the duty of liquidating the government-owned fleet, the Board was directed to investigate and determine as promptly as possible the full nature and extent of the shipping services from American ports which were desirable for the promotion and maintenance of the foreign and coastwise trade and postal services of the United States. If no American citizen was prepared to operate any service deemed necessary by the Board, then the Board was empowered itself to operate the service until it was established and could be sold as a going concern to an American operator.

---

[1] This quotation and that which follows are from the Act and its preamble.

War and Reconstruction

From its revenue from the sales of ships and the operation of shipping services the Board was empowered to set aside a construction loan fund not exceeding 25 million dollars over five years to be used by the Board to assist in the construction of vessels required to maintain services considered by the Board to be desirable.

The operations of the Board and of American shipping services need not be considered in detail. American maritime policy had its birth in the increment of tonnage during the war. The policy established in the period of reconstruction after the war was a deliberate attempt to reverse the pre-war trend in American shipping and to establish and maintain a mercantile marine in peace time in defiance of economic considerations because '. . . it is necessary for the national defence and for the proper growth of its foreign and domestic commerce that the United States shall have a merchant marine . . . sufficient to carry the greater portion of its commerce and serve as a naval or military auxiliary in time of war or national emergency, ultimately to be owned and operated privately by citizens of the United States'.

(b) *Japanese Shipping*

Japanese shipping did very well indeed out of the war. In the four years 1915–18 net earnings by the leading Japanese shipping companies averaged 111 million yen per annum, over ten times the annual average net earnings in the period 1900 to 1914; in 1918 alone net earnings were more than 30 per cent greater than the total net earnings for the fifteen years 1900 to 1914 inclusive.[1] The needs of war increasingly led to British ships being withdrawn from trades which did not directly serve the Allied cause. These conditions suited the Japanese admirably and they built ships furiously as long as their supplies of constructional materials held out. Not only did the share of the world's carrying trade travelling in Japanese ships increase, but Japan was able to supply to markets cut off from former supplies by war. Japanese exports increased from $315·3 million in 1913 to $799·1 million in 1917.[2] With the passing of the La Follette

---

[1] Saugstad, *Shipping and Shipbuilding Subsidies*, p. 326.
[2] U.S. Commerce Report, February 1918, p. 665.

Act, which prevented American shipping from employing Asiatic crews, the Pacific became almost a Japanese lake in which war risks were small and opportunities great. Japanese lines were able to enter traditionally British trades in India, the Far East and the Pacific, and in the years when British competition was removed to build up the shore organizations necessary for liner trades. With low labour and building costs, the assistance of subsidies, the advantage of integrated merchanting and shipping organizations, and extensive reserves built up out of wartime operations at inflated freight rates,[1] Japanese shipping became during the war a formidable force.

(c) *French Shipping*

British shipowners viewed the wartime experiences of the American, Japanese and some other fleets with alarm, but that of the French fleet with anger. France ended the war with a fleet virtually unchanged in size from pre-war, but which, with reparations tonnage, new building and purchases by the French Government from British and other owners, had increased by one million tons by 1920. The French Government gave direct assistance to shipowners in replacing war losses, including the purchase of ships on Government account which were later resold at bargain prices to private owners. Furthermore, and this was the cause of British anger, during the war a substantial part of French merchant shipping was free from requisition and able to trade at free market rates while two million tons of British shipping, requisitioned at Blue Book rates (see p. 49), were lent to the French Government to maintain essential wartime services. In addition to the efforts made by the French lines to replace shipping losses, the French Government in its purchases paid prices for ships which no British owner could afford while his ships were subject to requisition and, consequently, helped to establish an inflated level of prices of secondhand tonnage. French shipowners in 1920 seemed to be exceptionally well placed to take advantage of what opportunities existed and to gain in strength during the inter-war years.

[1] Japanese ships were kept largely outside the Allied shipping pool and were thus able to take full advantage of the high free market rates.

War and Reconstruction

(d) *Italian Shipping*

The experience of Italian shipping during the war was very much like that of French shipping. Even as late as 1917 Italian shipping was free from control and able to profit from wartime freight rates, while in 1916 some 400,000 tons of British shipping, chartered at Blue Book rates, was lent to Italy to maintain essential services. Apart from the considerable advantage of wartime profits, the chief benefit to Italian shipping came with the dissolution of the fleet of Austria-Hungary, most of which went to Italy, together with the port of Trieste and the trades from that port. The close connection which had existed before the war between the Austrian Lloyd line and an Italian line made it easy for the ships, trade and organization of the Austrian line to be taken over ready made, as it were. Under the reparations arrangements Italy received ton for ton compensation for ships lost.

(e) *Neutral Shipping*

The neutral countries Norway, Denmark, Sweden and the Netherlands all suffered severe shipping losses during the war and all except the Netherlands ended with fleets smaller than in 1914. Nevertheless, the fleets of all four countries were able to earn substantial profits from the carriage of cargoes for the belligerent countries. As the war went on and the British control of the seas became stronger, the trade to Germany was stopped, but this was fully compensated by the demand for shipping from British sources.

By 1914, Norway had become the fourth most important ship-owning country in the world. The disposition of the Norwegian mercantile fleet was especially favourable for profiting from the high wartime freight rates, most of the ships being engaged in tramping trades, largely on foreign account. Norwegian ships were able to trade at free market rates until 1917 and, in consequence, the gross freight earnings in foreign trade increased from 211·5 million kroner in 1914 to 1,107·2 million kroner in 1917 and 904·9 million kroner in 1918;[1] 1920 was an even better year with gross earnings of 1,280 million kroner. Although costs rose, they did not keep pace with rates so that large profits

[1] Wilhelm Keilham, *Norway and the World War* (Oslo, 1927), p. 346.

were earned and set aside for fleet replacement even after dividends of 200 per cent and over had been paid on capital.[1] The Government insurance payments for war losses were more generous than those in Britain and payments for losses usually exceeded the value of the vessels lost. Norwegian owners ordered over one million tons of shipping from American yards for delivery in 1918 and 1919, and a similar volume from British yards for delivery in later years, in this way covering the war-time loss of one-half of the fleet.

In 1917 some Norwegian tonnage was requisitioned by the government at fixed rates in order to dampen the rise in the cost of living. The loss of opportunities which this involved for the owners of requisitioned ships '. . . was pro-rated on all ship-owners according to their registered tonnage. This innovation . . . entirely changed the character of the requisitions, making them a sort of special tax'.[2] This policy may be contrasted with that of the British Government, to be discussed later.

It is commonly believed in Britain that it was the reserves built up from wartime profits which enabled Norwegian shipping to expand in the inter-war period. How true is this? The first thing to note is that the high free market rates were only earned by a part of the fleet; by the end of the war one-half of the pre-war fleet had been sunk. Second, Norwegian shipowners were more heavily taxed than were British shipowners during most of the war period and the rate of tax on company income rose from 14 per cent in 1913 to 57 per cent in 1918 while the tax on capital values rose from 0·3 per cent to 0·8 per cent with capital values increased each year for price increases before the tax was calculated.[3] The change in the Excess Profits Duty in Britain in 1917 lessened, but did not reverse, the difference between the tax positions. Third, costs of ship operation rose during the war, particularly the cost of coal and the wage rates of seamen which became generally higher than those paid in British ships. As a result, the rise in profits was smaller than the rise in gross earnings. Fourth, heavy losses were made by owners who had ordered ships in America and Britain during

---

[1] 'When Shipping Prospered', *Shipbuilding and Shipping Record* (14 December 1939), p. 619.
[2] Keilham, op. cit., p. 381.   [3] *Den Norske Amerikalinje* (Oslo, 1960), p. 326.

the war for delivery in the post-war period. Many owners had placed building contracts in 1917 and 1918 when the sterling-kroner exchange rate was under 16 kroner to the pound. The subsequent depreciation of the kroner, which fell to an average rate of 31·71 kroner to the pound in 1924[1] practically doubled the price to the shipowners of the ships. Many were unable to complete their contracts on those terms and had to pay substantial forfeits to the builders. Others, who took delivery of the ships contracted, were unable ever to make profits on them sufficient to restore even their pre-war positions. The incidence of losses from these contracts was most unevenly spread and while the total losses appear to have been about equal to the war-time gains so that the Norwegian industry as a whole was no better off in 1924 than in 1914, this was not true of all companies. It is significant, however, that the main expansion in the inter-war period came from new owners who entered the industry in the period and could not have had any war-time gains. When the older companies did expand it was more often on the basis of new capital obtained by borrowing than by the use of wartime reserves. The extent to which wartime profits accounted for the greater growth of the Norwegian than of the British fleet in the inter-war period is obviously limited.

The shipping of Denmark and Sweden profited from the high levels of freight rates during the war, although they found that costs rose steeply. In Denmark shipowners were specially taxed, the proceeds of the tax being used to stabilize food prices. Shipowners in both countries were affected by the embargoes placed by the British Government on neutral firms which had traded with the enemy and by the unwillingness to sell bunker coal unless the ship requiring the coal agreed to make a voyage on British account. In the later period of the war the German policy of unrestricted submarine warfare led to much Danish and Swedish shipping being laid up. Overall, it is probable that shipowners in Denmark and Sweden strengthened their positions during the war to a greater extent than did owners in either Britain or Norway.

The position in the Netherlands was very similar to that in

[1] Average price on Oslo Bourse for the year. The depreciation was in respect of the currencies of all countries in which ships had been ordered.

Denmark and Sweden. Dutch owners were able to expand their liner services during the war and to secure footholds in trades which had been served by British ships before 1914. Data respecting twelve Dutch shipping companies owning 70 per cent of the Dutch fleet show that in the period 1915–19 inclusive 198 million guilders were added to special purpose reserves and statutory reserves increased by 75 million guilders. Between 1919 and 1924 the book value of the fleets of these twelve companies increased from 89 million guilders (122 million guilders in 1914) to 351 million guilders, that is, by about the same amount as the increase in reserves from wartime profits.[1] The Dutch fleet increased from 1·59 million tons in 1919 to 2·56 million tons in 1924, that is, an increase of 61 per cent. This increase was apparently financed entirely from wartime reserves and exhausted those reserves.

If the profits put to reserve by Danish and Swedish shipowners during the war were similar, that is would have financed a 61 per cent expansion of those fleets, then wartime profits could have accounted for the increase in these fleets from 1·7 million tons in 1919 to 2·7 million tons in 1930. As the combined fleets amounted to only 2·75 million tons in 1939 it is probably true that in these two cases the entire expansion in the inter-war period was financed from wartime profits. This was not true, however, of either Norwegian or Dutch shipping.

Greek shipping also did well out of the war. Prior to the Boer war, Greek shipping had made little progress due to a lack of capital. During the freight boom at the turn of the century, Greek owners were able to make profits which enabled them to take a greater part in world shipping so that by 1914 the fleet amounted to 836,868 tons. During the 1914–18 war, 388,000 tons of shipping were lost and 260,000 tons sold to foreign buyers, reducing the fleet to 323,796 tons in 1919. The insurance recoveries from vessels lost and the receipts from sales between 1915 and 1919 yielded profits estimated at $38·6 million at pre-war exchange rates, while profits from charters during the same period were estimated as $190 million,[2] a substantial proportion

[1] Information by courtesy of Koninlijke Nederlandsche Reedersvereeniging, The Hague.
[2] Saugstad, *Shipping and Shipbuilding Subsidies*, p. 497.

of which was available for post-war expansion with tonnage of a better class than that which had yielded the wartime profits.

In minor shipowning countries, including some British Dominions, fleets were generally increased during the war or the immediate post-war years, frequently with government support. The expansion was often a defence against future withdrawals of tonnage and disruption of trade, such as occurred during the war, and to avoid the payment overseas of freights at the levels ruling during the war. A special motive for Australia's entry into overseas shipping was the fear of a monopoly of shipping services arising from the increasing concentration of shipping companies in Britain during the war (see Chapter XIV).

(f) *Enemy Shipping*

The enemy countries entered the war with 6·5 million tons of shipping, of which over 2 million tons were lost through seizure and sinking, including a substantial volume of German tonnage idle in American ports from the beginning of the war which was seized when America entered the war. For most of the war, however, enemy shipping was absent from the oceans of the world because of the effectiveness of the British blockade and the enemy countries had to rely on neutral shipping and land transport for their overseas supplies.

At the end of the war, the fleets of Germany, Austria-Hungary and Turkey were seized by the Allies as reparations for shipping losses during the war. The terms of the German surrender were that the German Government agreed to cede to the Allied and Associated Governments all German merchant ships of 1,600 tons and upwards and one-half, reckoned in tonnage, of the ships between 1,000 tons and 1,600 tons. In all, Germany ceded to the Allies 2·5 million tons of completed shipping and 250,000 tons of the 360,000 tons under construction, being left with 400,000 tons of shipping, with hardly any ship fit for overseas trade, and about 112,000 tons under construction.

In the reconstruction period the German Government paid to shipowners compensation for the ships lost, but the value of these payments was reduced by inflation and the severe domestic troubles in the country. Those shipowners who got in first with their rebuilding programmes were able to replace about one-third of their fleets from the money received, but those whose ships were last in the programme could only rebuild about one-seventh of their fleets. By the end of 1923, when the reconstruction as such was virtually completed, the German fleet amounted to 2·8 million tons, just over one-half of the size of the pre-war fleet, although consisting almost entirely of modern, economical vessels.

The fleet of Austria-Hungary was never replaced and the principal shipping lines passed, with the port of Trieste, under Italian management. The Turkish fleet was never sufficiently important to warrant separate treatment here.

By means of these reparations arrangements, the chief competitor to British liner services in the pre-war years was removed from the scene, but the advantage which might have been reaped was partly nullified by the entry of neutral and Japanese ships to former German trades from which they proved difficult to dislodge after the war. The full advantage of the disappearance of the Austrian fleet was reaped by Italy.

(g) *British Shipping*

The experience of Britain in terms of shipping losses was considered at the beginning of the chapter. Here, the intention is to consider particularly the financial experience of British shipping.

The effects of the war on British shipping companies differed from one company to another; some companies did very well indeed out of the war, some less well and a few badly. There is no general picture which is true for all and while broad generalizations will be made it must be recognized that exceptions to these exist.

The overall position is that from the outbreak of the war any British merchant ship became subject to requisition for the purposes of the state. Initially, requisition simply meant that some ships were taken over for naval purposes for use as armed merchant cruisers, troopships, hospital ships, stores transports and so on. The scope of the requisition was extended as the war progressed. In 1915, for example, all refrigerated space was requisitioned at Blue Book rates (see page 49) while the ships themselves continued to trade for their owners who could fill the non-refrigerated space at market rates. Later, the grain space on the North Atlantic trades was requisitioned, again leaving the balance of space available to the owners. In 1917 a Shipping Controller was appointed and for the last twelve months or so of the war about 96 per cent of the cargo handled was carried at Government rates.

Before general requisitioning in 1917, its impact was most unevenly distributed. Shipowners could discern no pattern in the requisition policy: if a ship was at hand she might be requisitioned. It became, therefore, a game of skill to keep ships out of British ports as much as possible and so free from the risk of requisition. The owner whose ship was requisitioned received only Blue Book rates; the owner whose ship was free received full rates. As a consequence, very high profits were earned by owners with free ships and shipowners were widely accused of profiteering. The wider spread of requisitioning later cut into these profit opportunities, while the Excess Profits Duty from 1915 skimmed off some of the cream.

Early in the war it was the tramp owners who had the greatest opportunities to make profits because of their ability to keep their ships clear of requisitioning, but later in the war the greater opportunities were available to liner owners. Owners of liners engaged on completely indirect trades also profited in the early part of the war because their ships did not use British ports but they lost both their high rates and their trade connections when their ships were diverted to direct trades to serve the war effort. The owners of refrigerated meat ships could not do very well because the refrigerated space was requisitioned. Tanker owners, also, had limited opportunities to profit, but at this time virtually all British tankers were owned by the great international oil companies or by the Admiralty, so the inability to profit was of little consequence to the British shipping industry. Passenger ships, by and large, fared badly because many were requisitioned while for the remainder the decline in the number of passengers willing to travel in a ship owned by a belligerent nation reduced their opportunities for profit. Liner owners, however, who had part of the capacity of their ships free had excellent opportunities to profit by carrying some cargo at inflated rates. Immediately on the outbreak of war, all conference rates had been subjected to heavy surcharges, 50 per cent being common, which were beyond those needed to cover increased working costs at the time[1] and further increases occurred during the war. After 1917, however, the opportunities for earning large profits scarcely existed for any class of British ship.

On requisition and control the picture is that the incidence of the sacrifice was uneven. The actual sacrifice, that is, the difference between what British ships were earning and what they might have earned had they been free to take advantage of market rates was estimated in 1917 as amounting to £300 million per annum.[2] In the absence of an equalization scheme, such as that operated in Norway, the unevenness of the sacrifice was not mitigated.

A second source of sacrifice was in the inevitable unevenness of shipping losses coupled with the inadequacy of the insurance payments recovered under the war risks scheme. The Liverpool Steamship Owners' Association stated that the replacement cost of the ships lost during the war '. . . amounted to £280 million, towards which £146 million only were available from war risks insurance recoveries'.[3] There were two separate sources of discontent here. On the one hand, the compensation for war losses of requisitioned ships was usually based on an estimate of their future earnings at requisitioned rates which fell short of their replacement costs at the time of loss, while the Government made a profit on the war risks insurance estimated to be nearly £16 million. On the other hand, ships usually could not be replaced at the time of their loss because the Admiralty had requisitioned many building berths for naval purposes, while after 1917 no ships could be built for private account at all. The consequence was that by the time the ships could be replaced after the war, shipbuilding costs were higher than at the time the ships were lost and the inadequacy of the insurance payments received thereby emphasized. The difference between replacement cost and insurance receipts had to be found by the companies from their reserves and their taxed profits during the

---

[1] Fayle, *The War and the Shipping Industry*, pp. 109–10.

[2] J. H. Welsford in *Fairplay* (8 March 1917), p. 421.

[3] *Liverpool Steamship Owners' Association, 1858–1958*, p. 28. Replacement cost was calculated at the peak 1919–20 figures.

war. The importance of the estimated deficiency between insurance recoveries and the replacement cost of the ships lost may be seen by comparing the suggested insurance deficiency of £134 million with the value of the merchant fleet before the war. The most accurate of the several estimates of this value is that used for the insurance of the fleet under the war risks scheme. This was £153·5 million. On this basis the insurance deficiency was nearly 90 per cent of the pre-war fleet value. While saying this, it must not be overlooked that for losses replaced by reparations tonnage and by building undertaken before 1917 and after 1921, the cost per ton was less than the £30 used in the Liverpool estimate. Further, insurance receipts were intended to cover only the depreciated value of the ships lost, whereas the figure of replacement cost is for new vessels. For both these reasons, the true insurance deficit was considerably smaller than £134 million, while much, perhaps all, of the true deficit was covered by refunds of Excess Profit Duty after the war (see p. 51).

The freight rate problem was a relative rather than an absolute problem. The Blue Book rates, which were paid on ships requisitioned by the Government and for cargoes carried on Government account, were determined in 1915 by a committee of shipowners. The year 1914 had been a poor one for shipping and rates were relatively low throughout the year, falling even further after the outbreak of war. When the shipowners met to determine fair rates for Government hire, they met in an atmosphere of generally unremunerative operation. The rates they fixed, which were accepted by the Government, were sufficiently above the free market rate to provide a satisfactory return to shipowners. These rates, however, were soon overtaken by rising free market rates so that the owners of requisitioned ships were worse off, not better off as anticipated, than the owners of free ships. In addition, costs also rose so that in some cases the Blue Book rates became actually unremunerative to shipowners before they were revised in 1918. The Government refused earlier revision of the rates on two grounds; first, that the shipowners had themselves set and accepted these rates for the duration of the war and, second, that they appeared to be making adequate profits.

The many doleful tales from shipowners regarding the actual losses made by running at Blue Book rates, as distinct from the loss of opportunities of profiting from free market rates, must be discounted as most owners, and the industry as a whole, were able to make greater profits during the war than in the pre-war years although wartime profits were not always greater than those earned in the highly favourable years 1912 and 1913.[1] Between 1914 and 1918, for a sample of liner owners having just over five million tons of shipping, reserves increased from £14·5 million to £38·3 million and paid-up capital increased from £30·2 million to £40·4 million, this increase being the result of revaluation, not of an influx of new money. The increase in net worth was, therefore, about £34 million for companies with a declared net worth of £62 million in 1914. In the same period for a sample of tramp shipowners owning 2·1 million tons in 1914 and 1·5 million tons in 1918, the book value of the fleet rose by £9 million while £8·7 million was added to depreciation reserves, giving an increase in net value of at least £17·7 million on a fleet valued at £15·6 million in 1914 and nearly 25 per cent smaller in actual size in 1918. No figures of voyage profits are available for liner companies, although the rise in dividends from £2·6 million in 1914, based on the favourable 1913 results to £5·3 million in 1917 is indicative of the high rate of profit being earned. For the sample of tramp owners, voyage profits rose from £3·8 million in 1914 to £11 million in 1916, although profits in other wartime years were substantially smaller.[2] These figures cover the earnings of about one-half of the liner fleet and one-fifth of the tramp fleet.

Under the Excess Profits Duty imposed by the Finance Act, 1915, the taxpayer had the option of selecting as his standard profit which could be earned in any year before liability to Excess Profits Duty arose the mean of any two pre-war years. Because shipping had two very good years before the war the liability to the extra tax was that much reduced. Despite the favourable basis for calculation, over £100 million of Excess

---

[1] These two good years followed a depression in shipping after 1904, from which the industry did not fully recover until 1911. This had the distinction of being the first truly international shipping depression.

[2] Figures from *Fairplay* Annual Returns.

Profits Duty was paid in 1915–16 alone, clearly indicative of the high profits being earned in the peak period for earnings. The net earnings of British shipping in 1916 were estimated at £188 million on a capital of £300 million[1] while Ernest Bevin, a biassed witness, stated that '. . . during the first thirty-one months of the war . . . to April 1917, . . . I am advised that the shipowners pocketed . . . £350,000,000'.[2] It should be noted here that the favourable treatment with respect to the Excess Profits Duty was over-corrected by the Finance Act, 1917, and the liabilities of shipowners for Excess Profits Duty became '. . . more onerous than those of any other trade'.[3] Under the Revenue Obsolescence Agreement, 1922, substantial refunds of Excess Profits Duty were made: the distribution to shipping was of the order of magnitude of £80 million.[4]

British shipowners made handsome profits during the war; their real grievance is that they were more restricted in taking advantage of the high free market rates than were their foreign competitors, while the rates paid to neutrals under the Inter-Allied Chartering Committee exceeded substantially those paid to British owners. On the other hand, if shipowners had treated

[1] E. Crammond, 'Effect of the War on the Economic Position of the United Kingdom', *Journal of the Royal Society of Arts*, LXV. The capital figure of £300 million is approximately twice the value of the fleet as estimated earlier, which seems about right as both fleet values and reserves are traditionally understated, but to an unknown extent, in the accounts of shipping companies. The net earnings of £188 million are more uncertain. On the basis of *Fairplay* data, tramp ship earnings were about £55 million before tax while as nearly as can be calculated liner earnings were £42 million after tax. This is about £30 million in excess of the post tax average profits for 1912 and 1913, and suggests an income figure for 1916 of no more than £100 million. On this basis, total earnings in 1916 were no more than £150 million. A higher figure than this can be obtained by making a rough calculation of the Excess Profits Duty paid by tramp ships, namely £25 million, and then adding the remainder of the duty, £75 million to the liner earnings net of tax, giving a figure of about £115 million for liner earnings and total earnings of about £170 million. There is every reason to believe, however, that the earnings of the companies included in the *Fairplay* sample at this time were somewhat greater than average and that, therefore, both of the estimates based on the *Fairplay* data overstate the profits earned. In any case, 1916 was by far the most profitable year of the war for shipping and it is doubtful whether average earnings over the whole period exceeded 60 per cent of the 1916 earnings.

[2] Transport Workers, Court of Inquiry. Report and Minutes of Evidence, Cmd. 936, 1920, evidence of Ernest Bevin, p. 7. The basis of this calculation is not given.

[3] Cmd. 9092, Third Report, para. 57, p. 61.

[4] Royal Commission on Taxation of Profits and Income, 1951–5. Minutes of Evidence, Questions 4071 to 4077, p. 389.

War and Reconstruction

their profits during the war as a windfall to be preserved for
fleet replacement, instead of doubling their dividends and
using their liquid resources to buy the ships and goodwill of
other lines at inflated prices, they would have been at least as
well placed at the end of the war as any of their foreign rivals.
Certainly they appear to have made sufficient profits during the
war to have made good the deficiency between insurance
receipts and replacement costs for ships lost, while still maintaining the pre-war dividend rates, leaving the post-war taxation
refund as an unexpected and extraordinarily valuable present.

The complicated structure of the Blue Book scales and the
absence of a satisfactory index of free market rates makes a
proper comparison between them impossible. However, if the
Blue Book rates and the free market rates are treated as approximately equivalent in 1915, not until 1918 were the Blue Book
rates raised, and then only to 123 or 148 (1915 = base 100)
depending on the ship type, whereas free market rates had risen
to over 400. Another comparison of the same nature is that
between the 8s. per deadweight ton per month of the Blue Book
and the 35s. per deadweight ton paid to neutrals by the Inter-
Allied Chartering Committee; before the Inter-Allied control
was started rates of up to 100s. per cargo ton had been reported.
In 1919, the rate, River Plate to Continental ports, reached
280s., whereas the British directed rate was 62s. 6d. The course
of freight rates during the war worsened the competitive position of British shipping relative to foreign shipping in the post-
war period and this, rather than any inability to make profits,
was the burden of complaint.

The high profits being earned by some sections of the industry
in 1915 and 1916 encouraged the entry of speculators into the
industry '. . . whose eager demand for tonnage, new or secondhand, accentuated the inflation of values and helped to prepare
the way for a disastrous crack after the war'.[1] In 1915 alone,
ninety-four shipping companies were formed. The result of the
activities of speculators in Britain and overseas was to force the
prices of secondhand tonnage to unheard of heights. During the
three years 1915–17, the price per deadweight ton of secondhand ships sold rose from between £3 and £7, within which lay

[1] Fayle, op. cit., p. 177.

all but three of the fifty-nine recorded sales in the first quarter of 1915, to a price between £50 and £59 within which range lay eleven of the seventy-four recorded sales in the last quarter of 1917, only three of the sales in this quarter being at less than £10 per ton. The rise in prices which took place made it difficult for the more traditionally minded shipowners, or the shipowners whose ships were requisitioned, to buy to replace their war losses. Rather than buy ships, many old-established owners considered it '. . . more profitable to sell their fleets than to run them, and the result was to increase the speculative at the expense of the more stable interests in the industry'.[1] The entry of new capital to the industry which this speculative activity involved might have benefited the industry had not values collapsed after the war; as it was the speculative enterprises were over-capitalized in relation to values in the inter-war years. This affected mainly some tramp companies, although the spate of amalgamations among liner companies which occurred during the war, extended the speculative dangers to these normally sober concerns. In addition to amalgamations between liner companies, the companies were active in the war in buying tramp tonnage, partly to maintain services jeopardized by Government requisitions, partly to take advantage of the profits being earned by tramp shipping; this latter factor was particularly important in the immediate post-war period. Such was the importance of expectations in determining ship prices that many tramp owners sold their ships and earned higher returns by using the proceeds to buy Government bonds. Uncertainty regarding the intention of the Government with respect to the ships built on its account after 1917[2] gave tramp owners an additional incentive to remove capital from shipping while the going was so good.

The events of this period of speculation raise questions about the effects of these on the subsequent position of British shipping. How far did the pursuit of speculative profits in the war years affect the capacity of the industry a few years later to meet the challenge of difficult trading conditions? To what extent did the

[1] Fayle, op. cit., p. 177.
[2] After 1917 the construction of merchant vessels was limited to standard types built for the government. About 2·4 million tons were built.

unwieldly capital structures brought about by amalgamations at the top of the boom inhibit a rapid adjustment to changing conditions in the inter-war years? What effects did the large capital losses suffered by investors who bought shipping shares at inflated prices during the boom have on the ability of the industry to attract new capital during the subsequent years? The answers to these questions are unknown, but in each case can hardly be other than adverse.

Another effect of the war was the withdrawal from traditional trades which foreign companies entered in the British absence. This affected the liner side of the industry, not tramp ships. The liner owners did their best to maintain their established services. Increasingly, however, ships engaged in indirect trades were directed to British import trades leaving the trade routes unattended. In order to economize on shipping, ships were directed to the short-haul rather than the long-haul trades, for example, fetching wheat from America rather than from Australia. The British entrepôt trade, which in 1913 comprised 14 per cent of total British trade, was largely lost and through shipping lines, established by neutrals or by Japan or the United States, took its place. For example, Australian wool destined for America had formerly been shipped via London, whereas under wartime conditions it began to be shipped direct; American cotton for Europe which had frequently been transhipped at Liverpool, became a through trade from America. In all, twenty-five new liner services were started by foreign owners during the war in replacement of British services which had been suspended. Neutral tonnage was able to secure all the share of world trade formerly carried by German ships and a great part, in some cases three-quarters or more, of the share formerly carried by British ships. British shipping companies were confronted in the post-war period with the job of winning the trade back. Despite these difficulties, the volume of British shipping in the Pacific in 1920 was four times as great as in 1914, which does not suggest that the immediate difficulty of winning back trade routes was great.[1]

[1] Alongside this figure should be set the six-fold increase in American tonnage and seven-fold increase in Japanese tonnage in the Pacific between 1914 and 1920. The volume of trade did not expand proportionately and British ships suffered from the low costs of Japanese shipping and the subsidies to American shipping.

War and Reconstruction

That the entrepôt trade suffered is undoubted, but was this really a consequence of the war? It has been shown already that one reason for the success of German shipping before the war was that it established through shipping services from South American and other countries to continental Europe and that the reaction of the British liner owners to this challenge was to agree to share territories. Entrepôt trading involves the landing of cargoes from a number of different places in one central port and then the regrouping of the goods into cargoes for different destinations. This arrangement is ideal when the demand for shipping in each individual trade is too small to permit a regular shipping service, and can usefully and profitably be maintained in these conditions. It can also be maintained if there is a lack of competition in liner trades from shipowners in a position to establish viable through shipping services. In the pre-war period, Britain was overwhelmingly the most important liner owner and for this reason could maintain trading practices which, when competition from other liner owners occurred, were bound to change; this had occurred, for example, when German liner services were started between South America and Europe. War or no war, the competition from other liner owners would have increased and through services increasingly replaced those based on entrepôt arrangements. It must be a matter of pure speculation whether British liner owners would have established such services or not.

RECONSTRUCTION

The 1914–18 war closed an era: to the British the world has never since seemed quite as rich or quite as secure as it seemed before. To some extent in all branches of human activity the pre-1914 security was that of the blind man who cannot see danger approaching and has developed no extrasensory mechanisms for its perception. In shipping this was certainly so and the contemporary pressure to return to normalcy,[1] a pressure increased by Government advocacy, accorded with the desires of shipowners themselves. The normalcy to which it was desired

[1] The ugly contemporary expression is retained to emphasize that there is no thought here that pre-1913 conditions were normal.

to return was not the position outlined in the previous chapter, but one in which British shipping would resume an unchallenged and unchallengeable position. All the changes between the pre-war and the post-war situations were attributed to the war, the ease with which the war could be blamed preventing men from seeing and taking steps to meet the essential threats to the British position, some of which had arisen before the war. The attitudes which went into the reconstruction of the British fleet after the war set the pattern for British shipping for practically twenty years.

British shipping was not released from control immediately the war was over; control was maintained by means of direction and rate limitation during the transitional period and passenger ships were retained for repatriating troops and similar duties. The control was less far-reaching than during the war but in 1919 approximately 25 per cent of British imports were carried at Blue Book rates and a further 25 per cent at rates below the market level. Despite these limitations on profits, 1919 was the year of greatest speculation in shipping companies and of record Stock Exchange prices for shipping shares. Although 1919 was a favourable year for British shipping, the shipping of foreign rivals enjoyed much greater profits in the reconstruction period. When all controls were finally removed from British shipping in 1920 freight rates had fallen, often to below the level of the controlled rates. The sharpness of the break in rates can be attributed, at least in part, to the artificial nature of the boom. The shipping shortage in 1919 and 1920 was partly real but was partly due to port congestion which reduced the effectiveness of each ton of shipping. When the congestion problem was solved, the real situation of an increased volume of shipping chasing a reduced volume of trade (see Table 4) was revealed.[1] The ensuing break in rates marked the end of the easy profit days and killed off a number of the speculative shipping ventures started during the war and in 1919.

British shipowners had recourse to four sources of ships to replace their wartime losses.

The first source of tonnage was the ships built during the war

[1] D. H. Aldcroft, 'Port Congestion and the Shipping Boom of 1919–20', *Business History*, III, No. 2 (June 1961), pp. 97–106.

by the British Government. These consisted of standard types which had been heavily criticized by British shipowners as conforming to the ideas of theorists in the Admiralty rather than to the requirements of British shipowners and British trades as determined by past experience. The sale of these ships to private owners was handled without recompense by Lord Inchcape, himself a shipowner, and yielded a sum of £35 million for 1·4 million deadweight tons. At an average of £25 per deadweight ton, this was below the cost of building or buying ships from other sources. In view of the standard nature of the ships, however, and their alleged lack of suitability for specialized trades, the transaction may have been better business for the government than for shipowners, who had reason to feel aggrieved that these ships were not allotted to owners in proportion to their unreplaced losses at the historic cost of the ships, less normal depreciation, which is the figure at which the ships would have stood in the accounts of shipowners had they been allowed to build to replace war losses after 1917. At the time, however, shipowners were concerned to prevent the Government operating these ships on its own account, so much so that the method of disposal was that Lord Inchcape bought all the ships himself from the Government and then resold them on a non-profit basis to other shipowners. This method ensured that, whatever happened, the ships would not remain in Government ownership. It is worth pointing out here that these much-criticized ships were instrumental in setting reasonable standards for crew accommodation which all shipowners, usually unwillingly, had to adopt in order to attract crew and, being generally faster than the standard design of the British tramp owner (and that of many liner owners also), were often able to remain competitive after other British ships, designed in the light of experience, had proved too slow to meet the needs of trade.

Second came the ceded German ships, 2·5 million tons of which were sold to British owners for a sum of about £20 million. The first offer of these ships was made in September 1920, after the freight market had broken and ship prices fallen (see p. 59) and Lord Inchcape, who conducted these sales also, had difficulty in interesting British owners in all the tonnage which was available. In June 1921, foreigners, including German nationals, were allowed to purchase vessels ceded to Britain because British owners would not take up the total which was available. It seems that British owners were never very keen to acquire these ships and did so largely '. . . in order to relieve the Government of the possible necessity of running them themselves, which . . . would have been disastrous from every point of view'.[1] Shipowners were naturally more worried at the prospect of competition from a Government-owned fleet than in saving the Government from making losses. By 1922-3 the wisdom of this course was being questioned and some shipowners were regretting that they had been '. . . tempted to buy some of the ships, although others were more fortunate in their deals. . . . Many people would be prepared to contend that the disadvantages of getting the fleet largely outweighed any advantages'.[2] From the point of view of the shipowners, the German ships represented an immediate source of tonnage available at bargain prices at a time when the delivery of new ships was slow. Had the ships been regarded as a stop-gap only, all might have been well. Instead, they saddled the British industry throughout the 1920s and 1930s with a large block of pre-war tonnage which often could not compete with more modern ships and in which capital, which at any time after 1921 could have been used to build modern tonnage at a not much higher price, was completely tied up. For the shipbuilding industry, the acquisition of these ships by British owners was an unmitigated tragedy.

It is perhaps unkind, but probably true, to say that in the immediate post-war years British shipowners spent £55 million on ships which were not ideal for their purposes, largely in order to prevent the Government from running the ships.

The third source of additional tonnage was purchases from foreign owners. It has already been shown that the merchant fleets of Greece and Spain were reduced during the war, partly by sales to British and French interests of aged ships at high prices. In the reconstruction period, ships could be obtained from the same sources, from Scandinavian owners who were frequently willing to sell the ships ordered during the war from

[1] 'Standard Ships and Ex-Enemy Tonnage: Lord Inchcape's Sales,' *Brassey, 1920-2*, p. 317.
[2] Presidential Address, *Chamber of Shipping Report, 1922-3*, p. 187.

American yards, and from American sources. The ships obtained from all these sources were bought at inflated prices. The individual British owner could restore his fleet by purchasing the whole of another shipping enterprise and diverting the ships purchased to his own trades; a number of such purchases occurred in 1919.

The best index of the demand for ships in a period of high demand is the difference between the price of a ship to build and the same type of ship newly completed. *Fairplay* for many years has calculated the building cost of a representative type cargo ship and the price which the same ship, ready for delivery, would fetch in the market. In the period being discussed, the *Fairplay* ship was a 7,500 deadweight-ton steamer. In December 1919, such a ship would have cost about £195,000 to build, whereas a ready ship was worth £232,500. Within three months the price of the ready ship had risen to £258,750. Subsequently, despite a rise in building costs to £225,000 in December 1920, the price of a ready ship fell to £105,000. By the end of 1922 both the building cost and the ready price had fallen to £70,000. At the peak, in March 1920, owners were prepared to pay nearly 30 per cent over cost to secure a ship immediately to take advantage of booming rates rather than wait for a ship to be constructed. This bonus represents an estimate of the earning capacity of a ship during the construction period and, with the inflated building costs, shows how high were profit expectations in 1919 and early 1920. The subsequent sharp fall is equally noticeable.

The break in ship prices which occurred in 1920 may be shown in other ways. Prices rose up to the first quarter of 1920, the average price per ton of ships sold in that period being £58·18, from which a continuous decline to £10·8 per ton in the second quarter of 1921 occurred.[1] In April 1921, a company sold for £80,000 two ships bought in February 1920 for £344,500;[2] the capital loss which was suffered was considered worthy of note because of the swiftness of the retribution on a company which had paid £28 per deadweight ton for a fourteen-year-old ship rather than because of anything exceptional about the fall in value.

[1] *Brassey, 1924,* article by L. Isserlis.
[2] *Shipbuilding and Shipping Record* (7 April 1921), p. 423.

The fourth source of tonnage was new building. In 1919 over seven million tons of merchant tonnage were launched in the world, of which four million tons were launched in the United States and 1·6 million tons in Britain. The British launchings were below the 1913 record total of 1·9 million tons, due largely to the work on hand in reconditioning and repairing ships after wartime service. Delivery times had lengthened and whereas the tonnage under construction and the tonnage launched from British yards had been approximately equal in pre-war years, in 1919 and for several years thereafter tonnage under construction was approximately twice the volume of the tonnage launched. Little attempt appears to have been made, however, to take advantage of the more favourable situation in Japanese yards, from which 0·6 million tons were launched in 1919 leaving only 0·3 million tons under construction, or of the availability of ships from America.

The return to normalcy was seen as an attempt to re-establish the proportion of the world fleet owned in Britain to its 1913 level, regardless of changes in the world fleet as a whole and of the changes in the world trading patterns becoming evident before the war and emphasized by the war. It is easy now to see the mistakes which were made, but it cannot have been easy then to see that these things were mistakes and the war itself prevented some of the circumstances which pointed to the hopelessness of the pursuit of normalcy from being discerned. However, in view of the pre-war trends in trade, discussed in the previous chapter, and the growth of the American fleet during the war it is difficult to see how British shipowners could have anticipated re-establishing the pre-war importance of the British mercantile marine otherwise than by venturing into new trades and adopting new types of ships. However, in looking for a return to pre-war conditions shipowners were doing neither more nor less than most other sections of British industry.

IV

The Troubled Years: the Inter-war Period

THE troubled years cover the period from the end of the immediate post-war boom to the outbreak of another war. It is a period in which the development, indeed the maintenance, of international trade was hampered by a widening net of tariffs, quotas and exchange restrictions as each country tried to handle the problems of unemployment and to satisfy its nationalistic ambitions. Shipping suffered from the depression and the restrictions on trade, but it suffered in other ways also, for example, by the decline in international migration and the growing use of subsidies and other devices to encourage the fleets of individual countries at the expense of those of nations, such as Britain, Norway, Greece, Denmark, Sweden and Holland which depended substantially upon the carriage of foreign-owned goods to maintain their shipping fleets.

THE TREND OF BRITISH SHIPPING

The changing position of British shipping in the period was shown in Figure 1. For convenience, the position in a few important years is repeated here; it was as follows:

1919	16·3 million tons; 34·0 per cent of world total						
1930	20·4 ,,	,,	29·9 ,,	,,	,,	,,	,,
1936	17·3 ,,	,,	26·8 ,,	,,	,,	,,	,,
1939	18·0 ,,	,,	26·1 ,,	,,	,,	,,	,,

Far from being restored to its pre-war position, by 1939 the British mercantile marine, after increasing up to 1930, was slightly smaller than in 1913 and as a proportion of the world fleet declined continuously throughout the period.

The fall in the proportion of the world fleet which was British-owned and registered can be separated into two parts.

The Troubled Years: the Inter-war Period

It was shown in Chapter II that before 1914 the rate of growth of British and non-British shipping was such that the proportion of British shipping in the world was declining. A continuation of this pre-1914 trend into the inter-war period would have resulted in the proportion of world shipping which was British-owned in 1939 being below that of 1913. With a continuing growth of the world economy there was no reason to expect a reversal of this trend. The trend of the growth of tonnage in the pre-1914 period is determined by finding the equations of the lines of best fit to the data for the period 1890–1913. The trend lines show the average annual increment rates as follows:[1]

World tonnage	1·028 million tons
Non-British tonnage	0·679 ,, ,,
British tonnage	0·348 ,, ,,

A problem arises in projecting these trends to 1939, namely that such a course ignores completely any effects of the 1914–18 war on either the total or the distribution of world tonnage. Between 1913 and 1919, British-owned tonnage fell so that in 1919 it was 4·6 million tons below the trend tonnage for that year. Non-British tonnage in 1919 was 4·6 million tons above the trend value, but this figure included about 4·5 million tons of shipping laid up in America which was never operational. This shadow fleet cannot be considered as constituting part of the total of world tonnage. If this idle tonnage is excluded from both the non-British total and the world total for 1919, then non-British tonnage is shown as 0·1 million tons above its trend value and world tonnage as 4·5 million tons below its trend value.

If the trend lines obtained for the period 1890 to 1913 are extrapolated from 1919 (active fleet) instead of from 1913, the wartime changes in tonnage are fully accounted for. This procedure is justified on two grounds. First, the wartime changes in active fleet sizes were largely irreversible; in particular the expanded American fleet was maintained in world trade by

[1] The equations of the trend lines are: $W = 20 + 1·028n$
$$N = 9·8 + 0·679n$$
$$B = 10·2 + 0·348n$$
where W, N, B, are World, Non-British and British tonnage respectively in millions of tons in any year and 'n' is the number of years since 1890.

means of subsidies. Second, the growth of world trade, which provided employment for world shipping, was interrupted by the war and did not resume from its 1913 level.

The trend lines extrapolated from 1919[1] instead of from 1913 yield the values for 1939 shown below in comparison with the actual values:

	Tonnage in 1939 (million tons)		As percentages of world total	
	Trend	Actual[2]	Trend	Actual
			%	%
World	67·0	69·4		
Non-British	43·9	51·4	65·5	73·9
British	23·1	18·0	34·5	26·1

On this basis, a combination of the pre-1914 trend and the irreversible effects of the war would have produced a British fleet in 1939 of 23·1 million tons, comprising 34·5 per cent of the world total. If the pre-war growth trend had continued in this way there would be no reason to feel that the relative decline which would have occurred needed any special explanation. In fact, however, the British fleet declined to 26·1 per cent of the world total in 1939. The second part of the fall in the proportion of the world fleet which was British-owned is the difference between the trend proportion of 34·5 per cent and the actual proportion of 26·1 per cent. The task in this chapter and the next is to look at the factors which might have contributed to this result.

TRADE, FREIGHTS AND TONNAGE

Data on trade, shipping and freight rates for the period 1920 to 1938 are given in Table 4. The trade index shows the recovery of

---

[1] The question may be asked, 'Why not extrapolate from 1920 instead of from 1919 and thus take account of the allocation of enemy fleets among the Allies?' The answer is that the purchase of allocated tonnage by shipowners was voluntary and part of the attempt to re-establish fleets and should be considered as reducing the discrepancy between trend tonnages and actual tonnages, not as a factor determining the trend tonnage.

[2] It is interesting to notice that if laid-up tonnage in 1939 is deducted from the total actual tonnage, the active fleet is revealed as being almost exactly of trend size. This can perhaps be regarded as a third justification for using 1919 instead of 1913 (but not 1919 instead of 1920) as the basis for the extrapolation.

world trade from the war, the growth to 1925, the hesitation in 1926 and the continued growth to 1929. During this period the world's active fleet continued to grow, the idle tonnage being largely, but not entirely, owned by the U.S. Shipping Board. The growth in world trade by 35 per cent between 1913 and 1929, while world tonnage grew by 45 per cent in total and the efficiency of the world fleet increased by about 20 per cent[1] should, presumably, have led to a fall in freight rates of perhaps 15 to 20 per cent. However, costs of ship operation had risen by between 30 and 40 per cent from 1913 and the cost of ship-building by about 20 per cent—although in 1926 ships could be built at prices no more than 5 per cent above pre-war—all factors tending to raise the minimum supply price, that is, the freight rate at which an owner was indifferent between laying his ship up and keeping it in trade. The result was that freight rates, after falling between 1920 and 1924, continued at a level above that of 1913 until 1927 when they began to fall due to the pressure of tonnage upon available trade.

It is interesting in this period to compare the British, German and Norwegian freight indices. That of Norway remained consistently above the 1913 level,[2] showing clearly that there were trades more prosperous than those in which British ships, the employment of which determined the weighting of *The Economist* index, were engaged. A comparison of the British and the German indices shows the effect of the devaluation of sterling in 1931 so that whereas the British index fell by 25 per cent from 1929 to the low of 1933, the German index fell by 51 per cent in the same period. A similar comparison can be made between the German and Norwegian indices.

A comparison of the German liner and tramp indices shows

---

[1] This figure is very uncertain. Average ship speeds and the average size of ships increased during the period and these changes increased the efficiency, in terms of carrying capacity per annum, of a given total gross tonnage. On the other hand, delays in port in handling cargo appear to have increased and this reduced the carrying capacity of a given total tonnage. The outcome of these opposing movements can only be guessed.

[2] The Norwegian kroner depreciated in terms of sterling from 1919 to 1924 as a result of internal inflation. After 1924 an appreciation was secured and the pre-war parity was restored in 1928 and maintained through the subsequent devaluation of sterling. Variations in exchange rates, therefore, contributed to the high level of the Norwegian index for the period 1924 to 1927 inclusive.

The Troubled Years: the Inter-war Period

TABLE 4. Indices[1] of world trade, shipping and freight rates, 1920–38
1913 = 100

Year	Index of world seaborne trade	Index of shipping tonnage		Indices of freight rates			
		Total	Active	The Economist	German liner	German tramp	Nor-wegian
	(1)	(2)	(3)	(4)	(5)	(6)	(7)
1920	83	122	n.a.	438·7	n.a.	n.a.	n.a.
1921	82	132	n.a.	158·4	n.a.	n.a.	n.a.
1922	92	135	119	122·0	n.a.	n.a.	n.a.
1923	94	139	126	109·7	n.a.	n.a.	n.a.
1924	106	134	126	113·4	n.a.	103	247
1925	114	136	128	102·2	n.a.	96	206
1926	115	136	128	109·7	n.a.	110	178
1927	127	139	133	109·6	120	99	170
1928	130	143	137	98·8	113	96	152
1929	135	145	141	96·8	114	100	151
1930	126	148	140	79·1	112	77	125
1931	112	150	130	79·6	95	73	102
1932	101	148	122	75·4	69	60	107
1933	103	145	123	72·7	66	49	110
1934	112	140	126	74·2	62	48	120
1935	118	136	130	74·4	63	50	125
1936	124	139	134	84·6	66	62	140
1937	141	141	140	128·3	73	86	n.a.
1938	135	144	142	97·6	77	64	n.a.

n.a. = not available.

Sources: (1) See footnote 1.
(2) Calculated from *Lloyd's Register*.
(3) Calculated as above, less tonnage laid up, figures of which from Brassey, Chamber of Shipping reports, etc.
(4) *The Economist*.
(5) and (6) German Statistical Year Book.
(7) *Der Wettbewerb in der Seeschiffahrt*, Institut fur Konjunkturforschung (Jena, 1940).

[1] The index of world sea-borne trade in the table is a composite. Use was made of United Nations' figures for the years 1930 to 1938 and the estimate of world sea-borne trade in 1912 given in Chapter II together with a German index of world trade for the period 1912 to 1937 and the League of Nations index of world trade volume for 1913, 1924 to 1929 and 1932 to 1936. Both the German and the League figures included land-borne trade which had to be excluded. The overlap in the data and the close correspondences between data from different sources in the overlapping years enabled a sea-borne trade index to be computed covering the

the manner in which liner freights were maintained relatively to tramp rates both in the 1920s and the 1930s. This better experience with regard to rates does not, however, mean that liners were less affected by the depression in shipping than were tramps, because liners were more frequently sailing with part cargoes than before 1914. This point will be taken up again later.

After 1929 world trade fell heavily and in 1932 was at about the same level as in 1913 while the volume of tonnage available was 48 per cent greater. In consequence, nearly 20 per cent of the world fleet was laid up, while freight rates were pushed, by the pressure of excess tonnage, to unprecedentedly low levels. At the depth of the depression in July 1932, 3·56 million tons of British shipping was laid up, that is, 17 per cent of the merchant fleet. This, however, compares favourably with 1922 when over 20 per cent of the British fleet was idle. Putting these two figures side by side in this way shows the effects on British shipping of the over-valued exchange rate of the 1920s, during which period British shipping as a whole fared rather worse than world shipping, compared with the period after devaluation when British shipping suffered rather less than that of other countries. In 1932, the percentages of shipping laid up in some leading maritime countries were:

Countries which had devalued:

Britain	17 per cent
Japan	6 „ „
Norway	20 „ „
Greece	35 „ „

Countries which had not devalued:

France	26 per cent
Italy	26 „ „
Germany	30 „ „
Holland	29 „ „

whole period 1920 to 1938. The tonnage indices are straightforward; the active tonnage index is compiled by deducting various estimates of idle tonnage from the total tonnage. *The Economist* freight index is used instead of the more representative index of the Chamber of Shipping because the latter was not calculated before 1920 and the use of 1920 as base year makes the depression of freights in subsequent years appear unduly severe, given the popular tendency to consider that the base year of an index is, in some way 'normal'. However, the movements of the two indices were very closely correlated.

The manner in which shipping suffered in countries which, for one reason or another, maintained the foreign exchange value of their currencies, is clear. It is not a coincidence that operating subsidies for tramps were introduced in Italy in 1932, Germany and Holland in 1933 and France in 1934.

Although world trade began to recover in 1933, the recovery in rates was delayed until 1934 due to the withdrawal of ships from lay up when freights showed any prospect of picking up. The anxiety of owners to bring their ships back into commission prevented a rise in rates from gathering any momentum. A second factor was the adoption of subsidies in a number of countries which enabled owners in those countries to accept low rates and still make profits. Recovery to prosperity in shipping was, therefore, slow, but by 1937, as a result of expanding world trade and the wholesale scrapping of ships in preceding years, the indices of world trade and of world shipping were once more in harmony and freight rates were at profitable levels for tramps, although the slower-moving liner rates had not recovered their 1913 level. After 1937 another down turn in world trade and in freight rates occurred, a decline arrested by the outbreak of war, while world tonnage continued to increase.

One result of the greater increase in shipping than in trade during the period 1920 to 1938 was an increase in the number of ballast voyages and in the number of liners travelling with part cargoes only.

The changing pattern of trade, in particular the growth of oil shipments, itself increased the number of ballast voyages as oil tankers cannot carry return cargoes when they have discharged their oil. This, however, was merely a normal feature of the market and calls for no special discussion here. The ballast voyages which created a problem were those in the tramp trades. Tramp ships made frequent voyages of a speculative nature in search of cargoes and then, faced with the prospect of further ballast voyages, were prepared to cut freight rates to levels below voyage costs because, when lying in a port other than the home port, crew costs and fuel costs to travel home were fixed costs which could not be avoided and almost any freight rate, no matter how low, was better than sailing home in ballast. This willingness to accept rates below voyage costs has always been a feature of liner operations and is one of the justifications for the existence of the conference system (see Chapter XIII). The habit of making speculative ballast voyages which grew up in the 1930s extended this particular problem to tramp trades also and the Tramp Shipping Administrative Committee (see Chapter V), which had been set up in Britain in 1935 with full international support and co-operation, found it necessary to proscribe ballast voyages by unfixed vessels in the administered trades.

In the case of liners, the frequency with which part cargoes only were available at conference rates was a major cause of the undercutting of those rates. The extent to which shipping employed was being less fully utilized in the depression can be seen by comparing the weight of British imports and exports with the tonnages of ships entered and cleared with cargo, that is, excluding ships in ballast. The weights of cargo carried per ton of shipping entering and leaving British ports with cargo for various years were:

1913	1·28 tons	1929	1·08 tons
1921	1·00	1931	0·94
1923	1·24	1933	0·92
1925	1·05	1935	0·96
1927	1·05	1937	1·00

This change was a consequence of the overtonnaging of trades and meant that liner rates which would have been satisfactory with full cargoes became unsatisfactory when only part cargoes were being carried.

During the inter-war years there was a sharp increase in the proportion of dry-cargo tonnage which was engaged in liner services. This occurred, first, through the operation of subsidized liner tonnage and, second, through tramp shipowners establishing liner services. The result was a continuing pressure on tonnage in liner trades which prevented liner rates from rising substantially when world trade picked up during the 1930s. Although liner conferences theoretically possessed the power to raise rates, while world trades were over-tonnaged this power was circumscribed by the fear of the higher-cost operators in each conference that if rates were raised the lower cost (or subsidized) members would consider it more profitable to secede and run at lower rates outside the conference. For this reason operators with relatively high costs, for example, most British lines, often could not raise rates when trade expanded while the lower-cost operators had no particular incentive to initiate such a rise nor, at existing rates, to break away and cut rates outside the conferences.

For British shipping the import and export trades of Britain were the most important sources of employment. These trades were relatively more important in the inter-war years than in the years before 1914 because the establishment of merchant fleets in other countries, particularly in America, reduced the British participation in the trades of those countries and British shipowners generally did not seek new trades to replace those which had been lost. The result was an increase in the significance of British direct trades to British shipping. In Table 5 the tonnages of British imports and exports are shown, together with an index of British sea-borne trade which may be compared with the index of world sea-borne trade reproduced from Table 4.

In 1923 only did British trade equal its 1913 level in volume, and that was due to special factors relating to coal exports. Comparing the years 1913, 1929 and 1937, the three being 'peak' years, British trade volume was made up of the following percentages:

	Imports	Exports Coal	Other
1913	37	51	12
1929	43	45	12
1937	57	33	10

showing clearly the increasing proportion of trade represented by imports. The increase in import volume between 1913 and 1937 was 19·3 million tons, of which 9·4 million tons consisted of an increase in oil imports.

For British shipping these changes had several consequences. First, the overall decrease in trade volume clearly was more adverse to British shipping than to that of other countries.

TABLE 5. British trade in quantum terms, 1913, 1920–38

Year	Imports (mil. tons)	Exports (mil. tons)			Total trade (mil. tons)	Index	Index world seaborne trade
		Coal	Other	Total			
						(1913 = 100)	
1913	56·0	76·7	16·9	93·6	149·6	100	100
1920	45·5	28·9	12·3	41·2	86·7	58	83
1921	39·3	26·2	8·0	34·3	73·6	49	82
1922	44·0	67·9	11·7	79·6	123·6	82	92
1923	52·0	84·5	14·0	98·5	150·5	100	94
1924	58·5	65·5	14·6	80·1	138·6	92	106
1925	55·0	54·1	14·9	69·0	124·0	82	114
1926	52·5	21·9	12·7	34·6	87·1	58	115
1927	61·5	54·3	14·9	68·2	129·7	86	127
1928	56·5	53·7	15·6	69·3	125·8	84	130
1929	60·5	64·4	17·0	81·4	141·9	94	135
1930	58·7	58·4	13·9	72·3	131·0	87	126
1931	55·2	45·9	10·4	56·3	111·5	74	112
1932	52·3	41·9	10·1	52·0	104·3	70	101
1933	55·4	42·1	9·8	51·9	107·3	71	103
1934	62·4	42·6	11·0	53·6	116·0	77	112
1935	62·8	41·9	11·5	53·4	116·2	77	118
1936	72·0	37·4	11·6	49·0	121·0	74	124
1937	75·3	43·5	13·5	57·0	132·3	88	141
1938	67·3	38·2	11·5	49·7	117·0	78	135

Source: Liverpool Steamship Owners' Association, Annual Reports, various dates.

Second, the change in the proportion between imports and exports meant that voluntary, induced or compelled insistence by foreign shippers on c.i.f. shipments tended to reduce the part of the trade available for British ships, while the scope for British shippers to assist British shipping by insisting on c.i.f. was reduced by the fall in British exports. Third, the marked decline in coal exports removed a competitive advantage which British tramps had enjoyed. Fourth, the increase in oil shipments, both absolutely and relatively, provided opportunities for a type of ship largely neglected by British shipowners (see below). Oil imports increased from 1·7 million tons, 1·1 per cent of British sea-borne trade in 1913 to 11·1 million tons, 9·5 per cent of trade, in 1938.

It may also be noted at this point that the change in trade volume carried with it a change in entrances and clearances of tonnage. The figures for 1913, 1929 and 1937 are:

| | Entered (mil. net tons) | | Cleared (mil. net tons) | | Percentage of British ships to total | |
	British	Foreign	British	Foreign	Entered	Cleared
					%	%
1913	32·3	16·8	40·1	27·7	65·8	59·2
1929	40·7	21·9	45·3	23·3	65·0	66·0
1937	39·3	31·1	36·0	25·4	55·8	58·6

It has already been pointed out that the utilization of ships decreased by nearly 25 per cent between 1913 and 1937, that is, 25 per cent more shipping was used for a given volume of trade; this accounts for the disparity between the changes in these figures and the corresponding changes in trade volumes. The figures of entrances show that between 1913 and 1937, British entrances increased by 22 per cent while foreign entrances increased by 85 per cent; this may have been due to the effects of subsidies, to overseas shippers selling on c.i.f. terms and specifying their own ships, or to the ability of other countries to provide better or cheaper services. In fact, it was chiefly in the countries subsidizing their shipping that c.i.f. shipments in national ships were encouraged. This means that the limitation on the growth of British shipping which was due to insistence on c.i.f. shipment for exports cannot be determined independently of the effects of subsidies. The effects of the two factors together on British trades are considered in Chapter V. In the case of clearances, the share of British ships was the same in 1937 as in 1913; the increase in the share obtained up to 1929 was lost in the 1930s.

It is clear from the trade figures that the tonnage of British shipping which was engaged in British trade could not grow during the period because British trade did not grow. The fact that British trade volume did not respond after the depression in the manner of that of the remainder of the world partially explains why the tonnage of British shipping, which lay above the trend value each year from 1919 to 1931, was below the line in subsequent years. British shipping could only have grown in the period had shipowners found new outlets in non-British trades.

An aspect of international trade in the inter-war years which needs specific mention is the growth of tariffs. This is not the place to consider the reasons why free trade principles were abandoned in the inter-war years, nor to consider the extent to which the growth of nationalistic sentiments and tariff barriers to protect domestic employment levels contributed to limiting the growth of world trade. It is the course of the volume of world trade, as shown by the index numbers in Table 4, which is important here, not the reasons for that course. The course of trade is, however, only one side of the picture. In addition to reducing the volume of world sea-borne trade, tariffs had the effect of raising prices and wages in the protected countries making it more difficult for shipping enterprises in those countries to survive as they had to secure their resources in a protected market but sell their services in an unprotected market.

The effects of tariffs are seen clearly in America and the protectionist policy of that country, was, and is, a major factor in keeping American wage rates at levels which priced American shipping out of world markets. British shipping had gained from this. In assessing the effects of American subsidy policies (Chapter V) it must be borne in mind that the proper comparison, although it cannot be made, is between the mercantile marine which a protectionist American economy maintained by subsidies and the hypothetical shipping fleet which a free trade American economy could have supported, adjusted to account for the reduction in imports arising from the tariff policy. America was not the only country concerned, however, and the countries which subsidized their shipping were generally those which protected their home industries. Britain also abandoned free trade during the period and this, in itself, handicapped British shipping in competition with the shipping of relatively low-wage countries on the one hand, and of protectionist countries which subsidized their shipping on the other hand. With respect to tariffs the misfortune visiting British shipping came doubly not singly.

The Troubled Years: the Inter-war Period

FUEL TRADES

The most important change in world trading patterns in the inter-war years was the decline in the relative importance of the coal trade and the growth of the trade in oil with a consequent need for specialized tankers to transport the oil.

The coal exports of the United Kingdom for the years 1913 and 1920 to 1938 were shown in Table 5. In the post-war period only in 1923, the year of the Ruhr crisis, did coal exports reach their pre-war level. The volume of exports was subject to cyclical variations and to changes arising from random factors. Despite these variations, however, the downward trend of the total is unmistakable.

Within the overall decline in total exports was a relatively larger decline in exports to distant destinations, such as South America, than in exports to nearer destinations. British tramp shipping was adversely affected in two ways by these changes. First, the long-haul coal trades had provided outward cargoes for tramps bringing grain and other bulk products home and in these trades British tramps had predominated. The coal exports before 1914 had given a competitive advantage to British tramps which had offset the advantages of the lower crew costs of Greek and Norwegian tramps. Second, the short-haul coal trades, in which the relative decline in coal exports was smaller than in the long-haul trades, were trades in which even in 1913 British ships had carried less than 40 per cent of the total.

In 1913 British coal exports to all destinations provided continuous employment for some 5 million tons of tramp shipping,[1]

---

[1] Clearances with coal to South America in 1913 were 2·8 million net tons, that is, about 4·5 million gross tons. Each ship could make between three and four trips per annum, so that between 1 million and 1·5 million gross tons were employed. In other distant trades more coal was carried, but the average distance was less, so that the tonnage required was smaller, probably between 0·75 million and 1 million tons. The long-haul trades, therefore, used between 1·75 and 2·5 million tons of shipping, to carry 14·7 million tons of coal in the year. In the shorter trades, ships could have made, on average, twelve voyages per annum—although sea time is reduced when trips are shorter, dead time in port per trip is unaltered and so becomes a higher proportion of the total time. To carry 58·7 million tons of coal in these trades, between 2·5 million and 3 million tons of shipping was required. The total tonnage employed was, therefore, between 4·25 million and 5·5 million tons, of which 90 per cent of that employed in the long-haul trades and 40 per cent of that used in the short-haul trades was British-owned.

of which about 3 million tons was British-owned. On the same basis, in the 'boom' year of 1937, about 2·5 million tons of shipping was employed in carrying British coal exports; about 1·5 million tons of this shipping was British-owned. The decline in the British coal trade, together with the intensified competition from foreign tramps, probably accounted for a decline of up to 1·5 million tons in the size of the British tramp fleet.

While the coal trade of Britain declined, world oil trades increased. World crude oil production before 1914 had grown from under one million tons in 1870 to about 45 million tons in 1914. In 1920 production was 95 million tons and the increase continued throughout the inter-war years with only a slight dip in 1932 as a result of the depression. By 1937 production had reached 276 million tons. Exports of oil by sea rose from some 14 million tons before 1914 to 60 million tons in 1931 and 84 million tons in 1937.[1] The world oil trade, therefore, was a trade which developed in the inter-war years, rising from less than 5 per cent of the total tonnage of world sea-borne trade in 1913 to about 21 per cent in 1937 and about 25 per cent in the years 1938 and 1939 when world trade generally was below the 1937 level.

The world tanker fleet in 1914 was 1·5 million tons, of which one-half was owned in Britain, almost entirely by the oil companies and the Admiralty. At this stage British shipping companies were not interested in tankers, but this was largely true of shipping companies throughout the world. In the inter-war period, alongside the growth in world oil trades was an increase in the world tanker fleet, from 1·4 million tons gross in 1913 to 10·7 million tons in 1938 and 11·4 million tons in 1939. This increase occurred fairly continuously throughout the period with a particularly rapid expansion between 1928 and 1931.

---

[1] Another estimate puts world exports of oil at 37 million tons in 1921, which ties up reasonably well with the figure of 14 million tons suggested for 1913, 100 million tons in 1930, 93 million tons in 1931 and 119 million tons in 1935. (T. Koopmans, *Tanker Freight Rates and Tankship Building* (Haarlem, 1939), p. 187.) On a similar basis, sea-borne exports in 1937 must have been about 142 million tons, that is, 36 per cent of total world sea-borne trade. This seems too high in view of the size of the world tanker fleet and the fact that the average distance which oil was carried increased by about 10 per cent during the period. The United Nations figure for world sea-borne trade in oil in 1937 is 105 million metric tons (102 million British tons), which includes American coastal trade in oil.

Britain, which had owned 50 per cent of the world tanker fleet in 1913, owned only 25 per cent in 1939, the relative decline being particularly heavy in the years 1928 to 1931.

TABLE 6. Dry-cargo and tanker fleets, 1913 to 1938
(Ships of over 100 tons gross)

Year	World fleet (million tons)			British fleet (million tons)			British percentage of world fleet		
	Tanker	Dry cargo	Total	Tanker	Dry cargo	Total	Tanker	Dry cargo	Total
1913	1·4	45·4	46·9	0·7	18·0	18·7	50·0	39·6	39·8
1923	5·2	60·0	65·2	1·7	17·6	19·3	32·7	29·3	29·6
1928	6·6	60·4	67·0	2·1	17·8	19·9	31·8	29·4	29·7
1933	8·9	59·0	67·9	2·3	16·4	18·7	25·8	27·8	27·5
1938	10·7	57·1	67·8	2·7	15·1	17·8	25·2	26·4	26·2

Source: Lloyd's Register.

Before the war, the world tanker fleet had been almost entirely made up of naval vessels and those owned, either directly or through subsidiaries, by the oil companies. The only independent tankers were those owned, mainly in Norway and Japan, by whale-oil enterprises. In the inter-war years a fleet of independent tankers grew up, owned by shipping enterprises and chartered on time or voyage charter to the oil companies. With the rapid growth in the demand for oil in the inter-war period and the increasing need for tanker tonnage, the big oil companies found it increasingly convenient to be relieved of the need to provide themselves for their full transport requirements. The practice grew up, therefore, of the oil companies owning tankers capable of providing from one-quarter to two-fifths of their annual transport requirements, taking further tankers on time charters for periods of up to ten years, and securing the remainder of their requirements by taking tankers on voyage charters. The historical sequence was from entirely owned fleets before 1914, through fleets partly owned and partly time-chartered in the 1920s, to the three-tiered arrangement, which is general today, in the 1930s.

For the story here, an important move by an oil company in the direction of deliberately meeting its transport requirements by the use of time-chartered vessels was the offer by the Anglo-

Saxon Oil Co. in 1926 of thirty-seven of its tankers for sale with ten-year time-charters back to the company. The tankers were offered internationally at an average price of £65,000 each, payment by a 20 per cent deposit at the time of sale and the balance over five to ten years to be deducted from the charter hire payable. The time-charter rates provided only a slender margin of profit on reasonable expectations regarding running costs, repairs and depreciation. Twenty-six of the ships were bought by Norwegian owners, while one bought by a British owner was afterwards resold to a Norwegian owner. Generally, the Norwegian purchasers were new men, not existing ship-owners. The capital for the deposits was raised from the pur-chasers' own resources, from Norwegian ship brokers who took an interest in the sales, from the British ship brokers handling the sales and from sundry sources in Norway and other coun-tries. The money was not easy to collect and the Norwegian purchasers had access to no special sources of funds which British owners, given a willingness to perform the labour of collecting the money in small amounts from diverse sources, could not have tapped. Perhaps the Norwegian tanker fleet would have developed as it subsequently did without these pur-chases, but that is speculation. What is certain, however, is that the willingness of Norwegian owners to accept the risks and the low profit margin expected extended the ownership of tankers to southern Norwegian ports. With falling costs in the early 1930s and more economical operation than under Anglo-Saxon ownership, profits exceeded expectations, averaging about £12,500 per annum before providing interest and amortization. The success of the tankers encouraged emulation in Norway and helped the Norwegians to consolidate an international reputa-tion as tanker owners willing to own vessels let on time charters.[1] The consequence was that both British and American oil com-panies afterwards approached Norwegian owners directly when they wanted an increase in the tonnage held on charter.

Why did the British owners fail to take the opportunity which proved so profitable for Norwegians? One reason for their lack of interest in the Anglo-Saxon transaction was that the profit

[1] For a fuller account, see Leif Nørgård, *Tankfartens etablerings- og introduksjon-periode i norsk skipsfart 1912–1913 og 1927–1930* (Bergen, 1961).

margin offered was smaller than British owners were accustomed to expect, while British ship brokers had neither the resources nor the outlook necessary to locate small shipowners with a little money who might have run the risks involved. Other reasons can best be considered in seeking an answer to the question, 'Why did British shipowners not copy the Norwegians and subsequently build tankers?'

Until 1932 Britain was allegedly not a very good country in which to own tankers, the allegation depending on the assumption that neglect of the safety factors implicit in load line rules was favourable to owners. There were no international rules regarding load lines. The Board of Trade had a set of rules dating from 1906 which applied to all British vessels, but not to ships owned in other countries, although most countries observed the British or the similar German rules and the British rules were enforced, when necessary, on foreign ships visiting British ports. Norwegian tankers observed the British rules, although smaller vessels with moulded depths of less than 24 feet could load slightly deeper. American tankers were permitted to load to deeper draughts than were British tankers and for a short period, between the signing of the International Load Line Convention in 1930 and the incorporation of the international rules into British legislation in 1932, American tankers could load to a freeboard 20 per cent less than the normal. This advantage was considerable, but of such short duration that it was, in fact, unimportant. Little, therefore, can be made of British load-line rules as a factor inhibiting the growth of an independently-owned British tanker fleet, particularly *vis-à-vis* the Norwegian fleet. The reason why British oil interests preferred chartering foreign-owned tonnage to building a greater volume of tonnage themselves was that they wanted to conserve their own capital resources for exploration while few independent British tankers were available for charter.

Tankers were not an obvious venture for liner owners. In addition, for British liner owners the replacement and improvement of their liner fleets had first call on their resources and the generally low level of profits being earned in the 1930s did not provide the internal finance necessary for entry into tanker trades. They traditionally rejected, indeed scarcely even considered, borrowing on the security of time charters as Norwegian owners were willing to do.

The tramp section of the industry, which might have been expected to show an interest in tankers to replace the declining trade for colliers, was also inhibited. The booms in coal exports in 1923 and 1929 and the extent to which labour unrest contributed to the low level of exports in the intervening years distracted attention from the change in the pattern of world fuel demands. Within the tanker chartering market the only charterers were the large oil companies which also owned vessels. There was, therefore, a substantial difference between the relative bargaining strengths of the charterers and the shipowners offering ships for charter which made the market unattractive to owners used to the more competitive tramp markets. Having built tramps in the early 1920s which were never really profitable, the tramp owners lacked the capital to switch into tankers and the enterprise necessary to enter enthusiastically into a new venture. The tramp owners as a whole were cheeseparing by nature, meeting competitive pressures by continuous economies within traditional ship types, but rarely taking a longer view and endeavouring to reduce costs (or increase receipts) by spending money on ships designed for existing conditions. In any case, spending money on new ships would usually have entailed raising more capital and after the losses in shipping enterprises caused by the break of the speculative boom in 1920 money was difficult to raise from traditional sources. However, the guarantee arrangements of the Trade Facilities Acts enabled companies which wished to raise new money to do so before the provisions were terminated in 1931, and Norwegian owners, who had also suffered heavy losses after 1919, found it possible to raise money, sometimes from British sources.

While there were objective factors which influenced British shipowners, these factors clearly do not account for the almost complete neglect of the tanker. Underlying the objective factors, and of much greater importance, was that British shipowners scarcely thought of tankers, which they seem to have regarded as hardly being ships at all, much as the American sailing shipowners in the nineteenth century turned their backs on steamships which they regarded as floating kettles not worthy of their consideration.

In 1938 the tonnage of tankers of over 2,000 tons gross in the world was 10·2 million tons. Of this total, 5·3 million tons were owned by oil companies and 4·9 million tons were independently owned, that is, owned by predominantly shipping enterprises. Only 0·9 million tons of the independently-owned tanker tonnage was owned in Britain and of this some 0·4 million tons consisted of Admiralty tankers and bulk liquid carriers used in molasses and whale-oil trades. In contrast to the figure of 0·5 million tons of British independently-owned tankers engaged in mineral-oil trades, are the following figures of the independently-owned fleets of other countries:

Norway	1·75 million tons		France	0·25 million tons	
America	0·63	,, ,,	Japan	0·18	,, ,,
Italy	0·34	,, ,,	Sweden	0·16	,, ,,

all these being countries with very much smaller total merchant fleets than that of Britain. The independent fleets of Italy and France enjoyed state subsidies. About 20 per cent of the American fleet of independent tankers was owned by the U.S. Navy, while the balance was engaged in the reserved coastal trades and did not compete in the world market. Japan, with low labour costs, had strong competitive advantages in the field of tankers, but tankers comprised only 7 per cent of the total sea-going fleet and most of the independent tankers were engaged in whale-oil trades. Japanese shipping, however, was engaged almost entirely in Japanese trades and in composite trades arising within trading routes with one end in Japan, and this marked absence from indirect trades helps to explain the relatively small tanker fleet; further, the Japanese fleet was expanding vigorously in other directions. The Swedish independent fleet, although seventh in order of world importance, was small and requires no special explanation. It is the Norwegian fleet of independently-owned tankers which was of greatest importance.

Before the 1914–18 war most Norwegian shipowners, like British owners, were not interested in tankers. However, the Norwegian tanker fleet doubled between 1914 and 1920 and again between 1920 and 1925, during the whole of which period the British tanker fleet only doubled. The real boom in Norwegian tankers started after 1926. The tonnage, including ships of under 2,000 tons and whale-oil carriers, owned in Norway grew in the following manner over the period:

1925	0·26 million tons		1933	1·51 million tons	
1927	0·40	,, ,,	1935	1·56	,, ,,
1929	0·78	,, ,,	1937	1·86	,, ,,
1931	1·45	,, ,,	1939	2·12	,, ,,

The boom in Norway was part of a world boom in tanker construction engendered by the rising world demand for oil with a consequent rise in freight rates. This boom scarcely touched the British or the American tanker fleets. Its failure to touch the American fleet was a consequence of the level of American running costs which led the oil companies there to seek to reduce costs by taking up Norwegian, rather than American, independently-owned tankers on time charters. Norwegian owners were able to borrow in America to aid the construction of their tanker fleet while shipbuilders with slack order books were willing to extend credit of up to 90 per cent of the building cost; there was nothing here which British owners could not have enjoyed had they sought it, however. The tanker boom got out of hand so that by 1933 nearly one-fifth of the total world tanker tonnage was laid up. The British fleet suffered proportionately more seriously at this time than any other and one-quarter of British tanker tonnage was idle, largely because it consisted mainly of steam tankers with higher operating costs than those of the motor tankers owned in Norway.

In competition with Norwegian vessels, British tankers were said to be at a disadvantage with respect to crew costs because both wage rates and manning scales were lower in Norway than in Britain. However, international crew-cost comparisons are very difficult to interpret as like can seldom be, and even more rarely is, compared with like. It is possible that the British disadvantage compared with the Norwegians amounted to 25 per cent of crew costs, but this is an outside figure and probably bears little relation to the actual difference. Even if the difference was of this magnitude it only raised voyage costs by about 10 per cent and total costs by about 5 per cent. Much more important than any economic disadvantage which Britain suffered through higher crew costs[1] was the British preference for steam as against motor tankers. Of the tankers in the Tanker Pool Scheme,[2] 55 per cent of the British vessels were diesel engined, against 83 per cent of the Norwegian vessels in the Pool. The lower running costs of diesel-engined ships are discussed below. The average size of British independently-owned tankers in 1938 was 6,400 tons (9,200 deadweight tons), whereas the average size of Norwegian independent tankers was 7,500 tons (11,400 deadweight tons), showing a greater average carrying capacity in relation to gross tonnage (and hence in relation to building costs) and giving lower running costs per ton mile at equal wage and other costs per week. Theoretical analysis suggests that a country with higher wage costs can only remain competitive in shipping if it adopts the most economical method of propulsion and builds generally larger and faster ships than its lower-wage rivals. British owners did exactly the opposite.

The change in world fuel trades had two effects on British shipping. First, through the decline in coal exports employment for about 1·5 million tons of British tramps was lost. Second, the failure of British shipowners to enter the fuel trade as independent tanker owners created a vacuum which Norwegian entrepreneurs filled; about 1·8 million tons of tankers were added to the Norwegian fleet. These ships, and the other tankers of the world, replaced colliers and catered for new fuel requirements which did not exist before the war.

[1] If the Norwegian purchasers of the Anglo-Saxon tankers had crew costs 25 per cent higher than those actually incurred, operating profits per vessel would have been reduced from about £12,500 to about £11,500 per annum, that is, from about 20 per cent to 18 per cent of the cost of the tankers. Clearly, the tankers would have been profitable at British wage rates.

[2] The principle of the Tanker Pool, first established in May 1934, was the payment of a laying up allowance financed by a levy on freights earned by vessels in trade. The laid-up allowance covered the cost of keeping a vessel inactive, removing from owners the incentive to operate vessels so long as the operating losses were less than the laying up costs. In this way the supply of tankers offering for charter was reduced, rates were raised and all tanker-owners profited. The success of the scheme was dependent on the support of the oil companies which, as both major tanker-owners and the only charterers of tankers, had the ability either to make or mar the scheme. The cost of the scheme to the oil companies was the price the companies paid for the long-run maintenance of the independent tanker fleet.

THE MOTOR SHIP

The major technical innovation of the inter-war years was the widespread adoption of diesel propulsion for ships. The diesel engine had been introduced immediately prior to the war, the way being shown by Germany and the Scandinavian countries. The popularity of the diesel in Scandinavia was practically instantaneous because the tonnage of fuel consumed per horse power produced was relatively low, an important consideration in countries which had to import all their fuel requirements, while fuel costs were from 30 per cent to 50 per cent lower than in the case of steamers.

For British shipping, the development of diesel propulsion had several consequences.

First, Britain having no worth-while indigenous oil supplies had no advantage in fuelling over other ship-owning countries whereas, so long as coal was the predominant fuel, the high quality of Welsh steam coal available at home gave British ships an advantage over less favourably placed rivals. The advantage was never critical because of the widespread availability of coal supplies throughout the world and the fact that ships could carry coal bunkers for only relatively short periods at sea while both British and foreign ships were on equal terms when bunkering in other than British ports. With the introduction of oil fuel the advantage was lost.

Second, and most important, British shipbuilders and ship-owners were generally slower than their Continental rivals to realize the advantages of the diesel engine. This point must be treated with care. Some British liner owners adopted the diesel-engined ship with great enthusiasm, the most notable being the members of the Kylsant (Royal Mail) group. Where British owners were relatively slow to adopt diesel engines was in tramps and tankers. For these types of ship, because of the economy in the running of diesel engines and the long range without refuelling, those owners who had built motor ships had an advantage. Some British cargo-ship owners did realize the benefits of diesel propulsion and the Bank Line Limited, in 1923, secured a guarantee under the Trade Facilities Act for a public issue of capital to build a fleet of nineteen motor vessels.

Despite the fact that Scandinavian motor vessels '. . . were known to be kept well employed and were understood to have proved more efficient in every way, . . .[1] few British owners followed the lead of the Bank Line.

Using British wage rates, the economy of the diesel engine can be seen from the figures in Table 7. The comparison is made between a diesel-engined vessel and a comparable steam vessel using the most economical engines. The advantage of the motor ship is clear and the ship shown in the table could survive on a freight rate of 1s. per ton less than that at which the steamship was viable. This calculation covers only direct voyage costs. In fact, diesel engines were more expensive in first cost than steam engines although this was partly offset by the fact that for ships with similar dimensions more cargo could be carried in a diesel ship than in a steamer. In the leanest years between the wars, however, freights were sufficiently low that only voyage costs could be covered by most tramp ships and as depreciation had to be written off whether ships were laid up or not it was only voyage costs that mattered in determining whether ships could accept employment at the ruling freight rates. The economy of the diesel vessel was, therefore, a vital competitive factor.

TABLE 7. Comparative costs of running for a voyage of 30 days of a motor ship and an economical steamship, deadweight capacity 8,000 tons, speed 10·5 knots

Cost items	Diesel ship oil fired	Steamship coal fired
Fuel used on voyage (tons)	282	1,005
Cost of fuel (£)	916·5	1,256·25
Cost of lubricating oil (£)	45	19·5
Engine room staff (number)	8	21
Wages and victualling cost of engine room staff (£)	181	307·25
Total engine room costs of voyage (£)	1,132·5	1,583
Engine room cost per ton carried (£)	0·141	0·198

Source: Brassey (1935), p. 337. Figures apparently relate to about 1930.

The manner in which diesel propulsion was adopted in a number of leading maritime countries is shown in Table 8. It is

[1] *Shipbuilding and Shipping Record* (2 January 1924), p. 8.

significant that the four leading countries in the adoption of the diesel engine were countries which did not subsidize their shipping and which paid relatively high wage rates,[1] although generally lower than those paid in the United States or Britain. It was by these means that shipowners in these countries sought to overcome the competition from subsidized shipping on the one hand, and the low wage costs of Greek and Yugoslavian tramps on the other hand.

TABLE 8. Percentages of tonnage equipped with diesel engines, selected years, 1923 to 1939

| | *Percentage of fleet using diesel propulsion* | | | | | | | | |
	1923	*1925*	*1927*	*1929*	*1931*	*1933*	*1935*	*1937*	*1939*
	%	%	%	%	%	%	%	%	%
Norway	8·3	12·9	21·1	29·9	40·3	43·0	48·6	56·0	62·2
Denmark	16·0	18·1	22·2	29·2	35·9	39·5	41·9	48·7	52·2
Sweden	16·1	21·4	22·7	27·1	31·7	33·3	36·6	39·8	46·6
Holland	2·9	5·3	8·0	13·2	22·0	26·0	33·0	38·8	45·5
Japan	0·8	1·7	3·0	5·4	12·0	14·3	20·4	24·9	27·2
Germany	4·2	9·0	10·6	14·4	14·8	17·2	18·5	22·3	26·2
Great Britain	2·0	3·9	6·1	9·5	12·4	14·0	16·6	21·3	25·6
Italy	3·1	4·7	11·0	14·4	16·7	19·3	22·3	20·3	20·8
World	2·6	4·2	6·6	9·7	13·4	15·0	17·4	20·7	24·4

Source: compiled from *Lloyd's Register*.

Part, at least, of the responsibility for the failure of British shipowners to adopt the diesel more enthusiastically must be attributed to British shipbuilders and marine engineers. Diesel type units were made in this country under licence from Continental producers and an indigenous British design was available. They were, however, made on a small scale, generally cost more than similar units made abroad and did not always perform to expectations. This is not the place to enter into a discussion of British shipbuilding and its failings; if British shipowners had really felt that they were being hindered by the

[1] In 1925 wage rates were highest in America, followed by Britain, Sweden, Netherlands, Denmark, Norway, Belgium, Italy, France and Germany in that order (*The Times*, 5 September 1925). Subsequent reductions in British wages narrowed the gap between Britain and countries lower in the list, the appreciation of the Norwegian kroner up to 1928 raised Norwegian rates in terms of sterling, while currency devaluations in 1931 altered the order substantially.

conservatism of shipbuilders there was no reason why they should not have built their ships abroad and thus jolted the British industry to greater efforts. Complacency, however, met complacency, and a reading of the contemporary statements of shipowners gives a strong impression that they felt it almost sinful of the Scandinavian and German owners to have adopted diesel propulsion. The competitive advantage gained by the shipowner who had built the right type of ship to meet existing conditions was rarely distinguished by the British industry from the advantages which other owners gained from subsidies and state help in general.

THE EXPERIENCE OF BRITISH SHIPPING

For British shipowners as a whole, the years of the 1920s were difficult despite the relatively favourable level of freights up until 1927, and British shipping was perhaps more depressed than that of any other leading maritime country. A wage reduction in 1925 helped to lower costs, but the over-valued sterling exchange rate put British tramp ships at a disadvantage in world markets. Most companies had to cut their dividends in 1924 and in subsequent years dividends remained generally below the levels ruling in the war and immediate post-war years. However, capitals had increased sharply as a result of speculation and amalgamations at inflated prices during the war, and a low dividend rate often was no more than a reflection of a capitalization which was inappropriate and from which the water had not been squeezed. Further, the depreciation which was being written off before profits were declared was based on the historic cost of ships owned, a significant proportion of which had been built or had changed hands at the high prices ruling between 1914 and 1921. In the case of liners, for example, the average book value of each ton of shipping was £10·1 in the period 1909–13 and £25 in the period 1924–8. Whatever may be thought about the absolute levels of these valuations, the increase had justification neither in terms of the earning power of the ships represented nor of their replacement cost. In the case of tramps, the increase in valuation was even greater and the many complaints of the industry that depreciation could not be covered from earnings during the 1920s must be seen in the light of the irrelevance to current conditions of the values at which ships were standing in the books of most companies. The acknowledgment of the capital losses and the heavy writing down of capitals would have given the industry a truer picture of its situation and improved its competitive position.

The 1930s were a great deal worse, but British shipping suffered in company with that of the remainder of the world although the depreciation of the pound sterling in 1931 eased the position somewhat and helped British ships in relation to the shipping of countries which did not devalue. Average dividends of liner companies owning about 6 million tons of shipping fell from 6·23 per cent in 1929 to 1·56 per cent in 1933, based on 1932 results,[1] although, as in the earlier years, the failure to write down fleet values, and hence capitals, was partly responsible for the low rate. In 1933 the average book value of the liners in the *Fairplay* sample was £14·6 per ton, whereas in terms of earning power a figure of about £6 per ton would have been more realistic.

The backbone of British liner trades was the carriage of British exports other than coal. In 1913 the weight of British non-coal exports was 16·9 million tons. This figure was exceeded in 1929 when 17 million tons were exported, but thereafter declined to 9·8 million tons in 1933, from which level it recovered to 13·5 million tons in 1937 (see Table 5). In addition, much British entrepôt trade was lost through the establishment of through services by foreign ships. The change in the entrepôt position is indicated, but not exactly measured, by the change in the tonnage of re-exports in the period. The indices for the tonnages of total exports, home-produced exports and re-exports, coal always excluded, base 1913 = 100, were as follows:

	1913	*1929*	*1938*
Home-produced exports	100	102	70
Re-exports	100	85	54
Total exports	100	100	68

Source: Liverpool Steamship Owners' Association; figures adjusted to 1913 base.

[1] All figures from *Fairplay*.

In conferences, the undercutting of rates was common, and those British shipowners who had relied on the shelter of conferences to protect them from the full blast of world depression were placed in a precarious position. The competition came from various sources, some from the subsidized ships, but the rest from non-subsidized Scandinavian and Dutch tonnage which, by the use of modern, economical and fast vessels and aggressive competitive methods, succeeded in wresting increasing shares of world trade from British hands. Table 10 (see page 92) shows the changes in the shares of British and Norwegian shipping in a number of world trades and these figures show convincingly that it was possible for unsubsidized shipping to expand in the face of subsidized competition.

British liner-owners suffered on the one hand from the subsidies and higher speeds of competitors' ships and on the other from a failure of traditional trades which was not compensated by a vigorous search for new openings. With regard to the subsidy/speed problem, higher speeds were frequently adopted by unsubsidized foreign liner owners to meet the competition of subsidized vessels, while subsidized owners also put higher-speed vessels into service. Paradoxically, it was chiefly those British liner companies operating on routes, such as those to Australasia, where foreign competition was least important, which adopted the fast diesel solution for cargo liners, while on routes, such as those to the Far East and America and in the Pacific in which foreign competition was strongest, the fast British-owned diesel-engined cargo or passenger liner was a rarity.

British-owned tramps suffered even more severely than liners because in tramp trades the advantage of being established is negligible and trading connections built up over the years non-existent. While liners were able to survive without a subsidy, tramp shipping was provided with a subsidy of £2 million per annum in 1935, although this came too late to be of very much use. Within the overall decline in British-owned tonnage in the period, tramp tonnage is believed to have decreased to a greater extent than liner tonnage, although no clear picture can be obtained as the classification, tramps and liners, is based on employment, not on type of ship, and ships can readily be switched from one category to the other. Further, some tramping companies established liner services, thus reducing the tramp fleet without reducing the total fleet. The inter-war years, in fact, were marked by an increase in liner services throughout the world which cut at the trades which had formerly been the preserve of tramp shipping.

To explain fully the position of British tramps in the inter-war period would entail a detailed comparison of running costs in different countries. Tramp ships are generally slow and wage costs are the largest single item of total voyage costs for a new ship, although the relative importance of wages declines as the vessel gets older and repair costs begin to rise. Differences in wage costs between countries are important in determining the distribution of tramp ship ownership so long as ships within the same age group are being considered. No reliable data regarding relative manning costs of tramp ships under various flags are available for the inter-war period (indeed for any period), although it seems clear that British manning costs were lower than those in America, roughly equal to those in Norway and the Netherlands after the appreciation of the kroner and the guilder, perhaps a little above those in France, Germany and Italy and substantially above those in Yugoslavia, Greece and Japan (see Chapter XIV for a fuller discussion). In the case of Yugoslavia and Greece, however, capital shortage meant that elderly ships were generally owned so that high repair costs provided at least a partial offset to the lower wage costs.

Although British wage rates were apparently high in relation to those paid in some other countries, they were not high enough to attract more British labour into shipping and when shipping began to revive in the mid-thirties British owners sometimes experienced difficulty in finding crews. This produced the paradox that higher wage rates to attract more labour would have raised costs, worsened the competitive position of British shipping and perhaps made the extra labour unnecessary.[1] At existing wage levels, however, crew shortage set a definite limit to the expansion of the British mercantile marine after 1935. A way out of this difficulty was the use of more capital intensive

---

[1] It is assumed that if higher rates had been paid to attract additional crews these rates would then have been paid to all existing crews. This assumption is valid for ratings, but not necessarily true for deck and engineering officers.

vessels in tramp and tanker trades, that is, the building of larger and faster vessels than were built for owners with lower wage costs and on which higher wage rates could have been borne. The traditional rule of thumb operating calculations of so many British owners, however, were not adapted to the discovery of this possibility. The problem was solved after 1939 when service in the merchant marine became a lucrative alternative to service in the forces and this alternative continued to the ending of National Service.

It is not possible to make detailed yearly comparisons of the share of British shipping in all the different trades in which it participated. In Table 9 estimates are given for the years 1912, 1929 and 1936 of the relative importance of various trades and of the proportions of those trades carried in British ships. These percentages are derived from value figures and so conceal variations in actual tonnages carried, which are important for determining the employment of shipping, while they do not distinguish between dry-cargo and mineral-oil trades.

TABLE 9. Relative importance of various trades, and proportions carried in British ships, 1912, 1929, 1936, in value terms

	1912		1929		1936	
Trade between:	%a	%b	%a	%b	%a	%b
Foreign countries	46	30	45	25	44	12
Britain and Empire countries	12	94	13	95	16	95
Britain and foreign countries	28	66	25	57	22	55
Empire countries	3	85	2	56	3	77
Empire and foreign countries	11	55	15	56	15	38
Total world trade	100	52	100	47	100	40
Index of world sea-borne trade in quantum termsc	97		135		124	

a Trade between areas as a percentage of world sea-borne trade.
b Percentage of trade carried in British ships.
c 1913 = base 100.

Source: Calculated from Board of Trade figures.

The first, third and fifth lines in the table show the areas in which British shipping declined in importance. The first line shows the trade between non-British countries which, as a percentage of world trade in value terms, remained remarkably steady over a period and in which the proportion carried by British ships fell from 30 per cent in 1912 to 12 per cent in 1936. In the British trade with foreign countries, which declined in value terms over the period, the proportion carried in British ships fell from 66 per cent to 55 per cent. The trade between Empire countries and foreign countries, also an indirect trade for ships registered in the United Kingdom, increased slightly as a proportion of world trade, but the British share in carrying that trade declined from 55 per cent to 38 per cent. In the minor trade between Empire countries themselves, the share carried in British ships also declined. The only trade in which British shipping held its own was that between Britain and Empire countries which increased as a proportion of world trade. As a consequence of these changes, the share of world trade carried in British ships fell from 52 per cent in value terms in 1912 to 40 per cent in 1936. In terms of volume the decline must have been greater, brought about by the smaller volume of trade of Britain (see Table 5) in 1936 than in 1913, the increasing competition of foreign tramp ships in the River Plate grain trade, and the comparatively small share—20 per cent to 25 per cent— of world oil shipments carried in British tankers.

A good example of the failure of British shipowners to provide the right type of ship for the available trade is the experience in Mediterranean fruit trade. Citrus shipments from Palestine to Britain increased from 0·2 million boxes in 1919–20, all carried in British ships, to 6·7 million boxes in 1937–8, of which 5 million were carried in foreign ships. In the fruit service between Italy and Britain, the British vessels engaged in 1939 had a maximum speed of 11 knots and no refrigerated holds, except for an occasional service to Liverpool, whereas the Scandinavian ships in the trade were 13-knot ships with refrigerated holds.[1] The valuable fruit trades, which increased considerably during the inter-war years, were thus lost to British shipping because of the backwardness of British liner owners in providing the right kind of tonnage.

Mention should be made of a trade in which British shipping showed considerable initiative, namely, the cruising trades.

[1] Italian comment on Chamber of Shipping Fact Finding Committee Report (Confidential), quoted *Shipbuilding and Shipping Record* (16 February 1939), p. 200.

Passenger liners rendered redundant by the decline in migrant and other passenger traffic were sent cruising in order to keep them in employment. The alternative to this was scrapping. Until it was clear that the ships would never be required again for normal service, cruising was profitable so long as voyage receipts exceeded voyage costs *minus* the daily cost of laying up. The business was overdone, of course, and highly unsuitable liners were sent on highly inappropriate cruises. At its best, however, liners unwanted in their regular trades found a profitable niche in cruising. The actual tonnage continuously employed was small in relation to total tonnage, and the contribution of cruising to arresting the decline in British-owned tonnage was no more than 150,000 tons. However, because of the large crews carried by cruising ships the contribution to the employment of seamen was significant.

SCANDINAVIAN SHIPPING

During the inter-war period some of the strongest competition to British shipping came from the fleets owned in the Scandinavian countries. The particular relevance of this competition is that Scandinavian shipping, like that owned in Britain, enjoyed virtually no state assistance or protection. The competition was completely fair. It was competition between an old-established mercantile marine, with strong traditions and backed by a substantial national trade, and relatively new fleets without deep roots and lacking the background support of strong national trades. The reasons why the Scandinavian fleet rose from 3·6 million tons in 1919 to 7·6 million tons in 1939, and the consideration of the spheres in which this fleet increased its importance, throw considerable light on the failure of British shipping to grow in this period. Most of the discussion will concern Norwegian shipping because it was Norwegian shipping in particular which provided the keenest competition to British shipping.

The increase in the importance of Scandinavian shipping was most marked in the world's oil trade (see above). In world fruit trades using refrigerated tonnage Scandinavian ships came to hold a dominant position in this period. Ships from these countries were also strongly represented in general cargo trades,

The Troubled Years: the Inter-war Period

especially in the timber trade to Britain and in liner trades to Canada and East Asia and in the Pacific.

In Table 10 the changes in the relative positions of Norwegian and British shipping in thirteen trades between 1913 and 1936 are shown. In all the trades shown, the share held by British ships declined between 1920 and 1936 whereas the share carried by Norwegian ships increased in all but three of the trades during that period. The inclusion of the changes between 1913 and 1920 shows that the greater success of the Norwegians cannot be explained in terms of a wartime encroachment on trades denied to British ships. Between 1913 and 1920 both British and Norwegian shipping improved their relative positions in six trades but whereas British shipping lost ground in those trades after 1920, Norwegian shipping lost ground in only three of them. In fact, the only three trades in which Norwegian shipping declined in relative importance between 1920 and 1936 were trades in which the position of that shipping had improved between 1913 and 1920.

TABLE 10. Changes between 1913 and 1920, and 1920 and 1936 in shares of thirteen trades held by British and Norwegian ships respectively

	Change in percentage of trade held by:			
	British ships		Norwegian ships	
Trade	1913–20	1920–36	1913–20	1920–36
	%	%	%	%
German	−8·9	−1·4	−1·6	+1·7
British	+2·9	−5·2	+0·8	−2·2
Dutch	−3·7	−4·5	−0·7	+1·6
Belgian	+1·7	−21·1	+1·4	+3·3
French	+7·0	−7·9	+2·3	−2·4
Norwegian	−5·4	−1·4	+1·8	−2·8
Swedish	−0·7	−0·9	−3·0	+2·5
American	−22·6	−1·7	−2·9	+5·8
Brazilian	−5·9	−8·7	+1·5	+0·6
South African	+1·8	−16·8	−0·9	+3·2
Indian	+3·7	−11·9	+0·3	+1·7
Japanese	−11·0	−4·6	−0·4	+3·9
Australian	+0·6	0·0	−1·6	+4·6

Source: Der Wettbewerb in der Seeschiffahrt, pp. 122–3.

92

The Troubled Years: the Inter-war Period

It is interesting at this point to look at the changes in the employment of the Norwegian fleet during the period. The figures in Table 11 show how the intra-European trade declined in importance between 1913 and 1939 and was replaced by trades outside Europe. The greatest expansion was in the trans-Atlantic trade which employed 7 per cent of the Norwegian fleet in 1913 and 25·4 per cent in 1939. The term covered trades between North America and Europe, and between Africa and Europe, both trades on which subsidized competition was strong. A considerable expansion occurred in trades with the Middle East, this partly arising, as in the expansion in the trans-Atlantic trade, from the growth in oil shipments. The percentage of Norwegian tonnage engaged in the Far Eastern trades rose from 6·2 per cent in 1913, to 7·4 per cent in 1939, again in the face of subsidized competition, while Norwegian ships increased or maintained their shares in all American trades, in each case regaining in the 1930s the ground lost in the 1920s to the expanded American fleet. Comparable information respecting the employment of the British fleet is not available.

TABLE 11. Employment of Norwegian shipping, 1913–39

Trade	1913	1925	1933	1939
	%	%	%	%
Intra-European	41·9	31·7	20·2	12·6
Europe—non-Europe	27·5	37·5	38·1	47·1
Outside Europe	28·1	27·5	21·6	30·6
Laid up	2·5	3·3	20·1	9·7
Total	100·0	100·0	100·0	100·0

Sources: Norges Rederforbund, quoted A. S. Svendsen, *Seeverkehr und Schiffahrtswirtschaft* (Bremen, 1958), pp. 443–4. Primary source for 1913 and 1925, *Verdenshandelens Forskyvning* (Oslo, 1940).

The usual reason advanced in Britain for the success of Scandinavian shipping is the profits which were made during the war and which were available for fleet expansion in later years. It was shown in the previous chapter that wartime profits possibly accounted for the expansion of the Danish and Swedish fleets

93

but could not account for the much more spectacular growth of Norwegian shipping.

An important reason accounting for the difference between the experiences of Scandinavian and British shipping during the period is the adoption by Scandinavian owners of the fast diesel solution to the problems being faced by all shipowners. While the typical British tramp remained, in 1939 as in 1913, a 9-knot steamer, the typical Scandinavian tramp was an 11- to 13-knot ship and 16-knot tramps were built. British cargo liners were faster, particularly refrigerated vessels, and speeds of 15 knots were quite common. For the rest, the position was shown clearly in the British-dominated Australian trade in which, during the 1930s, Swedish motor ships customarily won the race for carrying the first part of the Australian wool clip to Europe. As pointed out earlier, in the Australasian trades generally British owners were more progressive in questions of speed than in many other important trades.

Another factor of importance was the readiness with which Norwegian owners entered tanker ownership using borrowed money to finance tankers let on long-term charters to British and American oil companies. At least one major Norwegian shipowner today started in this way, while a number of smaller fleets were also built up on this basis.

When all is said the impression is that Scandinavian owners succeeded where many British owners failed largely because they were not inhibited by traditional attitudes and were more flexible and enterprising in seeking new trades and in adapting their shipping enterprises to seize opportunities. 'Norwegian owners have specialized in types of vessels least affected by foreign subsidized competition. . . . The growth of Norwegian shipping has been fairly earned as a result of enterprise.'[1]

CONCLUSION

The task of this chapter was to discover why British shipping tonnage in 1939 was 5·1 million tons below the level (the trend tonnage) at which it would have stood had the growth rate experienced between 1890 and 1913 been maintained after

---

[1] O. Mance, *International Sea Transport* (London, 1945), p. 81.

1919. The conclusion which can be derived from this chapter is only partial as the effects of subsidies in the inter-war years have not yet been considered. All that can be done here is to see what explanations, other than the subsidy policies of other countries, can be advanced to explain the failure of the industry to grow during the period.

Part of the difference between the actual tonnage and the trend tonnage arose from circumstances beyond the control of the British shipping industry. These circumstances include the subsidy and preferential policies of other countries to be considered in the next chapter. They also include the declining relative importance in world trade of the trade of Britain, particularly in the recovery in the 1930s. This reduced the proportion of world trade to which British shipping looked for a substantial part of its employment and in which British ships had some advantages. The decline in the British coal trade, in particular, reduced the advantage which British tramp ships had enjoyed while the low wage costs of Greek and Yugoslavian tramps enabled them to operate at freights at which British tramp owners could not afford to offer their ships. Protection to the British economy meant that British shipowners had to hire their labour in a protected market, which raised its price, while trying to sell their services in a generally over-tonnaged world market.

Clearly, the period was one of great difficulty for British shipowners through no fault of their own. There were, however, other factors, within the control of shipowners, which contributed to the relative decline of British shipping in the period. There was a failure of enterprise and a lack of flexibility in parts of the industry which contributed to the decline. This failure was partly due to habits of superiority acquired before 1913 and not changed when the situation changed, partly to a failure to escape from conventional ideas about the types and speeds of ships suitable for various trades and, indeed, about the trades themselves, partly to the extensive amalgamations which had occurred in the industry, particularly in the liner section. The failure of the important Royal Mail group, which included lines prominent in most British trades, had far-reaching repercussions. It was alleged that as a result of the amalgamations within the industry shippers often found that the services rendered had deteriorated and that companies, with interests in a great variety of trades, did not give the detailed attention to the needs of shippers in individual trades which is the essence of successful ship owning.[1] Passengers and cargo shippers alike frequently found foreign shipowners more ready to meet their needs and less endowed with an inherited take-it-or-leave-it attitude.

The picture one gets is of an industry which, immediately after the war, planned for a future which would be an endless succession of pre-war years. The possibility that subsidies might succeed in keeping rival shipping enterprises in operation was scarcely considered and little was done to determine how the effects of subsidies might best be countered or avoided.[2] The encroachment of American shipping on trades formerly served by British ships was considered to be only a temporary interruption until the American Government 'came to its senses'. But the American Government did not 'come to its senses'. Progress in ship design was significant in the period, yet the typical British tramp, even in 1939, was a 9-knot coal-burning steamer. Normalcy and 1913 never returned and the bewildered industry was not structured to display the flexibility and imagination needed to meet the situation. There was an attitude of complacency, that the British industry was the best by definition, had the most suitable ships and generally knew best, together with an introverted concern with servicing British trades which was in marked contrast to the extrovert attitude of younger shipping enterprises in other countries. To the generalizations of this and the preceding paragraphs there were, of course, notable exceptions. However, except for occasional flashes of enterprise, the great liner companies and the best-known tramp owners were rarely among the exceptions. Indeed, if the generalizations were wholly inapplicable to these owners the whole history of the period, and hence the generalizations, would have been different.

The difference in enterprise between shipowners, whether in

---

[1] See *Shipbuilding and Shipping Record* (16 January 1936), p. 57.

[2] 'We know of no method by which Governments can *foster* shipping . . .': this statement from a memorandum by the Chamber of Shipping and the Liverpool Steamship Owners' Association in 1923 sums up the prevailing attitude.

Scandinavian or in other countries, trying to expand in an over-tonnaged world without the support of subsidies or the advantages of being established and shipowners with traditional positions which they expected to be allowed to maintain, was the critical factor in accounting for that part of the decline in the relative position of the British industry which lay within the control of British shipowners. But the relative failure of enterprise within the British industry was itself in part a reaction to, and a direct consequence of, the impact of the factors which lay outside the control of the industry.

V

Nationalism in Shipping in the Inter-war years

THE inter-war period was marked by a growth of national consciousness and, in particular, by a widespread desire among nations to see their flags represented, or represented more powerfully, in the mercantile marines of the world. The reasons for this were many and need not be discussed here. The consequence was the spread of subsidies, preference legislation and the adoption of trading methods favouring national shipping. Among the latter, particular reference should be made to the extension to other countries of the British practice of selling exports c.i.f. and buying imports f.o.b. so that the nomination of the carrying ships was the prerogative of a national. British shipping found it hard to counter this movement which was an extension of a trading condition on which British shipowners had insisted when they were in a position to insist. The attempts of British shipping interests to induce British traders always to adopt such terms in their international trading transactions were largely unsuccessful. This lack of success arose from the curiously ambivalent attitude of non-shipping interests in Britain to British shipping; on the one hand was an unquestioning belief in the superiority of British shipping and British ships, while on the other was a marked lack of sympathy for British shipowners. The second part of this attitude arose from a multitude of causes, including the imperious attitude of many liner companies, the manner in which shipping interests had profited in the early years of the war, the bad taste left by the speculative deals of the immediate post-war years and the general distrust of the concentration and cartellization of much of the industry. Despite, perhaps because of, this ambivalent attitude, there was the same type of jingoist propaganda for shipping in Britain as in other countries. This was reflected, for example, in the Government loan to Cunard and in the conditions of the tramp shipping subsidy (see page 110). When considering the nature and extent of nationalism in assisting the shipping of other countries, it must not be overlooked that British shipping was not free of these influences: the real difference was in the degree of success achieved by different national shipping interests in enlisting the sympathies of their fellow nationals.

The nature of the formal assistance given to shipping in the inter-war years is indicated in Table 12. In this table, countries giving postal subventions alone have been excluded and subventions of this type are noted only when other forms of assistance were also given, or where postal subventions were deliberately used as an alternative to declared navigation subsidies. Reservation of coastal trades and subsidies to maintain coastal services are also generally omitted. An entry in the table does not imply that the type of assistance was rendered continuously over the period; indeed, many of the acts of assistance noted were *ad hoc* measures of only a short duration.

As the table below shows, most maritime countries took steps at some time at least during the period to aid their shipping. With so many entries in the table it is clearly impossible to consider here all the cases noted. The method adopted in considering the pre-1914 situation, that is, discussing each type of assistance separately is not, therefore, suitable for this period. It seems most convenient to classify the countries listed in Table 12 into four groups as under:

Group A: *Minor shipowning countries giving relatively unimportant assistance:*

Australia	Egypt	Poland
Belgium	Estonia	Rumania
Bulgaria	Finland	Turkey
Canada	Mexico	Yugoslavia

Group B: *Minor shipowning countries the practices of which adversely affected British shipping:*

Argentine	Portugal
Brazil	Spain
Chile	Russia
Peru	

Nationalism in Shipping in the Inter-war years

Group C: *Important shipowning countries giving relatively unimportant assistance:*

Denmark	Norway
Greece	Sweden
Netherlands	United Kingdom

Group D: *Important shipowning countries the practices of which adversely affected British shipping:*

France	Japan
Germany	United States
Italy	

Each group of countries can now be discussed in turn.

COUNTRIES IN GROUP A

The countries in this group were all minor ship-owning nations, some of them new countries created by the re-drawing of European frontiers after the war. The aims of each country in supporting shipping services differed somewhat, although fundamentally most were concerned with providing direct services to home ports which foreign lines were not providing. In this way some trans-shipment services were lost by British ships, but these were not of major importance to British shipping as a whole.

The Australian venture into passenger shipping on the Britain-Australia route by means of five medium-sized vessels was potentially serious. It arose from dissatisfaction in Australia with the service provided by the co-operating British lines to which outside competition was unimportant. However, the costs to the Australian Government of running the fleet with Australian crews were sufficiently high for it to be pleased enough in 1928 to sell the ships at bargain prices to a British company. This Australian experience showed the impossibility of a high wage economy successfully operating slow passenger ships in which crew costs are a large part of total voyage costs. The sale of the ships to British interests within five years of the formation of the line meant that little damage was done to British shipping: indeed, the competition of these ships before they were sold was an important factor leading British owners to improve the quality of the ships engaged on the Australian trade. Without this improvement the British lines would have

TABLE 12. Aid to shipping, 1919 to 1939

Country	Postal subventions	Operating subsidies	Construction subsidies	Indirect subsidies	State fleet	Preferences
Argentine					×	
Australia	×	×			×	
Belgium				×	×	
Brazil	×	×	×	×	×	
Bulgaria		×		×		
Chile	×	×		×		×
Canada	×	×		×		
Denmark	×			×		×
Egypt		×				×
Estonia				×		
Finland		×		×		
France	×	×	×	×	×	×
Germany	×	×	×	×		×
Greece	×	×				
Italy	×	×	×	×.	×	×
Japan	×	×	×	×		
Mexico						×
Netherlands	×	×		×		
Norway	×	×		×		
Peru		×			×	×
Poland		×	×	×	×	×
Portugal	×	×	×	×		×
Rumania					×	
Russia					×	×
Spain	×	×	×	×		×
Sweden				×		
Turkey				×	×	
United Kingdom	×	×	×	×		
United States	×	×	×		×	a
Yugoslavia		×	×	×		

a Preference legislated but not utilized.

Sources: various, including: Imperial Shipping Committee, *British Shipping in the Orient* (1939); Brassey, various dates; U.S. Federal Maritime Board Reports; Committee on Industry and Trade, *Survey of Overseas Markets* (H.M.S.O., 1926); Saugstad; Mance; E. W. Schiedewitz, *Subsidies to Shipping and Shipbuilding, 1919–30* (Hamburg, 1931), and supplemented by W. Winkler (Hamburg, 1933); *Shipbuilding and Shipping Record*, various dates; *Fairplay*, various dates.

been hard pressed to maintain their position in the trade when foreign competition increased in the 1930s.

The subsidies given to Yugoslavian shipping did not affect British shipping. However, because of their low wage costs, Yugoslavian tramps were serious competitors to British tramps and the natural advantage thereby enjoyed was increased by indirect assistance in the form of the exemption of shipping profits from taxation. On the other hand, both profits and tax rates were sufficiently low over most of the period that in practice the advantage of tax exemption was negligible.

The assistance given by other members of the group need not be specifically considered.

COUNTRIES IN GROUP B

Of the seven countries in this group, four are South American republics and two are Iberian countries with important South American trading connections. The subsidies given were chiefly for services which did not compete with established British services, although a subsidized Brazilian line, Lloyd Brasileiro, engaged in European services, thereby diverting traffic from, and restricting the opportunities open to, British lines. The Spanish bounties to tramp ships increased general tramp competition, but the subsidies to Compañia Transatlantica for services from Spain to North and South America affected Italian and French rather than British shipping. Much of the assistance to Portuguese shipping was designed to maintain colonial services.

The preferences which four of these six countries granted were somewhat more important and, by diverting both passengers and cargoes to national flag ships, adversely affected the old-established British trades to South America and the trans-shipment trade from Iberia via Britain to both North and South America. The Portuguese preferences, which dated from 1922, included higher customs duties on goods imported in foreign ships, higher port dues on foreign than on national ships, taxes on passenger tickets sold for foreign lines and priority to Portuguese ships in berthing arrangements. After 1930, as a result of international pressure, the preference arrangements were gradually replaced by subsidies. The purpose of the measures was to establish and maintain in world trades the fleet, consisting largely of captured German tonnage, which Portugal had acquired during the war.[1] The measures succeeded in this aim, but the fleet hardly grew from its 1919 size during the whole inter-war period. In the case of Chile, the Government initially had an arrangement with the British-owned Pacific Steam Navigation Company under which, in return for concessions regarding mails and rates on Government cargoes and personnel, the line was granted preferential treatment. After the expiration of this contract in 1926, subsidized Chilean services were provided and preference was given for the carriage of Government cargoes in Chilean vessels. By and large, however, the preferences given by countries in this group affected the services of only a few regular British lines and some tramp ship cargoes, for example coal. Their real importance lay in the effect on the economics of whole voyages of the loss of even a minor trade covered as part of that voyage. Difficulties in Portuguese and Brazilian trades upset the whole pattern of South Atlantic trades and the final consequences of such difficulties may have been disproportionate to their apparently modest initial impact.

The position of Russia in this group merits special discussion. In 1913 the Russian fleet amounted to 0·97 million tons. By 1919 it had fallen to 0·54 million tons, a decline which continued until 1927, in which year the fleet amounted to only 0·31 million tons. By 1939, the fleet had grown to 1·32 million tons. After the Revolution the mercantile fleet passed entirely into state control. Prior to the Revolution, British ships had enjoyed a valuable share of the Russian overseas trade and the trade itself was of significant volume. After the Revolution the overseas trade of Russia declined greatly and when it recovered preferences were given to Soviet tonnage in the carriage of imports so that whereas in 1913 only 15·9 per cent of Russian imports were carried in Russian ships, by 1933 the figure had reached 88·6 per cent, although it fell slightly in subsequent years. In this way what had formerly been a valuable trade to a group of lines on the north-east coast of Britain was lost.

[1] Saugstad, op. cit., p. 509.

COUNTRIES IN GROUP C

Group C includes the three Scandinavian countries, the Netherlands and Greece, countries the fleets of which provided serious competition for British shipping.

Assistance to Danish shipping was limited to a '. . . tendency in Denmark to keep liner shipments in Danish vessels . . .' which increased steadily during the inter-war period, so that by 1938 90 per cent of Danish agricultural produce was carried in Danish ships and only 10 per cent in British ships under mutual arrangements as regards sailings.[1] Why this Danish predominance occurred is not clear, but there is no evidence of deliberate official flag discrimination. Some minor indirect assistance was given to Danish shipping, but it had only a marginal influence.

Assistance to Greek shipping took the form of direct subsidies to ships on coastal or short sea routes and a mail-cum-operating subsidy for a transatlantic mail service from Greece employing one secondhand liner. The former measures had no effect on non-Greek shipping at all, while the latter measure perhaps affected Italian transatlantic services.

In the Netherlands, mail contracts were granted to a number of lines, generally at about International Postal Union rates. Straight subsidies were paid to three lines in the 1920s. In one case, the subsidies were to prevent the company concerned terminating its Amsterdam calls and were not specifically directed to helping the line. A second line which received a subsidy was engaged in the cross-Channel service and so lies outside the terms of this book. The only real subsidy of any concern here was that of one million guilders per annum granted to the Holland South Africa Line for the five years 1921–5 inclusive, to save the company from going into liquidation. This measure preserved the competitive position of the line in the South African trades. However, had the line been allowed to go into liquidation, the German lines engaged in the trade were much better placed than the British lines to take advantage of the situation. In 1933, to assist Dutch shipowners whose wage costs were some 25 per cent above those in other European maritime

---

[1] *Shipbuilding and Shipping Record* (26 January 1939), commenting on Chamber of Shipping, Shipping Policy Reports which were not made public.

countries which had gone off the gold standard, loans of up to 20 per cent of the wages paid were made. Later the interest on those loans was remitted and later again most of the principle was also waived. Some building loans at low interest rates were made and some Dutch lines benefited from an agreement with German lines under which German importers instructed over- seas shippers to ship either in German or in Dutch ships.

The Norwegian Government subsidized Norwegian coastal services and paid direct subsidies to the Bergenske S.S. Co. for the Bergen–Newcastle service, to Spanskelinjen A/S for a mail and cargo service to Spain, Portugal and Italy to ensure that the ships called at small Norwegian ports which they would otherwise have missed, and to a third line for the mail service to Frederikshavn. In the case of the Mediterranean route, the subsidy was no more than compensation to the line for the extra costs involved in calling at several small ports, and was an alternative to further subsidized coastal services. The only Nor- wegian subsidy which affected British shipping was that paid for the Bergen–Newcastle mail service, on which two small ships were employed. Apart from the subsidies mentioned, no other assistance was given to Norwegian overseas shipping. Norwegian policy was that '. . . Norway cannot afford to enter a subsidy war and hence must take particular care not to give foreign nations any excuse for attack'.[1] Loans for shipbuilding at $5\frac{1}{2}$ per cent and 6 per cent were provided.

Swedish ocean shipping was completely unsubsidized in the period. Finance for shipbuilding was, however, made available at rates of 4 per cent and 5 per cent.

The count of the assistance measures granted by these five countries shows them to have been of a minor nature and, in themselves, of little effect on British shipping; certainly they did not in any way account for the competition which the ships of these five countries provided for British-owned ships in the period. It is now necessary to turn to the sixth member of the group, the United Kingdom.

Postal subventions to British shipping continued in the inter- war years although the '. . . British authorities pointed out that

[1] U.S. Maritime Commission, *Economic Survey of the American Merchant Marine* (Kennedy Report), 1937, p. 58.

the rates paid to shipping companies for the conveyance of mail
. . . compared favourably with the rates fixed by the Postal
Union Convention for the carriage of transit mail. . . .'[1] It was
argued that if British postal subventions had been paid at the
rates ruling in the United States between 1928 and 1936, they
would have been between two and three times as high; this
claim, however, does not dispose of the argument that the mail
payments assisted British shipping because, in fact, American
mail subventions were estimated to be approximately forty times
the value, at International Postal Union rates, of the work
done.[2] As the total amount involved was only about £1 million
per annum, the true subsidy element cannot have been absolutely
large when spread over all British mail services.

The Trade Facilities Acts and the Irish Loan Guaranty Acts
passed between 1921 and 1926 were of assistance to shipping.
Under these Acts, the Government guaranteed loans from
private lenders to companies willing to use the proceeds in
placing orders with industries experiencing high rates of unemployment. The guarantee probably saved borrowers about
2 per cent in interest charges. The depressed shipbuilding
industry was one of the chief beneficiaries under the Acts and in
all £35 million in loans were guaranteed for shipbuilding. Of
the amount guaranteed, £2·3 million covered loans direct to
shipbuilders for modernizing their plants, £3·6 million was to
cover ships built to foreign order, while £29 million was
guaranteed on behalf of British shipowners. Of this latter
amount, over £13 million was in respect of loans to members of
the Kylsant group, £2·75 million to the Blue Star Line and
£2·6 million to the Bank Line. A number of other companies
raised smaller amounts under the Acts, but with the exception
of the companies noted and the Silver Line and Henderson
Bros., the opportunity to raise loans to rebuild or expand fleets
was not generally taken. In part, this was because by the time
the Acts were passed most British shipowners had replaced their
war losses, either with Government standard ships, from
reparations tonnage or by new building. Further, the use of

[1] Mance, op. cit., p. 121.
[2] Subventions were about $3 million per annum for work worth $73,000 per
annum. See Eversheim, op. cit., p. 19.

loan capital is anathema to most British shipowners while the use of the facilities under the Acts was opposed by the Chamber of Shipping, which subsequently expressed pleasure that no further guarantees were granted after 1931.[1] The facilities given under the Acts helped British shipbuilders during a bad patch and contributed directly to the building of the major part of the motor tonnage owned in Britain during the 1920s and early 1930s. The Chamber of Shipping blamed the Acts for contributing to the world surplus of shipping and, in so far as ships were built which would not otherwise have been built, that is true. However, where old ships were scrapped and replaced by motor ships the British fleet was improved, while if motor ships were built without any other ships being scrapped, then the number of economic, as opposed to uneconomic, units of the fleet was increased and its total competitive position improved. The number of vessels laid up in Britain during the inter-war years would scarcely have been less had the Bank Line, for example, not built a fleet of motor ships, but the number of British ships actually employed would certainly have been less. The negative attitude of the Chamber of Shipping was no more than a summary of the attitudes of the majority of its members, most of whom were blinded by traditional prejudices to the opportunity offered. In fairness to the attitude of shipowners it can be added that the Government did not prove an accommodating guarantor and its refusal during the depression to assist borrowers to extend the repayment time of money borrowed under the Acts was the immediate, but not the only, cause of the collapse of the Royal Mail (Kylsant) Group.

In 1930, the Government agreed to take up at commercial rates that part of the insurance of the planned Cunard liner (later named *Queen Mary*) which the market could not absorb. Then in 1933/34 further action was taken with respect to the *Queen Mary*, whose building had been suspended by the Cunard Line. In the immediate post-war years Cunard had developed a technique for using the bill market to finance new construction, redeeming the bills in annual instalments from their depreciation allowances. At one stage during the 1920s nearly £5 million was outstanding in bills, but by 1928 when the building of the

[1] Report in *Fairplay* (23 February 1933), p. 459.

Queen Mary was being considered, all the liabilities had been extinguished. The plan to build the *Queen Mary* was that the cost, estimated at £4·5 million when the contract was signed in 1930, would be financed by bills as required to cover the periodic payments due under the construction contract. In December 1931, only three months before the projected launching of the ship, work was suspended because the decline in earnings made it impossible for the company to set aside as depreciation allowances sufficient funds to cover its bill liabilities and to allow it to issue the bills required to finance the completion of the vessel. At the time the Government refused to assist Cunard to complete the ship and for over two years the almost completed hull lay on the stocks. Then in 1934, the Government agreed to advance up to £3 million for the completion of the *Queen Mary* and up to £5 million towards the cost of building a sister ship. Before this was done, however, a merger of the competing Cunard and White Star Lines was demanded and this was secured in 1933. In 1934 a further £1·5 million was advanced to the merger company for working capital.

The necessity for this exceptional action arose from the conditions of world trade generally, the impact of subsidized French and German competition[1] in the North Atlantic express service and the general over-tonnaging of the route following the imposition of immigration quotas in the United States. The position of the White Star Line was parlous at the time, as it had suffered heavily from its membership of the International Mercantile Marine in which its carefully husbanded reserves had been dissipated to support unprofitable members of the group. The merger between Cunard and White Star put a quick end to a famous line, the dying struggles of which might otherwise have brought down Cunard also.

In 1935 the Government provided assistance for tramps in the form of a plan for scrapping and building on the pattern of that adopted in Japan (see p. 121) and a scheme of operating bounties. The bill embodying these plans was enacted as the British Shipping (Assistance) Act, 1935.

Under the Scrap and Build Scheme it was provided that the

---

[1] The German record-breakers, *Bremen* and *Europa* were constructed before German shipping was subsidised.

Treasury might advance moneys on guaranteed loans to British owners who were prepared to scrap two tons of old shipping for every one built, or who wished to modernize existing ships. Although intended primarily to assist tramp owners, the scheme was not restricted to tramps. Provision was made for advances not exceeding £10 million in total, this figure being the amount of the estimated deficiency in the depreciation allocations of the tramp fleet between 1930 and 1935. Only £6·2 million was applied for under the scheme. The caution of shipowners in using the facilities was matched by the timidity of the administrators of the scheme and only £3·55 million was actually lent. This amount financed the construction of fifty new vessels of 186,000 tons, while ninety-seven vessels of 385,625 tons were scrapped. The scrapping provisions were a farce and far from British owners taking the opportunity to improve their fleets at the low interest rates at which the money could be obtained, more often than not they bought old ships overseas for scrapping and kept their own veterans in the fleets; only six of the ninety-seven vessels scrapped were the property of the applicant companies. Perhaps if the scheme had contained a stronger subsidy element it would have worked better, although in their comments on foreign subsidies British shipowners seemed to regard low interest loans as a very valuable subsidy indeed. Part of the failure of the scheme can be attributed to the fact that by the time it came into operation freight rates had begun to rise and ageing ships could make profits. However, there was nothing in the structure of the British fleet to suggest that no improvements were desirable; in particular, the British tramp fleet was badly supplied with just the type of economical motor ship with which Scandinavian, Dutch and Japanese owners were able to cut freight rates. No applications for loans towards the costs of modernizing old ships were made. The scheme was abandoned in 1937 after operating for only twenty-two months. Its chief beneficiaries were the foreign owners of ancient ships who were able to sell them above scrap prices to British owners.

The bounty provisions of the 1935 Act provided that 'If in the opinion of the Board of Trade at the end of the subsidy year the average level of freight rates for the year (expressed as an index number representing a percentage) was less than the average for 1929 (represented by 100 per cent), then the total sum payable by the Treasury for the year will be a sum not exceeding a quarter of a million pounds for every unit per cent by which the average for the subsidy year is less than the average for 1929, subject to a maximum of £2,000,000.'[1] The amount of £2 million was determined as being the amount by which tramp earnings in 1934 failed to provide the amount needed to cover depreciation at 5 per cent per annum. The full amount of the subsidy was paid in 1935 and 1936 but although the provision was extended to 1937 the rise in freight rates to above the 1929 level meant that no payments were, in fact, made. A Bill to restore the bounties for a period of five years from 1939 was not proceeded with on account of the war.

As a condition for receiving the subsidy the Government insisted that the tramp shipping industry should produce a scheme to prevent the subsidy from being dissipated by the competition of British tramps with each other. Prior to this insistence by the British Government numerous schemes for international co-operation in the rationalization of shipping services had been proposed, but none had found sufficient support among shipowners. Faced with the necessity to produce an organization to terminate competition among British ships, a scheme was instituted in Britain which rapidly developed into an instrument of international co-operation.

To satisfy the Government requirements, the industry set up a Tramp Shipping Administrative Committee which would 'as its main function, actively promote co-operation among shipowners in

   (*a*) minimizing domestic competition;
   (*b*) improving freight rates and conditions; and
   (*c*) promoting as against foreign subsidized competition the fullest possible employment of British tramp shipping'.[2]

Despite these fine-sounding words, there was little that could be done by the British industry on its own which would not simply have constituted rationalization to disappearance.

[1] Memorandum on the Financial Resolution accompanying the Subsidy Act, Cmd. 4754, 1934, Section 2, Part I, para. 14.
[2] Ibid., Section 2, Part II, para. 3.

The opportunity for full international co-operation occurred early in 1935. The late Argentine wheat crop had caused rates of freight to fall to the uneconomically low level of 12s. a ton in February, compared with 16s. 6d. on average in 1934, which had barely covered the expenses of an average British steamer in the trade and allowed nothing towards fixed costs. The British tramp shipowners were committed to the principle of organization and the presentation of a united front to raise the rate. In the circumstances such a course would have assisted foreign shipping more than British shipping, so that the Greek initiative to set up an international committee to cover the Plate trade, the committee being a sub-committee of the Tramp Shipping Administrative Committee, was accepted. The basic rate Plate to United Kingdom or Continent was fixed at 16s. 6d. per ton and from mid-February all shipowners agreed not to accept lower rates. In the first few months for which the scheme was operating nearly 600 charters were agreed with only a single violation of the agreed terms.

The immediate success of the minimum freight scheme in raising rates in the Argentine grain trade led to its extension to the St. Lawrence trade and the Australian trade in March 1935. In each case care was taken '. . . to stabilize the rates at a level which was no higher than that of rates actually paid during 1934 . . .' which represented '. . . a bare living wage for shipowners without allowing for depreciation or interest'.[1] The St. Lawrence scheme was extended into a general North Atlantic scheme covering all grain shipments eastwards and coal shipments westwards. With each of the three minimum freight schemes subsequent increases in rates above the 1934 levels were obtained. The attempt to establish a similar scheme in Baltic trades failed because of Soviet refusal to recognize the minimum rates or to employ ships operating under such conditions.

The three minimum freight schemes were valuable, but insufficient in themselves. It was shown in the previous chapter that liners in the 1930s were frequently trading with only part cargoes and so were in a position to undercut tramp rates in order to fill their empty space, any rate above the direct

[1] Interim Report of Tramp Shipping Administrative Committee, Cmd. 5004, 1935, p. 6.

handling charge of the cargo being better than unused space. In order to prevent liner owners from wrecking the schemes minimum rates had also to be agreed for parcels of grain carried in liners on the routes concerned. These rates were below the tramp rates, the differential representing the higher cost of loading tramps and the convenience to charterers of being able to despatch them to any port, which was often not chosen until the ship was at sea. This provision benefited both liners and tramps. The second difficulty was that the controlled rates attracted unfixed tramps to make speculative voyages in ballast in order to profit from the agreed rates. The pressure of a substantial volume of unfixed tonnage would have wrecked the scheme, and it became necessary to prohibit unfixed ballast voyages to Argentine and Australian ports. This prohibition introduced a measure of control into tramp ship operations and a limitation on the freedom of owners which was often resented (see below). 'Such restrictions . . . proved to be one of the most necessary and beneficial of the Committee's activities. . . . Experience has shown that this is the only satisfactory and effective way of adjusting supply to demand.'[1] These were the main, but by no means the only, difficulties which the schemes met.[2]

When the subsidy arrangements were terminated at the end of 1937, the enforced co-operation among British shipowners ended. However, it was agreed by shipowners in the leading maritime countries to continue the co-operative system and the minimum freight schemes. The scheme continued on this voluntary basis up to the outbreak of the war.

The effects of the subsidy to tramps must be considered as a whole with the organizational arrangements which took place. It was claimed that the whole arrangements gave tramp shipping '. . . a fine lesson in self-reliance . . .'[3] and both British and foreign owners had benefited from the arrangements. It was also claimed that the subsidy payments themselves prevented '. . . the abnormal transference of large blocks of British tonnage

[1] Fourth Report of Tramp Shipping Administrative Committee, Cmd. 5363, 1937, p. 4.
[2] For an account of other difficulties, see H. Gripaios, *Tramp Shipping* (London, 1959), pp. 79–81.
[3] *Shipbuilding and Shipping Record* (19 November 1936), p. 609.

to foreign flags. . . .'[1] As a rule, contemporary discussions of the arrangements rarely differentiated between the subsidy arrangements and the international co-operation among tramp owners which was secured. The latter had the obvious intention, and the effect, of reducing competition, primarily by eliminating speculative voyages in ballast, although the ballast restriction did lead to continued cutting of coal freight rates, to the disadvantage of British tramps. Clearly there was a certain amount of muddle in the operation of the co-operative scheme. However, by limiting the competition among tramps and so keeping up rates, the scheme probably saved the British tramp fleet, which was increasingly non-competitive in world markets because of relatively high wages and an addiction to 9-knot steamships. Those shipowners who complained that it was humiliating '. . . to go hat in hand to a committee . . . to beg for liberty to do this or that . . .'[2] missed the point. The subsidy helped British tramps during a period of abnormally low rates, but it was the limitation of competition which enabled the British tramp fleet as a whole to survive the period.

COUNTRIES IN GROUP D

The shipping policies of the five countries in this group were sufficiently important for the position of each country to be considered separately.

(a) *France*

The experience of French shipping in the inter-war years was very mixed and, although extensive subsidies were paid, by 1939 France had less shipping than in 1920.

Liner services from France to French colonies and protectorates in the East, to Brazil and the Plate, to Mexico, Central America and the West Indies, to New York and within the Mediterranean were subsidized under mail contracts which provided payment in excess of International Postal Union rates.

---

[1] Cmd. 5004, cit. p. 10.

[2] 'Observations by Sir John Latta on the Government Tramp Subsidy Scheme' (London, 1937), p. 4. This pamphlet is an excellent example of the emotive expression, muddled thinking and rabid nationalism that unfortunately pervaded much of British shipping in the inter-war period.

In the period from the end of the war to 1923 the total of subsidy payments each year was small, but it increased thereafter, with a particularly sharp jump after 1931. In addition to these payments, liner companies received assistance towards the construction of liners for the South American and New York services. The bulk of the payments under the mail contracts were made to Messageries Maritimes for the Eastern services and to Compagnie Générale Transatlantique for the Atlantic service, both of them lines operating on overcrowded routes. These two lines, with two others, found that the acceptance of the pottage of subsidies cost them their birthright of freedom and the lines passed increasingly under Government control after 1937.

The French construction and navigation bounties as paid before the war on non-contract services were terminated after the war, the former in 1920 and the latter in 1930. However, in 1925 a tax was placed on petroleum and a part of the proceeds was allocated to pay a small operating subsidy to French-built tankers or to foreign-built tankers taken on the French registry before 1926. Then in 1934 the Tasso Law provided subsidies for ships not benefiting from other measures, that is, tramp ships. The need for this subsidy arose from the increases in French wage costs due to the Blum social security measures which were disastrous for French shipping and had led to 28 per cent of the fleet being idle in 1933.

In addition to the subsidy arrangements, some form of discrimination was adopted by giving French ships preference in the carriage of Government-owned cargoes; in 1936 this was extended by the provision that 40 per cent of the coal imported on private account had to travel in French ships. Imports into French colonies were assessed for tariff at a lower rate if transshipped to a French vessel at a French port than if they arrived in a foreign vessel. As a result, although Blue Funnel vessels called at Saigon for cargo on homeward passages, on outward passages the call was omitted and goods from Britain were taken only to France to complete the journey to Saigon in a French ship.

In the inter-war years, French tramp competition was not particularly serious to British shipping. In liner trades, French competition was important but, except in the North Atlantic service, appeared to affect German and Italian shipping rather more than British shipping.

(b) *Germany*

German competition to British shipping was important for practically the whole of the inter-war period. The German mercantile fleet had been reduced from its 1913 size of 5·1 million tons to 0·7 million tons in 1920. A rapid recovery occurred and by 1931 the fleet had reached 4·3 million tons. In carrying out this reconstruction shipowners received state assistance in the form of payments in compensation for ships requisitioned for reparation purposes but these did not cover the cost of replacing the lost ships. After 1925 shipowners were given assistance in the form of loans from the Government for new construction at rates of interest between 2 per cent and 4 per cent below open market rates. In 1932 nearly one-half of the loans made to the Norddeutscher Lloyd and Hamburg-Amerika lines were written off, thus being converted into bounties. Throughout the 1920s, however, German shipping was prosperous and in the falling freight markets gained from the general economical running of the post-war ships.

The depression hit German shipping in 1930 which was further affected by the currency depreciations of 1931. By 1932, 30 per cent of German shipping was laid up. The beginning of extensive state assistance was partly a consequence of the handicaps imposed on shipping by the over-valued exchange rate and partly of the nationalistic fervour of the Nazis who obtained power in 1933.

In 1932 a scrap-and-build scheme was inaugurated with interest-free loans to owners. Then in 1933 a general operating bounty was provided, consisting of a straight bounty per ton for each day at sea plus an allowance towards wages. The total bounty payments amounted to as much as 25 per cent of the operating costs of some ships. However, the main part of this bounty was not a subsidy but compensation for the overvaluation of the Reichsmark in relation to sterling and other important currencies. The growth of Nazi power and the development of a controlled economy led to the adoption of barter deals in commodities with shipping clauses giving preference to German ships, to state contributions of capital to the leading lines and to the pursuance of national power politics in the building of ships irrespective of the needs of the trade. The limitations on foreign dealings in Reichsmarks imposed to protect the currency also assisted shipping; foreigners holding blocked balances had a direct incentive to employ German ships in order to activate the balances by using them for freight payments.

The extent of the assistance given to German shipping cannot be accurately determined. The generally accepted estimate is that in 1936 it amounted to £9·3 million,[1] of which about one-half was compensation for the effects of the over-valued exchange rate.

One must be wary of attributing too much importance to German subsidies and economic policy as factors assisting shipping. The German fleet declined from 4·3 million tons in 1931 to 3·7 million tons in 1934 and although it recovered to 4·5 million tons in 1939, this was still below the 1913 tonnage and Germany was a net demander rather than a net supplier of shipping services. The main German challenge on the North Atlantic, in the trades to South America, and in the South and East African trades, came before subsidies were started. Some of the ships providing this competition were built with the aid of cheap loans and it was the outstanding balance of these loans which was written off in 1932. Thus the ships were subsidized eventually, although this writing-off of the loans could not have influenced the decision to build and operate the ships. Had the outstanding part of the loans not been remitted in 1932, at the worst the companies concerned would have been forced into liquidation and the ships sold, probably to newly-formed German companies, at bargain prices.

The competition of German shipping was severe throughout most of the inter-war years; the figures in Table 13, however, bring out the fact that, by and large, its chief effects were felt before the subsidy policy started. It can be seen that except in the German, Dutch and Norwegian trades, the main recovery of German shipping occurred before 1931, while subsidy policies after 1931 did little more than enable the ground won to be

[1] G. Candace, *La Marine française* (1938), pp. 176–7.

retained. German shipping gained from having modern tonnage and from enterprising management. In addition, German
shipping was helped by rate cutting in the Far Eastern and
New Zealand liner trades, by a campaign in Germany to induce
importers to instruct shippers overseas that goods be sent in
German or Dutch ships, and by the readiness of German liner
owners to break conference rules wherever it suited them. The
German success was a compound of many ingredients, several
of which could have been adopted by British shipowners. It was
galling to British shipowners that German shipping, after being
decimated by reparations, should have risen again to pro-
minence, but the reasons for the phoenix-like re-emergence
should not be misunderstood.

TABLE 13. Percentages of entrance and clearance at national ports
by German flag ships 1913, 1920–36

Ports	1913	1920	1931	1936
	%	%	%	%
German	61·0	52·9	56·5	64·1
British	11·0	0·6	7·9	8·0
Dutch	21·3	6·0	20·2	22·2
Norwegian	4·3	12·4	7·9	13·6
Swedish	14·3	20·3	17·0	15·9
American	12·2	0·1	10·5	9·0
South African	13·5	0·1	6·2	5·7
Indian	10·3	0·2	7·0	6·4
Japanese	6·8	0·0	1·9	2·2

Source: Der Wettbewerb in der Seeschiffahrt, p. 121.

(c) *Italy*

'From the commercial point of view the subsidy is designed
mainly to promote the trade of Italians with one another, in as
much as the geographical scope of the system is confined chiefly
to the Mediterranean and those parts of Africa, Asia and
Southern Europe where for centuries Italians have been established and are increasing in numbers.'[1] In the pre-Fascist
period, subsidies were paid in two forms. First, to the liner services operated under contract, mainly to the areas mentioned

[1] Saugstad, op. cit., p. 265.

above, payments were made to cover the cost of mails and to compensate the lines for the losses involved in maintaining uneconomic services. Second, navigation bounties on a small scale were paid to ships not in receipt of contract payments. In 1926, the contract system was revised and actual payments to contract lines immediately rose by 50 per cent. Provision was made under the contracts for the construction of new vessels. Ships engaged on the Australian service received a refund of Suez Canal dues under the new arrangements. In 1934 assistance for the reconstruction and renovation of liners was provided. In 1936 the liner companies were reorganized into four groups, the major part of the shares of which were held by the Institute for Industrial Reconstruction, thus making these lines virtually departments of the State.

Tramp shipping was not ignored, although being less prestigious it was less generously assisted. From 1932 a temporary bounty, reconsidered annually, was granted to meet the difficulties of tramp owners which arose because they had '. . . to bear expenses in gold currencies and to collect freight rates in paper currencies'.[1] Under these conditions, however, the tramp fleet neither improved in quality nor expanded and after a scrapping subsidy had been introduced in 1932 over 600,000 tons of shipping were scrapped within two years.

The position of Italian shipping is well depicted by the following account. 'After this formidable economic crisis (aggravated by the depreciation of the British pound in 1931 and of the dollar in 1933) and the coming into power of the Fascist dictatorship . . . a complete antiliberal economic trend took place in Italy. . . . In the early thirties, first under the pretext of protecting the shipping industry, but actually to comply with the political principles of the corporative régime, the Government took over the merchant marine by means of Government subsidies and by a series of special laws. At the same time the Fascist government began to take over the management of the national shipping also, allegedly for emergency reasons. By 1937 this process of assuming control was completed under the direction of the Ministry of Communications. A Government monopoly had thus been established and the formation of tariffs [fares and

[1] *Shipbuilding and Shipping Record* (27 December 1934), p. 692.

freights] was not subject to the economic laws alone, but, and above all, to Government policy.'[1]

Discrimination in favour of Italian ships affected only migrant trades. General restrictions on immigration into America imposed in 1921 and 1924 reduced the annual average intake from over 1 million in 1913 to 0·45 million in 1920–3, 0·16 million in 1924–30 and 0·03 million in the period 1931–8. In order to protect their shipping in the face of these restrictions, the Italian Government restricted the rights of foreign ships to carry emigrants and in 1925 it became almost impossible for British ships to secure any of the Italian emigrant trade. The difficulties for British ships extended also to the Australian trade and Italian emigrants, and those returning to Italy on holiday, travelled mainly in Italian ships.

The competition of Italian shipping to that of other nations was keenest in the early 1930s before the withdrawal of shipping for the Abyssinian campaign. Subsidies to liners permitted them to operate uneconomic through-services to Italy. This reduced the trade available on these routes to ships which had formerly trans-shipped passengers and cargo for carriage to Italy or had handled the traffic on composite voyages. A determined effort was made in the 1930s to improve the quality of Italian merchant ships, both in comfort for passengers and in speed. In 1932, Italian sources boasted that Italian ships had '... acquired absolute predominance in respect of the conveyance of passengers from India to Europe and from Europe to India, . . .'[2] largely through the provision of a faster service than that provided by the ships of the P. and O. and other British lines.

British tramps in the 1930s suffered from the competition of Italian tramps which, paying lower wage rates[3] and in receipt of subsidies, were able to accept freight rates at which British ships could not operate. However, in the only tramp trade for

[1] Monopoly Problems in Regulated Industries, Hearings before the Antitrust Subcommittee of the Committee on the Judiciary, House of Representatives, 86th Congress, Ocean Freight Industry (Celler Committee), part 1, vol. 1, p. 880, from statement submitted by Law Librarian, Library of Congress. First bracketed insertion from previous sentence in source.

[2] *Shipbuilding and Shipping Record* (19 May 1932), p. 530.

[3] Although Italian wage rates were lower than British wage rates, Italian shipowners were liable for heavy social charges in respect of each man employed. These charges may have doubled the wage cost of the lower paid grades of labour.

which detailed figures are available, the Italian competition appears to have declined in importance after 1933; in that year Italian ships took 10 per cent of the River Plate grain fixtures, whereas in 1935 the percentage was only 1 per cent due to the withdrawal of tonnage for the Abyssinian war, while in 1937 Italian fixtures had recovered to only 4 per cent of the total.[1]

In liner trades, Italian competition was apparently most serious in the trades to South America, Australia and India, with extensive rate-cutting by Italian lines in the trades to Australia and India which diverted traffic from British to Continental ports, particularly passenger traffic. Passengers were attracted as much by lower fares and faster ships as by the freer atmosphere of Italian (and other) ships compared with the 'stuffy' atmosphere of many British ships, particularly in Far Eastern trades. Emigrants from Italy generally travelled in Italian ships and Italian importers were subjected to a campaign to instruct exporters in other countries to ship the goods concerned in Italian ships.

By 1939, the Italian merchant fleet had been built up to 3·4 million tons from a total of 1·4 million tons in 1919 and Italy was a net supplier of shipping services to the world. Without subsidies, the Italian merchant marine would have consisted mainly of tramps and slow passenger steamships, in the running of which the low levels of Italian wage rates would have been an advantage. Note, however, that depreciation of the currency might have been required to realize this advantage and that social charges eliminated much of the wage rate advantage. Subsidies enabled Italian shipping to compete with British (and Dutch, French and German) lines in fast liner services, while currency restrictions to protect the over-valued exchange rate hampered other shipping.

(d) *Japan*

The Japanese fleet expanded rapidly between 1920 and 1939, rising from 2·2 million tons to 5·6 million tons. Although Japanese shipping had been subsidized since 1891, prior to 1932 '. . . there was nothing remarkable in the dimensions of the

[1] Sixth Report of Tramp Shipping Administrative Committee, Cmd. 5750, 1938, p. 9.

subsidies'[1] which were not a major factor in accounting for the growth of the Japanese fleet.

In 1931 a rationalization movement started in Japanese shipping. Government control of shipping increased during the 1930s so that by 1932 all shipping was ordered by the Department of Communications; 'the only way of navigating safely through the hazy sea of the economic and financial difficulties is to steer her [Japan] correctly and firmly with the combined effort of the statesmen and the general public'.[2] Under the tighter Government control of shipping, operating and construction subsidies were given and in 1937–8 subsidies for tramp ships, which had not formerly been assisted, were provided. In 1937–8 also, the policy of construction subsidies for the building of large, fast liners, quite openly intended for use in war, reached its apogee. The Imperial Shipping Committee reported that although Japanese operating subsidies to liners were fairly substantial, the subsidy paid to Japanese tramps was at about the same rate as that paid to British tramps.[3]

In 1932 a subsidized 'scrap and build' scheme was started, providing for the scrapping of 400,000 tons of ships of twenty-five years of age and the building of 200,000 tons of new ships. This aim was achieved. In 1935 a second scheme for scrapping 50,000 tons and building 50,000 tons was launched, this time with the payment of subsidies on an increasing scale the faster, in relation to their length, were the ships built. A third scheme, identical with the second was promulgated in 1936.

The success of Japanese shipping in the inter-war years was the result of many factors. The Government shipping policies, although not a major factor, were nevertheless important. First, they permitted an expansive and generally profitable industry to expand faster than it otherwise would have done. Second, they encouraged the building of fast liner tonnage in which the Japanese advantages were less marked and shipowners not particularly interested. In addition to this, however, the operating bounties introduced in 1937 enabled Japanese shipping, already

[1] Mance, op. cit., p. 80.
[2] Y. Taji, 'Japanese Shipbuilding and Shipping', *Shipbuilding and Shipping Record* (14 April 1932), p. 423.
[3] Imperial Shipping Committee, *British Shipping in the Orient*, para. 198, p. 62.

closely integrated with manufacturing and trading interests, to quote particularly low freight rates which assisted the Japanese export trade. This trade was also assisted by the slight under-valuation of the Japanese yen after the 1931 currency devaluation. British lines complained of rate cutting and sharp practices by Japanese shipping in the trades between America and the Far East, and of the patronage by Japanese traders of through shipping services established by Japanese ships from the Far East to South America, avoiding the entrepôt trans-shipment at Singapore which the British lines provided. Japanese ship-owners were quicker than those in most other countries to foresee the end of the depression and the rise in rates which commenced in 1934 and had already begun to increase their fleets; this action by the shipping lines was fully in accord with the general pattern of industrial modernization carried out in Japan between 1926 and 1932. Japanese success was in part due to subsidies, in part to sharp practices and rate cutting, but much of it was due to efficiency and enterprise and to '. . . the short-sighted policies of her rivals'.[1]

(e) *United States of America*

The American fleet (Great Lake tonnage always excluded) increased during the war, from 3·0 million tons in 1913 to 10·8 million tons in 1919. The increase carried on until the fleet reached 14·7 million tons in 1922; by 1939, however, the size of the fleet had fallen to 9·4 million tons. Of the fleet at its peak, over 4 million tons was laid up, a further 1·2 million tons was made up of small coasting ships and about 2 million tons of sea-going tonnage was used in coastwise services, including voyages between the east and west coasts of America. At its peak, there-fore, about 7 million tons of American-owned shipping was in service on the ocean trade routes of the world. By 1932 this had fallen to about 5·5 million tons and by 1939 to about 2·5 million tons.

American shipping policy dates from the Shipping Act of 1916 under which the U.S. Shipping Board was set up to develop the merchant marine. After the war the Board, either itself or through private shipping companies, set up steamship

[1] Mance, op. cit., p. 93.

services from America as directed in the Act of 1920. The private shipping companies received subsidies to cover the differences between their costs and their receipts. The losses of the Board on the services directly operated and on the maintenance of idle tonnage were met by the Treasury.

The heavy cost of the system to the American Treasury led to its revision. In 1928 the Jones-White Act was passed changing the basis of support to a postal subvention. Subsidies were paid under forty-one contracts for ocean mail services, the payment being determined by the sizes and speeds of vessels employed. Neither the lengths of the routes served, nor the volume of mail actually carried, were determinants of the subsidy payment. Provision was also made for assistance to the contracting lines to enable them to build new tonnage for the contract services. This system was also expensive and less than fully effective in securing the desired aim, and in 1936 a further change was made.

The Merchant Marine Act, 1936, terminated all the mail contracts and replaced them by direct construction and operating subsidy payments. The construction subsidies were really subsidies to American shipyards and were necessitated by Government rules that operating subsidies were payable only on ships built in the United States. Attached to the construction subsidy was the provision of low interest loans for 20-year periods, covering three-quarters of the total construction cost less that part of the cost borne by the Federal Maritime Commission (which had replaced the U.S. Shipping Board). The operating subsidies provided in 1936 were available for ships engaged on essential trade routes approved by the Commission. Neither tramps nor tankers received operating subsidies, although construction subsidies were paid on tramp tonnage. The operating subsidy covered the difference between American and foreign costs, thereby putting U.S. ships on a par with other ships in the search for cargo. In 1938 a further Act was passed to provide additional encouragement for the construction of new ships.

There were two reasons for the change of policy in 1936. First, postal subventions had proved an inefficient and expensive method of maintaining a mercantile fleet; in 1935 postal subventions amounted to $29·5 million for work worth $2·8 million at International Postal Union rates. It was hoped that this cost would be cut by almost one-half under the new arrangements. In fact, operating subsidies averaged $14·7 million per annum over the ten years 1938–42 and 1947–51 inclusive. Second, contracting shipowners had not been building the new tonnage required under their contracts because the service payments provided no solution to the problem of building ships at the very high prices ruling in American yards.

Throughout the whole period, only liner services (but not all liner services) received operating subsidies. The American liners then operated at conference rates instead of at rates appropriate to their costs. The conferences had to admit the American tonnage which was able to secure a share of the trades which it entered. The efforts to win trade were reinforced by a considerable volume of jingoist propaganda to persuade American shippers to patronize American ships and importers to specify American tonnage for the carriage of the goods purchased. This policy succeeded in attracting a larger share of imports than of exports to American ships because a higher proportion of American exports than of imports consisted of tramp and tanker cargoes. American flag ships did not participate in tramp trades in the period, and only to a limited extent in the international oil trade. The tramps, the construction of which had been subsidized, were either employed carrying Government-sponsored cargoes at bonus rates or were transferred to Panamanian registry.

EFFECTS OF SHIPPING POLICIES

The adverse effects on British shipping of the shipping policies of countries in groups A, B and C were relatively slight and, in aggregate, were more than offset by the favourable effects of the assistance granted to British ships. In the South American trade, however, the old-established Royal Mail Line and Pacific Steam Navigation Company were affected by preference legislation, and the development of national fleets. The lines were also affected, however, by the inherent weakness of the Kylsant group, of which they were members, and by competition of the Blue Star Line established by the Vestey meat interests. These two factors were more important than any action by other countries engaging in that trade in weakening these lines.

The adverse effects of the policies of countries in group D cannot be similarly dismissed. The discussion of the shipping policies of the five countries in this group has indicated that the competition from America can be attributed directly to subsidies and that it affected the trade between Britain and America (a direct trade for British ships), and the indirect trades (for British ships) between British Dominions and foreign countries and America. The Italian competition affected chiefly those British trades which had involved trans-shipment at some point and composite trades which were replaced by direct shipping routes served by Italian ships. French competition affected particularly the North Atlantic and Far Eastern liner trades. German and Japanese competition was less a consequence of subsidies than of enterprise and special advantages, for example, low labour costs in Japan. In each case, an important competitive element was speed, a factor which British shipowners had largely neglected in their post-war rebuilding plans. A second factor was the establishment of through services between ports which British ships had covered only by trans-shipment services or as parts of longer routes.

The services started by these five countries during the period were almost entirely direct services, that is, services to and from the subsidizing countries. For British ships this meant extra competition on that part of the trade of each subsidizing country which was with Britain, in addition to extra competition on many parts of the network of liner services which British shipowners had built up in the past. Wherever the competitive pressure was felt, British shipowners had every reason to feel annoyed if they were put out of business by the entry of higher cost shipping which could only be maintained with the aid of subsidies. However, they had no legitimate ground for their much more frequently expressed annoyance that foreigners were taking a larger part of their own trades from British ships and also taking part of British trades.[1] It seemed to be regarded as quite in order for British ships to carry foreign cargoes but wrong for foreign ships, whether subsidized or not, to carry British

[1] See League of Nations, *Notes on the Merchant Shipping Crisis* (Geneva, 1934).

cargoes. The justification for British shipowners taking part in carrying the trade of all other countries, namely that the provision of shipping is a separate transaction and not an integral part of the commodity transaction, was rejected when applied to British trades. On the whole, British shipowners seemed to be annoyed about subsidized competition for the wrong reasons and to complain where the grounds for their strictures were weak. This alienated sympathies which they might otherwise have commanded and provided a rationalization of the difficulties being faced which, by removing all responsibility for those difficulties from British shipowners themselves, prevented any effective action being taken to meet the situation.

The effects of subsidized competition in British trades can best be seen by studying the import trade. In the import trade of Britain, the shipping of America, France, Germany, Italy and Japan together increased its share over the inter-war years as shown in Table 14. On its own this fact suggests that the impact of subsidized shipping on British shipping in British trades was severe. The table shows further, however, that between 1913 and 1929 the share of the British import trade held by British ships did not change significantly, the increase in the share of the trade taken by subsidized shipping being at the expense of unsubsidized foreign shipping. In the period between 1929 and 1937 the share of the trade taken by British shipping declined by 9·2 per cent, of which only 3 per cent was taken by subsidized foreign[1] shipping, the other 6·2 per cent of the relative British decline being matched by an increase in the share of the trade held by unsubsidized foreign ships. It is, therefore, impossible to attribute to the subsidy policies of other countries the whole of the decline in the share of the trade held by British ships. Had this been the sole cause of the decline then unsubsidized foreign entrances would have declined equally with British entrances.

The competition of subsidized shipping was alleged to be particularly strong in Far Eastern trades. The Imperial Shipping Committee, referring in particular to German and Italian subsidized competition, considered that '. . . foreign competition in the Far Eastern trades has not yet made it impossible for the

---

[1] 'Subsidized foreign' means the shipping of America, France, Germany, Italy and Japan, not all of which was assisted throughout the periods being considered.

British lines to carry on without subsidy, but it may well be that that situation is approaching'.[1] A pertinent comment on the general position of British shipping in the Far Eastern trades, however, is that British liner owners failed to keep pace with the rapid growth of traffic because of the persistence and skilful policies of competitors, with the consequence that '. . . a decline in efficiency has followed on the relative failure in competition and a vicious circle of cause and effect had ensued'.[2] A part of this decline in efficiency can be attributed to the dampening effects of conference arrangements on the competitive spirit of British shipowners (see Chapter XIII).

TABLE 14. Entrances at British ports, by percentages, 1913, 1929 and 1937

Identity of vessels	1913	1929	1937
British	65·8	65·0	55·8
Subsidized foreign	7·5	14·2	17·2
Unsubsidized foreign	26·7	20·8	27·0

Table 15 shows the position in Indian trades. It is clear from these figures that the decline in the relative British position occurred before 1929 when much of the 'subsidized' shipping was, in fact, in receipt of small subsidies only. The picture is that the decline in the German share of the trade between 1913 and 1920 was taken almost completely by American and Japanese ships. During the 1920s unsubsidized German shipping again secured a significant share of the trade, mainly at the expense of British shipping. In the 1930s, the British share of the trade increased at the expense of both subsidized and unsubsidized foreign shipping, only the share held jointly by Italy and Japan being maintained.[3] The position of British shipping in the Indian trade was adversely affected during the 1920s, mainly by an intensification of competition as the Germans tried to win back

[1] Imperial Shipping Committee, *British Shipping in the Orient*, para. 75, p. 21.
[2] Sir Halford Mackinder, Chairman, Imperial Shipping Committee, reported in *Shipbuilding and Shipping Record* (6 July 1939), p. 1.
[3] The shares of these countries are added because each withdrew shipping at a different period on account of their wars while the other appeared to be the chief beneficiary of such withdrawal.

some of their pre-1914 share of the trade and Japanese and American ships attempted to retain their wartime gains. The German success in this attempt was almost completely at the expense of British shipping, but this was not due to subsidies as German shipping was not assisted in the 1920s.

TABLE 15. Entrances and clearances at Indian ports, by percentages, 1913, 1920–38

Identity of vessels	1913	1920	1929	1936	1938
British	73·0	76·7	67·0	64·8	70·4
Subsidized foreign	16·6	15·1	24·4	24·4	22·7
Unsubsidized foreign	10·4	8·2	8·6	10·8	6·9

Source: Indian Trade and Navigation Accounts.

Data concerning the Japanese trades show a British decline during the 1920s when subsidies were not particularly important and a recovery during the 1930s when subsidies were greater (see Table 16). The 1937 figure for British participation is exceptionally high and the indication that a full recovery of lost ground was made must be doubted. The Japanese figures show a substantial growth by the unsubsidized Norwegian fleet and a continuous decline in the share of the trade held by subsidized American vessels.

TABLE 16. Entrances and clearances at Japanese ports by nationality of carrying vessels, 1924 to 1937

Year	Japanese	British	German	Dutch	Norwegian	American
	%	%	%	%	%	%
1924	60·9	20·1	1·7	2·0	2·0	8·6
1929	66·3	17·0	2·7	2·0	1·8	6·4
1931	70·9	12·6	1·9	0·5	1·6	5·7
1934	69·1	14·9	2·6	0·8	3·0	5·2
1937	63·1	21·6	3·1	0·4	5·9	3·0

Source: Sempei Sawa, 'System of Shipping Theory', *Kyoto University Economic Review*, xx, no. 2 (October 1950), p. 11.

The figures relating to the Indian and Japanese trades make it difficult to accept fully the argument of the Imperial Shipping

Committee that British shipping was being driven from Far
Eastern trades by subsidized competition during the 1930s.

American policy had a particularly serious impact on British
shipping because a high proportion of American trade, which
was about 20 per cent of world trade by volume, had been
carried in British ships before 1914. In 1913, British ships had
made up 51·7 per cent of the entrances and clearances at
American ports, but by 1923 the British share had fallen to
33·3 per cent. In 1924, American imports amounted to 41 million tons, of which 21 per cent only was carried in British ships
and 54 per cent in American ships; exports were 52 million tons
carried, 36 per cent in British ships and 35 per cent in American
ships. In no other year in the inter-war period, however, did the
share of American trade carried in American ships reach this
level. The peak year for American trade was 1929: imports
amounted to 51 million tons carried, 23 per cent in British ships,
49 per cent in American ships and 28 per cent in ships flying
other flags, and exports were 58 million tons carried, 35 per cent,
31 per cent and 34 per cent in ships flying British, American and
other flags respectively. These British proportions are substantially below the pre-war levels, much of the trade formerly
handled by the British lines having been pre-empted by the
American mercantile marine. Although the share of American
ships in carrying American trade fell with the decline in the size
of the American fleet, the share carried by British ships also
continued to fall, so that by 1935 it was only 20 per cent in terms
of tonnage carried, this excluding the extensive British participation in the passenger traffic into and out of American ports.
Although the entry of uneconomic American shipping to world
trades certainly restricted the opportunities open to British shipping, the subsequent decline in American shipping was not coincident with an increase in the British share of American trades.
In Table 17 the percentages of entrances and clearances at
American ports of the ships of five nations are shown. It can be
seen that Norwegian shipping, which was unsubsidized, trebled
its share of the American carrying trade between 1920 and 1938.
The share of Japanese shipping also increased, while that of German shipping, although it increased sixty times from its 1920
level, never succeeded in regaining its importance. The

K

shipping of both Germany and Japan was subsidized, but, in the German case, the bulk of the growth shown in Table 17 occurred *before* subsidies started and was associated with a resumption of trade after the war. The Japanese growth also occurred mainly in the period in which subsidies to Japanese shipping were relatively small.

TABLE 17. Employment of shipping in American trades—percentages of entrances and clearances, 1913, 1920–38

Nationality of tonnage	1913	1920	1929	1933	1936	1938
	%	%	%	%	%	%
American	14·0	50·8	37·6	36·8	31·2	26·6
British	51·7	29·1	30·2	26·8	27·4	27·5
German	12·2	0·1	4·7	6·5	6·0	6·0
Norwegian	7·4	4·5	6·7	7·3	10·3	12·5
Japanese	—	2·7	4·2	4·7	5·2	5·1

Source: Statistical Abstract of the United States, various dates.

One reason for the growth in the Norwegian participation in American trades is interesting and throws some light on the failure of British shipping to recapture its former share of the trade when American shipping declined. The changes in American shipping policy in 1928 and 1936 led to reductions in the subsidized services; these are shown in Table 17. Many shipping enterprises established in America in the 1920s found it impossible to maintain their cargo liner services after these changes but were unwilling to sacrifice completely the organizations and connections they had built up in the preceding years. In order to preserve as much as possible, they were willing to enter agreements with foreign lines to take over the services formerly operated with American flag tonnage, provided those foreign lines agreed to employ the American lines as their general cargo agents in the United States and elsewhere. Norwegian shipowners seized the opportunities to establish liner services on these conditions and to build or buy tonnage for the trades. The American concerns assisted the Norwegian enterprises to raise loans in America to finance the construction of ships for the trades. The associations proved profitable for both

parties and many of the relations between American and Norwegian shipping interests thus established still exist. There were
no economic or political reasons why British lines should not
have taken these opportunities rather than the Norwegians. The
British lines established in the American trade, however, had
their own cargo organizations and were unwilling to deal with
former competitors in a new guise while British owners not
engaged in American trades did not take advantage of the
changes in the position of American lines.

The impact of American policies on particular trades was
often serious. This can be seen in its clearest form in the competition in the Pacific between the Union Steam Ship Co. (a
New Zealand company which had become a member of the
P. and O. group in 1917) and the American-owned Matson
Line. The Union Company had been maintaining a mail and
passenger service between Australia, New Zealand and the
United States since the nineteenth century and had succeeded in
holding its place against the competition of the Matson Line.
Under the subsidy arrangements instituted in 1928, however,
the Matson Line received postal subventions which averaged
$800,000 per annum between 1928 and 1932 for work worth
$175,000 on American, not International Postal Union, pound-
age rates and over $1 million per annum for the period 1932–5
for work worth $135,000, the increase arising because larger and
faster ships were put on the service. In putting these new ships
on the service the Matson Line received loans from the U.S.
Shipping Board of $11,677,000, half at 2 per cent and the other
half at less than 1 per cent interest, towards the cost of constructing two liners which cost $16·25 million to build.[1] In addition,
trade on the San Francisco to Hawaii leg of the trans-Pacific
route was reserved for American ships, thus preventing the New
Zealand ships from sharing in the lucrative tourist traffic on this
section of the route.

Detailed evidence concerning British participation in trades
between America and East Asia is presented in Table 18.

Three other factors must be taken into account before the
figures in the table are discussed. First, the relative importance

[1] Imperial Shipping Committee, 35th Report, *The Possibilities of a British Passenger
and Cargo Service between Western Canada and Australia and New Zealand* (1936), p. 12.

of the three districts in the American trade with East Asia changed over the period. The figures are:

District	Exports 1922	Exports 1938	Imports 1922	Imports 1938
	%	%	%	%
Pacific	57·8	36·8	53·4	29·6
Atlantic	30·7	38·9	46·6	62·5
Gulf	11·5	24·3	0·1	7·9

Source: W. A. Radius, *United States Shipping in Trans-Pacific Trade 1922-1938* (Stanford U.P., 1944), table 34, p. 74.

These changes were brought about by a decline in exports from the Pacific coast, largely due to a fall in lumber shipments, while exports from the other districts increased and a smaller increase in imports to the Pacific coast than to the other areas. Second, the figures cover only dry-cargo exports, except in the years 1930–5 inclusive in which cased oil carried in dry-cargo vessels is included. Bulk oil shipments in tankers is not included. Third, the pattern of participation by American ships is that the fall in the American share of the trade which can be attributed to the 1928 Act was small, whereas that following the 1936 Act was substantial. In 1922 American ships carried 30 per cent of the exports and 34 per cent of the imports on the routes, compared with 30 per cent and 52 per cent respectively in 1928, 28 per cent and 42 per cent respectively in 1930 and 9 per cent and 15 per cent respectively in 1938 when the full effects of the 1936 Act had been realized.

It is now possible to interpret the figures in the table. First, British participation in the trades from the Pacific coast was well maintained over the period, despite the presence of subsidized American and Japanese ships. This was a trade in which British ships had participated before 1913 and although it is not possible from the data to draw any conclusion about the affects of the entry of subsidized American competition after the war on the share of the trade held by British ships, what is clear is that the subsequent decline in the American share of the trade benefited British rather than other non-American shipping. However, the Pacific coast trade declined both absolutely and relatively in the period.

TABLE 18. British participation in American trans-Pacific[1] trades, 1922 to 1938. Dry cargo only

Year	Percentage of exports carried in British ships from:			Percentage of imports carried in British ships to:		
	Pacific coast	Atlantic district	Gulf district	Pacific coast	Atlantic district	Gulf district
	%	%	%	%	%	%
Fiscal						
1922	7·7	40·0	10·4	8·0	35·6	
1923	7·9	52·8	17·1	7·6	34·9	
1924	13·3	49·2	12·8	8·0	45·9	Average
1925	6·9	46·8	18·9	6·4	41·8	over
1926	10·9	43·3	8·1	7·5	36·5	nine-year
1927	9·3	43·9	14·2	6·8	32·7	period
1928	10·9	46·4	21·0	7·8	31·7	3·3%
1929	10·5	45·2	18·4	5·6	27·3	
1930	8·1	45·4	32·9	3·7	25·1	
Calendar						
1930[a]	..	43·2	28·9	..	26·1	18·0
1931[a]	..	41·1	26·4	..	21·2	0·7
1932[a]	..	36·4	33·1	..	24·9	..
1933[a]	..	23·2	29·9	..	20·8	15·6
1934[a]	..	28·6	27·1	..	21·7	17·9
1935[a]	..	28·6	18·3	..	9·4	15·3
1936	17·8	27·9	17·0	7·5	16·1	14·8
1937	19·5	34·6	32·6	12·6	10·2	20·6
1938	25·7	23·7	20·5	16·3	16·2	7·9

.. = not available.

[a] Includes 'tanker cargoes' carried in dry-cargo ships.

Source: Radius, tables 5, 14, 21, 24, 27, 32, pp. 33, 40, 53, 56, 65, 68 respectively. For original sources see footnotes to tables.

Second, in the expanding trades of the Atlantic and Gulf districts the British participation appears to have been well maintained over the period in so far as the trade moving across the Atlantic to East Asia was concerned. In the new trade routes created by the opening of the Panama Canal, however, British

[1] The term trans-Pacific is taken from the source. It covers trade between America and the Asian countries on the other side of the Pacific, whether the ships employed used the Pacific or Atlantic Ocean routes.

participation was smaller and the decline in both the American and the British shares of the trade was matched by a doubling of the share carried in other non-American ships which developed the increasingly important Panama routes. These ships were owned principally in Japan, the Netherlands and Norway, with Japanese shipping as the most important. It cannot be doubted that the substantial competition of Japanese ships was a potent factor preventing an expansion of the British share of the trades: equally, however, the failure of both British and American ship-owners to take advantage of the opportunities offered by the opening of the Panama Canal and, in the British case, the concentration largely on the trades which had existed before 1914, provided an opening for the entry of Japanese and other ships. In 1936, for example, 88 per cent of the imports of the Atlantic district from East Asia moved via the Panama Canal. None of this trade was carried by British liners, whereas all other non-American liners trading from East Asia to the Atlantic district travelled via the Panama Canal and 90 per cent of the tramp trade was also via the Panama.

Third, the figures in Table 18 cover only a part of American trade, namely the trade with East Asian areas carried in dry-cargo liners, whereas the figures in Table 17 cover all trades and all cargoes. This suggests that the failure of British shipping to profit from the contraction of American shipping, which was shown in the earlier table, was partly due to other factors than the neglect of the Panama routes, in particular, the failure to secure a sufficient expansion of the tanker fleet and to provide the right type of tramp ships for world trade requirements.

The general conclusion from the detailed data on the trans-Pacific trades is that during the inter-war period British ships more or less maintained their places in the liner trades existing before 1914, but failed to secure a substantial share '. . . in the development of the new trade via the Panama Canal'.[1] This conclusion says nothing about the relative positions of British shipping in the pre-1914 period and the post-1920 period and, therefore, in no way controverts the earlier conclusion that the entry of subsidized American lines had a seriously deleterious effect on the position of British shipping.

[1] Radius, op. cit., p. 61.

Nationalism in Shipping in the Inter-war years

In terms of totals the changes in the position of non-British shipping between 1919 and 1939 are as shown in Table 19.

TABLE 19. Changes in non-British shipping, 1919–39

	1919 (million tons)	1939 (million tons)	Percentage increase
Subsidizing countries:			
America	10·8	9·3	− 13·9
Others	9·4	16·5	75·5
Non-subsidizing countries	14·1	25·7	82·3
Total non-British	34·3	51·5	50·1

The non-British fleet increased by 50 per cent over the period, made up of a decline in the American fleet (including inactive vessels) of 14 per cent, an increase of 75 per cent in the combined fleets of France, Germany, Italy and Japan, and an increase of over 80 per cent in the fleets of non-subsidizing countries. On the surface, these figures may seem to support a conclusion that the subsidy policies of the four countries prevented their fleets from growing as fast as they might have done. Such a conclusion would be in accordance with the view of the Chamber of Shipping and the Liverpool Steamship Owners' Association expressed in 1923, namely, 'We know no method by which Governments can *foster* shipping—but there have been many examples of the damage done by Government intervention'.[1] Such a conclusion is rejected here.

On the evidence available is it possible to say explicitly how far subsidized competition prevented British shipping from expanding as it might have done in the period?

The American subsidy policy was intended to maintain in operation the ships built during the war. As was shown earlier, before 1914 American trades were very important for British shipping so that the growth of the American fleet hit British shipping directly and hard. However, this growth occurred

---

[1] Memorandum by Chamber of Shipping and Liverpool Steamship Owners' Association to Imperial Economic Conference, clause 5A (II), quoted in *Report of Chamber of Shipping, 1923–4*, p. 89.

during the war and was accepted as irreversible when 1919, instead of 1913, tonnages were used as the basis for the extrapolation of the pre-war trend in the previous chapter. This means that only if the active American fleet in 1939 had exceeded that in 1919 would American shipping have had any further impact on British shipping. In fact, American participation in world trade declined in the period.

With respect to the shipping of other subsidizing countries, the evidence of the timing of the British losses in some important trades suggests that the direct damage to British shipping from their subsidy policies was not extensive. The fleets of these countries expanded in the period and secured an increasing share of world trade. Some of this expansion was clearly in traditionally British trades, but much of it was in new trades. Only if it could be shown that British shipowners were continuously and actively seeking new fields to conquer, and were frustrated because the fruits of their enterprise were stolen by the owners of subsidized ships, could the subsidies of these other countries be considered as a major factor accounting for the relative decline in British tonnage in the period. There is no evidence that British shipowners were engaged in this restless search, but the evidence of Table 19 shows clearly that opportunities for the expansion of non-subsidized fleets existed despite the encroachment of subsidized competition in world trade.

Alongside the direct effects of subsidies were indirect effects. The most important of these was that the subsidies enabled ships surplus to the requirements of trade to remain in service and to exert a depressive influence on freight rates. It has been shown, however, that subsidies were paid mainly to liners operating within conferences at rates determined by those conferences. Within the conferences, neither the owners of ships receiving subsidies, nor the governments behind those owners, had any incentive to resist rate increases to enable partly loaded ships to operate profitably. There is, therefore, no *a priori* reason for accepting that subsidized liners had any depressive effects on rates, given the inelastic demand for the sea transport. What remains then is that over-tonnaging led to part cargoes only being carried, giving smaller returns at any set of rates than full cargoes would have yielded. Whether rates were, in fact, higher or lower than they would have been had fewer ships been available is impossible to say.

Clearly, the effects of subsidized competition were more serious for liner owners than for tramp or tanker owners. They were, therefore, more serious for countries with a substantial part of their shipping engaged in liner services, than for countries with smaller liner interests. The essence of successful enterprise, however, is flexibility and there was complete freedom of entry into all non-liner activities and into non-conference liner services. The enterprising shipowner, if he found one of his services damaged by subsidies, would have moved to other services. If enough British owners had responded in this way, no decline in the position of the British fleet in the inter-war years need have occurred.

VI

The Birth of the Liberty

THIS chapter covers the period from the outbreak of war to the completion of the transition from war to peace, taken here as the end of 1948.

WAR

The consideration will be restricted to two matters only, changes in tonnages during the war and the financial experiences of the war.[1]

(a) *Shipping Losses and New Building*

During the war the losses of Commonwealth-owned ships amounted to 11·9 million tons. A further 9·8 million tons of Allied and neutral shipping was lost and approximately 10 million tons of enemy shipping, making a total of about 32 million tons. This was just over one-half of the pre-war fleet as shown in Table 20. These losses must be considered alongside the building which occurred during the war. In 1946 the world fleet was estimated to be 72·9 million tons, an increase of 11·5 million tons over the 1939 total. This puts the total of new construction during the war at about 43 million tons.

The building during the war was mainly of standard types of cargo vessels and tankers. There was rather more variety in the American building than in the British because the pressure in America was not so great nor the shortage of materials so acute. The war-built American ships included the famous Liberty ships and tankers, in addition to fast cargo ships and transports suitable for use in peacetime liner trades and, in many cases, for conversion into passenger vessels.

[1] For other matters the reader is referred to C. B. A. Behrens, *Merchant Shipping and the Demands of War* (London, 1955), and to the numerous unofficial war histories, particularly those dealing with the experiences of individual company fleets.

TABLE 20. World tonnage by nationality, 3 September 1939, 30 June 1946 and 31 December 1948. Ships of 500 tons and over; Great Lakes tonnage excluded

	1939		*1946*[a]		*1948*	
Country	*Tonnage (000's tons)*	*Percentage of total*	*Tonnage (000's tons)*	*Percentage of total*	*Tonnage (000's tons)*	*Percentage of total*
		%		%		%
Argentine	246	0·4	354	0·5	677	0·9
Belgium	386	0·6	219	0·3	407	0·6
Brazil	446	0·7	511	0·7	676	0·9
British Dominions	1,716	2·8	2,944	4·0	3,203	4·4
Denmark	1,093	1·8	733	1·0	1,037	1·4
Finland	553	0·9	278	0·4	446	0·6
France	2,748	4·5	1,216	1·7	2,462	3·4
Germany	4,185	6·8	413	0·6	141	0·2
Greece	1,763	2·8	532	0·7	1,298	1·8
Italy	3,322	5·4	321	0·4	2,085	2·9
Japan	5,427	8·8	1,200	1·7	1,370[b]	1·9
Netherlands	2,792	4·6	1,563	2·1	2,640	3·6
Norway	4,686	7·6	2,809	3·9	4,213	5·8
Panama	722	1·2	834	1·1	2,843	3·9
Portugal	213	0·3	264	0·4	422	0·6
Russia	1,154	1·9	938	1·3	1,250	1·7
Spain	932	1·5	899	1·2	985	1·4
Sweden	1,442	2·3	1,462	2·0	1,841	2·5
United Kingdom	16,892	27·5	13,340	18·3	16,046	22·0
United States[c]	8,722	14·2	40,882	56·1	26,199[d]	36·0
Others	1,986	3·2	1,206	1·7	2,308	3·2
	61,426	100·0	72,918	100·0	72,941	100·0

[a] Estimates; excludes Russian tonnage the whereabouts of which had not been reported for some time; German figures exclude vessels temporarily transferred to other flags pending final allocation.

[b] Estimate; the Chamber of Shipping gives a figure of 1,200 tons as in 1946. In an article in *Kyoto University Economic Review* (October 1958) a figure of 1,385 thousand tons is given for 1946 and 1,555 thousand tons for 1948, but these figures include ships of over 50 tons. It has been assumed that the difference between the Kyoto figure and the Chamber of Shipping figure for 1946 is due to these very small vessels and that the tonnage of such vessels did not change between 1946 and 1948. J. B. Cohen in *Japan's*

Economy in War and Reconstruction (Minneapolis, 1949) gives total Japanese tonnage as 1,494 thousand tons at 15 August 1945, of which only 557,000 tons was operable. On this basis presumably less than 400,000 tons of the shipping shown in the table was available for immediate use.

c Vessels of 1,000 tons and over.

d Reserve fleet of 13·1 million tons included.

Source: Chamber of Shipping Annual Reports.

Within the overall net increase of 11·5 million tons in the world merchant fleet between 1939 and 1946 there were considerable changes in the distribution between different countries. These changes may be summarized as follows:

1. Fleets showing substantial declines:

Country	Percentage decline	Country	Percentage decline
Belgium	43	Italy	91
Denmark	33	Japan	78
Finland	50	Netherlands	44
France	56	Norway	40
Germany	90	United Kingdom	21
Greece	70		

2. Fleets showing substantial increases:

Country	Percentage increase	Country	Percentage increase
British Dominions	72	United States	369

The fleets of all of Britain's important rivals in the inter-war period, except that of the United States, suffered heavier proportionate losses during the war than did the British fleet. The majority of those losses were directly due to the effects of war although it is alleged that the decline in the Greek fleet was partly due to profitable sales. This allegation is not supported by the statistics of Greek ships chartered to the British Government during the war.[1]

[1] See Behrens, op. cit., pp. 113–18.

Although the British fleet suffered losses amounting to about 11 million tons (Dominion-owned tonnage excluded),[1] the net decline in the fleet as shown in Table 20 was 3·6 million tons, the difference being made up of wartime building, purchases from America, enemy prize tonnage, and ships allocated to the United Kingdom by the Inter-Allied Reparations Agency. From 1942 a scheme was in operation for selling Government-owned vessels to private owners for fleet replacement. The ships were sold at cost, less depreciation, with delivery at the end of the war. The first three allocations during the war resulted in most of the ships offered being sold, but the fourth allocation was less successful because the ships, built late in the war, had high cost prices which made them unattractive to buyers who feared that the end of the war would be followed by a fall in prices. In 1945 three further allocations were made, including allocations of ex-German tonnage and the ships of the fourth wartime allocation which had not been sold. Under the 1945 scheme the ships were sold by tender on an auction system with the offer of bare-boat charter (i.e. charter of unmanned vessels with maintenance responsibility on the charterer) for three or five years on unsold ships. Under the three post-war invitations to tender, 1·96 million deadweight tons of ocean-going vessels (about 1·2 million gross tons) were sold and realized £34 million, while a further 1·59 million deadweight tons were chartered at an annual charge of £2·54 million.

The only countries whose fleets expanded substantially during the war were the United States and the British Dominions. The Dominions principally concerned were Australia,

---

[1] Total war losses of Commonwealth vessels were as follows:

		million tons
U.K. commercially-owned vessels	8·90	
Ministry of Transport vessels	2·18	
Total U.K. owned		11·08
Non-U.K. vessels	0·76	
Others	0·02	
Total Commonwealth		11·86

In addition 0·633 million tons of U.K. commercially owned vessels were lost by 'marine risks', that is, under conditions in which their loss was not covered by War Risk Insurance. (See M. G. Kendall, 'Losses of U.K. Merchant Ships in World War II', *Economica* (November 1948), pp. 289–93.)

Canada and India. In the post-war years the fleets of Australia and Canada were used chiefly in coastal trades or were transferred to British registry because it was impossible to operate profitably at the wage levels ruling in those countries. The increase in the American fleet was of crucial importance both to the successful prosecution of the war and to the economy of post-war ship operations; the sale of these ships after 1946 is considered below.

(b) *Wartime Financial Arrangements*

Financial arrangements in wartime covered two questions, namely, the determination of rates of hire for vessels employed on Government business and the compensation to shipowners for ships lost.

Initially a distinction was drawn between Government business and other business as in the 1914–18 war. However, in order to prevent a recurrence of the experience in that war, freight rates were controlled and a licensing system was introduced to enable the Government to secure the vessels it needed. The rates paid by the Government for British-owned tonnage were below those which it paid for neutral tonnage; for example, the neutral rate, River Plate to United Kingdom was 55*s*. compared with the British rate of 32*s*. 6*d*., while the rates for Montreal to United Kingdom were 4*s*. 6*d*. for British ships and 10*s*. 6*d*., raised to 11*s*. for neutral ships.[1] These differences annoyed British shipowners who were also aggrieved at being unable to profit from the high rates ruling in neutral trades, for example, the scrap trade from America to Japan and the coal trade from Hampton Roads to South America in which neutral ships were earning handsome profits.

From the Government's point of view, the informal system was not a success. It had been adopted because of a widespread disbelief in the expert calculations of a shipping shortage. The Government, however, found it difficult to get ships to trade on dangerous routes at the rates paid when shipowners were left with some freedom. With the spread of the war a shipping shortage became manifest and early in 1940, a full requisitioning scheme was enforced.

[1] *Shipbuilding and Shipping Record* (9 November 1939), p. 496.

The scheme of hiring was not finally settled between the Government and the industry until August 1940, although most of its features were operative before that date. Under the scheme, all British-owned vessels were taken under charter by the Government, freight rates being determined to allow owners a profit of 5 per cent on the agreed value of each ship and depreciation at 5 per cent. The Government did not wish to manage directly the whole British merchant fleet. It was therefore arranged that liner tonnage remained under the control of its owners, except when requisitioned for Naval Commissioned Services, and the owners were paid a management allowance based on average management costs and not intended to yield a profit. Tramp ship owners did not usually have the necessary shore organizations to carry out the day to day arrangements, including the assembling and loading of cargoes. In consequence most tramp ships were placed under the management of liner companies by the Government. This was a necessary step, but it meant that tramp owners were left without any real functions with respect to their ships. The effects of six years spent drawing charter hire without taking operational responsibility are believed in the industry to have debilitated the enterprise of tramp owners and largely to account for their hesitancy and general lack of initiative when the war was over.

The structure of rates agreed was complex and need not be considered. It was kept under continual review during the war period and the basic rates covered the ships' expenses that they were designed to cover, but did no more than this.

The relation between the rates paid to British ships and those paid to ships flying other flags was not simple. Early in the war when countries such as Norway and Greece were neutral, the rates paid to hire the ships exceeded those paid for British ships. When the countries became Allies in 1940 a problem arose: the rates paid could hardly be less than they had been previously, but those rates were in excess of those paid to British owners. In the event, the rates paid were the subject of inter-governmental negotiation and in some cases different rates were paid for ships chartered before and after the fall of the countries concerned. For Danish and French ships there was no government to which they could be responsible and the ships were put under the British flag and paid British rates. For the others the general tendency was to maintain throughout the war the rates being paid early in 1940, but not to increase those rates as costs rose. The gap between British and foreign rates was, therefore, narrowed but never completely eliminated.

After the American entry into the war there was scarcely any neutral tonnage remaining to earn high profits as in the previous war. The Swedes time-chartered over one-half of their fleet outside the Baltic to the British Government at profitable, but not excessive rates. The other neutral fleets, for example, those of Spain and Portugal, were not chartered to the British Government and took advantage of whatever high rates they could obtain.

The second part of the financial arrangements covered the replacement of tonnage lost. Under the Government Tonnage Replacement Scheme the values of ships for insurance purposes were divided into two parts. First, was the basic value representing generally, the pre-war value of the ship for insurance purposes, that is, its depreciated historic cost in 1939, not its cost of replacement by a new ship. Second, was an additional value, which averaged about 25 per cent of the basic figure, to cover the increase in insurance values of ships during the war. With regard to the basic value, the implicit assumption was made that owners had available, as depreciation reserves, the difference between the insured values and the replacement costs. It was recognized that many owners had been unable to make the necessary depreciation allowances during the 1930s, but specifically provided that the freight rates agreed should not cover these arrears of depreciation.

When a ship was lost only the basic element of the insurance was paid to the owners in cash. The second part of the value was credited to the owners and held in a 'kitty'. Credits could be withdrawn only when a lost ship was replaced, it being provided that any credits not drawn seven years after the end of the war should be cancelled. On the 8·74 million tons of British commercially-owned vessels lost through war risks, the total recovery by owners was £268·6 million, giving an average of £30·74 per ton. The average for passenger and mixed passenger and cargo liners over 3,500 tons was £44 per ton, while that for other classes was lower.[1]

How well did British shipping do under these conditions? Figures of the profits earned by British shipping companies are not particularly informative as there is a strong tradition of non-disclosure to prevent competitors assessing the actual position. For this reason the financial experience shown in company accounts may not represent the true position.

For liner companies in the *Fairplay* sample, the following changes may be noted:

Reserves:

1939	£30 million
1946	£113 million

Debentures and Loans:

1939	£37 million
1946	£11 million

Dividends:

1939	£2·7 million
average 1940–6 inclusive	£4·0 million

Investments and cash:

1939	£59 million
1946	£151 million

The position may be summarized by saying that during the war period the companies concerned increased their reserves by £83 million and reduced their capital indebtedness by £26 million, that is, an increase in net worth of £109 million. On the assets side of the industry's balance sheet cash and investments had risen by £92 million. The ships lost by the companies in the sample had been worth in 1939 about £31 million while depreciation on the remaining ships, based on 1939 values, should have amounted to a further £30 million between 1939 and 1946. These figures do not include depreciation reserves in 1939. The fleet in 1939 had a book value of £77 million, which is reasonable in terms of replacement cost at the time, so that by 1946

[1] Figures from Kendall, op. cit.

L

the value of the remaining ships, that is, their depreciated historic cost, should have been about £16 million. In fact, the value is shown as £45 million. This difference of £29 million could have arisen in either of two ways, namely, by including the value of some investments with fleet values, or by revaluing the fleet to take account of its increased earning power and replacement cost. Given the accounting conventions of shipping companies, the second possibility seems unlikely, but it is known that in some cases values of investments were included with fleet values.

In terms of a balance sheet, the position of the sample of liner companies was:

Changes in the balances, 1939 to 1946			
Reserves	+83	Investments	+92
Debentures and loans	−26	Fleet value	−61
		Investments included with fleet	+29
	+57		+60

The discrepancy between the two sides of the account arises from rounding the figures and changes in items not included. In addition to the amounts shown, the companies had available in the 'kitty' an unknown further sum, probably about £10–£15 million, from War Risks Insurance. This makes the total sum available for replacement and expansion £121 million (£92 million plus £29 million) plus the amount in 'kitty'. Between 1939 and 1946 the Chamber of Shipping index of shipbuilding prices doubled so that replacing the lost ships at 1946 prices would have absorbed approximately £62 million, leaving £59 million plus the 'kitty' and depreciation reserves in 1939 to replace the surviving ships when their replacement became necessary. At 1946 prices this would have cost about £90 million while the amount available to cover this was the depreciated value of the fleet in 1946, £16 million, plus £59 million of wartime reserves not required to replace war losses, plus the 'kitty', plus the accumulated depreciation reserves in 1939 on the whole of the fleet. As can be seen, it was a close thing, although the position of the companies had been improved by the repayment of £26 million in loans and debentures which would otherwise have been available in cash. Additionally, there were probably some hidden reserves in the investment values shown.

It may be concluded that the wartime financial arrangements were such that the companies in this sample (which is reasonably representative of the whole) were able to hold their own in the face of shipping losses and rising building costs, while increasing their dividends by 50 per cent over the 1939 level. However, in no year during the war did the dividends exceed 4 per cent of the capital used as disclosed by the accounts; however ,'the capital used as disclosed by published accounts is not necessarily any true indication of the amount of actual capital employed in the business'.[1] Only in 1943 did dividends as a percentage of disclosed capital exceed their 1938 level and through the war they were lower than the annual averages for the periods 1909–13, 1914–18 and 1919–30. On the basis of these calculations it does not appear that the liner companies made exorbitant gains during the war.

For tramp companies the picture is less clear. In 1938 voyage profits for the companies in the *Fairplay* tramp ship sample had amounted to £2·7 per ton, a figure exceeded in 1946 with profits of £3 per ton, but this was after the wartime controls had ended. During the war, however, the companies had enjoyed a period of reasonable prosperity which enabled them to write off their arrears of depreciation and increase their reserves from £6·4 million to £18·3 million. Ships worth £6·7 million at 1939 valuations were lost during the war and the replacement of these absorbed the increase in reserves. There is nothing further of a qualitative nature that can be said. It seems, however, that although the wartime period was profitable, the financial results were no better than in a good pre-war year and not as good as in 1937.

The whole financial arrangements were reviewed by the Select Committee on National Expenditure in 1944–5. The Committee surveyed the published accounts of a large number of shipping companies and obtained additional information in four cases because the abbreviated financial statements of the kind generally available did not provide a sufficient picture of

---

[1] Fifth Report from the Select Committee on National Expenditure, Session 1944–5, *War-time Financial Arrangements with British Shipowners.*

the finances of the companies. In most cases the Committee concluded that the financial experiences called for no special remark and only in the four cases did they consider it necessary to make specific comments. Even in the four cases, after taking account of all factors, including profits from ancillary operations and the relation between the share capital and the actual capital employed, the Committee concluded that the wartime profits did not suggest an excessive or improper inflation. In a special inquiry into the profits of liner companies it was estimated that profits as percentages of capital values[1] of the fleets were:

For financial years ending between
    30 September 1940 and 31 March 1941, 3·6 per cent
    30 September 1942 and 31 March 1943, 4·5 per cent

The Committee noted without comment the use of liquid resources by companies for the repayment of redeemable debentures. It was concluded that the earnings of shipping companies had not been disproportionate to those of other enterprises engaged in war service and that the financial arrangements made had proved fair and reasonable.

The Select Committee had nothing constructive to say about the replacement scheme. Kendall argued that the probable cost of replacement of ships lost from war risks and ordinary marine risks during the war was about £600 million, towards which insurance recoveries totalling £287 million and depreciation reserves, which he estimated at £210 million, were available. This left a deficiency of £103 million which shipowners had to find from their general reserves to replace their war losses.[2]

The implicit attribution of the whole of the deficiency to the inadequacy of insurance recoveries is, of course, not justified. At the most the insurance scheme could only have provided for replacing each vessel on the day it was lost with another vessel of the same type, size and age, leaving the difference between the price of such a vessel and a new vessel of the same type and size to be met from depreciation reserves. Because shipbuilding

---

[1] The capital values were those on which the Inland Revenue based depreciation allowances.

[2] Kendall, op. cit.

prices had risen, depreciation reserves based on historic cost were inadequate in amount. By and large, the insurance recoveries would have replaced ships at the time of their loss and also, generally, in 1946, but each year that replacement was deferred shipbuilding prices rose.[1] During the war, losses could be replaced only by standard ships, poor substitutes for liners although good substitutes for tramp losses. Even after the war had ended, some deferment of replacement was unavoidable because the capacity of British yards did not exceed 1·2 million tons per annum until 1949, and approximately one-quarter of this capacity was reserved for ships for export. There was, therefore, no question of replacing all ships lost at 1946 prices, or even at 1948 prices. Shipbuilding prices themselves were undoubtedly pushed up by the heavy demand for ships in the immediate post-war years, a demand which would not have occurred had it not been necessary to replace war losses. While, therefore, part of the deficiency shown by Kendall's calculation was due to the inadequacy of earmarked depreciation reserves based on historic cost, a substantial part arose from the pressure of demand to replace war losses on an inelastic supply position, and might reasonably have been covered by a special subvention from the Treasury awarded under conditions which did not give hesitant owners (see below) any further cause to delay replacement. This conclusion must be modified in so far as American ships were available for purchase to replace tonnage which had been lost.

The argument above is not intended to allocate the whole of the deficiency to the direct effects of the war because after the war shipping did not return to the depressed conditions of the years, excepting 1937 and 1938, which had preceded the war. The increased prosperity of shipping in the post-war years raised the prices of ships, the capital goods of the industry, and this reduced the real value of the equity originally subscribed and of any loans raised subsequently. If such rises in capital values could not be accommodated from earnings, for example

[1] It should be noted that the fall in interest rates after the war provided holders of investments with capital profits so that insurance recoveries invested in bonds increased in money value. For ships replaced after 1946 this factor should be taken into account in the calculation of any discrepancy between replacement costs and insurance recoveries.

by the capitalization of money profits, then extra capital should have been raised. Shipping companies, however, *repaid* capital, a course of events only justifiable if shipbuilding prices were falling and even then betokening a lack of willingness to consider fleet expansion.

Had Kendall calculated his depreciation reserves on the basis of 1946 valuations instead of those of 1939 for the fleet existing in 1946 he would have obtained a figure of about £315 million which, with insurance recoveries, would have replaced the fleet. It is only that part of the difference between the 1939 and the 1946 building prices directly attributable to the post-war scramble to replace lost tonnage which, it can be argued, might have been covered by a subvention additional to the insurance recoveries, and then only in so far as the additional values allowed for in the insurance recoveries did not cover the rise in building costs and the losses could not be replaced by the purchase of American tonnage.

The problem may be looked at in another way. On the basis of the average book values shown in the *Fairplay* samples for 1939, the value of the fleet at the outbreak of the war was about £210 million. Approximately one-half of this fleet was lost and, assuming that the percentage of losses was the same for all types of ship lost, the value of the lost tonnage, at 1939 valuations, was about £105 million, against which insurance recoveries amounted to £287 million. Shipbuilding prices doubled between 1939 and 1946, so to replace lost vessels with identical tonnage would have cost about £210 million, leaving £77 million towards meeting the deficiency of depreciation reserves. This calculation accords with Kendall's figures as the 1939 valuation of the lost vessels shown above, £105 million, plus his estimate of the depreciation reserves on those vessels, £210 million, agrees fairly well with his estimated £300 million as the cost of building the lost vessels in 1939. This then leaves intact his estimated deficiency, £103 million to be met from general reserves, but shows that the real deficiency in depreciation allowances was £180 million, of which £77 million was met from insurance recoveries. The actual amount which remained and which might have been met from a subvention as argued above must, therefore, have been relatively small.

The conclusion is that in so far as freight rates were concerned they were fair but shipping companies did not make fortunes. For replacements, the compensation was reasonable but rising prices in relation to depreciation reserves meant that in 1946 practically the whole of the wartime gains were needed to restore fleets to their pre-war strengths while subsequent increases in replacement costs could only be met by drawing on general reserves accumulated before 1939, by increasing capital, or directly from post-war profits.

How did the shipping of Britain's competitors fare during the war? It has been shown that the fleets of Germany, Italy and Japan were heavily reduced in size. After the war neither the fleets, nor the owners of the fleets, were in a favourable position, although American support and the use of American aid funds were important factors in the reconstruction of the Italian and Japanese fleets and the Italian fleet was able to make a rapid recovery (see Table 21). The position of American shipping has been considered in quantum terms: in financial terms, wartime profits, particularly before America entered the war, enabled subsidies to be dispensed with by many lines and permitted tramp operators to enter business and survive until they could transfer their ships to Panamanian registry. French shipping suffered heavy losses and that which remained was partly under the British flag, chartered at British rates, while the remainder was idle or operating at rates which enabled it to dispense with subsidies. Greek shipping also suffered heavy losses, but substantial profits were made on the ships which survived. A part of these profits was lost in the post-war upheavals in Greece but the remainder was used to establish fleets under flags of convenience. No real information is available about this but the sudden emergence of Greek entrepreneurs in shipping after 1946 is explicable only in terms of the use of wartime profits. Swedish shipping did reasonably well out of the war, but not so well as in the 1914–18 war; in the post-war years Swedish shipping grew at a rate above that at which world shipping grew and wartime profits aided this growth. However, Swedish shipping was not a major competitor to British shipping in the period. The two chief competitors which have not been accounted for are the Netherlands and Norway.

The Birth of the Liberty

When Holland was invaded, 20 per cent of the Dutch fleet was seized by the Germans. Prior to that, the fleet had avoided employment in the Allied cause and had earned substantial profits in neutral trades. After the capture of Holland, about one million tons of Dutch shipping were placed under British control and the remainder of the free tonnage continued trading in the Pacific. In June 1942, all Dutch ships were requisitioned by the Government, although those time-chartered to Britain remained in that service. In the period 1940–5, the profits available for dividend payment amounted to 23·8 per cent of the share capital in the case of twelve companies owning 80 per cent of the dry-cargo fleet. The greater part of these profits had been earned before June 1942, after which profits were very moderate. After the war, the accumulated resources of these twelve companies amounted to 280 million guilders, while the sum necessary to restore the fleet was 525 million guilders. Of the deficiency of 245 million guilders, 29 million guilders was obtained from the profits available for dividends which were distributed as shares, not in cash, and the balance from pre-war reserves and new issues of capital.[1] This position was clearly less favourable than that of British shipping.

It has already been pointed out that the rates paid to Norwegian ships by the British Government exceeded those paid to British owners. After the loss of Norway, all vessels which had escaped capture were requisitioned by the Norwegian Government in London and were managed by the Norwegian Shipping and Trade Mission (Nortraship). Freights earned were paid to Nortraship which was an agency of the Norwegian Government. About one-half of the amount received was retained and used towards the expenses of the Norwegian Government and the other aspects of the Norwegian war effort.

The payment to shipowners for the use of their ships was not made until after the war when it was fixed at 11 per cent and 12 per cent of 1939 insurance values for steam tramps and other ships respectively. These amounts were bareboat rates and may be compared with the rate paid on British vessels taken on bareboat charter which was 10 per cent. As shown below, however, the insured values of Norwegian ships exceeded those for British

[1] Information by courtesy of Koninklijke Nederlandsche Reedersvereeniging.

ships so that the slightly higher rates of charter hire were calculated on the basis of greater capital values, giving the Norwegian owners charter rates perhaps 3 per cent to 4 per cent above British rates. The calculation of the rates paid to Norwegian ships were based on the earnings of a considerable sample of shipping companies collected over the years 1935–9.[1] This meant that although the rates exceeded those paid to British ships they did not exceed the average earnings of Norwegian shipping over a period which included both good years and bad. It seems to follow, therefore, that any advantage which Norwegian shipping enjoyed compared to British shipping in the determination of wartime rates was no more than it had enjoyed in the pre-war years as a result of enterprising management. Both British and Norwegian owners were taxed on their earnings, while Norwegian owners also paid a property tax each year on their capital values.

The replacement terms for ships lost while requisitioned by Nortraship worked out at about £38·9 per ton on average, compared with the British average of £30·74 per ton. However, the Norwegian fleet had a higher proportion of motor tonnage than the British fleet and this cost about 35 per cent more on average than steam tonnage. The average age of Norwegian ships requisitioned was about 2·5 years less than that of British ships. Assuming an even spread of losses among motor ships and steamships and among ships of various ages, the different structures of the fleets would account for an excess of Norwegian values over British values of about 22 per cent, 14 per cent arising from the higher proportion of motor ships and 8 per cent from the difference in age structure. On the other hand, the British average included recoveries on higher-valued passenger vessels which, for a proper comparison, should be excluded. Taking account of these factors, on a reasonably comparable basis, Norwegian shipowners were paid an average of £31·6 per ton and British shipowners £27·7 per ton for ships lost, both figures applying to non-passenger ships stabilized for propulsion and age. Ships which were lost while not under requisition by Nortraship were compensated at values about 20 per cent below that given above, but even when this is taken into account

[1] E. W. Paulson, *Studier i Skipsfartens Økonomi* (Bergen, 1949).

Norwegian owners as a whole received on average 7 per cent to 8 per cent more than British owners for the loss of comparable vessels.[1]

What conclusions can be drawn about the respective financial experiences of British and Norwegian ships? Although Norwegian ships did slightly better both in terms of freight rates and compensation for losses than British ships, Norwegian owners had two disadvantages compared with British owners. First, British owners who received bareboat charters had no administrative expenses while those who had administrative expenses managed ships for the Ministry of Transport which covered the expenses on a non-profit basis; Norwegian owners, on the other hand, had their organizations in Norway to maintain without receiving any payment for the use of those organizations. Second, British payments for the use of ships and compensation for losses were made as they accrued, enabling shipowners to earn interest on the money until it was distributed to shareholders or used to replace lost ships, whereas payments to Norwegian owners were not made until 1946. Interest at 0·75 per cent was paid by the Norwegian Government on all amounts owing from 1 October 1945 to the date of payment, and a payment of 5 per cent per annum on 80 per cent of the insurance value of ships lost was made from the date of loss until September 1945, which offset most of the advantage British owners enjoyed from receiving immediate payment. On balance, the advantage of Norwegian shipowners was relatively small and probably no more, and perhaps less, than they would have enjoyed had there been no war, profits earned between September 1939 and April 1940 always excepted.

The examination of the financial experiences of shipping during the war reveals that, by and large, the British industry neither suffered heavily nor gained greatly and that the shipping of other important maritime countries did not generally end up in relatively much more favourable positions; the only exceptions to this were America and Sweden. The divergences of financial experiences of the first world war were not repeated.

[1] Details of the Norwegian settlement from *Instilling om Oppgjøret mellom Staten og de Norske Skipsrederier* (Oslo, 1946).

The Birth of the Liberty

TRANSITION TO PEACE

The transition period may most conveniently be regarded as lasting until the end of 1948. By this time the British fleet had been restored to 95 per cent of its pre-war size; subsequent expansion was slow and it was not until 1954 that the 1939 tonnage was passed. By the end of 1948 also the tonnage built during the war had been distributed among private owners and the surplus American tonnage had been placed in reserve. Control over British ships had ended chiefly in 1945 although it was not until January 1949 that tanker rates were freed completely from the control of the Ministry of Transport.[1] By the end of 1948, however, most world shipping had settled down to peacetime conditions of operation.

In America, the Merchant Ship Sales Act, 1946, provided for the sale of war-built American vessels to American and non-American citizens, vessels not sold to be withdrawn from commercial service and placed in reserve. This was the origin of the U.S. Reserve Fleet to which 13 million tons of shipping were transferred. The American Government placed certain restrictions on the classes of ships which could be sold to foreigners and, in general, American owners had first option on the better type of ships suitable for liner trades and the vessels sold overseas were chiefly Liberty ships. Between 1 July 1945 and 30 June 1953, 11 million tons of American shipping were transferred to foreign registers.[2]

Of the total transferred 3·5 million tons were privately owned ships transferred mainly to flags of convenience but often remaining within American ownership; this category included 1·05 million tons of vessels built for foreign registry between 1950 and 1953. These transfers formed the basis for the expansion of the flags of convenience fleets (see Chapter IX).

[1] British tankers engaged in cross-trades were freed from control in June 1948, and those engaged in the United Kingdom trade in January 1949. Norwegian tankers were freed in January 1947 and so were able to profit from the high rates of 1947 and 1948 which were denied to British tankers. This scarcely affected British shipping companies because few independent tankers were owned in Britain. It may, however, have deterred the building of tankers, although there is no evidence of this.

[2] Figures from Merchant Marine Studies, Hearings before Senate Committee on Interstate and Foreign Commerce, 83rd Congress, Washington, 1953, pp. 285-7, and *Bulletin of American Bureau of Shipping* (January 1949).

The other 7·5 million tons of tonnage transferred was government owned, and was more widely distributed among world shipowners with Panamanian (Greek or American ownership), Italian, British, French, Greek and Norwegian buyers predominating. It is uncertain precisely how much tonnage British owners purchased. One official American figure is 0·76 million tons, although an earlier figure of 1·56 million tons checks rather better with what fragmentary data are available in this country and should, therefore, be accepted. There is considerable doubt concerning the quantity of tonnage British owners were permitted to buy. The tonnage offered for sale varied greatly in quality and it seems that the British Government limited the purchase by classes of vessels instead of giving a blanket permission to buy any available ships. British shipowners could not always secure as many vessels of some classes as they were allowed, while with other classes they had the opportunity to purchase, and would willingly have taken, more ships than they were authorized by the British Government. The Americans were prepared to sell the ships on a loan basis provided the loans were guaranteed by the Governments of the shipowners. The British Treasury refused to give this guarantee because it considered that the terms of the loan were too severe. The ships purchased had, therefore, to be paid for in cash for which the necessary dollars were made available. This provision itself limited both the total that could be purchased and the use each shipowner could make of his resources.

For British shipping, the transition period was one of great uncertainty, despite the tremendous profits being earned. British tramps covered by the *Fairplay* sample recorded voyage profits of over 60 per cent of the paid-up capital for the years 1946, 1947 and 1948, while liners were scarcely less remunerative.

With memories of the collapse of the previous post-war boom, shipowners generally adopted a cautious attitude towards fleet expansion, and often towards replacement. Although most liner companies were eager to replace their ships as fast as they could be built, some feared a depression and a break in shipbuilding prices, the current level of which they regarded as unreasonable; '. . . directors could not blindly embark on building programmes at costs at which they knew the ships could not be operated'.[1] Tramp ship owners were much more hesitant. Part of this hesitation arose very reasonably from the long order-books of the builders and many owners feared that, although the present moment was propitious for fleet expansion, the situation would have changed before a ship was delivered, perhaps three or more years after being ordered. Shipowners, like many other business men, were less confident than academic economists about the prospects of maintaining full employment and, there-fore, did not believe that remunerative freight rates could last without a government guarantee. It must not be overlooked either that building abroad in this period was restricted while the British shipyards were expected to devote part of their capacity to export orders, so that British owners were queueing for only part of the building capacity. In early 1948 it was commented that those shipowners who had contracted for new ships immediately after the end of the war need not '. . . consider that they were unduly venturesome. Yet the number of these was restricted. Some were restrained by uncertainties as to how long demand for tonnage and world commerce would continue active, by the level of prices and by the existence of a large volume of surplus tonnage.'[2] Despite the surplus tonnage, repre-sented by the U.S. Reserve Fleet, there was an acute shortage of some types of cargo ships and tankers under the British flag because losses had not been replaced, nor had orders for replace-ment been placed.

Although some bold decisions were taken, for example, two tramp owners established liner services in the Far Eastern trades to take advantage of the opportunities created by the with-drawal of Japanese shipping, a preponderance of British owners once again looked backwards, this time to the 1939 situation of world tonnage and the post-1919 experiences. The experience of history suggested delay as the wisest course: those British owners who took this course were not alone and in most mari-time countries some shipowners took a similar view. Perhaps the main differences between the aggregated reactions of various national shipping industries arose from the varying relative

[1] Chairman, Ellerman Lines, reported in *Shipbuilding and Shipping Record* (26 June 1947), p. 641.
[2] *Shipbuilding and Shipping Record* (26 February 1948), p. 245.

importance of owners who had entered the industry after the collapse of freight rates in 1920. There were few such owners in Britain.

In Table 21 the extent to which the fleets of a number of leading maritime countries were replaced in the years to the end of 1948 are compared. Nine of the eleven countries listed earlier as suffering substantial declines during the war are included; the countries excluded are the ex-enemy countries, Germany and Japan. It can be seen from the table that the replacement factor[1] for the British fleet was smaller than that of any other important fleet which had suffered during the war.

TABLE 21. Fleet restoration in some leading maritime countries

| Country | Post War Fleets as percentages of 1939 fleets | | Replacement Factors |
	31 December 1946	31 December 1948	
	%	%	
Belgium	57	106	1·8
Denmark	67	95	1·4
Finland	50	81	1·6
France	44	90	2·0
Greece	30	74	2·4
Italy	9	63	7·0
Netherlands	56	95	1·6
Norway	60	90	1·5
United Kingdom	79	95	1·2

Source: Calculated from figures in Table 20.

When all the immediate post-war transfers of tonnage had been completed and the earliest of the post-war ships had entered service, the fleets of the leading maritime countries were as shown in Table 20 for the end of 1948. From the table it can be seen that the British fleet had declined to 22 per cent of the total world fleet. However, the world fleet of 72·9 million tons included the U.S. Reserve Fleet of 13·1 million tons. If this tonnage is excluded, the world active fleet at the end of 1948 is shown as being about 3 million tons smaller than at the outbreak

[1] The replacement factors have been calculated by dividing the percentages which the 1948 fleets bore to the 1939 fleets by the percentages which the 1946 fleets bore to the 1939 fleets.

of war in 1939, while the British fleet constituted 26·9 per cent of this fleet, only a little smaller than the percentage in 1939. Despite the hesitations of the period, by the end of 1948 the British fleet was relatively as strongly placed as in 1939. There is, therefore, no *prima facie* reason why British shipping should not have retained its relative position, at least at the 1939 level. History, however, is a continuous process, not something which can be neatly cut into discrete periods, and the doubts of the transition period did not end in 1948, nor were their effects fully realized by then.

VII

The Prosperous Age: the Post-war Period

THE period from the end of the war into 1960 was generally prosperous for shipping with the Korean War and Suez crisis as high lights, followed in each case by a period of lower prosperity as a consequence of the over-building in the booms and, additionally, in the post-Suez period, of a slackening in the growth of world trade. The result was that in 1958 and subsequent years profits became increasingly difficult to earn and the problem of excess tonnage became important for the first time since before the war. By the close of 1960, when this narrative ends, the situation was one of considerable uncertainty and the need for a reappraisal of the whole world shipping position was apparent.

World Trade and Shipping

The volume of world sea-borne trade passed its 1938 level in 1948 and has almost doubled since then as shown in Table 22. Until 1957 the increase in trade was great enough to provide remunerative rates for all ships owned outside the really high-wage countries, such as America. Shipping capacity also increased, partly by a straight increase in tonnage as shown in Table 22, partly by an increase in speed and a reduction in 'dead' time spent in port due to improvements in port facilities; these increases are not shown in the table. As a result, when dry-cargo trade turned down after 1957 and the tanker trade failed to maintain its previous growth, there was a sudden end to the abundant prosperity of earlier years. By mid-1959, the depth of the depression, 9 per cent of the world fleet, excluding the U.S. Reserve Fleet, was idle.

The faster growth of the oil trade than of dry-cargo trades is apparent from the table. Between 1937 and 1957 the tonnage of oil moving in international sea-borne trade exactly quadrupled, while in the same period the tonnage of dry cargo carried increased by only 50 per cent. It is clear that the world trading pattern since the war has been such as to provide a solid basis for expansion in shipping and to provide greater opportunities for tanker owners than for owners of dry-cargo tonnage. This gave a substantial incremental advantage to those shipowners who had become established in tanker trades, and known to the oil companies, before the war. However, during most of the period the shortage of tankers was such that almost any owner prepared to satisfy an oil company regarding the type of tanker built could have secured a pre-construction time charter.

TABLE 22. Indices of trade and shipping tonnage, 1948 to 1959
1950 = 100

Year	Dry cargo		Tanker		Total	
	Trade	Shipping	Trade	Shipping	Trade	Shipping
1948		98		88	89	95
1949		98		92	91	96
1950	100	100	100	100	100	100
1951	120	114	113	111	115	113
1952	117	108	127	121	121	111
1953	120	109	131	131	125	115
1954	130	112	142	145	135	121
1955	150	117	155	157	152	128
1956	163	125	173	170	168	137
1957	170	133	187	182	177	148
1958	163	140	195	210	172	159
1959	165	143	209	226	184	165

Note: U.S. Reserve Fleet excluded from shipping tonnage.
Sources: Chamber of Shipping Report and *United Nations Bulletin of Statistics.*

The course of British trade in the period is shown in Table 23. Oil imports have more than quadrupled since 1938, again indicative of the importance of the oil tanker to post-war shipping. Dry-cargo imports, on the other hand, scarcely rose from their 1938 level until 1960. Imports of foodstuffs, which have been affected by the inelasticity of demand in response to rising incomes together with the subsidized increase in British

M

agricultural output, have actually declined, but imports of manufactured goods and basic material, particularly iron ore, have
increased, the increase in 1960 over 1959 being particularly-
sharp. The weight of exports, other than coal, more than
doubled during the period, but although these are generally
goods on which relatively high freight rates are earned (except
during boom periods), the actual weight of such exports is not
an important factor in determining the size of the British fleet.
Coal exports continued the decline noticed in Chapter IV and
have become unimportant as a source of employment for British
ships.

TABLE 23. United Kingdom trade, 1938, 1948 to 1960
(in million tons)

	Imports			Exports			Total trade
Year	Oil	Other	Total	Coal	Other	Total	
1938	11·8	55·5	67·3	38·2	11·5	49·7	117·0
1948	17·2	44·7	61·9	11·6	11·9	23·4	85·3
1949	17·7	47·6	65·3	16·0	12·9	28·9	94·2
1950	18·9	44·3	63·2	16·2	15·5	31·7	94·9
1951	28·5	51·1	79·6	9·1	19·1	28·2	107·8
1952	30·5	49·6	81·1	13·7	19·7	33·4	114·5
1953	33·8	54·5	86·3	15·7	21·7	37·4	123·7
1954	39·3	52·1	91·4	15·6	22·9	38·4	129·8
1955	50·3	59·6	109·9	14·3	22·7	37·1	147·0
1956	45·5	49·0	104·5	11·2	24·7	35·9	140·4
1957	43·9	60·4	104·3	10·0	23·1	33·1	137·4
1958	47·3	56·9	104·2	5·8	24·2	30·1	134·3
1959	53·7	58·2	111·9	5·0	25·1	30·1	142·0
1960	60·2	68·0	128·2	6·8	25·7	32·5	160·7

Source: Liverpool Steamship Owners' Association, Annual Reports.

Two things are clear from the figures in the two tables. The
first is that greater opportunities for expansion existed in tanker
than in dry-cargo trades. The second is that although British
dry cargo imports expanded by nearly 25 per cent between 1938
and 1960, largely due to increased imports of iron ore, total
British dry-cargo trade was smaller in volume in 1960 than in
1938. If British shipping was to expand in the period it had to do

one or more of three things, namely, increase or maintain its relative position in tanker trades, increase or maintain its share of the British dry-cargo import trade, or find increasing employment outside British trades.

For the British mercantile marine the carriage of passengers is more important than for the shipping of any other country. Information on the number of passengers travelling by sea is less complete than is that for the volume of goods transported. The number of passengers crossing the North Atlantic, which had fallen from 2·6 million in 1913 to 0·66 million in 1937, was only 0·56 million in 1950, largely owing to shipping and foreign exchange difficulties. Subsequently, the total traffic rose, reaching 2·25 million in 1958 and 2·8 million in 1960, excluding those passengers travelling by non-conference liners. However, whereas before 1939 practically all the traffic was sea-borne, since the war air travel has increased sharply, from carrying one-third of the total traffic in 1952 to taking over one-half in 1958 and later years; between 1957 (the peak year for sea travel) and 1960, the number of passengers travelling by sea declined by 17 per cent while the number travelling by air increased by 35 per cent.

In other passenger trades the position has been similar. The number of passengers travelling by sea between Britain and non-European countries increased until 1955 for arrivals and until 1957 for departures, thereafter declining, while the number travelling by air increased continuously so that now more people fly than travel by ship. The figures are given in Table 24. For passengers leaving Britain, emigration helped to swell both the total number and the number travelling by sea and explains why the number departing by sea increased until 1957 whereas arrivals by sea began to decline in number after 1955. Over 80 per cent of the passengers travelling by sea between Britain and countries outside Europe travelled in British ships, but it is clear that since 1957 over one-half of the total passenger traffic is air-borne and that, given a decline in emigration, the air-borne proportion will increase further. It seems, therefore, that while increasing levels of real income per head in the advanced industrial countries will lead to more than proportional increases in passenger traffic, the share of this traffic travelling by sea will fall and will probably fall at a faster rate than the increase in the total. Clearly the maritime passenger trades have not been, and are not likely to become, expansive trades in so far as mere transport is concerned.

TABLE 24. Passengers entering and leaving the United Kingdom, from and to non-European countries, 1950-9 (thousands)

	1950	*1953*	*1956*	*1959*
Arrivals:				
by sea	269	302	325	312
by air	125	176	250	428
Departures:				
by sea	333	369	386	334
by air	130	185	260	414

Source: Annual Abstract of Statistics, no. 97 (1960), p. 39.

It is necessary at this point to recognize that although ships are being superseded by aeroplanes for the transport of passengers, ships can provide cruising facilities which aircraft cannot. Cruises can take, roughly, two forms. First, there is the pure holiday cruise from a port which returns to that port within, say, a fortnight. Second, there is the cruise either as part of a voyage or as a lengthy holiday. The first type of cruise can be operated by vessels during the slack periods in their normal trades, or by specially equipped vessels. The second type of cruise requires a passenger vessel in which the emphasis is not simply on providing a tolerable means of transport, but on providing active pleasure; this calls both for vessels designed with this in mind and for routes which are pleasant in themselves. These considerations have been reflected in the new tonnage provided for the Cape route and in the 'Round-the-World' services started by British and Dutch lines. They can also be seen in the relatively better experience of passenger liners travelling between America and southern Europe than of those travelling to Britain and northern European ports. British vessels have scarcely participated in this southern trade since 1914.

The Prosperous Age: the Post-war Period

At the end of 1948, when the post-war transition period may be said to have ended, British shipping comprised 26·9 per cent of the world total, the U.S. Reserve Fleet being excluded. This may be compared with the proportion at the outbreak of war, 27·5 per cent. This shows quite clearly that at the beginning of the period of post-war expansion British shipping was in nearly the same relative position as in 1939. By the end of 1960 the percentage had fallen to 18·2 per cent, the relative fall being caused by a growth in the British fleet of only 12·4 per cent, compared with a growth in the world fleet of 86·3 per cent. In the period, the world dry-cargo fleet increased in size from 44·95 million tons to 68·53 milllion tons, an increase of 52·4 per cent, while the tanker fleet increased from 14·75 million tons to 40·98 million tons, an increase of 177·8 per cent. The increase in the British fleet was 3·4 per cent for dry-cargo vessels and 96·6 per cent for tankers. The more impressive growth in the tanker fleet must be considered in the context that about 70 per cent of the British tanker fleet is owned by the oil companies, compared with a world figure of under 40 per cent for company-owned tankers. In other words, the growth of the tanker fleet was largely the result of the oil companies' expansion of their tonnage, not of British shipowners' provision of an independently owned fleet of substantial dimensions.

The relative decline in the British fleet is marked in both dry-cargo vessels and in tankers. Within the category of dry-cargo vessels the same pattern is discernible for individual types. The amount of refrigerated space in British ships expanded significantly less quickly than that of the world as a whole; between 1953 and 1958 the refrigerated capacity in British ships expanded by 4 per cent compared with an expansion of 120 per cent in the Norwegian fleet. The passenger-carrying capacity of the British fleet increased less rapidly than that of the world fleet. The percentage changes in the number of passenger berths is, however, misleading, since much of the expansion of the world passenger fleet occurred as new ships were built for British owners and older, slower, ships were sold to foreign owners.

The total dry-cargo fleet under the British flag declined in size until 1952, largely because the decline in the tramp fleet was greater than the slight increase in the liner fleet. After 1952 the dry-cargo fleet increased in size, the increase being a complex of varying patterns for liners and tramps. Liner tonnage increased until 1957, but between mid-1957 and mid-1960 decreased by just under 5 per cent. Tramp tonnage continued to decline until 1956, but between mid-1956 and mid-1960 increased by 14 per cent. Through the Korean and Suez booms, when almost every-one was making money from tramps and the index of real freights (see Table 27) was high, the British tramp fleet declined. In 1956, after a twelve-year period of almost continuous pros-perity, the British tramp fleet began to expand. The expansion came in time for the break in freight rates in 1957, since when the largest increases in the fleet have occurred: long delays between the ordering and delivery of ships are a factor in the explanation of this bad timing.

The poor timing of the increase in the tramp fleet was matched by a neglect of the most suitable type of vessel. Theoretical analysis, if not common sense, indicates that a high-wage country needs to own larger and faster tramps than low-wage countries if it is to be able to compete. Although Britain has not been a really high-wage country for most of the post-war period, British wage costs were substantially higher than those in countries such as Greece and on a par with those in most west-ern European countries. In 1957 the largest tramp owned and registered in Britain was under 12,000 deadweight tons, the modal size being between 7,000 and 8,000 deadweight tons. By mid-1960, one tramp of over 12,000 deadweight tons had taken its place in the fleet, while the modal size of new constructions was between 10,000 and 11,000 deadweight tons. At the end of 1960 the world tramp fleet included 229 bulk carriers of over 14,000 deadweight tons, a size class not represented in the fleet owned and registered in Britain, although some ships of this class were owned by overseas subsidiaries of British companies and registered in Britain.

It is difficult to find any valid explanation of the foregoing position in terms of external factors. If tramp owners did not have the necessary resources to build more tonnage, they could have borrowed, either using their own credit or, if that would not suffice, by obtaining loans based on pre-construction time charters, although this possibility was less readily available for general purpose tramps than for specialized bulk carriers. Much of the growth of the world tramp fleet occurred in the flags of convenience countries and the ships registered under such flags enjoyed immunity from taxation. The position of these ship-owners may have limited the growth possibilities for British tramps, but cannot explain either the faulty timing or the neglect of the most economical ship type. Further, shipowners in countries such as Norway, the Netherlands and Sweden were equally affected by the flags of convenience fleets, yet managed to expand their tramp fleets. The concentration on smaller vessels than those which were economically optimal can be explained as arising from the limited capacity of British ports to handle the larger vessels,[1] but this does not explain why tramp shipowners, whose ships are supposed to be truly international traders, should have accepted the limitation.

In the case of liners, it is possible to point to the effects of sub-sidized competition and flag discrimination as imposing limitations on growth. This question is considered at length in Chapter VIII. Here, it may merely be noted that despite these limitations some British liner fleets expanded in the period, while the liner fleets of countries such as Denmark, the Nether-lands, Norway and Sweden also expanded without the aid of subsidies or favourable discriminatory arrangements.

The British tanker fleet was shown to have expanded by 96·6 per cent between the end of 1948 and the end of 1960. The growth in individual years is shown in Table 25 together with the index of tanker freight rates. Although the British fleet expanded in each year, the growth was smaller each year than that of the world fleet, except in 1959 when the boom had broken and the British tanker fleet expanded by 12 per cent. In fact, there is evidence of a lag of approximately three years between a boom in freights and the expansion of the British fleet, although how much of this can be attributed to delays in ordering as opposed to construction delays cannot be ascertained.

---

[1] In 1962 only one British ore port could handle 35,000 deadweight ton bulk carriers, whereas Continental ports handling 65,000 tonners were available.

The Prosperous Age: the Post-war Period

The 1951–5 lag was about the same for total tonnage as for British tonnage, but the post-1956 lag was much shorter for total than for British tonnage and the difference can, perhaps, be attributed to delays in ordering.

TABLE 25. Annual percentage growth of tanker tonnage and the tanker freight index, 1949 to 1960

Year	Percentage growth in tonnage: World	Britain	Tanker market index in December
	%	%	Scale = 100
1949	4·8	2·7	112·7
1950	8·7	7·1	301·8
1951	9·9	6·1	407·4
1952	9·9	5·8	150·8
1953	8·9	4·7	85·8
1954	10·4	8·8	110·6
1955	9·7	1·8	247·7
1956	6·7	3·7	435·4
1957	11·7	5·8	51·0
1958	12·7	6·9	65·9
1959	7·6	12·0	59·4
1960	7·3	4·6	75·4

Source: Calculated from Chamber of Shipping figures.

The boom in British tanker ownership in 1959 was largely a consequence of the sudden interest in tankers displayed by British liner owners after 1956. Those liner owners who had secured preconstruction time charters during the boom for tankers which did not, in fact, enter service until 1959 or 1960 will undoubtedly profit from their ventures. For tankers built as speculative ventures it is clear that the combination of a lengthy gestation period for the idea and a long construction period caused the ships to miss the boom for which they were designed, although this does not mean that the vessels will never be profitable.

The possibility of British shipowners profiting in the future from their ownership of tankers is, however, somewhat limited by the size structure of the British fleet. At the end of 1960, 48 per cent of the world tanker tonnage comprised vessels of

20,000 deadweight tons and over, whereas the comparable figure for vessels owned and registered[1] in Britain was 37 per cent. If the British owned and registered tankers are arranged in size groups, a bi-modal distribution results, with the peaks at 12,000 to 12,999 deadweight tons and 16,000 to 16,999 deadweight tons.[2] Although these are largely older ships, an unduly large proportion of the tanker tonnage owned by independent shipowners and oil companies in Britain is below 25,000 deadweight tons. Only two British tankers were of over 45,000 deadweight tons in 1960, that is, were approaching the optimum size for a tanker when account is taken of the level of British wage costs.

The reasons for the comparative neglect of tankers by British shipowners were discussed in Chapter IV with reference to the inter-war period and that discussion is applicable to the post-1948 situation. The reason why so many of the tankers which have been built are smaller than the optimum economic size is that shipowners were unduly conscious of the limitations of British oil terminals in handling the biggest tankers. Two comments are relevant to this point. First, the tanker market is an international one and there is no more reason[3] for British shipowners to think in terms of chartering their vessels to British oil companies than there is for British oil companies to refrain from employing foreign tankers. It should also be noted that the international character of the oil companies means that a British company chartering a British vessel will not necessarily use it in British trades. Second, while the British tanker fleet increased by 131 per cent from 1939 to 1960, British oil imports increased by nearly 350 per cent, so that clear opportunities for expansion with employment only in British trades were missed.

[1] The difference between the tonnage of tankers registered in Britain and that owned and registered is 650,000 tons, which are owned by overseas associates of British companies, for example, Bermudan companies. In making the calculation in the text, 250,000 tons of Admiralty owned tankers were also excluded.

[2] During 1961 and 1962 there has been a steady stream of these small tankers towards the breaking yards.

[3] Bunkering contracts between oil companies and shipowners may lead to favourable charter terms being offered to shipowners if they decide to build tankers. This means that British shipowners may have a substantial bias in favour of chartering to British oil companies, each of which wishes to retain the bunkering contracts held.

The Prosperous Age: the Post-war Period

Since the war there has been a continuous increase in the proportion of British trade carried in foreign ships as the figures in Table 26 show. It may be noted that foreign participation was smaller in 1949 than in 1938. The ensuing increase is greatest in British import trades, this arising mainly from the failure of the British tanker fleet to match the rate of expansion of the world tanker fleet. It will be argued later (Chapter XI) that a decline

TABLE 26. Movement of foreign shipping in the foreign trade of the United Kingdom, 1938, 1949 to 1960

	Entrances with cargo		Clearances with cargo	
Year	Net tons (millions)	Percentage of foreign tonnage	Net tons (millions)	Percentage of foreign tonnage
1938	68·4	43·1	58·9	41·4
1949	54·9	34·2	41·5	30·0
1950	57·5	37·4	45·3	30·4
1951	63·6	41·7	43·6	30·2
1952	64·2	42·1	47·0	33·9
1953	69·4	43·5	50·2	35·9
1954	72·4	44·1	51·1	36·4
1955	79·3	45·0	50·1	37·6
1956	77·1	46·2	49·9	36·7
1957	78·4	47·5	50·7	37·8
1958	79·9	47·8	51·4	37·5
1959	84·8	48·9	54·0	38·6
1960	91·6	51·0	54·8	40·3

Source: Board of Trade, Trade and Navigation Returns.

in the proportion of the oil and bulk cargo imports to Britain carried in British ships is appropriate, because of the economic disadvantage of British owners in the operation of the smaller types of tankers and bulk carriers which are all that many British ports can handle. However, there is no such economic reason for a decline in the British flag participation in export trades, while, if the industry had absorbed correctly the implications of the economic position, the decline in the share of British imports held would have been offset by an increase in the participation of British ships in the large tanker and bulk carrier trades of the world. An explanation of the increase in foreign participation in imports based on the encroachment of tonnage registered under flags of convenience cannot be maintained because until 1957 foreign exchange difficulties limited the competition which these ships offered to British ships (see Chapter IX). The preference policies of other countries had some effect on the proportion of British exports travelling in foreign ships, but this, again, is inadequate as an explanation of the increase which occurred (see Chapter VIII).

Can an explanation of the failure of British shipping to grow in the period be found in the environment in which it had to operate? The questions of the shipping policies of other countries and the growth of the flags of convenience fleets, both of which affected that environment, are considered in Chapters VIII and IX respectively. The factor which calls for consideration here is the extent to which the policy of the British Government created difficulties for British shipping. It is worth noting that the policy to be discussed is not specifically related to shipping, but was rather the application to shipping of policies determined by general, financial and strategic considerations.

The attitude of the Government towards the purchase of war-built American ships was discussed in Chapter VI. Among subsequent policy matters, access to finance for expansion and restrictions in ship transfers are cited by the General Council of British Shipping as matters on which British shipowners have been hindered. They contrast the unhappy position of British shipowners with that of their Norwegian counterparts. 'There has been a much closer association of Norwegian shipping interests with their Government than is the case in this country. For instance, Norwegian owners wishing after the war to build tramps, both dry cargo and tanker, did not find much difficulty in borrowing money for the purpose. In contrast with their British counterparts, they could borrow dollars, and, it is understood, they were encouraged to do so by their Government who, unlike the British Government in the early post-war years, did not impose a rigid control on the transfer of ships from the national register. Although Norwegian owners did not avail themselves to any appreciable extent of the right to transfer ships, when built, to foreign flags, the fact that they could do so much more easily than was possible in the case of a ship registered in the United Kingdom made loans to Norwegian shipowners a more attractive investment.'[1] The several aspects of this complaint are considered below.

In the immediate post-war period any British shipowners wishing to build abroad had to obtain permission which was usually refused.[2] Purchases of secondhand ships abroad also required permission: this permission was invariably refused in the case of ships from dollar countries and was not always granted for other purchases. Since August 1951, all restrictions on building or purchasing abroad have been lifted in respect of soft-currency countries. It is clear, therefore, that initially the British industry was restricted completely to the tonnage which could be obtained from British sources, plus secondhand tonnage purchased abroad under licence. Since 1951, however, the industry has enjoyed almost complete freedom to contract overseas; the only important exception was the import of ships from Japan for which licences were not granted until the autumn of 1956.

Borrowing overseas for ships built in Britain was possible throughout the whole post-war period, while in the 1950s it became permissible to borrow for overseas building also; until 1959, however, Treasury permission for loans had to be obtained. In practice, however, the inclusion of ship mortgages within the general transfer restriction limited the extent to which overseas borrowing was possible. The policy in this regard was gradually liberalized during the 1950s, but an owner wishing to obtain sanction for an overseas construction financed by a loan, with the ship mortgaged as security, could not be certain until the ship was built whether the necessary permission would be given or withheld. In theory this was a substantial limitation; in practice there is no evidence of permission being refused, while the *Survey of British Shipping* does not cite this as a restriction. The silence of the *Survey* on this point surely implies that the uncertainty did not stop shipowners because they did not seriously contemplate such transactions in the period when restrictions were most stringent.

[1] General Council of British Shipping, *Survey of British Shipping* (December 1960), para. 39, pp. 16–17.
[2] Factual information about British Government policy as it affected shipping is by courtesy of the Ministry of Transport; the Ministry is not responsible for the way in which the facts are interpreted here.

The transfer of British ships to overseas ownership or registry was prohibited in 1939; this was in line with the policy in practically every maritime country. After the war the restrictions were maintained, although they were gradually liberalized during the 1950s, particularly after 1954. Until September 1958 permission was required before such a transfer could be made and although permission was generally given in the case of slow, old ships, there was a bias towards refusing to transfer ships of over 12 knots or ships with particular strategic value, for example, ships with heavy lift gear and fast passenger vessels. The proceeds from the sale of ships overseas before 1954 were placed in blocked accounts which could only be used for building in Britain. Prior to 1954, also, sales for scrap had to be made to BISCO, while after 1954 BISCO had to be given first option on all ships destined for scrapping. After September 1958, owners were allowed to transfer their ships freely (except for former naval craft) to all countries outside the Sino-Soviet bloc; these remaining restrictions were removed, except for certain special categories of ships, in June 1959.

The position during the post-war years up until September 1958 was complicated. Two points are worth making about it. First, the transfer restrictions were designed primarily to preserve the strategic value of the British fleet and were not intended either to help or hinder shipowners. Second, the recital of the policy and the fixing of dates of changes gives an impression of a much more clear-cut policy than existed. The 1950s were marked by a gradual liberalizing of the interpretation placed on the policy as Government departments sought, in the changing world situation, to interpret the spirit rather than the letter of the regulations. Dates for policy changes between 1948 and 1958 are rather dates at which particular interpretations of policy were first given than dates at which the basic policy changed. It is often impossible to say whether the date at which a shipowner was allowed to do something formerly banned marked the first date when that would have been allowed, or simply the first application for permission for some time. During the 1950s the interpretation placed on the transfer policy did not prevent any owner selling old ships overseas for further trading and so obtaining better prices than could have been obtained if the ships were scrapped. The restriction on the transfer of faster ships meant that, by and large, the types of ships which are uneconomic for British owners could be sold to overseas buyers and replaced by faster vessels. It is difficult to see how these restrictions affected adversely the growth of British shipping. The *Survey of British Shipping* does not analyse the question, although the authors apparently believed that the absence of similar restrictions in Norway helped Norwegian shipping to expand faster than British shipping.

The *Survey of British Shipping*, while not analysing the effects of the purchasing and transfer restrictions on British shipping, contrasts the situation in Britain with that in Norway. 'With their greater freedom from post-war controls and their much more ready access to finance, it seems that the Norwegians were able to avail themselves of opportunities to build which were not open to British owners.'[1] How far is this description of the Norwegian position valid?

The regulations in Norway have been changed a number of times since the war. Immediately the war was over, Norwegian owners could purchase ships from America under licence, provided they borrowed 75 per cent of the purchase price in America. This was unpopular with Norwegian owners who had reserves of kroner which they wished to, but could not, use for the purchases, except for the deposits of 25 per cent for which foreign exchange was made available. For contracts in Britain the sterling reserves from war insurances recoveries could be used.

In the autumn of 1947 strict rules were imposed on Norwegian shipowners who could build abroad only if 100 per cent of the contract price[2] was raised overseas, either by loans or by the sale of old ships. The latter provision was easier than that facing

---

[1] Ibid., December 1960, para. 41, p. 17.

[2] Some of the misunderstanding in Britain of the Norwegian position may be semasiological. In Norway it is customary to use the term 'self-financing' to refer to the raising of loans overseas, that is, the provision by the shipowner himself of the necessary foreign exchange without calling on the official reserves. In Britain, the term 'self-financing' means using one's own capital resources. If a British owner said that he had self-financed the building of a ship in Sweden it would be presumed that he had used his own capital resources and obtained the necessary foreign exchange from the Bank of England. If a Norwegian owner said he had self-financed the building of a ship in Sweden it would mean that he had borrowed the whole of the contract price in Sweden.

British shipowners. However, whereas the British industry had access to the British shipbuilding industry with a capacity of over one million tons per annum, the Norwegian shipbuilding industry was producing only 33,000 tons per annum.

In October 1948, a complete stop was put on new foreign contracts by Norwegian owners, the existing contracts which were sufficient to restore the fleet to its pre-war level being maintained. This ban on new foreign contracts, which in practice was a ban on practically all new building, lasted until March 1950. It was this restriction, in particular, to which Mr. Niarchos referred in his famous letter to *The Times* in 1958 (see page 222) as contributing to the need for people like himself to enter ship owning to cater for the needs of world trade. The restriction was more severe than anything which the British industry suffered as, although British owners could not build abroad in the period, they could build in Britain.

In the spring of 1950 the Norwegian Government allowed contracts to be placed if long-term time charters were available and provided all the finance was borrowed overseas. Then in December 1950, licences were given freely, but always on condition that all the finance was raised overseas.

In 1951, as a result of the O.E.E.C. trade liberalization policies, Norway became committed to allow more imports of ships. The base year for liberalization was 1948 in which year there had been heavy imports of dry-cargo tonnage. Accordingly, in February 1952, ordinary dry-cargo vessels were placed on the free list and shipowners could use their kroner reserves for such purchases. However, the 100 per cent financing rule continued to be applied for tankers, ore carriers, reefer ships, passenger ships and all secondhand ships. This position still continues, although the 100 per cent rule is relaxed when the foreign exchange reserves are favourable. Most shipowners had used up their reserves of kroner by 1956 so that, in effect, they had to borrow also for dry-cargo tonnage.[1]

Given the limited size of the Norwegian shipbuilding industry and the necessity for Norwegian owners to contract abroad both to maintain and to expand their fleets, it is clear that the general

[1] A full account of the Norwegian position can be found in A. S. Svendsen, *Skipsfartspolitiken i Norge etter krigen* (Bergen, 1957).

policy of the Norwegian Government was not generous. In fact, the expansively minded industry made a virtue out of necessity and, pressed by eager shipbrokers, perfected borrowing techniques on the basis of pre-construction time charters. In this way, foreign loans were used for building outside Norway, while the kroner reserves were gradually used up in Norway and, after 1952, on foreign-built dry-cargo tonnage. This, however, was not the intention of the regulations and Norwegian shipping expanded in spite of, not because of, the actions of the Government. Borrowing appears to have been easier because the alternative to borrowing was stagnation and, this being rejected, the former was adopted and made easy by usage. The old adage, 'Where there's a will there's a way' has rarely been more completely illustrated. Since 1951, in which period the Norwegian fleet almost doubled in size, Norwegian owners had access to few sources of funds which were not available to British owners had they sought them.

With respect to taxation, British shipping has been subject to normal taxation rates. Depreciation is allowed by either the straight line method or the reducing balance method. Under the former, depreciation at the rate of 5 per cent for dry-cargo vessels and 6·25 per cent for tankers can be written off against income each year. Under the latter method the figures are 12·5 per cent and 15 per cent respectively, depreciation in this case being calculated each year on the opening value. In 1945 an initial allowance of 20 per cent was given, increased to 40 per cent in 1949. The allowance was suspended in 1952 but restored at 20 per cent in 1953. Initial allowances simply allowed accelerated depreciation, with only the original price being written off in total. In 1954 the initial allowance was replaced by an investment allowance of 20 per cent which allowed accelerated write off and 120 per cent of cost to be charged against income over the depreciation period. In 1956, investment allowances were suspended, except for shipping and certain fuel economy installations. In 1957 the 'unique position' of shipping was recognized by increasing the investment allowance to 40 per cent.

Using the straight line method the full cost of a dry-cargo ship can be written off in twelve years and of a tanker in ten years, and, because of the investment allowance, 40 per cent of the original cost remains to be charged against income in later years. Using the reducing balance method, 100 per cent of the cost of dry-cargo vessels can be written off in seven years and of tankers in six years, again with a further 40 per cent of cost to be charged against income in subsequent years. These write-off periods compare with ten years for a tanker and thirteen years for a dry-cargo vessel in Norway.

The final aspect of taxation is the balancing charge (allowance) which is levied (given) when a ship is sold, scrapped or sunk and the sale or insurance receipts are more (less) than the written down cost, excluding the investment allowance. The rules governing the charge (allowance) are the same as for plant and machinery in general. This charge is a source of justifiable irritation to shipowners as a profit on parting with a ship is rightly regarded, in times of rising prices, as being no more than a contribution to the cost of the replacement. If the ship is replaced, the balancing charge need not be paid at once, but can be deducted from the cost of the replacement for calculating ordinary depreciation allowances. It may be noted that the Norwegian tax system contains an almost identical provision.

The question of international tax comparisons is taken up in Chapter XV. Here, the further discussion will be limited to comments on the British system as it affects shipping. First, whatever the tax position of British shipping *vis-à-vis* that of shipping in other countries, the taxation liabilities of shipping are calculated in the same way as those of other British industries. Shipping should not, therefore, have found that taxation on earnings made it less attractive to investors than alternative domestic investment projects. It is possible that the methods of calculating liability to taxation have meant that shipping is more adversely affected than other industries. In particular shipping is a capital intensive industry with lumpy replacement, the natural lumpiness being exacerbated by the effects of the war on the age distribution of the fleet, and highly variable earnings. These disabilities are not unique to shipping, but there are few industries in which they are combined in quite the same way. Special treatment with regard to balancing charges would help to lessen the disabilities and can be justified because it would be rare for another British taxpayer to claim depreciation allowances on a ship bought at a price exceeding its written down value as recognized by the Commissioners of Inland Revenue.[1] Second, as compared with ships under flags of convenience, investment in ships under the British flag clearly has been less favourable. However, the main source of funds for the former has been loans and as interest is treated as a cost, not as a distribution of profits, the ability to maintain loan interest (but not repayments) is not influenced by taxation. Third, both the initial allowance and the investment allowance systems presented to shipowners the opportunity of reducing their liability to income tax by expanding their fleets. In Norway shipowners treated high taxation, particularly the annual property tax levied on current values, as an incentive to invest, not as a deterrent, for they realized that only by investing and securing constantly increasing depreciation allowances could they reduce their tax liabilities.

FREIGHT RATES

The course of tramp freight rates since the war is shown in Table 27. The Italian index enables comparisons with the period before the war to be made. There is no continuous British index covering the whole post-war period, but the movements of the Italian and the British indices during the period 1952 to 1958 are sufficiently close that the former can be treated as reasonably representative of the course of British rates in the years before 1952. The indices show that freight rates remained at more than double the 1938 level throughout the post-war period and reached six times that level in 1951 as a result of Korea and over five times that level as a result of the Suez crisis.

The freight rates on which these indices are based are calculated in money terms and give no indication of the value to

---

[1] The purpose of the balancing charge is to prevent more than the original cost of an asset (plus the Investment Allowance where appropriate) from being written off against taxation. This would occur, for example, if a British shipowner sold a ship to another British owner for more than its depreciated value and the new owner claimed deductions based on the purchase price of the asset. Taxing the vendor on his profit prevents this. In shipping such a situation would rarely arise and a general balancing charge could easily be replaced by one made only when a ship is sold to another British owner.

shipowners of those rates. To overcome this difficulty, an index
of real freight rates has been calculated by deflating the indices
calculated from money rates by an index of tramp shipping
costs.[1] The results are shown in Table 27.

TABLE 27. Indices of money and real freight rates, 1938, 1948 to 1960

Year	Italian freight index	British freight index	Index of tramp costs		Indices of real freights:	
	1938 =100	1952 =100	1938 =100	1952 =100	1938 =100	1952 =100
1938	100		100		100	
1948	317		248		128	
1949	275		252		109	
1950	293		276		107	
1951	611		302		202	
1952	376	100	324	100	116	100
1953	298	77·5	334	103	90	74
1954	315	86·1	353	109	90	79
1955	466	127·7	374	115	125	110
1956	537	157·0	405	125	132	125
1957	417	112·7	433	134	97	84
1958	240	67·1	435	134	55	50
1959		71·9	453	140		51
1960		74·2	455	141		53

Sources of rate indices: Chamber of Shipping, Annual Report, 1960–1.
Weltschiffahrts-Archiv, *Facts and Figures* (1959), p. 300.

The real freight index based on 1938 shows that in the four
post-war years 1953, 1954, 1957 and 1958 real rates were below
their 1938 level, while the same applies to 1959 and 1960 for
which the calculation was not made. The 1938 level of freights
may be regarded as having been generally satisfactory. Most
British tramp owners were able to cover their total costs and to

[1] The index of tramp shipping cost is calculated from the cost items, capital cost,
wages, stores and fuel, given weights of 48, 20, 20 and 12 respectively. For capital
cost, the Chamber of Shipping index of shipbuilding prices is used. For wages an
index of the wages paid to an able seaman receiving maximum efficient service pay
as listed by the National Maritime Board is taken. For stores the price index of the
Central Statistical Office has had to be used. For fuel the prices of diesel oil and
marine fuel oil in the United Kingdom are used.

make 'normal' profits. An index of real freights no more than
ten points below the 1938 level may be regarded as providing no
cause for immediate alarm among shipowners, although profits
would be thin at this level and, in the long term, capital would
move out of the industry. Real rates within ten points either side
of the 1938 level are unlikely to induce any significant changes
in the size of the tramp fleet. If, when real rates are rising within
the neutral range, owners anticipate that the increase will continue this may lead to substantial increases in tonnage in
expectation of better times ahead. On the other hand, if owners
are not expansively minded (have inelastic supply curves and
are not maximizing profits) rates above the normal range will
not lead to expansions in tonnage—as has been seen in the case
of British-owned tramps.

The conclusions from the 1938-based index may be transferred to the 1952-based index. The two indices are not exactly
parallel because of the different weights used in calculating the
original freight indices. On the 1952 index of real freights, the
'normal' profit level is about 85, with a neutral range of about
8 points either side of this level. As the index rises above 85
tramps earn profits in excess of the minimum required to induce
owners to replace worn-out ships. When rates are below about
77 tramps are doing badly. There is something of a paradox
here: according to the index tramp shipping was unprofitable
in each of the years 1958–60, yet tramp companies earned
profits, although below the level of those earned in 1957 and
earlier years. The resolution of this paradox lies in a realization
of the nature of the capital values used in constructing the cost
index. By using always current values, not historic cost, the cost
index in a period of rising prices shows greater cost increases
than are shown by a company calculating depreciation on historic cost. Hence the discrepancy between the real index and the
performance of companies is due to the failure of the companies
to calculate depreciation each year on the basis of replacement
cost: even if they did, of course, they could not charge such
depreciation for tax purposes.

The index of real freights fell below the neutral range in 1958
and has remained below in subsequent years. The low real rates
do not mean, however, that all tramp shipping was unprofitable

but emphasize the necessity of maintaining real earnings by building ships with lower real costs per ton mile. The most important cost items causing rises in the index of tramp costs have been shipbuilding prices and wages and to avoid the effects of rising prices in these two sectors ships with low building and manning costs per ton mile must be built, that is, big and relatively fast ships. It is the 9,000 deadweight ton tramp, the cost ratios of which were used in calculating the cost index, not the big ship, which has become most unprofitable. The course of real freights in the period supports the theoretical argument (see Chapters X and XI) regarding the necessity for building bigger ships.

There is little that can be said about liner freights. These tend to follow tramp freights, but in a damped, lagged, fashion (see Chapter XIII). In a period of boom, such as 1951 and 1956, the damping of liner rates is extremely heavy and liner owners do not profit from the boom, except in so far as their ships operate fully laden instead of part-laden, unless ships can be spared from liner services to operate as tramps. The fact that it was the liner fleet which increased during the high-rate period and the tramp fleet which decreased, while in the low-rate period the opposite has been the case, means that the British fleet was less well adapted to profit from the boom and more susceptible to the effects of the slump than it might have been. While it must have been difficult to know what was the right thing to do at any one time, it is remarkable that the industry as a whole should have been so completely wrong in its timing in the post-1948 period.

PROFITS OF BRITISH SHIPPING

It is not possible to say anything very useful about the profits of British shipping in the period 1948 to 1960. Figures of voyage profits and of dividends are available and although the latter are clear-cut, there is no single definition or formula for calculating the former and it is never clear exactly what the level of actual profits is. Shipping companies claim that greater disclosure of their operating results would give vital information to foreign competitors. That may well be, but it makes it difficult to determine whether shipping was sufficiently profitable to have attracted capital in free competition. In Chapter X the figures of voyage profits are used to calculate a 'real' profit rate, but this is a somewhat sophisticated concept which could hardly take its place in a prospectus in which past performances and future prospects were exhibited as lures to attract new capital.

In Table 28 the average dividends paid on capital for the *Fairplay* samples of liner and tramp companies are shown, together with the extent to which the dividends were covered by voyage profits, which are not necessarily the same as net earnings after deducting depreciation.

TABLE 28. Dividends and dividend cover for British liner and tramp companies, 1948 to 1960

	Liner Companies		Tramp Companies	
Year	*Dividends*[a]	*Dividend cover*[b]	*Dividends*[a]	*Dividend cover*[b]
	%		%	
1948	8·03	5·9	15·68	4·4
1949	9·04	5·4	15·20	4·1
1950	8·46	5·7	11·12	3·1
1951	9·67	4·6	12·02	3·0
1952	10·59	5·6	13·24	7·7
1953	9·60	5·9	13·86	5·1
1954	9·66	4·1	9·36	3·0
1955	9·16	3·3	9·13	2·6
1956	8·41	3·1	11·71	4·3
1957	10·39	4·1	13·12	4·9
1958	10·85	0·9	7·31	5·5
1959	9·06	3·3	4·53	3·0
1960	8·59	2·6	3·77	2·9

[a] Dividends before tax as percentages of paid up capital.
[b] Voyage profits divided by dividend payments.

Source: Fairplay, Annual Returns Issue (12 January 1961), p. 127, with liner voyage profits from earlier issues.

The figures for liners cover a sample the tonnage of which increased from 3·94 million tons in 1948 to 5·51 million tons in 1960 and the paid up capital of which increased from £54·5 million to £131·4 million. The increase in paid-up capital, arising almost entirely from bonus share issues, reduced the dividend rate, particularly in the later years in the table. This cannot be overcome by expressing dividends as percentages of paid-up capital plus reserves because the book figures of reserves did not fall when capitals were increased; in other words, there are substantial secret reserves which have clearly varied in relation to disclosed reserves.

The liner figures show a satisfactory dividend rate and, in all years except 1958 when dividends exceeded voyage profits, a good cover, exceeding three in eleven of the thirteen years shown. Voyage profits are not the total of earnings. For the companies in the sample the composite item Debtors, Investments, Stores and Cash varied between £171 million and £251 million in the period. Neither the book value of the investments in this composite item, nor the extent to which the book value falls short of the real value of the investments to create secret reserves, is known. It is clear, however, that the investments held provided another source of income and a further cover for dividends. The rate of return on the composite item as a whole which was needed to cover the dividends paid was as follows:

	%		%
1948	2·5	1955	4·5
1949	2·9	1956	4·7
1950	2·5	1957	4·8
1951	2·9	1958	5·1
1952	3·0	1959	4·5
1953	3·0	1960	4·7
1954	3·6		

While it is clear that some constituents of the composite item were non-earning, it is not beyond the bounds of possibility that investment income alone was sufficient to cover dividends, particularly before the sharp increases in dividends in 1954 and the further increases in 1957 and 1958.

For tramps the period was also clearly profitable. In eleven of the thirteen years shown the dividend cover was three or more while paid-up capitals increased from £9·9 million in 1948 to £28·6 million in 1960, almost entirely due to the issue of bonus shares.

There is no real way in which these figures can be compared with earnings in other parts of the economy[1] to determine

[1] Data published quarterly by the *Economist* of company earnings in a number of industries seemed to suggest such a way, but after consideration were rejected because they do not enable the dividend cover to be calculated on a comparable basis.

whether shipping could have raised capital in Britain in competition with other industries. First, it is not possible to estimate the extent to which figures of paid-up capital in different industries have varied as proportions of the real capital employed. The ordinary difficulties of such a comparison are increased to the point of impossibility because the period has been one in which many companies in most industries have made bonus issues; in the case of shipping the dividend *rate* would have been between two and three times as high in the last few years if these bonus issues had not been made. Second, industry figures such as those in Table 27 conceal variations between companies and it is companies which raise capital, not industries.

Despite the difficulties of comparison, something can be said about the post-war potential of shipping to raise money for expansion. First, the bulk of the post-war expansion of world shipping has been financed from loan capital, either the ship mortgage or the loan on the security of a pre-construction time charter. Although no positive information is available, it appears that the latter source of funds has been practically ignored by leading British shipping companies. The earnings of British shipping have been sufficiently regular and the gearing ratio[1] so low that borrowing in any form would have been both safe and possible. Second, with voyage profits in most years being over 35 per cent of capital and reaching over 50 per cent for liners and 90 per cent for tramps, most companies could have made a good enough showing in a prospectus to attract new money. Third, new companies were established, one of them in 1959 when earnings were low, and succeeded in attracting capital.

The general conclusion is that while individual shipping companies may have found difficulty in raising capital for expansion, the earnings record of the companies in the sample is sufficiently good that, at least up to 1957, they could have raised capital, either loan or equity, had they wished to. In a lenders' market, people wanting capital had to look for it, they could not sit back and wait for it to be offered. To have sought new capital would have entailed greater disclosure of their operating positions than British shipowners are normally willing to make.

---

[1] The gearing of a capital structure is the relation of equity to borrowing. A low-geared capital is one in which borrowing is small in relation to equity.

SHIPPING AND THE BALANCE OF PAYMENTS

In the post-war period the necessary pre-occupation with foreign exchange reserves has focused attention on shipping's contribution to Britain's invisible earnings. Two separate calculations of this are made, one by the Treasury and the other by the Chamber of Shipping. The results of these two calculations differ substantially because a different basis of calculation is used for each. However, neither is a real measure of shipping's contribution to the external balance. The most recent results of the two calculations are:[1]

	1958 £m.	*1959* £m.	*1960* £m.	*1961* £m.
Chamber of Shipping	134·8	99·5	72·3	52·2
Treasury	22	3	− 56	− 50

The relevant calculation is of the extent to which the British balance of payments would be less favourable if a British fleet did not exist. This calculation is based on the assumption that the purchaser of internationally traded goods ultimately pays the freight on those goods. On this assumption, if no British fleet existed, the whole of the freight cost of British imports would be a charge on the British balance of payments. The cost of the absence of the British fleet is the cost of the shipping services required by Britain, plus the net receipts of foreign exchange earned by British shipping in carrying non-British goods. The resulting figure is the total of the cost to the balance of payments if the fleet did not exist. The additional cost to the balance of payments of the disappearance of the existing fleet is then obtained by deducting the payments already made to foreigners for the carriage of British goods and passengers. The net result is shipping's contribution to the balance of payments.

The relevant calculation is set out in Table 56 in an appendix at the end of the book. On the basis of these calculations the contribution of British shipping to the balance of payments was:

	£ million
1952	360
1958	288
1960	249

[1] Calculation by the Chamber of Shipping set out in Annual Report, 1961–62, and in *Fairplay* (2 August 1962), p. 12; Treasury figures from *United Kingdom Balance of Payments: 1958 to 1960*, Cmnd. 1329; *1959 to 1960*, Cmnd. 1671; table 8, p. 16.

The Prosperous Age: the Post-war Period

The decline in the foreign exchange contribution of British shipping is clear. The additional cost to the balance of payments of the disappearance of British shipping declined by 31 per cent in the eight-year period between 1952 and 1960. In 1952 actual outgoings on the shipping services required were £377 million, of which £239 million, 63 per cent, was paid to British ship-owners, whereas in 1960 the figures were £485 million, £286 million and 59 per cent, respectively. The figure of 59 per cent would have been very much lower had tramp and tanker rates in 1960 not been 50 per cent below their 1952 levels. In 1952 shipping's contribution to the balance of payments amounted to 12·2 per cent of the total import bill, whereas in 1960 it amounted to only 6·1 per cent of the total import bill. Whichever way it is regarded, however, it is clear that there has been a significant decline, brought about by increases in charter hire and freight payments to foreign shipowners. In fact, the total freight bill for imports increased by 30 per cent between 1952 and 1960 while the increase in freights paid to foreigners was 46 per cent.

The greater increase in import freights paid to foreigners than in the total import freight payment is a consequence of the falling proportion of British imports carried in British ships. This has arisen because changes in international cost conditions have swung the balance of advantage in the running of smaller ships of many types in favour of other countries. The result is that British shipowners are increasingly less able to compete in the operation of the type of ships which can be handled at many British ports. This should have been compensated by a substantial increase in freight earnings in cross-trades as British shipowners employed larger ships in non-British trades; in fact the increase was limited to 13 per cent despite the maintenance of liner rates. The changes in the payments of import freights over the period support nicely the theoretical arguments of Chapters X and XI.

The increase in charter hire paid for foreign ships is related also to the question of ship sizes. In 1958 £137 million was paid in chartering foreign ships, despite the existence of over one million tons of British shipping laid up at the end of the year. An important reason for this anomalous position was that only

12 per cent by number of British tramp ships were between 10,000 and 15,000 tons. This is the size which liner owners who want extra tonnage prefer to charter and which, for a large proportion of the world's bulk trades, is now the most economical. The chartering of foreign tankers by British oil companies, whether for use in British or in foreign trade increased outgoings on chartering. This arose partly because the expansion of the independently owned British tanker fleet was not great enough to match the demands of the resident oil companies, partly because only 2 per cent of British tankers (including oil company tonnage) were over 25,000 tons. The consequence of these two structural defects in the mercantile fleet was a substantial net outgoing on charter hire to foreign shipowners.[1]

---

[1] Since this section was written it has become possible to make the calculation for 1961. This is given in 'British Shipping and the Balance of Payments', *The Bankers' Magazine* (October 1962), together with a reconciliation of the present method and those employed by the Chamber of Shipping and the Treasury. In some respects, too, further knowledge has changed slightly the interpretation of the results.

VIII

Enemies of Competition in the Post-war years

STATE interference with the competitive process in shipping continued after the second world war, as Tables 29 and 30 show. The experiences in the post-war years differed from those in the inter-war years in that whereas in the 1930s subsidies were the main form of assistance and preferences were relatively unimportant, in the post-war period preferences have become more important than subsidies, certainly in a numerical sense. This change has been brought about by a fundamental change of policy in Germany and Japan, and by the difference in the world economic situation in the post-war period as compared with the inter-war years; in particular the high levels of freights throughout most of the period have assured the viability of shipping enterprises which, in less prosperous conditions, would have needed subsidies if they were to survive.

SUBSIDIES

The countries which have granted subsidies to national shipping enterprises are listed in Table 29.

In the period since 1945 the extent of subsidies to shipping has declined in all countries except the United States.

In France a construction differential subsidy is paid to cover the difference between the cost of building in a French yard and that of building overseas. Operating subsidies are given to a limited number of 'national interest' services, including the transatlantic mail and passenger service. The main shipping lines, which were taken under Government control in 1937, have been fully nationalized since the war. To a large extent, therefore, the subsidies have been paid to enterprises in

Government ownership. The total amount currently paid in aid to French shipping appears to be less than the tax relief from the investment allowances of British shipowners.[1]

TABLE 29. Aid to shipping, 1945 to 1960: Subsidies
(Postal subventions excluded)

Country	Type of subsidy: Operating	Construction	Indirect	State-owned fleet
Argentina				×
Australia	×	×		×
Belgium			×	
Brazil				×
Canada	×		×	
Denmark			×	
France	×	×	×	×
Germany, West			×	
Greece			×	
India		×	×	×
Italy	×	×	×	×
Japan	×		×	
Pakistan				×
Spain	×		×	
Sweden			×	
Turkey				×
United Kingdom			×	
United States	×	×	×	
U.S.S.R.				×
Yugoslavia		×	×	×

Sources: U.S. Maritime Administration, *International Shipping and Shipbuilding Subsidies and Aids* (Washington, 1959); Chamber of Shipping, *Survey of British Shipping* (December 1960); Bonner Committee Hearings, part 2; *Indian Shipping, Syren and Shipping, Fairplay, Shipping World*—various dates.

In Italy after the war, E.R.P. Funds were used to build new ships and to buy American war-built tonnage. Loans and subsidies for new construction were given in the immediate post-war years. However, as shown in Chapter VI, the Italian mercantile fleet suffered heavy losses during the war and without either state assistance or insurance recoveries those losses could

[1] See *Fairplay* (26 April 1962), p. 37.

not have been replaced. Since 1954 construction differential subsidies have been given. The Government has retained the full control of shipping enterprises, which was instituted in the Fascist era, and for a large part of the cargo carried fixes the rates to be charged. Where rates are fixed in this way, it is impossible to determine whether any subsidies are paid or not.

In Japan, the Government supplied 84 per cent of the finance needed for the construction and repair of ships between 1945 and 1949, but this was no more than belated insurance payments for war losses; in any event, the amount of construction before 1950 was slight. Between April 1948 and December 1951, the American Government contributed $22·8 million[1] towards the rebuilding of the Japanese fleet, allowing the fleet to increase in size by one million tons in the period. However, it was not until 1958 that the Japanese fleet again reached its pre-war size. The operating subsidies noted in the table represent the difference between the operating costs of ships and the freight rates allowed by the Government in the period before 1950. Apart from some indirect assistance, such as accelerated depreciation allowances and loans below market interest rates for ship-building, Japanese shipping has been virtually unaided since 1950.

In the United States the system of construction differential and operating subsidies started in 1936 was extended after the war to cover more trades, and American-flag ships were able to strengthen their positions in the Pacific trades left open by the annihilation of the Japanese fleet. During the eleven-year period from the beginning of 1948 through 1958, American shipping was assisted by operating subsidies to the extent of $788 million, with a further $102 million paid in construction subsidies by the Federal Maritime Board, in addition to the special subsidies paid by the U.S. Navy to cover the costs of additional special features, usually extra speed. Operating subsidies are available in America only to ships engaged on Essential Trade Routes[2]

[1] Merchant Marine Studies, 83rd Congress, op. cit., evidence of James A. Farrell, p. 125.

[2] In July 1960, thirty-three Essential Trade Routes were recognized, plus two Round-the-World services and one Tri-Continent Service. For details see U.S. Dept. of Commerce, *Essential U.S. Foreign Trade Routes* (Washington, 1960). In 1961 a bill was passed in the House of Representatives to permit subsidized liners to

and to the extent that American costs exceed costs in other countries. In return for the subsidies, the lines have to make an undertaking to provide a service of the pre-determined frequency and cannot, for example, thin out cargo sailings when freight is short. Further, the line in receipt of a subsidy is restricted to the agreed route and if it finds itself unable to make a profit on that route cannot vary the ports of call without permission; the American Banner Line, for example, was refused permission in 1960 to add a call at Southampton in an attempt to make its subsidized transatlantic service to Zeebrugge viable. The position in America is often misunderstood in other countries because it is usually assumed that the construction of the American-owned Liberian tonnage has been subsidized, whereas in fact neither the Federal Maritime Board nor the U.S. Navy has the funds to subsidize the construction of such vessels.

The other countries granting direct operating subsidies include Australia and Canada which subsidize coastal services, and Spain which subsidizes direct services from that country which no liner owner would provide on a commercial basis. In addition to these, both India and Yugoslavia provide construction subsidies in order to protect their national shipbuilding industries.

The indirect subsidies given by a number of countries consist mainly of cheap loans and accelerated depreciation provisions. A good example of the latter is the Investment Allowance given to British shipowners since 1954 which is at least as generous as similar advantages given in other countries.

Since 1945, the extent of state-ownership of shipping fleets has increased. In each of the countries marked all, or a significant proportion, of the national flag fleet is state-owned. State-owned ships may run alongside privately-owned ships which may, or may not, be subsidized, the state service may be run in a commercial fashion and any subsidies granted be paid as though the vessels were privately-owned, or the state-owned fleet may be operated on a non-commercial basis. It is not possible to be clear

engage in the lucrative cruise business from New York. The entry of American ships to this business will be a severe blow to the British Cunard and Furness Withy lines, also to the Greek-owned cruising ships. There are American liners operating without subsidies on routes not classed as essential.

in all cases whether state-owned ships are subsidized or not: all that can be done is to note the possibility that operating losses can be met directly from taxation, without making any overt subsidy arrangements. In booming freight markets such a possibility is unimportant; in depressed markets it is highly likely to occur. The expanded fleets of the Communist countries are particularly important in this connection. The ships of these countries now regularly compete in international markets, but it is impossible, because of the absence of proper pricing systems in the home economies, to say whether the shipping is subsidized or not. As it follows directives, not the call of profits, the net effect is as though differential subsidies (taxes) were paid (charged) to load the price system to produce just the amount of international competition which, in fact, occurs.

Outside the United States, the effects of subsidies in the post-war period in limiting the growth opportunities of British ships have been slight. The American subsidies serve to maintain an active fleet about 15 per cent greater than in 1939, that is, the growth of the active American flag fleet has been smaller than the growth of American trade. The growth of the unsubsidized American-owned fleet flying flags of convenience will be considered in Chapter IX.

The overall conclusion that in the post-1945 period subsidies have not caused any further worsening of the British position and are much less important than in the 1930s must, however, be considered in the context of the general prosperity of shipping for most of the period. Given a prolonged period of depression in shipping, the extent of subsidies would certainly grow and the losses of state-owned fleets increase. In such a situation, the damaging effects of subsidies would become more important while their cost to national exchequers would almost certainly lead to further flag discrimination in order to guarantee cargoes for national fleets and so reduce the losses to be borne by the state. In this connection, the extent to which countries with state-owned fleets have adopted discriminatory shipping practices in the period is significant.

Enemies of Competition in the Post-war years

PREFERENCES

At first glance, Table 30 gives the impression that world trade as a whole is tangled in a tight web of preference legislation. This impression is largely illusory and many of the acts of discrimination noted were single *ad hoc* actions lasting for only a short period of time.

For some time after the war, the volume of world trade was limited by the available shipping space in all countries except America. Dollars, however, were scarce and all countries tried to economize on their use of dollars for freight payments to American ships because all such dollars had to come from current earnings; at the same time, many countries were willing to allow nationals to buy ships in America because the dollars for such purchases could be borrowed or obtained from Aid funds. These two factors together helped to produce a rash of discriminatory practices. Countries short of foreign exchange tried to ensure that all freight payments were made to national ships or in currencies which were soft to them. Sometimes the discrimination was directed specifically against the dollar, but more often countries adopted a general discrimination rather than a unilateral discrimination which would have annoyed Americans. The foreign exchange problem was particularly important in the years of high freight rates, for example, the first year or two after the war, in the Korean period and in the post-Suez period. Between these booms, falls in freight rates revealed the shaky economic basis of many of the expanded shipping fleets and subsidies were adopted, or flag discrimination maintained, to enable the fleets to survive.

The upsurge of national consciousness among small countries, many of them smarting under real or imagined injuries from the traditional maritime countries, led those countries to desire a place in their own trades. This motive is complicated because alongside national aspirations went the inability of traditional maritime countries for several years after the war to cater properly for the trades of smaller nations, many of which had built up their economies at great cost during the war. It became a matter of necessity for many of these countries to establish fleets of their own, both to avoid dislocations in their trade when

o

TABLE 30. Aid to shipping, 1945 to 1960: Preferences
(Reservation of coastal trade excluded)

Country	Bilateral trade treaties	Cargo reservation and preference	Exchange control preference	Tax and harbour concessions
Argentine	×			×
Brazil	×		×	×
Bulgaria	×			×
Burma				×
Ceylon	×			
Chile	×	×		
China	×			×
Colombia	×		×	
Cuba	×			
Czechoslovakia	×		×	
Ecuador		×		×
Egypt	×	×		×
France	×	×		×
Germany, East	×			
India	×			×
Indonesia	×			
Iran	×			
Israel	×			
Italy	×			
Japan	×			
Lebanon	×			
Libya	×			
Pakistan	×	×		
Peru	×	×		×
Philippines		×	×	
Poland	×		×	×
Portugal	×	×		×
Rumania	×			×
Spain	×		×	
Turkey	×	×	×	×
United States		×		
U.S.S.R.	×			×
Venezuela	×			
Yugoslavia	×			

Source: As in Table 29.

foreign tonnage was withdrawn and to save foreign exchange payments for shipping services.[1] As was shown in Chapter VI, there was a period of indecision in British shipping after the war when shipowners held back and failed to grasp the opportunities available. This left a vacuum into which exchange difficulties prevented the United States from stepping, which was partly filled by Norwegian and Greek tonnage, but for the remainder was filled by countries without established maritime traditions.

Many subsequent troubles would have been avoided if the traditional maritime countries had bowed to the inevitable; instead, when the new or expanded fleets became significant, attempts were often made to stifle their further growth by refusing to admit the fleets to the relevant conferences. This happened in the Indian trades, as Indian evidence makes abundantly clear, and it also happened in certain South American trades. In Nigeria there were complaints that the West African Lines Conference made '. . . calculated attempts to cripple the growth of indigenous shipping lines'.[2] When admitted to the Conference, the Nigerian National Line was restricted to handling only 2·5 per cent of Nigeria's total exports.

Against this background, the post-war discriminatory practices can be considered.

The most favoured discriminatory device has been the bilateral trade treaty containing a restrictive shipping clause; in Table 30, thirty countries are shown which have concluded such treaties. Under these treaties exclusive rights for the shipment of the goods covered by the treaty were reserved for vessels of the contracting countries. Argentina, for example, concluded such treaties with Brazil, Chile, Czechoslovakia, France, Italy, Japan, Rumania, Spain and Yugoslavia in 1949. Among the trade treaties agreed by Pakistan, one with Egypt contained an exclusive 50/50 shipping clause; a treaty covering the shipment of jute from Pakistan to Spain provided for the entire trade to travel in Spanish ships; a treaty covering coal shipments from South Africa to Pakistan provided that the coal should travel in

---

[1] See John D. Harbron, 'Argentina's State Merchant shipping', *Shipping World* (24 May 1961), pp. 475–6.
[2] Report in *Financial Times* (14 July 1959).

Pakistani ships. Indian bilateral trade treaties with Czechoslovakia, Egypt, Finland, Poland and Yugoslavia, provided that
Indian ships would be allowed to carry a reasonable proportion
of the trade between India and those countries. In 1960 a direct
shipping line was established between Russian Baltic ports and
the United Arab Republic, it being agreed that all cargoes would
be shared between the ships of the two countries. These examples
are only a few selected at random to illustrate the problem.

The actual number of bilateral arrangements, including
overt and covert agreements, is not known, and it is not certain
that the entries in the table cover all cases. The importance of
the large number of trade treaties containing shipping clauses
must not be exaggerated, however. First, in the disrupted
foreign exchange situation after 1945, which has continued to
the present time for some countries, such agreements probably
ensured that trade took place. Had the trade not been reserved
to ships of the trading countries but opened to free competition,
then in many cases it would not have taken place at all because
of exchange difficulties. Second, most, but by no means all, of
the treaties referred to specific items of trade or covered only a
short period. At no time in the period, for example, have all the
countries in the list been conducting a significant part of their
trade under bilateral treaties with limited shipping rights.

The British Government has generally refused to execute
trade treaties containing shipping clauses, a restraint for which
it has been criticized. 'Because *successive* British Governments
have been diffident about stipulating in trade treaties for a substantial quantity of British shipping to be used for the carriage of
our timber imports, we largely rely each year upon the use of
Scandinavian and Russian ships. In the opinion of most members of the Baltic Exchange, this omission on the part of White-
hall is one of disastrous importance. [It] . . . cuts deeply at the
root of our tramp shipping industry.'[1] Although the above may
not be a general view within the industry, neither is it a solitary
view and there is sufficient evidence to suggest the conclusion
that the opposition in Britain to shipping clauses in trade
treaties is often based on interest and not on principle.

[1] Captain Cuttle, 'The Timber Muddle', *Syren and Shipping* (14 December 1960)·
p. 460. My italics.

Another type of preference is that which restricts a certain portion of all inward or outward cargoes, or certain types of cargo, to national ships.

In America, tramp interests have been aided by the 50/50 legislation of 1948 covering, initially, only cargoes purchased from America with funds made available under relief schemes.[1] Between April 1948 and June 1958, 79 million tons of cargo financed by E.C.A. were transported from America to Europe. Of this amount, 55·8 per cent was carried in American ships.[2] The total shipments amounted to less than 4 per cent of American exports over the period, which is the basis for the common American claim that less than 3 per cent of their exports are, in fact, diverted to American ships by the operation of the 50/50 rule. While this claim is probably valid over the long period, for individual years, such as 1951/2, it certainly understates the extent of the diversion. Although intended to apply only to goods shipped by Government agencies, considerable ingenuity is often used in defining the nature of cargoes so that they come under the preference rules; for example, in February 1961, it was ruled by the Maritime Administration that any scrap derived by buyers of old Government-owned ships from the reserve fleet must, if exported, be shipped *entirely* in U.S. flag ships. Any liberality shown in the interpretation of the preference rules is vigorously attacked by both shipowners' associations and maritime trade unions. The shipowners have claimed that the American '. . . 50-50 laws are not to be considered as within the meaning of the term "flag discrimination" . . .' and that the American Government should not be a party to any discussions about the international effects of flag discrimination which include references to the American cargo preference legislation.[3] As an example of partial thinking this claim can have few rivals.

The direct damage to the shipping of other nations by the

---

[1] The present preference system of the U.S. really dates from 1934 when it was legislated that exports financed by loans made by the Reconstruction Finance Corporation, the Export-Import Bank, or any other agency of the U.S. Government, should be shipped exclusively on U.S. flag vessels. Except for retaliatory purposes, the Maritime Administration has usually ruled that these cargoes be divided 50/50, U.S./foreign.

[2] O.E.E.C., *Maritime Transport*, fifth year (1959), p. 54.

[3] Ralph E. Casey, President, American Merchant Marine Institute Inc., reported by *Fairplay* (13 October 1960), p. 46.

operation of the American 50/50 rule has probably been relatively small, but the indirect damage has been considerable. First, the manner in which the rule has been applied to an increasing range of cargoes, as the distinction between aid and trade has become blurred, has created uncertainty for other shipowners. Second, American ships, assured by the discriminatory rules of outward cargoes for which they have received premium rates of freight based on American costs not on world tramp ship rates, have provided competition to other shipping for return cargoes to America and have been able and willing to cut rates for such cargoes. For example, under the agreement in 1960 by which America sold 17 million tons of grain to India it was provided that 50 per cent of this must travel in American ships, this provision being derived from Public Law 480 which applies to the disposal of surplus agricultural produce. Being secured the trade, American ships were able to push the grain rate from America to India from the existing level of about $9, which other ships continued to receive, to $25.40. After unloading in India the American ships sought return cargoes and by their competition pushed the ore rate from India to America down from about $24 to about $9. 'Where the non-American ship had been obtaining some $33 for the round trip this was reduced to $18.'[1] Third, the example set by America to other nations has been wholly bad. When seeking means of protecting their own merchant fleets these other countries, particularly in South America, have been unable to comprehend the philosophical distinctions between 'aid' and 'trade', distinctions which many Americans themselves can no longer recognize, and have applied the 50/50 rule indiscriminately to all shipments.

Brazil has adopted both the bilateral treaty and an overall rule that 70 per cent of Brazilian imports must travel in Brazilian ships. It should be noted, however, that this 70 per cent rule was adopted in part at least, in retaliation to the action of the conference covering the trade between Brazil and Europe which in 1959 re-established the deferred rebate system and so shut the non-conference ships of Lloyd Brasileiro from the trade.

Preference to national ships through exchange control is more frequently the result of foreign exchange difficulties than of a

[1] *Survey of British Shipping*, p. 32.

desire to protect shipping, although such protection is often a welcome side effect. The preference may take the form of refusing to make foreign exchange available for freight payments, or of limiting the quantity made available each year, or of a rule such as that adopted in France, namely, that imports of manganese should be carried in French ships because only such ships would accept freight payments in francs. Before Brazil legislated for cargo preference, exchange difficulties had led to preference being given to shipments by Lloyd Brasileiro and the re-imposition of the deferred rebate system was the somewhat clumsy response of the conference to the effects of these Brazilian difficulties. The British foreign exchange regulations between the cessation of the short-lived period of convertibility of sterling in 1947 and the decision to support the transferable sterling rate in 1955 acted to the advantage of British shipping and to the disadvantage, in particular, of the flag of convenience fleets of Panama and Liberia.

Finally, there is the group of discriminatory practices relating to the taxation of ships in ports, of goods landed, and so on. Individually, most of these practices are minor irritants designed to give national flag ships an edge on foreign ships. In aggregate, however, with the other practices discussed, they serve to make the maintenance of multilateral shipping services difficult.

The main countries practising flag discrimination with any consistency are the Soviet Bloc countries, the United States, the majority of South American republics, some Middle Eastern countries, Spain, Portugal, France and Turkey. The importance of the discrimination of each differs greatly and the discrimination in some cases is restricted to trivial matters, or only to coastal trades, or to specific ships, for example, the flag of convenience fleets. In the 1950s the British Government made seventy-four formal protests to thirty-one countries respecting flag discrimination, but without a great deal of success. America has been more successful and her established discriminatory system has been used in retaliation when other countries have discriminated against American shipping; for example, America was able to force Argentina and Brazil to drop discriminatory arrangements regarding berthing rights and taxation. A particular shipping line faced with discrimination, or the possibility of discrimination, generally has the opportunity of protecting its position by setting up behind the discriminatory barrier. British shipping companies have been much less active in doing this than have industrial firms in setting up behind tariff walls, and there is no doubt that opportunities in India and Pakistan, for example, have been missed. In the South African trade, however, the British and Commonwealth Shipping Co. set up the Springbok Company at the end of 1958, shares in which were offered to South Africans. It was proposed that seven ships of the Bullard King Line, a member of the group, should be transferred to the Springbok Company which would then take over the Bullard King services between South Africa and the United Kingdom. This venture was obviously of a precautionary nature and the proposed transfer from Bullard King did not occur.[1] In addition to this, two cargo ships of Union Castle, another member of the group, were transferred to South African registry.[2]

Alongside the formal machinery for discrimination which has been discussed, there has been informal machinery designed to secure that the shipping of each country secures preference in that country's trade. Foreign importers, particularly state trading bodies which have become increasingly important since 1945, often impose as a condition of purchase that the goods travel in a national ship. In the seller's market of the first ten years after the war such conditions could not be imposed—in fact it was the seller who could insist on the goods travelling in a national flag ship—but in the more competitive trading conditions of the later 1950s, buyers have been able to dictate terms in this way. There has been a general move outside Britain since the war for importers to purchase f.o.b. and exporters to try to sell c.i.f., which makes it more likely that the carriage of the goods concerned will be diverted to nationally-owned ships. As has been observed in earlier chapters, the British mercantile marine was built up on the basis of f.o.b. imports and c.i.f. exports and so long as overseas traders who insist on retaining

[1] In 1961 the South African Marine Corporation (Safmarine) and the Springbok Line were consolidated. Safmarine was then owned by the Industrial Development Corporation of South Africa which had acquired the interest previously held by the American founders of the line.
[2] State of the Union Year-Book for South Africa, 1959–60, p. 255.

the option of choosing the ship themselves are guided by commercial motives, then the British shipowner has nothing about
which he can legitimately complain, even if a British ship is not
selected. However, with the plethora of state and semi-state
trading bodies which have grown up since the war, '. . . it is
abundantly clear that considerations other than the efficient
routing of cargo have prevailed'.[1] In Britain, the '. . . growing
tendency for industrialists to quote f.o.b. instead of c.i.f. . . .' has
been deplored and Chambers of Commerce in some parts of the
country have passed motions calling on exporters to retain the
shipping rights in the goods sold and to choose British ships.[2]
The industrialists, on the other hand, point out that f.o.b. is
often demanded by the customers and if they, as sellers, attempt
to insist on c.i.f. sales they risk losing many orders.

Unofficial discrimination has also been practised by conferences. Several examples have already been mentioned.
Another well-authenticated case is the attitude of the conference
lines in the Australian trade to the Greek steamer *Patris* which
started a service from Greece to Australia in December 1959.
Australian travel agents and shippers were threatened with
reprisals by the conference lines if they booked passengers and
cargo with the *Patris*. To thwart the conference boycott, the
owners of the ship entered the meat business themselves in order
to secure the cargoes other shippers were prevented from giving
them. In order to attract passengers, a vast advertising campaign was launched in Australia and passengers were offered a
three-day stay in Greece at no extra cost.[3] The success of the
measures encouraged the owners of the *Patris* to place a second
liner in the service. No difficulties were experienced in obtaining
passengers for the outward trips from Greece.

It is impossible to assess at all accurately the effects which discrimination has had on world trade in the post-war years. In the
early 1950s it was generally believed that no more than 5 per
cent of world trade was then affected by official discriminatory devices. Since then, world trade has probably increased
faster than discrimination, although the pinch of the shoe of

[1] *Survey of British Shipping*, p. 25.
[2] See report in *Shipping World* (2 December 1959), pp. 379–80.
[3] *Naftika Chronika* (15 January 1961), p. 52. (English Supplement edition.)

preferences is greater and is felt more sharply when shipping is slack, as in 1958–60, than when it is buoyant, as in the Korean period.

Some of the effects of discriminatory practices may be discovered by relating, for internationally traded goods, the countries of origin and destination and the flags of the ships transporting those goods. Information of this nature is available only for the United States, and only for one year, 1957; it is given in Table 31.

TABLE 31. Shipping and trade of the United States, 1957
(Commercial cargoes only)

Country	Share in U.S. trade		Proportion of U.S. trade carried		Proportion of U.S. trade with each country carried:			
					in national ships		in U.S. ships	
	1	2	3	4	5	6	7	8
	[a]M	X	M	X	M	X	M	X
	%	%	%	%	%	%	%	%
U.S.A.			23·2	16·9				
Liberia[b]			24·0	16·5				
Norway	1·3	0·6	11·5	10·2	33·4	51·9	2·6	6·2
Panama[b]			9·4	5·1				
U.K.	1·3	5·4	5·7	8·1	40·8	45·9	32·6	17·6
Sweden	0·5	1·4	4·1	3·3	76·9	61·8	1·5	10·9
Germany, W.	1·4	11·3	3·8	4·9	30·9	18·4	16·9	5·3
Italy	0·8	10·2	2·5	10·0	20·9	62·3	42·4	5·6
Netherlands	1·0	16·6	2·2	3·0	33·3	7·0	13·5	3·9
Japan	1·3	13·0	2·1	4·9	46·8	32·7	35·8	16·2
Greece	0·2	0·8	1·9	5·8	59·6	31·0	25·5	23·2
Denmark	0·0	0·6	1·7	1·4	59·7	33·0	0·5	5·1
Belgium	2·1	5·0	0·8	0·5	16·2	6·5	15·6	7·1
France	0·3	6·0	0·3	1·5	29·7	18·7	29·1	24·1
Spain	0·3	1·3	0·3	0·9	29·4	57·3	25·0	34·4
All others	89·5	27·8	6·5	7·0	5·1	12·7	23·4[c]	33·7[c]

[a] M = Imports, that is, goods unloaded in American ports.
  X = Exports, that is, goods loaded in American ports.
[b] Trade insignificant.
[c] Includes trade with Liberia and Panama.

Source: Celler Committee Hearings, part 1, vol. 1; compiled from information on pp. 750–3.

Enemies of Competition in the Post-war years

The figures in the table show clearly the importance of national shipping in national trades, both in countries such as the United Kingdom and Norway, not practising any form of discrimination, and in those, such as Spain, in which discrimination is practised. The information in the table cannot be interpreted to say anything about the effects of the American discriminatory legislation, as such legislation technically covers only non-commercial cargoes which are not included in the table.

Reference to the columns 1 and 2 in the table shows the overwhelming importance of 'all other' countries in the import trade and their high rating in the export trade. This group includes all the chief discriminators in the world, but the figures make it quite clear that the bulk of the trade of these countries was carried neither in national ships nor in American ships; 71·5 per cent of the imports and 53·6 per cent of the exports were carried by the ships of nations which were not parties to the trade. On the other hand, the ships owned by this 'all other' group of countries carried a higher proportion of U.S. exports than of imports, despite the fact that these countries took less than three-tenths of American exports while providing nearly nine-tenths of American imports. American imports of oil were entirely from the 'all other' countries, but the inclusion of these in the figures does not fully account for this difference; if only dry-cargo imports from 'all other' countries are considered, the group still contributed 33·6 per cent of the total American imports by weight. The situation, then, is that 'all other' countries had a larger share in the carriage of American exports than of imports, a difference which cannot be explained in terms of trade shares. Further, a higher proportion of American exports to 'all other' countries, than of imports from those countries, travelled in national ships. Flag discrimination is usually applied to imports, and American exports are imports to other countries. As the group 'all other' countries in the table includes the majority of the known discriminators in the world, it is most likely that the difference between the percentage of American exports and imports to and from 'all other' countries which were carried in the ships of those countries is largely due to the effects of flag discrimination.

Enemies of Competition in the Post-war years

The conclusion above is derived mainly from the relation between the pairs of figures in columns 5 and 6. Apart from the group 'all other' countries, the situation in which the share of American exports travelling in national ships exceeded the share of imports travelling in those ships existed also in Norway, Britain, Italy and Spain. Neither Norway nor the United Kingdom operated discriminatory measures and the situation noted arose partly from the nature of the cargoes carried, particularly the importance of tramp cargoes in the export trade to Britain, and partly from the custom which importers in Norway and Britain have of purchasing f.o.b. In the case of Spain, the result can fairly be attributed to flag discrimination. In Italy flag discrimination was not officially practised, yet Italy took almost exactly 10 per cent of American exports and Italian ships carried 10 per cent of American exports and nearly two-thirds of Italian imports from America. All of this suggests flag discrimination in that it is precisely the type of quantitative result to be expected when national ships are given preference in the carriage of imports.

The conclusion to be drawn from the examination of the figures in Table 31 is that there is evidence in the American trade of the effects of flag discrimination in diverting cargoes to particular ships, although the extent of the diversion cannot be measured.

The question can be looked at in another way by considering the trades of various countries. Figures for 1957 will again be used although later figures are available. However, when trade is considered in broad groups, as in Table 32 the differences from one year to another are slight. In 1957, the volume of world seaborne trade, excluding trade on the Great Lakes, was 930 million metric tons, divided as shown in the table.

From the figures in the table it can be seen that the known discriminators outside the United States account for about 10 per cent of world trade. If it is assumed that 50 per cent of the imports of these countries and 3 per cent[1] of the exports of America are carried in nationally-owned ships, then discrimination affected 5·7 per cent of world trade. It is clear, however,

---

[1] Based on American claims that the 50/50 rule diverts only 3 per cent of U.S. exports to U.S. ships. See above.

that the known discriminators did not possess the shipping capacity to lift 50 per cent of their imports, so the actual discrimination fell short of the potential and 5·7 per cent is obviously an overstatement of the proportion of world trade diverted by discriminatory practices.

TABLE 32. World trade, 1957 (in million metric tons)

	Imports	Exports
United States of America	168	155
'Free' countries[a]	618	452
Known discriminators[b]	95	98
Possible discriminators[c]	43	55
Unaccounted[d]	6	170
Total trade	930	930

[a] 'Free', i.e. non-discriminating, countries: such countries as O.E.E.C. countries, less Portugal, Spain and Turkey; British Commonwealth, less South Africa, India and Pakistan; oil exporters in respect of oil shipments.

[b] Known discriminators consist of most South American countries, French and Portuguese overseas possessions, the Communist countries.

[c] Possible discriminators consist of countries for which no definite information is available for 1957, India, Pakistan and South Africa where discrimination is frequently alleged.

[d] Unaccounted: trade of countries not given in detailed figures; almost entirely exports of oil products from Middle Eastern countries.

Source: Compiled from United Nations and O.E.E.C. trade figures and sources given in Table 29.

Another way of looking at the figures is to add to one-half of the imports of the known discriminators a proportion, say one-quarter, of the imports of the possible discriminators and the whole of the non-commercial exports of the United States,[1] most of which travelled either in American ships or in ships of the other parties to the deal. On this calculation, 79 million metric tons out of a total of 930 million metric tons, that is 8·5 per cent of world trade, is not available for free and open competition.

The figure of 8·5 per cent is based on an extreme view of the shipping policies of various countries. In view of the gaps which

[1] Non-commercial exports are determined by deducting the total of commercial cargoes, used in calculating the figures in Table 31, from the U.N. figures of U.S. exports. The result is more likely to be an overstatement than an understatement of the non-commercial cargoes.

existed between the aspirations and the achievements of many countries in the field of discrimination, the fact that only 50 per cent of American non-commercial exports were, in fact, fully tied, the possibility of double counting when exports and import figures are added and the arbitrary nature of the allocation to possible discriminators, the 8·5 per cent is obviously an over-statement.

No exact conclusion can be drawn, but it is doubtful if more than 5 per cent of world trade was removed from free competition by official discriminatory practices in 1957. This count does not include non-governmental acts of discrimination.

In the years since 1957, discrimination in the South American trades has increased but that in some other trades has declined. The flat condemnation of discriminatory practices by I.M.C.O.[1] appears to have had some results, although I.M.C.O. members, including Russia, India and the Argentine practise forms of flag discrimination, relying on a certain ambiguity in the wording of the relevant Article in the Convention.[2] Nevertheless, it seems unlikely that discrimination today concerns a higher proportion of world trade than in 1957.

This global statement ignores the fact that the impact of discrimination in individual trades is very much more important.[3] The Brazilian preference in respect of imports, for example, resulted in a halving of the relevant British service and the former fortnightly sailings at a profit became monthly sailings at a loss, a disequilibrium situation which can be followed either by a relaxation of the Brazilian rules or a further cut in non-Brazilian sailings. The Chilean 50 per cent rule applying to imports had a different effect. Chilean tonnage was insufficient to lift the required volume of cargo, so under an agreement with the conference lines the cargo was shared between Chilean and non-Chilean ships on a suitable basis, and the non-Chilean lines were required to pay a fine for all cargo carried in excess of the quota. The proceeds of this fine provided subsidies to the

[1] Inter-Government Maritime Consultative Organisation which was formally established in January 1959.

[2] *Survey of British Shipping*, p. 27.

[3] This paragraph records the position in 1959/60. Discriminatory rules change so frequently that there can be no certainty that the position will be the same when this book is published.

Chilean fleet which, with this assistance, will eventually grow to a size sufficient to enable it to carry its share of the cargo under the agreement. Guatemala levies a surcharge of 100 per cent on customs duties for goods from certain countries, including Britain, unless those goods are carried in Guatemalan ships. As most British exports to Guatemala are dutiable, this regulation means that such exports wait in Britain until a Guatemalan ship is available rather than travel in the first available British ship. Ecuador and the other countries participating in the Gran Colombiana Line do not exercise any official discrimination in favour of that line, but the Coffee Association has directed that preference be given to such ships when shipping coffee. However, Ecuador used to discriminate against foreign ships by means of preferential consular rates for goods travelling in Ecuadorian and Colombian vessels. The difference in the rates was only 1 per cent *ad valorem* but this approximated to 12 to 14 per cent of the total freight cost. Between 1947 and 1954 the American flag share of shipments from Atlantic ports to Guayaquil fell from 47·6 per cent to 7·7 per cent,[1] largely as a result of discriminatory practices. Pressure from the United States succeeded in making Ecuador drop its discriminatory practices. In the Argentine the overthrow of the Peron régime has led to a loosening of regulations and a decline in the importance of state cargoes in relation to commercial cargoes for which all ships can compete. However, shipments of material for railways, power stations and other public utilities which are state-owned continue to travel in Argentine ships and ships of the Argentine fleet are given preferences in Argentine ports. Discrimination, competition from air travel and the social and economic changes within the area have meant that whereas in 1939 Royal Mail employed nine passenger ships totalling 140,000 tons and numerous cargo ships on the South American run, in 1960 only three passenger ships were used; on the other hand, all three ships were newly built in 1960 for the trade which, despite all difficulties, is obviously not yet impossible.

Although the overall impact of discrimination may be that only 5 per cent of world trade is removed from free competition, the unevenness of the discrimination has meant that it has been

[1] Report in *Syren and Shipping* (4 November 1959), p. 167.

heavily localized in its impact. First, there has been the obvious geographical localization, for example, in the South American trades, or the Indonesian trades from which Dutch ships have been driven. Second, oil cargoes, which constitute about 45 per cent of world sea-borne trade by weight, are substantially less affected by discrimination than dry cargoes so that shipping fleets with a high proportion of tanker tonnage, such as the fleets of Norway and Liberia, are relatively affected less than dry-cargo fleets. Third, discriminatory action affects ships engaged in indirect trades more severely than those engaged in direct trades which means that a maritime nation with a substantial proportion of its fleet engaged in indirect trades is likely, other things being equal, to suffer more than a nation which takes little part in indirect trades. The essential trade routes of the United States, for example, all constitute direct trades so that American shipping has probably suffered less from discrimination than that of Norway, Greece, Britain and the Netherlands which depend to a considerable extent on indirect trades for the employment of existing fleets.

The question of the effects of discrimination cannot be considered only in static terms, as it is always possible for a single country, the shipping of which is being harmed by discrimination, to lessen that harm by adopting discrimination itself. This means that so long as any discriminatory practices exist the possibility of their multiplication cannot be ignored. This is more likely to happen in a shipping recession than in times of prosperity and at such times the effects of such extended discrimination would be felt severely by non-discriminating nations.

It is wrong, however, to consider official discrimination in shipping apart from world trading policies in general on the one hand, and the competitive policies of established shipping enterprises on the other. So long as tariffs, quotas, and other barriers to the free flow of international trade in goods exist, barriers to free international competitive shipping can be expected. No nation which, for example, restricts imports of cotton goods can reasonably complain if a producer of cotton goods restricts the free use by its nationals of foreign shipping services, either to protect its foreign exchange position or to raise its level of employment. Finally, so long as unofficial discrimination exists, or is believed to exist, either through conference rules or the attempts to persuade exporters to sell c.i.f. and importers to buy f.o.b., official discrimination is more likely to increase than to decrease.

IX

Flags of Convenience

'THE term "Flags of Convenience" is commonly used to describe the flags of such countries as Panama, Liberia, Honduras . . . whose laws allow—and indeed make it easy for—ships owned by foreign nationals or companies to fly these flags. This is in contrast to the practice in the maritime countries (and in many others) where the right to fly the national flag is subject to stringent conditions and involves far-reaching obligations.'[1] The term need not, however, be restricted to the flags of the three countries named although these are overwhelmingly the most important. The Costa Rican flag was used as a flag of convenience until 31 December 1958, at which date all foreign shipping licences were withdrawn and the foreign-owned ships flying the flag had to find other registration. Before 1914, British sailing ships were often transferred to British-financed companies in Norway to avoid the costs of survey and to take advantage of the cheap, high quality, Norwegian labour. In the inter-war period some British companies transferred their shipping operations to Hong Kong in order to take advantage of cheap labour. The Bermudan flag is used as a flag of convenience by a few British owners (see pp. 230–1), while some American and Canadian owners have formed Bermudan shipping companies. Since 1957 the Lebanese flag has been used by some Greek owners. Early in 1960 the flag of Surinam was adopted as a flag of convenience by a subsidiary of a Dutch company. These examples are by no means exhaustive, but serve to show that the use of flags other than the national flag of the shipowner is neither a new device nor one solely dependent upon the willingness of the three countries named to accept the registration of foreign-owned ships.

[1] O.E.E.C., 'Study on the expansion of the Flags of Convenience fleets and on various aspects thereof' (Paris, 1958), p. 2.

Flags of Convenience

'Flag of Convenience' is a term, certainly now regarded as a term of opprobrium, for the flag of any country which permits persons or companies, other than those with a genuine link with the country, to register their ships in its ports. What constitutes a genuine link, however, is a matter of definition. Some 600,000 tons of British flag shipping, for example, are owned by Greek nationals through companies set up in, and administered from, London. The British flag banana fleet of Elders and Fyffes (formed in 1901 by the merging of the West Indian interests of Elder Dempster with Fyffe & Hudson) is owned by the parent United Fruit Co., of America, while American interests control the British flag Silver Line. British interests own much of the tonnage registered in Hong Kong, including the Panholib[1] tonnage actually owned in Hong Kong (see Table 34). These examples could be multiplied. The criterion for a genuine link is the location of the immediate effective control over the ships, not the location of the ultimate control. Where there is control through a nationally registered company with the ability to exercise that control through resident directors, the link is, in the terms used, genuine. Where the immediate owning company is a name-plate and both immediate control and ultimate control lie elsewhere, the link is not genuine. There is, however, undoubtedly a lot of casuistry employed in determining the genuineness of existing links in individual cases.

The practice of registering ships under flags other than that of the owner's country dates from before the first world war, but the term 'Flag of Convenience' is of post-1945 origin: in the main, the 'problem' of the flag of convenience is largely a post-Korean growth. British shipowners generally ignored the competition from such ships until about 1957, although seamen's unions and some shipping correspondents were stressing the facts. There were two reasons for this neglect. First, the Panholib ships had been handicapped by foreign exchange restrictions in Britain and other countries. Second, until the fall in world dry-cargo shipments and the sharp increase in tanker tonnage after 1957 (see Table 22), there was no problem of sur-

---

[1] The descriptive adjective Panholib is a collective coined from the words Panama, Honduras and Liberia and is commonly used to stand for 'Flag of Convenience'.

plus capacity and shipowners were earning satisfactory profits. It is worth noting that in the period 1949 to 1954, when British shipowners scarcely worried about the Panholib tonnage, the annual compound growth rate of the British fleet was 1·2 per cent, compared with 2·4 per cent in the period 1954 to 1960 when the expansion of Panholib fleets was alleged to be hampering British growth.

The tonnage under the Panamanian flag at the outbreak of war was 722,000 tons, 1·2 per cent of the world total; that under the other Panholib flags was negligible, consisting of coasters only. By 30 June 1946, the tonnage of the Panamanian fleet had risen to 834,000 tons, still 1·2 per cent of the world total, while the fleets of Honduras, Liberia and Costa Rica were still negligible. The progress of these fleets since 1948 is shown in Table 33. The table shows quite clearly the expansion since 1950 and the large absolute and relative growth of the Liberian fleet which, however, was reversed in 1959. The initial post-war rise in the Panholib fleets occurred in Panama and consisted largely of U.S. war-built types which were able to make enormous profits in the immediate post-war years when the volume of international trade was limited by the tonnage available.

TABLE 33. Flag of Convenience fleets, 1948 to 1960 (Figures as at 31 December in million tons; lake and river craft excluded)

	Panama		Honduras		Liberia		Costa Rica		Total	
Year	Fleet	% of world	Fleet	% of world	Fleet	% of world	Fleet	% of world	Fleet	% of world
1948	2·8	3·8	0·4	0·5	0·0	0·0	0·0	0·0	3·2	4·3
1950	3·4	4·4	0·6	0·8	0·4	0·5	0·0	0·0	4·4	5·7
1952	3·8	4·6	0·5	0·5	1·1	1·2	0·1	0·0	5·5	6·3
1954	4·0	4·4	0·4	0·4	3·2	3·5	0·3	0·3	7·9	8·6
1956	4·0	4·1	0·4	0·4	6·4	6·5	0·5	0·5	11·3	11·5
1958	4·4	3·9	0·2	0·2	11·1	9·7	0·5	0·5	16·2	15·9
1960	4·1	3·3	0·1	0·1	10·6	8·6	0·1	0·1	14·9	12·0

Source: Annual Reports, Chamber of Shipping.

There are several points which must be considered with reference to these Panholib ships. First, the actual ownership of the ships. Second, the forces causing those owners not to use their national flags. Third, the attractions of the particular flags of Liberia, Panama and Honduras. Fourth, the causes of the growth in tonnage and its nature. Fifth, the effects of such registrations. Sixth, the British position in relation to the flag of convenience.

OWNERSHIP

The citizens of two countries, Greece and America, predominate as owners of Panholib tonnage. On the one hand, are the new Greek shipowners, men such as Niarchos, Onassis and Livanos; on the other hand are American owners such as Erling D. Naess, the American oil companies, Alcoa and companies owning bulk ore carriers. It is generally considered that about 40 per cent of the Panholib tonnage is American owned, about 45 per cent Greek owned, while every other nation customarily denies that their nationals own any of the remaining 15 per cent. Table 34 shows the results of an attempt to determine the actual ownership of ships registered under the Panholib flags in 1959–1960.

The exact figures shown must be treated with a certain caution for several reasons. First, the bulk of the tonnage is owned in small companies each of which owns only one or two ships. Thus, the main Niarchos fleet of 0·99 million tons is owned in forty-six companies, thirty-eight of which are single ship companies. The clues to the true ownership of the ships owned by these small companies registered in Monrovia, Puerto Limon or Panama are the nationality of the managing agents of the companies, the language used in naming the companies, the system of nomenclature of the ships and the funnel markings used. None of these things is conclusive in itself and even when all four point in the same direction there is still the possibility that they do not indicate the real owner of the ships. This means that there may be errors in the allocations between countries, although it is believed that these errors are likely to affect mainly the American and Greek figures on the one side and the Hong Kong, Italian and Swiss figures on the other. A second source of error arises from multiple entries for individual ships. Where, for example, a fleet in common ownership is entered under managing agents A, B and C in New York, London and Genoa respectively,

Flags of Convenience

double counting is relatively easy to avoid; where, however, the fleet is split in different ways between two or more agents in each port the problem is more difficult. A third error arises in the source itself in that the original information was apparently compiled without access to the authoritative Lloyd's Confidential List, the circulation of which is very restricted. In the event, the table shows a rather larger tonnage of Panholib ships than in fact existed. The error is partly due to double counting and partly to differences in the composition of figures taken from different sources.

TABLE 34. Ownership of Panholib tonnage, 1959–60

Country	Tonnage	Country	Tonnage
	000's tons		000's tons
Argentine	12	Lichtenstein	41
Bahamas	26	Monaco	18
Belgium	17	Netherlands	15
Brazil	102	Norway	86
Canada	72	Philippines	20
Cuba	8	Portugal	32
Denmark	2	Singapore	38
Egypt	2	Spain	227
France	56	Sweden	40
Germany	159	Switzerland	102
Greece	7,202	Turkey	14
Hong Kong	175	United Kingdom	156
Israel	47	United States of America	6,978
Italy	806	Yugoslavia	25
Lebanon	11	Unidentified	186

Total: 16·7 million tons.

Notes: 1. Total tonnage registered under Panholib flags returned as 16·3 million tons at 31 December 1959.
2. Greek owned tonnage under Panholib flags given in *Naftika Chronika* (15 January 1961), p. 51 as 8·26 million tons at 31.12.59 and 6·12 million tons at 31.12.60.

Source: Compiled from G. M. Grønvold, *Panama and Greek Ships* (Oslo, 1960).

Making allowances for these factors, the figures in the table support the widespread belief that Greek and American owners each own between 40 and 45 per cent of the total tonnage. Of the other 15 per cent, Italian owners appear to account for about one-third with the balance widely spread throughout the world.

The British figure of 156,000 tons calls for comment. This excludes all ships owned by companies registered in the United Kingdom which are, or appear to be, themselves dominated by foreign persons as directors. Thus, although the British flag tonnage, amounting to about 600,000 tons, owned by Greek interests is normally included in any list of British-owned ships, the Panholib ships owned by these same interests are treated here as Greek owned. In so far, therefore, as it is possible to tell, the tonnage which is shown as British owned but flying a 'phony' flag is genuinely British owned. Almost a third of the total is owned by one tramp ship owner. No other regular British owners appear to have owned Panholib tonnage, although, of course, it is impossible to tell how far, if at all, British shipping interests have contributed capital to enterprises under the management of London Greeks and owning Panholib tonnage.

REASONS FOR USING PANHOLIB FLAGS

There are two sides to the question of why shipowners sought flags other than their own national flag for registering their ships. On the one side are the repulsive pressure of their own flags and on the other the attractive powers of the Panholib flags. In this section only the repulsive forces are considered, that is, only those forces which would have led shipowners, in any case, to seek a flag other than their own national flag. The attractive powers of the Panholib flags, which have operated when no strong repulsive force existed, are considered below. A general impression is that repulsive forces have been most important for Greek and American owners, while a later realization of the attractions of Panholib registration has been influential with owners in other countries. The dichotomy between attraction and repulsion is not, of course, complete and these have not existed as two entirely separate sets of forces only one of which was operating at any one time.

Greek nationals adopted the flag of convenience because political conditions at home at the end of the war were sufficiently unstable that Greek registration was unattractive and finance from American sources was not available for building or purchasing ships to be registered in Greece. The ships, Greek owned but not Greek registered, fall into three distinct groups. Historically, the earliest were aged passenger liners bought from other countries for use in world-wide migrant trades, which were often given Panholib registration. Today the Greek passenger fleet contains few ships built for Greek owners but the emphasis is shifting from elderly migrant carriers to luxury cruise ships. The second group consists of Liberty and other wartime dry-cargo ships bought from the Americans at the end of the war for world-wide tramp trading; Greek owners bought 696,544 tons of U.S. Government-owned ships between 1 July 1946 and 30 June 1948, while a further 1,337,629 tons went to Panamanian ownership, the real owners being unidentified. The third group consisted of tankers and bulk carriers, some of which were American types included in the above figures, but subsequently consisting mainly of new building.

The American owners of Panholib tonnage were driven to adopt such registry by high American wage costs and the provision that 75 per cent of the crews and 100 per cent of the officers of ships flying the American flag must be American nationals and that such ships must conform to the generous American manning scales. American owners have been able to transfer tonnage in this way, despite the restrictions in the Merchant Marine Act, if they agreed to build in America for American registry replacements for the ships transferred, but not necessarily to an equivalent tonnage; this condition did not attach to the war-built tonnage which was transferred. American registry for ships which have not enjoyed a construction subsidy and do not enjoy an operating subsidy, which is the position with tramps, tankers and bulk carriers, is not generally economically possible[1] because labour has to be secured in competition with tariff-protected shore industries and subsidized liner services. It was the Americans who coined the phrase 'flag of

[1] It should be noted that some liners registered in America operate without subsidies. Some tramp ships are also registered in America and can operate unsubsidized because they obtain specially favourable freight rates on reserved cargoes (see p. 198). American-flag tankers and bulk carriers are generally owned by oil companies or industrial concerns, not by independent shipowners.

necessity' and the O.E.E.C. saw such registrations as '. . . the removal of a handicap rather than the gaining of an advantage. . . .'[1]

ATTRACTIONS OF PANHOLIB FLAGS

A strong attractive force of the Panholib flags is freedom from taxation. In Liberia a registration fee of \$1·20 per net ton and an annual tax of \$0·10 per net ton is charged, the government giving an undertaking not to increase the tax for a period of twenty years from the initial date of registration. The Panamanian fees and taxes are the same, but without the twenty-year guarantee. In Honduras the registration fee is \$0·25 per net ton and the annual tax \$0·05 per net ton, which tax may not be increased during a term of thirty years from the date of first registration of a vessel.[2] The freedom from other taxation of ships sailing under these flags enables the shipowners to arrange their business enterprises so that only profits repatriated are subject to taxation, that remaining with the shipping enterprises being tax free and fully available for fleet expansion. It is this which gives the flag of convenience its attraction, which accounts for the fears felt by tramp ship and tanker owners in other countries and which, partly at least, explains the growth which owners of such tonnage have been able to achieve in the post-war years.

The tax advantage, however, must not be exaggerated. Freedom from taxation was a considerable advantage in the years to 1958 when large profits were being earned by world shipping but in the relatively depressed years since then has ceased to be of great value. Partly as a result of this, and partly as a consequence of Greek shipping policy, the tonnage registered under the Liberian flag in fact fell in 1959 and 1960. Further, by registering their ships under a Panholib flag owners lose the advantage of any tax concessions given at home. For a British shipowner there is the 40 per cent investment allowance which would be lost. This may not be considered important: the Anglo-American Shipping Co. Ltd., formed in 1958, partly with

---

[1] O.E.E.C., op. cit., p. 5.
[2] O.E.E.C., ibid., p. 4. Fees and taxes in Costa Rica were equally modest. Figures relate to the position in 1958.

American finance, chose Bermuda rather than London as the headquarters, despite the loss of the investment allowance. The success of the Greek shipping policy of 1953 in attracting ships to the Greek registry away from Panholib registration has been considerable and in the years 1959 and 1960 the Greek-owned Panholib fleet fell by 3·45 million tons while the fleet registered in Greece rose by 3·3 million tons.[1]

The Greek shipping policy sought to minimize the advantages offered by the flags of convenience rather to attempt retaliatory action. In particular, the policy offers to Greek shipowners the freedom to buy or sell ships without Government permission, taxation fixed at rates no higher than those ruling on the day of admission of any vessel to the Greek flag, tax exemptions for vessels up to two years of age and reduced taxation upon all vessels under twenty years of age.[2] These advantages, together with the creation of political stability in Greece, have sufficed to produce a 250 per cent expansion of the Greek registered fleet since 1956; the increase mainly concerned dry-cargo tramp ships, although from 1959 an increasing volume of tanker tonnage was registered under the Greek flag.

Certain non-fiscal advantages are enjoyed by ships flying Panholib flags as the ships are free from national regulations concerning standards of equipment and from requirements regarding manning scales, wage rates and social service payments. 'Registration of ships in any of these countries . . . is a mere formality. Of obligations there are none, since these countries do not have any body of shipping legislation and are signatories to very few, if any, of the international maritime conventions.'[3] The freedom, however, is not absolute, being circumscribed by the requirements of insurance companies and by the insistence on the part of maritime countries that only ships complying with their regulations can use their ports. While, therefore, Panholib ships could possibly be sub-standard when the total tonnage involved was small, it is impossible for the

[1] *Naftika Chronika* (15 January 1961), pp. 50–51.

[2] See *Shipping World* (4 February 1959), p. 171 for further details. It is widely believed in Britain, perhaps without foundation, that the Greek Government also gave an undertaking not to prevent a subsequent retransfer to a flag of convenience if owners considered such a course desirable.

[3] Peter Duff, 'Flags of Convenience', *Financial Times* (17 December 1955).

existing volume to be sub-standard as the number of countries between which they would then find trade possible is insufficient to support more than a small fraction of the present fleet. The U.S. Bureau of Shipping has denied the contention that Panholib ships are generally sub-standard, pointing out that slightly over one-half of such ships are classified with the Bureau. Lloyd's agree with this general view.[1]

Nor is it true that standards for crews are always low in Panholib ships. When the International Transport Workers' Federation (I.T.F.) decided to boycott Panholib ships it originally intended that the boycott should apply only to ships in which conditions were sub-standard. In practice, it was found that conditions and wages in Panholib ships were generally above world standard and for the purposes of the boycott, staged in December 1958, sub-standard was interpreted to mean the absence of a collective agreement and of payment by the ship-owners to the Welfare Fund of the I.T.F. It is worth pointing out, however, that not all seamen on Panholib ships are un-protected; the Union of Greek Shipowners claimed in 1958 that some 27,000 to 30,000 Greek seamen were employed on Pan-holib ships under collective agreements with conditions superior to any except those prevailing in America.[2] A Greek ship broker living in London has claimed that '. . . all Greek-owned foreign flagged vessels are manned according to Greek law and are operated in strict accordance with international conventions and regulations'.[3] The I.T.F. agreed at the time of the boycott that they had concluded collective agreements of a satisfactory nature with '. . . about two hundred of the two thousand flags of convenience owners'.[4] The number of such agreements is increasing.

On the whole question of wages and conditions the position of Panholib owners against owners of ships registered in traditional maritime countries is not very clear. The International Shipping Federation, the international body of shipowners which deals with employment conditions, in opposing the boycott organized

[1] See report in *Fairplay* (12 February 1959), p. 415.
[2] Report, *Financial Times* (2 December 1958).
[3] J. A. Hadjipateras, *Syren and Shipping* (7 January 1959), p. 191.
[4] Report, 'Dockers of the World Almost Unite', *Manchester Guardian* (29 November 1958).

by the I.T.F. against Panholib ships stated that the '. . . advantage of flags of convenience lies essentially in lower taxation, not in bad employment conditions. . . .'[1] Owners of Panholib ships generally pay higher wages than other owners in order to attract crews, but not as high as those paid by shipowners in America where the operating differential subsidy arrangements have removed any incentive U.S. owners may have possessed to limit wage increases and where, in any case, wages of seamen must be comparable with those in shore-based occupations in order to attract crews. Panholib ships are free from manning laws and generally carry smaller crews than comparable ships registered under traditional flags. The higher wages, however, are not always based on collective agreements and so can quickly be reduced when there is unemployment among seamen. After the break in freight rates in mid-1957 wages in the flag of convenience fleet owned by Onassis were reduced without warning by 20 per cent; Onassis claimed that many other owners of tankers and tramps had made similar wage cuts. These cuts were made without consultation, as arbitrary decisions of the shipowners concerned in response to a fall in freights. This occurred at about the same time as time charters executed over the previous ten years expired, forcing the ships concerned into either the trip charter market or lay up.[2] On the other hand, the slack period in 1959–60 does not seem to have caused any pressure to be placed on wages.

Some of the advantages which Panholib owners enjoy over owners of ships registered in traditional maritime countries may be counteracted by discriminatory action against such ships on the part of seamen's and dockers' unions, for example, the boycott of December 1958. Direct government discrimination directed at the flag of convenience is believed to come only from Russia, which was reported to be charging Panholib ships three times the normal harbour dues in 1958.[3]

The I.T.F. is actively concerned about the position of seamen in the Panholib ships and would like to see the owners of these

[1] Report, *Financial Times* (5 November 1958).
[2] See Report of Proceedings, Annual General Meeting of National Union of Seamen, 1958, pp. 31, 131.
[3] Report by the Labour Correspondent, *Financial Times* (21 October 1958).

ships forced to comply fully with international regulations. Their concern is of longer standing than that of most ship-owners; in 1948, when most shipowners were not interested in the flag of convenience, anticipating that the prospects for the continual employment at remunerative rates of such ships were poor,[1] the I.T.F. meeting in Oslo passed a resolution calling for the boycott of such ships. In 1949 the I.T.F. drew up a list of obsolete ships which had been transferred to Panholib flags because they were obsolete and could no longer reach survey standards in traditional maritime countries.

CAUSES AND NATURE OF GROWTH

The growth in the post-war years of the Panholib fleet has represented a net addition to the shipping fleet of the world. The repulsive forces of some flags and the attractive powers of the flags of convenience, which explain why, when certain ship-owners expanded or created their fleets, the Panholib flags were adopted, have been considered. But why did the growth occur in such a way at all?

After the second world war there was an absolute shortage of shipping in relation to the trading needs of the world, this short-age affecting passenger, dry-cargo and tanker tonnage. Although the bulk of the passenger tonnage owned in Greece and some passenger tonnage owned in Italy and Switzerland is, or has been, registered under Panholib flags, these ships form a very small part of the total tonnage under these flags and it is the dry-cargo and tanker tonnage which is of real importance.

In the case of dry-cargo tonnage, several million tons of American war-built ships, principally the famous 'Liberty' ships, were available at the end of the war and prior to placing these in the Reserve Fleet the U.S. Government offered to ship-owners of the world an opportunity to purchase such ships as they desired. British and Norwegian owners, for example, pur-chased ships for national registration; Greek and American owners usually adopted Panamanian registration. Shipowners in some of the traditional maritime countries viewed the welded construction of the Liberty ships with suspicion. This, together

[1] See report by Shipping Correspondent, *The Times* (11 August 1948), p. 9.

with fears of a post-war slump, led them to refrain from purchasing enough American tonnage to take advantage of the trading opportunities available. This reluctance on the part of traditional owners presented an opportunity to non-traditional owners who registered the ships under Panholib flags; from the untaxed profits which the ships earned in the immediate post-war period and through the years of Korea and Suez their owners were able to expand their fleets by building modern tonnage.

The position with regard to tankers was different in some respects. Mr. Stavros Niarchos, the Greek shipowner, has argued that the Panholib tanker fleet was built as a response to certain basic economic conditions. Immediately after the war there was a tremendous need for sea transport, but the shipping industry of the maritime nations '. . . was stifled by unimaginative governmental restrictions and crippling taxation. It is a fact that in Britain, for instance, the major oil companies invited British owners first to assist in the transport requirements of the oil industry; the response, as we know, was meagre indeed. It was inevitable, then, that free enterprise should seek an outlet to fill the need'.[1] Norwegian owners were unable initially to supply the tonnage required because of severe Government restrictions on the placing of orders overseas (see Chapter VII), although they later did so by borrowing overseas to finance ship construction without drawing on the official exchange reserves. In Britain, most shipowners were not interested in tankers and so did not respond to the invitation. An opportunity was created and taken initially by Greek owners and slightly later by Norwegian owners. The Greek owners who stepped in to take advantage of the opportunity offered adopted mainly Panholib registration. The combined Greek and Panholib tanker fleet increased from 1·62 million tons in 1948 to 2·95 million tons in 1952, 6·04 million tons in 1956 and 8·03 million tons in 1960. The big rise in world tanker tonnage which these increases, together with those taking place in other countries, entailed resulted in surplus capacity in 1958 and subsequent years. The bulk of the surplus was represented by technically obsolete tonnage and the expectations of those who after the war saw the need for more

[1] Stavros Niarchos, letter to *The Times* (1 April 1958).

tanker tonnage and set out to satisfy it were more than justified
by events. The Norwegian experience, a growth of nearly 250
per cent in the tanker fleet between the end of 1948 and the end
of 1959, in which period the growth of the British fleet was less
than 100 per cent, shows that neither Panholib registration nor
an advantageous national shipping policy were necessary conditions for success. Contrary to some opinion in this country,[1]
Norwegian owners are not allowed to transfer ships to Panholib
registration unless the Panamanian company was in existence
before the war or the sale was a genuine sale to an independent
owner with no connection with the Norwegian seller.

A high proportion of the tanker construction was financed
with American loan capital and Greek owners appear to have
operated largely on the basis of securing a time charter for
seven or even fifteen years from an oil company, a 95 per cent
mortgage from American financiers on the security of the time
charter, then building a tanker to fit the charter and finally
sitting back to enjoy the profits. The Norwegians appear to have
relied less on American finance, although, as before the war, the
pre-construction time charter with a loan raised on its security
was the commonest arrangement.

Apart from Norwegian and Greek shipowners who stepped in
to provide the tankers needed to transport world fuel requirements two other sources must be mentioned. First, the profits
earned by tankers in the Korean and Suez booms attracted
speculators to the industry, frequently residents of non-maritime
countries or even inland territories and these people adopted
Panholib registration. Second, the American oil companies both
through their American and their foreign affiliates have placed
a substantial volume of tonnage under flags of convenience,
mainly in order to avoid the high wage costs which American
manning scales entail, but also to avoid taxation. Since the
decline in profits in 1958, some of these American-owned ships
have been transferred to the British and other flags.

No account of the growth of the Panholib fleet can be complete without a consideration of the American rôle. This has
occurred, first, in the provision by American financial institu-
tions of loans against long-term charters with the freight paid in

[1] See *Survey of British Shipping*, p. 17.

dollars, such loans not being available for ships to be registered in countries where political conditions were unstable; it was this condition which ruled out Greek registry. The second factor has been the leave given for ships built with American construction subsidies to be registered under a Panholib flag provided the owner agreed to build in America tonnage for American registry, perhaps one new ship for every three transferred. More important, however, has been a third factor, namely, the permission given for American-owned tonnage built without construction differential subsidies to be registered under a Panholib flag provided it is available in theory at least, to the U.S. in time of war. American shipowners have been prepared to build in American yards, despite the high costs involved, because during shipping booms American yards could give quicker delivery than could be obtained from other countries with lower building costs. In the Korean and Suez booms freight rates were sufficiently high that the prospect of securing delivery of a ship six months or a year earlier than would otherwise have been possible was considered to justify the extra cost involved by building at an American yard: the advantage was not simply one of obtaining some additional months service from the ship during a period of high rates but often of securing a time charter at those rates for a period of seven years or more. As far as the American government was concerned the deal was attractive because it provided employment for the shipyards and a ship theoretically available in wartime without the expenditure of any subsidy money.

Effects of Panholib Registrations

First and foremost among the effects is the cumulative advantage which tax-free operation gives as untaxed profits can be ploughed back to build more ships to earn more untaxed profits and so on. This has permitted a very rapid growth rate of these fleets, just over 400 per cent during the years 1948 to 1958. However, in the booming conditions for most of the period from the end of the war until 1958 shipping was able to attract capital in most countries of the world and if the growth in world shipping had not occurred under Panholib flags it would have occurred in other ways under other flags, partly at least through the provision of operating subsidies for American flag tankers. There is no reason, however, to assume that the fleet under the British flag would have grown very much faster than it did as British operators as a whole, apart from the oil companies, did not become greatly interested in the tanker until about 1956. It is possible, of course, that if flags of convenience had not existed some of the owners who used such flags would have set up companies in Britain to own their ships. This would have increased the British fleet shown in the statistical returns, but not the fleet owned by established British shipowners.

When considering the advantage of tax-free operation, special mention must be made of the highly-geared capital structures under which many Panholib ships were operated. On the basis of 5 per cent equity and 95 per cent borrowed, a little equity went a long way and in booming freight markets earned very high profits. Although precise information is lacking, it seems that shipping empires with weak foundations found their salvation in the Korean and Suez freight booms and have thus been enabled to withstand the slack years since 1957. Without Suez it is possible that there would have been a spate of bankruptcies among Panholib owners who had built ships without first securing a time charter. Since that time, some new owners who entered on the same basis have, in fact, found themselves in difficulties, for example, the Swiss-owned Arosa Line, while in America mortgagees have had to foreclose on an unknown number of tankers on which interest payments were not being maintained. The jeremiads in the British industry who neglected to grasp unconventional finance to seize unparalleled opportunities[1] have not been slow to point to the effects of Korea and Suez in preventing the financial crashes they confidently predicted.

A second effect of the volume of Panholib tonnage remains potential: it is the consequence of a substantial volume of tonnage without any national trade ties in a world of spreading flag

---

[1] In fairness, it must be pointed out that the deposits paid when American loans were secured had to be paid in dollars, which British owners did not have but which owners in other countries seem to have obtained from American grants for post-war reconstruction. However, America was not the only source of loans and British owners could probably have borrowed in countries such as Sweden had they wished.

discrimination. Every additional act of flag discrimination which increases the number of trading routes on which competition is restricted intensifies the competition in the remaining free areas because it reduces the area within which the entire Panholib fleet, the bulk of the Norwegian fleet and a substantial part of the British, Greek, Dutch and other fleets compete directly. For the present such a clash has not occurred simply because flag discrimination has scarcely affected tankers and in the dry-cargo trades has affected liner rather than tramp trades. If, in the future, discrimination should extend to cover the oil trades, with a consequent increase in national fleets which some Arabian oil producers are threatening, the Panholib fleet, un-attached to any trade, could lead to ruinous competition in the free trades of the world. By analogy with the Tanker Pool of 1934, the oil companies are unlikely to stand aside and allow competition to drive rates to levels which forced independent tankers owned in maritime countries out of the market.

A third effect could arise from the second, but could also arise in any recession in shipping, and that is a debasement of safety and crew standards among those Panholib ships which are subject to no control from the country in which their real ownership lies. Insurance requirements and port regulations exercise a check, but a lot of saving can be effected, and a lot can happen, between the four-yearly surveys on which insurance depends. A reduction in wages or in manning scales would be particularly difficult to prevent in such circumstances and unless followed by similar reductions in other countries (or the payment of operating differential subsidies) would concentrate unemployment in shipping among the fleets and seamen of the traditional maritime countries with well-established maritime codes.

A fourth effect arises from American policy. The alleged basis of American shipping policy is the provision of an adequate tonnage of ships for wartime needs. This requires the maintenance of a sufficient active fleet to provide enough seamen to man, with the dilution of untrained labour, a larger wartime fleet, part of which is kept inactive in reserve in time of peace. The size of the total merchant fleet, active plus inactive vessels, is determined by anticipated wartime needs while the proportion of active to inactive vessels is set by the rate at which trained seamen can safely be replaced by untrained men. Part of the total fleet is, however, registered under Panholib flags, a course which makes economic sense only if fewer American seamen are employed on each ship than would be the case if the ships were registered under the American flag. This could be secured by smaller, but all-American, crews than American flag ships carry, or by crews of any size made up of non-American nationals. However achieved, the result is that the Panholib ships cannot be regarded as available fully manned to America in time of war. This being so, given the rate at which untrained seamen can be substituted for trained seamen, the active part of the American-owned fleet must be larger, and the inactive part correspondingly smaller, if some of the active ships are under Panholib registry than if all the active ships were under American registry and were subsidized.[1] Given, therefore, the American intention to be in a position to have a given tonnage of shipping available for defence purposes, it would be better for other maritime countries if the active part of the fleet was subsidized under the American flag than that part of it should be unsubsidized under Panholib flags. This would not be so only if one of two conditions is satisfied, namely, that the Panholib ships owned in America are fully manned to American standards by crews as reliable in wartime as those manning American flag ships, or, that the American defence experts have not made their calculations realistically and accurately. The first

---

[1] Suppose (a) the U.S. war-time fleet requirement is 27m. tons;

   (b) manning rate in U.S. and Panholib ships is 1 man per 1,000 tons;

   (c) dilution rate is 2 trained to 1 untrained.

What is the minimum size of the peace-time active fleet?

   (a) 18m. tons (plus inactive reserve of 9m. tons) if all ships under U.S. flag.

   (b) 18m. tons under U.S. flag, plus Panholib tonnage (now 7m. tons) if none of the manpower in the Panholib ships can be relied on in war time; total active fleet 25m. tons, inactive fleet 2m. tons.

   (c) 16m. tons active under U.S. flag, plus 7m. tons active under Panholib flags, if 2 men in 7 on Panholib flag ships would be available in war time; total active fleet 23m. tons, inactive fleet 4m. tons.

Only if all American owned, Panholib flag, ships are fully manned by American standards with crews as reliable in wartime as those of American flag ships will the active fleet be no larger when part of it is under the Panholib flag than when it is all under the American flag.

condition is not satisfied, but some informed opinion within America believes that the second condition is satisfied.[1]

A fifth effect is the drain of trained seafarers to Panholib vessels, attracted by the higher wage rates offered. The owners of those vessels have made no contribution, neither directly nor indirectly, to the costs of training officers and ratings, whereas shipowners in traditional maritime countries have borne their share of such costs. This applies more to the ships owned by expatriate Greeks than to those owned by Americans which use a high proportion of American labour.

Finally, is the disturbance to international trading relations through the diversion of freight earnings from shipowners who would change them into their national currencies at their central banks to owners with no national ties. As a result, the earnings are not available to finance normal international trading transactions. Dollar freight payments outside America are reduced because American oil companies are able to employ their own tonnage which cannot be operated profitably under the American flag.

BRITAIN AND FLAGS OF CONVENIENCE

Few British owners have sought Panholib registration.[2] However, there has been a slight movement towards Bermudan registration. The movement has been slight for two reasons. First, it did not gather force until 1956, since when the 40 per cent investment allowance and the falling rate of profit have reduced the value of such a move. The first public suggestion of the advantages of Bermudan registration for British ships appears to have been contained in a letter to *The Times* in 1955 which pointed out that the '. . . benefits derived by others from operation through Liberian companies and Liberian registered ships can be matched by British subjects operating through, for example, resident Bermudan companies and British ships registered in Bermuda'.[3] In April 1956, it was reported that a

[1] See Wytze Gorter, 'United States Shipping Policy' (New York, 1956).
[2] In reply to a questionnaire from the I.L.O. in 1956 the British Government stated that no British owned ships could be registered under a flag of convenience. See 'Flag Transfer in Relation to Social Conditions and Safety' (Geneva, 1956). But compare the figures in Table 34 above.
[3] David Graham, Bermuda, letter in *The Times* (12 December 1955), p. 9.

number of leading British shipping lines were actively considering setting up new companies in parts of the Commonwealth
where income tax was low and the problem was to be considered
at a meeting in London. Until then, '. . . few British owners,
largely for reasons of prestige and convenience, gave it serious
thought . . .', but they had realized that the only alternative to
slow extinction over the next few decades was to put themselves
on an equal footing with their Panholib rivals.[1]

The second possible reason for the slightness of the movement
to Bermudan registry is a legal impediment to such transfers.
The impediment arises from Section 468 of the Income Tax
Act, 1952. The way in which that Section has been interpreted
so hedges with restrictions the possibilities, as to reduce to a very
great extent what otherwise would appear to be an opening for
British shipowners to put themselves on a tax parity with Panholib owners. The Section is designed to prevent, without
Treasury permission, a transfer of a trade or business from a
United Kingdom parent company to a subsidiary in a place
such as Bermuda. *Prima facie*, cash subscriptions to shares of such
a subsidiary would not constitute a transfer of a trade or business,
but this is one of the refinements of the Act dependent on the
source of the money used to buy shares. If a British company
owned a ship and sold it to produce that money, the legal view
is that the money so received would constitute a part of the trade
or business. On the other hand, cash by way of profits or
reserves in themselves would not do so. The main thing is that
transfer of a trade or business is not confined to the visible
physical assets but extends to constructive transfer, in relation to
which the border line between what can be done and what cannot be done is narrow and uncertain. On the one hand, on the
basis of constructive transfer a liner company could not set up a
Bermudan subsidiary to build, own and operate liner tonnage,
either in the same or a different trade. On the other hand, the
same liner company could regard entry into the tanker business
via a Bermudan subsidiary as not being a project involving

[1] Report in *The Times* (25 April 1956), p. 10. This report is useful for indicating
the time when British owners began to consider seriously the growth of the Panholib
fleets, but it is not necessary to subscribe to the reasons given for the neglect nor to
the implication that the Panholib fleets were, or are, a major menace to British
shipping threatening it with extinction.

constructive transfer of an existing trade. The two cases mentioned are relatively clear-cut; in the majority of cases the uncertainty surrounding the interpretation of constructive transfer in each instance acts to prevent people from taking the risk of finding themselves in breach of the law.

The largest Bermudan company in 1961 was Shell Bermuda (Overseas) Limited, set up in 1955 with a board resident in Bermuda exercising absolute control over the operations of the tankers owned; the company owned forty tankers with a total deadweight tonnage of 830,000 tons, all the ships being registered in London. A number of well-known British shipping companies have set up Bermudan subsidiaries with each subsidiary owning a few ships registered in London or Liverpool; the total tonnage owned by these Bermudan companies in 1960 was 220,000 tons. A Bermudan member of the P. and O. group owned four tankers of 123,000 deadweight tons all registered in London. The Salient Shipping Company (Bermuda) Ltd., a member of the Vestey (Blue Star) Group owned several dry-cargo ships, of which two were registered in London and five were registered in Bermuda. The British-flag, American-controlled, United Fruit Company had a Bermudan subsidiary owning five small reefer ships, all registered in London. The American-owned Naess group, which has British connections, had six Bermudan subsidiaries each owning one or two tankers totalling 266,000 tons deadweight. This group, by having a number of one- or two-ship subsidiaries is following the pattern noted earlier for registration under other flags of convenience. All the Naess-owned ships were, however, registered in London.

It is significant that apart from the Vestey group, none of the British shipping interests with Bermudan subsidiaries have adopted Bermudan registration for the ships technically owned in Bermuda and all but one of the foreign-owned Bermudan companies have adopted London registration.[1] A Bermudan company has its profits taxed at Bermudan rates, which is an advantage, but if its ships are registered in Bermuda must pay wages at rates comparable to those paid in Liberian ships in order to attract crews. London registry gets over this problem and enables labour to be engaged on British articles. The fact

[1] All information from *Syren and Shipping* (15 March 1961), pp. 627–9.

that a number of British and foreign companies have chosen to set up Bermudan subsidiaries to own ships, but then register those ships in Britain strongly suggests that the wage cost advantage which Liberian ships are often alleged to possess over British ships because of their lower manning scales is unimportant, if it exists at all.

Although nine British shipping companies, plus the internationally-owned Shell Company have set up Bermudan subsidiaries, the drift to Bermuda which shipping chairmen were threatening in their 1956 speeches has not occurred and while legal obstacles have had a part to play in this, there is little doubt that a way could be found around these. For example, a company could be set up in Bermuda with such capital as could be raised locally and from the profits of its United Kingdom parent. This company could than secure long-term bare boat charters[1] from its parent and use these charters as security for loans to finance the construction of the ships concerned. The United Kingdom company could then replace each of its ships as it reached retirement age by a chartered vessel owned by the Bermudan subsidiary, charter rates being determined from time to time to secure the desired balance between profits available for distribution in the United Kingdom and those available in Bermuda for expansion. In this connection it may be noted that some British liner owners are active in time chartering foreign-owned and manned vessels and putting them on berth in their regular services. This is sometimes done because suitable British ships are not available, but often because such a course is cheaper than extending its own fleet.

American owners have frequently expressed their willingness to adopt the British flag if satisfactory conditions regarding the use of the tonnage in wartime could be arranged. In Washington it is claimed that American-owned ships are registered under nine NATO flags, namely, the Belgian, British, Canadian, Danish, Dutch, French, German, Italian and Norwegian. Such registration concerns chiefly tankers owned by American oil companies and fruit ships owned by subsidiaries of United Fruit.

[1] Whether bare boat charters or charters of fully manned ships would be taken would depend on the relative manning costs in Britain and Bermuda; bare boat charters would presume that British manning costs were lower than Bermudan.

'Such registries represent flags of convenience for practical and economic purposes. However, none of these ships is under effective U.S. control.'[1] Canadian owners have already adopted the British flag to secure protection from Canadian crew costs. Something of the order of 600,000 tons of Greek-owned ships are registered in Britain through the intermediary of companies registered in London, which companies are recorded as the owners. There are many shipowners, however, in addition to Greeks who would concur with the view that '. . . if . . . a law was made permitting foreigners to be owners of British ships, with permission for a percentage of the officers and of the crew to be foreigners as well, I see many . . . running after this potentiality, irrespective of the burden of taxation. . . .'[2]

Is there a solution to the problem of the flag of convenience? Is there really a problem? Undoubtedly, to shipowners in heavily taxed countries the existence of ships owned in countries levying no taxes is a limitation on growth possibilities of a serious nature. However, the problem is only different in degree, not in kind, from that which is caused by variation in taxation rates between fully maritime countries and until all other countries levy identical taxes it is difficult to see how the flag of convenience can be regarded as a unique problem.

The problem for British shipowners is not so much that their profits are taxed at relatively high rates, but that replacement costs of ships have risen practically continuously since 1939 making depreciation reserves calculated, and exempted from taxation, on the basis of original cost, inadequate for the replacement of tonnage at higher prices. The failure of the British taxation authorities to abandon the accounting convention of historical cost as the basis for depreciation, and to allow companies to set up tax-free depreciation funds sufficient to maintain the real value of the assets concerned, has handicapped British shipping as effectively as the refusal of British shipping companies generally to see that in a period of rising prices past reserves, accumulated when prices and profits were lower, are

[1] Report in *Syren and Shipping* (11 May 1960), p. 208, of study 'Flags of Convenience' by the National Academy of Science, National Research Council, Washington.

[2] Mr. George Lemos, article in *Naftilia*, reported in *Syren and Shipping* (3 December 1958), p. 395. The critical condition here is that regarding nationality of crews.

inadequate for expansion. Mere tax-free replacement funds based on the present costs of vessels would not have enabled British companies to expand their fleets sufficiently to fill the need which the Panholib ships filled, and continue to fill. That would have required two things. First, a willingness to raise new capital from whatever source it could be obtained and in particular to use borrowed money the interest payments on which would have been charged to profits before taxation was assessed. Second, a readiness to place orders for ships anywhere in the world where orders could be accepted and quick delivery given. In the period during which the Panholib fleet emerged as a problem British owners displayed neither the willingness nor the readiness. Norwegian owners acted differently and succeeded in expanding their fleets, despite the menace of the flag of convenience.

X

Economics of Shipping Enterprises[1]

Two conditions are necessary if an industry is to be able to expand. First, it must be able to attract and retain capital and labour in competition with other industries. Second, it must be able to sell its product in competition with its competitors. If these two conditions are not satisfied then a failure to expand is inevitable. Put another way, if either of these conditions has not held for British shipping for any significant period, then the first possible answer to the question posed in Chapter I is clearly applicable. The task in this and the two subsequent chapters is to consider the nature of, and the variations in, the economic factors involved in the provision of shipping services in order to test the validity of the first possible answer to the question. Matters relating to the future of the British shipping industry arise in this analysis and, as promised in Chapter I, these will also be pursued so that both the dominant theme (the explanation of the past) and the subordinate theme (the prospects for the future) are intertwined.

This chapter will concentrate mainly on the domestic issues relevant to the first condition related above. This will be done by considering the economics of different ship types, their cost structures and the profitability of their operations. The international issues with which the second condition is concerned will be considered in the next chapter, while the statistical material concerning the most important cost item, labour, is presented in Chapter XII.

[1] In this chapter it is possible only to scratch the surface of the subject. A. S. Svendsen, *Sea Transport and Shipping Economics* (Seeverkehr und Schiffahrtswirtschaft, Bremen, 1958), covers the subject quite thoroughly. Thornton discusses the organization of liner companies. On tramp shipping, H. Gripaios, *Tramp Shipping* (London, 1959) and F. M. Fisser, *Tramp Shipping* (Trampschiffahrt, Bremen, 1957), may be consulted for further information. Fisser's work is more analytic and less descriptive than that of Gripaios. On tankers, Koopmans and R. S. Nielsen, *Oil Tanker Economics* (Bremen, 1959), can be referred to for matters not covered here.

LINERS

Liners constitute the largest single group in British shipping; over one-half of the total, and three-quarters of the dry-cargo, tonnage is classed as liner tonnage (see Table 50). The term 'Liner' covers a wide range of vessels, the element of homogeneity in the classification being found in the nature of the employment of the ships. Liners are ships plying a fixed route or routes, sailing according to a pre-determined schedule, which offer cargo and/or passenger space at fixed rates to those who wish to have goods transported or to make journeys.

It is usually said that liners sail on schedule whether full or empty, but this is an over-simplification when applied generally to all liners. Passenger liners normally observe fixed schedules and if they are also mail carriers the schedule will be invariably respected, barring incidents beyond the control of the shipowner. Cargo liners, which may carry no more than twelve passengers, operate somewhat more flexibly and there are usually margins of tolerance in sailing and arrival times which enable them to approach more nearly to full utilization of capacity than can a ship tied to a fixed schedule.

The previous paragraph implicitly assumes a complete dichotomy between the passenger vessel and the cargo vessel, recognizing only the cargo liner carrying twelve passengers or fewer as a composite type. In fact, the majority of passenger liners also carry cargo, but when they do so the needs of passengers tend to take precedence over the needs of cargo.

The provision of both passenger accommodation and cargo space in one vessel appears to be an obvious economy, both in first cost and in running cost, compared with providing two specialized ships. Historically, liners were developed in the third quarter of the nineteenth century when steamers replaced sailing ships on world trade routes. They were usually combined passenger and cargo carriers while those ships which carried only cargo were generally tramps. The cargo liner, as such, appeared at a somewhat later date and the main development occurred during the inter-war period when the decline in large-scale migration changed the relation between the passenger space and cargo capacity required in the world. The historical sequence means that when conferences were developed to cover the carriage of freight they were based on the particular economics of carrying cargo in ships with extensive passenger accommodation and which had, in consequence, to conform fairly rigidly to fixed schedules.

The greater flexibility of cargo than of passenger liners does not mean that they always sail fully loaded. A simple calculation may show the shipping manager that the extra freight earned by waiting to load some low-rated cargo would be less than the cost of holding the ship for another tide. Liner trade routes are often composite and a delay in one port may mean berthing difficulties, loss of cargo, or wasted time by having a dead week-end in port later in the voyage. Delays waiting for cargo may upset the conference trip-sharing agreements (see Chapter XIII) and so not be possible within the existing arrangements. None of these reasons for sailing with empty space are, however, reasons for which a shipper should be asked to pay. While it is undoubtedly true that partly laden vessels do sail so that shippers may be ensured of regular facilities, yet it is also true that once a ship ceases to be tied to a rigid schedule by the needs of passengers, the provision of regular services is only one reason why ships may sail with empty space.

Liners operate either within conferences or non-conference. The position of liners within conferences is discussed in Chapter XIII. The non-conference liner may be operating independently on a route not covered by other liners or the liner may be in competition with conference liners, cutting freight rates below conference levels, or offering to all shippers the lowest conference rate. This situation is always unstable and it may generally be assumed that where conference and non-conference liners are running side by side, sooner or later the non-conference shipowner will join the conference unless his competition is so limited that it cannot worry the conference or he himself has no desire to join the conference. In the latter situation, the non-conference operator faces the possibility that the conference will break down and a period of unrestrained competition ensue which forces him into a reconstituted conference.

Economics of Shipping Enterprises

(a) Passenger Liners

Outside the North Atlantic, the specialized passenger ship with no cargo accommodation was a rarity in regular services before the 1939-45 war. Since then, entirely passenger liners have been built by several British lines trading outside the North Atlantic, while Dutch liners excluded from the Indonesian trade have been refitted without cargo space for round-the-world services.

There are several advantages in separating passengers and cargo. First, the shipowner can meet the demands of passengers for higher speeds, without having to provide power to haul cargo around the world. Second, delays in port when the capital invested in passenger accommodation is not earning can be reduced. As a result, fewer vessels of the most expensive type are required because each passenger berth can carry more passengers each year. Third, the large staff of caterers and stewards are not left idle[1] while the ship is in port loading and discharging, or, if the port is other than a terminal port, the passengers are not eating without being transported. Fifth, the ship is less affected by unrest on the waterfront; a delay to any ship is expensive to a shipowner, but a delay to a ship full of passengers can be near-ruinous.

It was shown in Chapter VII that passenger travel by sea is generally declining in favour of air travel. This decline is most apparent in the case of first-class travel for which the elasticity of substitution between air and sea is high and favours air travel when the prices of the two are, as is generally the case, similar. The changing pattern of demand for sea travel has been recognized and in new, or reconstructed, ships the proportion of first-class to tourist class accommodation is smaller than on older vessels. The price elasticity of demand for cheaper passages is quite high; this is confirmed by the success of the block booking of liners in the South African trade which enables off-season

---

[1] Here the changing conditions of employment on ships is a relevant factor altering the economics of mixed passenger/cargo ships. Formerly, crew were engaged only for each voyage and were discharged as soon as the ship reached port. This meant that crew costs did not occur while the ship was in her home port. Now, however, conditions are more secure for crews so that shipowners cannot ignore crew costs in any port at all.

travel to be offered at greatly reduced fares. An extension of the scheme operated on the Cape route to the North Atlantic has not been favourably received by the British conference lines which claim that '. . . conference agreements would not allow them to offer their ships to the public at reduced fares. . . .'[1] In the 1930s the rigidity of the conference rules was avoided by classing Atlantic liners as cabin-class ships for which the conference provided no scale of fares. Shortly before the maiden voyage of the *Queen Mary* in 1936 Cunard announced its intention of running her as a cabin-class vessel and of withdrawing from the conference. The conference thereupon agreed to recognize the classification and cabin class became the top class on all principal North Atlantic ships; after the second world war the name first class was restored.[2] This experience shows that it is possible to throw off the dead hand of conference rules.

For the completely specialized passenger ship total costs are made up as follows:

Organization overheads:
    office and agency costs
    depreciation

Voyage overheads:
    insurance
    crew costs, including wages, victualling and social payments
    fuel
    repairs and maintenance
    port charges

Voyage variables:
    food, laundry and other passenger costs.

The relation of these categories for any ship will vary according to the speed, age and size of the ship and the amount of service provided on board. No real information is available about the actual division of total costs between these three categories. The following division covers some of the cost items for a 30,000 tons British liner of 21·5 knots employed in the Australian trade:

[1] *The Times* (20 April 1961).
[2] N. R. P. Bonsor, 'North Atlantic Seaway' (Prescot, 1955), p. 29.

	Percentage of total
Annual capital cost[a]	49·27
Crew costs	20·54
Repairs, stores, survey, etc.[b]	10·99
Fuel	19·20
	100·00

[a] Assumes 5 per cent depreciation and 5 per cent interest on capital.

[b] Includes survey allowance on an assumed annual cost of the first five years of the ship's life.

Source: See Table 41.

The items omitted from this classification are office overheads, insurance, port charges and passenger costs. If these were included and the interest on capital excluded, it is estimated that the resulting division of costs for a new liner registered in Britain and with a speed of about 20 knots would be approximately:

Organization overheads	30 per cent
Voyage overheads:	
crew costs	20 ,, ,,
fuel	20 ,, ,,
others	20 ,, ,,
Voyage variables	10 ,, ,,

The difference in cost between sailing with an empty ship and a full ship, once the ship is committed to the voyage and the crew engaged, is slight. It is clear, also, that the cost savings to be obtained by cutting standards of food (but not service) to passengers are minimal. The three most important single items of total cost are depreciation, crew costs and fuel.

The passenger liner owner, faced with this cost structure, can keep his costs down in three ways.

First, new ships need to be built with an eye to future adaptation to meet changing conditions. This means, generally, an initial reserve of speed to permit a quickening of voyage times. Further, it means that the internal structure of the ship must be such that changes in accommodation can readily be made without undue restriction from structural arrangements adopted to secure the necessary strength. A passenger liner maintained in good condition and regularly brought up to date can be reckoned to have a useful life of at least thirty years, although this will not apply if insufficient reserves of power were provided initially so that the ship has to be forced to maintain schedules later in her life. If the life span of the vessel can be lengthened in these ways, the annual depreciation charge is reduced.

Second, voyage times must be shortened by the adoption of higher speeds. This reduces the depreciation charge for the fleet as a whole by reducing the number of units needed. Within the individual vessel, it reduces wage costs per trip by shortening voyages. The cost of the extra speed is, of course, high and British shipowners in the past apparently have too often looked only at the extra cost of speed and rejected the fast ship on that basis, to discover later that faster ships would have paid better. The change in the planned speed of the *Pendennis Castle* which was on the stocks at the time of the merger between Union Castle and Clan Line (see Chapter XIV) shows neatly the difference between the traditional and the dynamic approach to the question of speed.

The high speed solution to rising costs is one related partly to the economics of the individual ship, but it concerns mainly the economics of the whole line. For any individual ship it is unlikely that the saving in wages by raising speed by 1 knot will offset the extra cost of that knot and it is not until speed is raised by several knots in order to eliminate a whole ship that the big economies start being made; on the North Atlantic in the 1930s Cunard had to jump from 22 knots to 28 knots in order to provide a weekly service with two ships instead of with three.

(b) *Cargo Liners*

In the first paragraph of this chapter liners were defined solely in terms of service and this is the relevant definition for most purposes. Cargo liners do, however, differ from other dry-cargo vessels, being generally differently equipped in the cargo holds and faster than tramp ships. Much of the former difference in speed has disappeared as a consequence of improvements in propulsive machinery. These improvements, together with increases in wage rates, have altered the economic balance between slow ships taking a long time for each voyage, and thus incurring crew costs for a long period, and faster ships making quicker voyages and thereby saving crew costs.

The type, as opposed to the functional, distinction between liners and tramps was not, however, only a matter of speed. Ships with extensive refrigerated capacity normally operate on liner services, as such ships are inherently unsuited to freelance work which places a premium on flexibility. Even within the category of refrigerated ships there is further specialization depending upon whether the vessel is a meat carrier, fruit carrier or a carrier of dairy produce. This means that refrigerated vessels are generally tied fairly closely to the trade for which they were originally designed and, by operating only on that, or perhaps another similar, route become functionally liners in this respect although they may not operate within a conference. But the more specialized ships become then, paradoxically, the less like liners they are in terms of cargo composition and freighting arrangements. Although highly specialized vessels resemble liners in following a constant route, voyage after voyage, they resemble tramps in lifting cargoes each of which is homogeneous. The practical decision whether such vessels are liners or tramps will then depend on the conditions under which the cargo is carried. If the shipper buys all the cargo space for one voyage, or for a series of voyages or a period of years, then there is little practical reason to think of the vessel concerned as a liner. If the ship's space is not hired as a whole, but a charge made per ton for the actual cargo carried, for practical purposes the ship is a liner. Where the goods, although homogeneous in nature are despatched by numerous shippers each sending small consignments, then a liner-type operation is required. Where, however, the shippers co-operate to form a producers' association for purposes of shipment, whole ships can be engaged and a liner-type operation is inappropriate. It is largely because the former mode of shipment was the more common in the past that British refrigerated vessels are owned mainly by liner companies while, for example, tankers are not.

Without arguing a case about other specialized ship types, the general conclusion can be reached that the more specialized is a vessel the less like the traditional concept of a liner she becomes. Specialization in this context needs careful interpretation. An exclusively passenger ship is clearly, in one sense, completely specialized, that is, she cannot carry iron ore, bulk petroleum, coal, or any other such commodity. However, she is not specialized within her function as a passenger carrier as she can carry any people[1] and, as argued above, can increasingly do this on any route, while it is the exception, not the rule, for a passenger vessel to be entirely booked by one organization. A cargo vessel which can, and normally does, handle cargo of different types for an assortment of shippers remains a liner in function, even if not adhering to a rigid schedule; a vessel which carries a homogeneous cargo on behalf of one shipper is not a liner in function. A ship could, of course, carry a homogeneous cargo on behalf of a number of shippers and so remain a liner. The increasing size of trading and manufacturing enterprises and the growth of exporters' co-operatives has reduced the number of individual parcels of bulk commodities travelling and increased the size of the individual parcel; this change has helped to make possible charter, rather than liner, freighting arrangements for cargoes of a homogeneous nature. Whenever the parcel carried on behalf of a single shipper (whether importer or exporter) reaches the size of a ship load, it ceases to be a liner cargo. It then becomes possible for the shipper to charter a ship to move the cargo, or, if such parcels are frequent, to take a ship on time charter or even to build his own fleet. He will take either of these latter courses if he finds that the fluctuations in tramp voyage rates create difficulties for forward planning, or if existing liner services cannot move his goods in the most convenient units to him or at rates which are not more than the cost to him of transporting the goods in his own ships.

At this point it may be asked why there has been a tendency toward specialization of function and why, if it is economic, it did not occur earlier? There are several factors which are important here.

First, for most goods the cost of sea transport is small in relation to the value of the goods. In the case of conference freight charges this is deliberate and 'what traffic will bear' is an important determinant of rates. Tramp rates are based on the supply and demand for tonnage and for much of the periods between about 1875 and 1914 and between 1921 and 1939 there

---

[1] Possible exceptions to this are the pilgrim ships which operate in Far Eastern waters and the troopships operated by the British India and Bibby lines.

was a surplus of shipping tonnage, or at least an adequacy, so that it was rare for tramp rates to be such that freight costs were a significant part of the final price of goods. The consequence was that producers seeking to reduce costs ignored freight charges because even large proportionate reductions in these would have been small in relation to the final prices of their products. Between 1945 and 1958, however, the same surplus of tonnage did not exist.

Second, throughout the twentieth century there has been a growth in the scale of enterprises, frequently by the amalgamation of smaller enterprises to secure economies of scale. This change reduced the number of individual shippers of cargoes, particularly of bulk cargoes such as coal, ore, newsprint, grain, wool, so that individual shippers increasingly found that their shipping requirements were continuous rather than occasional and, therefore, increasingly susceptible to their influence. Alongside of this change has been a dissemination of world markets, so that bulk products are less frequently shipped in small parcels by individual producers for sale in the great commercial centres of the world, but are bought before shipment and shipped on account of the purchasers.

Third, developments in marine engineering, in ship construction and in cargo-handling equipment have produced the possibility of constructing ships capable of carrying homogeneous cargoes of all types without incurring problems relating to trim, the movement of bulk cargoes and so on. It can, of course, equally be argued that this has been a consequential rather than a causal factor.

Finally, has been the growth in the volume of world sea-borne dry-cargo trade from about 300 million tons in 1913, of which about 100 million tons was coal, to about 500 million tons currently. More goods moving provided opportunities for specialized ships to move those goods.

All the changes which have taken place have meant that the liner owner as such has had, if he was to command an expanding fleet, to abandon many of the older ideas of liner ownership, to build specialized ships let on time or voyage charter while at the same time constantly revising his ideas about the most economical speeds for his ships. It is generally the case that an established enterprise is less likely to initiate changes than a new entrant. This means that the changes discussed above were less likely to produce a response among existing liner owners, and the shipping industry dominated by those owners, than in an industry with a smaller stake in the existing order. It then follows that the older industry, having resisted the change initially, suffered an increasing incremental disadvantage rendering it more difficult for it to make the change at a later date.

In summary of the argument so far, it may be said that the traditional rôle of the liner and of the liner company has been changing. The change was slow, but noticeable, between the wars but has quickened since 1945. The economically successful liner owner has been the one who has changed with the trend and adapted his fleet and his view of his functions over time.

If the generalized concept of 'liner' as maintained by the shipping industry is considered, that is, a return to the concept of the first paragraph, is it possible to say anything about the cost structure of cargo liner operations? The short answer to this question is, very little. Even if a great deal of information was available, it would be difficult to make any useful generalizations because the costs borne by shipowners vary greatly from trade to trade and for ships of different ages, speeds and general types. Further, some costs, such as wages, vary greatly from country to country while others, such as fuel costs, do not. This question of the international variability of costs is taken up in Chapter XI. Within the shipping of any one country the most highly variable elements of costs are the handling costs of cargo and port charges. The extent of the variation can be seen from the analysis in Table 35 of twenty-two operating accounts relating to the period 1949–56 and covering cargo liners owned by two American companies. It is clear from the figures in the table that there is no one percentage distribution of costs which can be regarded as representative even for American cargo liners generally.[1]

What is clear from the figures in the table, however, is the

---

[1] As a class American cargo liners are more homogeneous than those of any other country because they are all variations on a few basic designs of the Federal Maritime Board. For this reason, cost variations between ships should be smaller for American ships than for any others. Variations due to differential increases in the various costs over the period were not particularly important.

high proportion of costs which are independent of the volume of cargo carried.

TABLE 35. Analysis of twenty-two operating accounts of American vessels, 1949 to 1956

	Cost items:						
	Crew %	Fuel %	Repairs %	Insurance %	Port expenses %	Cargo handling %	Other %
Average of all accounts	30	12	6	8	10	25	9
Highest percentage	39	16	10	12	14	45	13
Lowest percentage	20	7	3	6	6	14	5
Range within which 50 per cent of observations lie	25–30	10–13	5–8	7–8	7–9	23–27	8–10

Source: Calculated from legible accounts appearing in the published evidence of the Celler Committee.

Cargo liner costs fall into the same three groups as passenger liner costs. First, are the organization overheads, which include interest, office and agency expenses, depreciation on vessels, that is, those items which can be changed only by altering the structure or scale of the organization. Second, are the voyage overheads, costs such as wages and victualling for the crew, fuel, insurance, repairs and maintenance and port charges; these are costs which are unalterable once the voyage has been scheduled. The third part of total costs is the cost of cargo handling and this is the only short period variable cost.

The relation between the three parts of the total costs will depend mainly on the nationality of the ship being considered, the proportion of port time to sea time, and the age, condition and type of ship. For a ship owned in a high-wage country, wage costs will be a higher proportion of total costs than for a comparable ship owned in a low-wage country. Repair costs for a new ship are relatively less important than for an old ship. A ship on a 10,000 mile route with calls only at the terminal ports will incur relatively lower port and cargo charges than will another ship on the same route which calls at a number of intermediate ports.

With all these limitations in mind, clearly nothing other than an approximate statement can be made about the percentages of the various classes of costs to total costs. Taking a modern cargo liner with only 'normal' repair costs, that is, only costs of general maintenance and repairing damage, the following division is suggested:

Organizational overheads	35–40 per cent
Voyage overheads	45–50 ,, ,,
Variable costs	10–20 ,, ,,

For any individual ship a widely different cost distribution may apply, but on the basis of the limited information available it seems unlikely that for any cargo liner company as a whole the cost distribution will diverge very far from this pattern.

Given a cost distribution of this nature, the problem of the determination of freight rates (discussed in Chapter XIII) is clear. With completely free competition rates can be forced down in the short period until they cover only 10–20 per cent of total costs because, so long as variable costs are covered it will always pay to carry cargo on a scheduled service rather than sail with empty space. This factor is the basic reason for the adoption of devices to regulate the competition between liner companies, and some limitation of competition is clearly necessary to maintain services in the long run. If the possibility exists of choosing between running the vessel or not running it, then it will pay to maintain the service in the short run provided rates are sufficient to cover 60–65 per cent of total costs. If full utilization of capacity could always be secured by thinning out services the range of variation of freight rates in response to trading conditions is then determined: they would vary between those required to cover, say, 110 per cent of total costs and 60 to 65 per cent of total costs, given always that competition is regulated to prevent rates being forced to variable costs. In practice, however, the need to maintain conference berth rights, to preserve the goodwill of shippers or to avoid giving an opening for non-conference competition means that services cannot be thinned out when trade is slack in order to preserve full utilization and the range of variation in rates is narrower than would be the case if full utilization could always be secured.

(c) *Liner Profits*

It is not possible to say anything meaningful about the profits of British liner companies before 1932. 'Unfortunately, the income of Liner Companies is so presented in the profit and loss accounts that it is absolutely impossible to ascertain how much profit or loss has been made during the year on the running of steamers.'[1] Since 1932 the position has been a little clearer, although the figures of profits from voyages which are published by each company are not based on any standard classification and it is not possible to amend them to produce a standardized series. Another difficulty is that profit figures can only acquire meaning by being related to some other series, preferably the real capital which was employed to earn those profits. There are no figures made public by the shipping companies which can be used for this purpose.

In the absence of better information it has been necessary to use the voyage profit figures of the shipping companies as they stand. These have been related (see Table 36) to a series of capital values constructed to take account of the current replacement costs of ships each year by similar vessels purchased in the market. The capital series used, therefore, is based on building costs of new ships adjusted to take account of the age of the ships actually in use and the market expectations about future earnings as shown by the difference between the building cost and the price of a ready new ship each year. This has produced what may be regarded as the real value of a ton of shipping each year and voyage profits per ton have been expressed as percentages of those annual values. The results are given in Table 36.

The figures in Table 36 bear no relation to what the companies themselves think of as their profit rates. The accountant's conception of the profit rate is profit expressed as a proportion of either paid-up capital or of the depreciated historic cost of the earning assets. The conception on which Table 36 is based is that of profit expressed as a proportion of the capital employed

[1] *Fairplay* (7 January 1932), p. 108.

as valued currently, that is, ignoring historic cost altogether. In times of falling ship values the profit figures shown in Table 36 would be higher than the accountants' figures, for example, in the 1930s; in times of rising ship values the profit rates shown by the accountants would exceed those shown in Table 36, for example, in the 1950s.

TABLE 36. Voyage profits as percentages of real capital values for liner companies, 1932–9 and 1948–60

Year	Per cent		Year	Per cent		Year	Per cent
1932	8		1948	20		1955	10
1933	10		1949	22		1956	8
1934	10		1950	18		1957	14
1935	9		1951	10		1958	4
1936	12		1952	15		1959	13
1937	16		1953	16		1960	11
1938	20		1954	13			
1939	14						

Note: The percentages are shown for the years in which the accounts were made up. Accounts presented, say, in 1932 refer to operations partly or wholly in 1931.

Source: Voyage profit data from *Fairplay* sample.

In calculating Table 36 no allowance was made for depreciation. The customary rate for shipping companies is 5 per cent per annum and at least this should be deducted from the profit rates shown in the table. Should the depreciation, however, be based on historic cost or on the current asset values? The economic answer is clear and having adopted an economic rather than an accountancy definition of the profit rate, the same definition is used for depreciation. On this basis, in 1958 alone the liner companies failed to cover depreciation. Other relatively poor years were 1932, 1935 and 1956, but apart from these years the liner companies in the sample earned more than enough to cover current interest on the capital employed after allowing proper depreciation.

At almost any time during the whole period the liner companies as a whole earned sufficient to justify new issues of capital for purposes of expansion and their alleged inability to raise new capital was a consequence of attempts to rely entirely on self-financing by limiting dividends not of any inability to earn profits. In fact, none of the liner companies listed in the Stock Exchange Year Book raised any new capital between 1945 and 1960, although at least one repaid capital and a number increased their capitals by making bonus share issues. The policy of self-financing is a traditional one, but not one permitting of great expansion. If the liner companies had wished to expand their operations this could have been done readily between 1948 and 1958, and again between 1936 and 1939, by distributing higher dividends to attract investors. The profit rates shown make it clear also that the liner companies as a whole could, with perfect safety, have borrowed money for fleet expansion. This could have been done either by borrowing against time charters on new vessels, or by the issue of debentures. In fact, the total of debentures and loans of the liner companies in the *Fairplay* sample fell from £37 million in 1939 to £17 million in 1960, there having been a decline to £5·2 million in 1955 followed by an increase in subsequent years. In the same period creditors rose £22 million to £105 million this item including bank overdrafts and other relatively short-term borrowing. An expansive force can be inferred from the increase in creditors, but as debtors, investments, stores and cash in the same period rose from £81 million to £238 million, it is by no means certain that the liner companies as a whole increased their net indebtedness.

(d) *Costs of Liner Tonnage*

A particular aspect of the expansion of liner fleets which needs to be considered here is the cost of liner tonnage in relation to other tonnage. No comprehensive figures are obtainable, but on the basis of limited information it appears that the relation between costs per ton of different classes of vessels, if all are expressed as percentages of the cost of passenger liner tonnage of the highest class, would be:

Passenger liners	100
Cargo liner	40–50
Tramp	30–35
Tanker or Bulk Carrier	25–30

Since the war British owners have built approximately one million tons of high-class liner tonnage. On the basis of the figures above, the same amount of capital would have built about two million tons of cargo liner tonnage, or three million tons of tramp tonnage or four million tons of tanker or bulk carrier tonnage. There is no suggestion that British liner owners were wrong to use their capital intensively rather than extensively, although it is undoubted that a greater fleet in terms of tonnage would have been owned if resources had been used to build cheaper vessels. Such a fleet would not necessarily have been more profitable or economical. Strangely, the difference in the values of different classes of tonnage is not reflected in the balance sheets of shipping companies; in 1960 the liner companies in the *Fairplay* sample valued their ships on average at £59·8 per ton while the tramp companies valued their fleets on average at £60·5 per ton. This situation arises partly from the respective age structures of the fleets but mainly from the financial conservatism of liner owners in establishing hidden reserves in the form of undervalued assets.

Although the capital resources of the liner companies would have gone further in terms of tonnage if they had been spread more thinly there was no reason why an either/or decision had to be made. As argued above, liner companies with their tremendous reputations for stability, and their profitability since the war, could have increased their capital resources either by borrowing[1] or by raising new equity capital. Then the decision to spread capital deeply in liners instead of thinly in tramps or tankers need not have meant that the enterprises had to foreswear expansion.

TRAMPS

The term tramp is often taken to have a pejorative connotation because in the past tramp tonnage was inferior to liner tonnage, either in terms of its original construction or because tramping was the last refuge before the breaker's yard of the aged cargo

---

[1] Although long-term borrowing has been avoided, overdrafts have been common, and much of the increase in creditors represented short-term credit used to cover the costs of new ships. For four lines in 1960, creditors exceeded the item Investments, Debtors, Stores and Cash, etc.

liner. Properly, however, the term tramp should be used as a functional, not as a qualitative, term.

The traditional function of a tramp ship is to move about the world in search of, or carrying, cargoes. A tramp is usually engaged to load a full cargo to be carried between any two ports. Chartering is traditionally by the trip, the charterer arranging in London, say, for a ship to lift a grain cargo from the Plate and carry it to a port to be specified within, say, a certain European range. The shipowner agrees the rate and makes the ship available at the Plate port at the agreed date. He is responsible for the manning, victualling, fuelling and so on of the ship, but not for handling the cargo which is the responsibility of the charterer. The ship is under charterer's orders from the commencement of the charter period until discharge is completed when she is handed back to the owner ready to undertake a different voyage. By not being tied to a fixed route, the tramp provides an important element of flexibility to sea-transport patterns.

The market for tramp ships is practically perfect as there are large numbers of owners and charterers while owners' brokers and charterers' brokers have almost complete knowledge of rates being paid in the main chartering centres for each different trade and of the ships receiving those rates. Each individual rate has to be sufficient to cover the addition to the costs of the shipowner of making the trip, with no problem of incomplete utilization arising.

The costs of a tramp ship can be divided into two classes, namely organization overheads and variable, or voyage, costs; there are no cargo handling charges. The additional costs of making a trip rather than lying idle are less than the paid out variable costs because the short-run alternative to making a voyage is not cost-free idleness. It follows, therefore, that the variable costs which must be covered if the trip is to be made are the paid-out variable costs less the costs which would be incurred if the ship laid up.

In the short run, tramps will continue to operate so long as losses through operations fall short of the losses through lay-up. In the long run the response of the industry to a slump by permanently removing excess capacity is slow. The natural slowness is reinforced because old ships with heavy repair costs, making their continued operation unprofitable for high-wage operators, are frequently not scrapped but sold to owners in lower-wage countries. Owners in such countries, unless they are receiving government assistance, can rarely afford to purchase ships unless they are available at prices only just above scrap value, but their low wage-costs enable them to sustain the high repair costs on old ships.

Ships are temporarily withdrawn from the market and laid up whenever rates fall below variable costs, although they tend to return quickly whenever rates show a sign of rising. The position is, however, complicated by the costs of periodic surveys. Although survey costs are not part of short-period variable costs unless rates are sufficient to cover the ordinary variable costs plus writing off the survey cost over the inter-survey period, the ship will be laid up. When rates rise again, a ship for which the survey has been postponed will not move out of lay-up unless the rise in rates is expected to be lasting.

The incidence of surveys has several effects on the movement of rates in slumps and recoveries. If a slump is a sudden one in which rates fall quickly to a low level, then ships not due for survey will be laid up. If recovery follows quickly ships can move speedily out of lay-up and so dampen the rise in rates; this, for example, happened in 1960 when trade began to recover from the post-1957 recession. On the other hand, a slow slump in which rates gradually sag downwards will be characterized by ships due for survey going into lay-up berths instead of having the survey. If the slump is a long one, by the time it ends most of the laid-up ships will be due for survey, whether they were due when laid up or not. In this case, the movement of ships out of lay-up in response to an upward movement of rates will be relatively slow. This can produce the position in which rates rise strongly because of a shortage of ready ships while there is a volume of laid-up tonnage. This was the position in the recovery between mid-1936 and mid-1937 when trade recovered more quickly than ships could be transferred from lay-up to active service.

At the recovery end of the cycle, an increase in the demand for tramp shipping leads to improving freight rates and, after all tonnage is employed, rates carry on rising until either the demand falls off or the supply of ships increases due to new building. The experience of all recorded periods of high rates is massive building of tonnage in excess of requirements and an eventual break in rates. The break in rates does not immediately stop the building of tonnage, however, for during the boom shipbuilding order books will have lengthened so that when the boom breaks shipbuilders have unstarted orders on their books. The contracts in respect of these might be cancelled but they are just as likely to continue. This may be because the contracting owners are holding time-charters on the vessels to be built, or because they have the money in hand and might as well use it to build a ship as in any other way, but it is just as likely to be because ups and downs are an integral part of the life of the tramp owner and, in the downturn from one boom, he can just as reasonably look forward to another boom in eighteen months or two years as to a continuation of depressed conditions. The result is that deliveries of new tonnage may continue for two or three years after the break of a boom, although no new orders are being placed, and the entry of these new ships to the markets exacerbates the depression in rates.

The result of these forces is extreme variations in the level of tramp profits year by year, short periods of high profits being generally followed by longer periods of low profits. This is illustrated by the figures in Table 37.

Over the fifty-one-year period profits per ton varied from £0·1 in 1933–4 to £16·2 in 1956–7. The sudden variations year by year are apparent, even though masked by the data which is compiled annually whereas breaks or rises in rates can occur at any time during the year.

The figures of percentages of profit per ton value are rougher than is the case with comparable figures for liners. Like the figures shown in Table 36 they do not correspond to the profit rates as shown by the companies themselves. For example, for 1926–7, when shipbuilding prices were falling, the real profit rate shown in the table is 46 per cent, whereas the accountant's rate for the year was 12 per cent; in 1951–2, however, when shipbuilding prices were rising, the respective rates are 34 per cent and 61 per cent.

Although the profit rate shown varied from 66 per cent in

1912–14 to 2 per cent in 1933–4, it is significant that in the table a positive rate of profit before deducting depreciation is shown for all years; profit net of depreciation at 5 per cent is positive for all years except the two years 1932–3 and 1933–4. It is also significant that in general the rate of profit shown in the table

TABLE 37. Tramp ship voyage profits per ton, 1909–10 to 1959–60

Year	£ per ton	% per[a] ton	Year	£ per ton	% per[a] ton	Year	£ per ton	% per[a] ton
1909–10	0·5	18	1926–27	1·5	42	1943–44	1·2	
1910–11	0·8		1927–28	1·9	46	1944–45	1·7	
1911–12	1·4		1928–29	0·7	17	1945–46	2·9	16
1912–13	2·6	66	1929–30	0·6	15	1946–47	7·3	32
1913–14	1·9	66	1930–31	0·3	7	1947–48	7·8	26
1914–15	2·0	37	1931–32	0·3	8	1948–49	5·8	21
1915–16	5·5	39	1932–33	0·1	3	1949–50	4·5	20
1916–17	3·3		1933–34	0·1	2	1950–51	5·2	15
1917–18	1·7		1934–35	0·3	8	1951–52	15·1	34
1918–19	3·0	25	1935–36	0·8	20	1952–53	11·0	26
1919–20	5·7	39	1936–37	1·6	32	1953–54	5·5	14
1920–21	3·8	28	1937–38	2·8	40	1954–55	4·9	10
1921–22	1·8	28	1938–39	1·3		1955–56	10·3	16
1922–23	1·5	34	1939–40	1·3		1956–57	16·2	26
1923–24	1·2	26	1940–41	1·6		1957–58	11·4	23
1924–25	1·1	26	1941–42	1·6		1958–59	3·8	8
1925–26	1·1	25	1942–43	1·5		1959–60	3·3	7

a Based on calculated real values per ton for each year.

Source: Calculated from *Fairplay* sample of cargo boat earnings and estimated prices of *Fairplay* standard ship adjusted for age, etc.

for the post-1945 period has been below that in the supposedly depressed twenties. There are two conclusions to be drawn from this. The first is that the profit rates for the 1920s support the argument of Chapter IV that one reason for the apparent distress of tramp shipping before 1930 was the failure of the enterprises concerned to write down their capitals to take account of the fall in values after 1920. This was more important for tramp companies than for liner companies because a substantial proportion of the tramp shipping of the period was owned by companies which had either been formed, or reorganized, in the period 1915–20 when values were generally high. The second conclusion is that the overall performance in the 1950s in relation to that in the 1920s shows clearly the way in which the economics of tramp ship ownership on the conventional pattern have moved against Britain.

The discussion so far has concerned the traditional type of tramp ship capable of carrying a wide variety of bulk cargoes or doubling on a liner service and hired on charters covering single voyages. However, there have been two developments away from this traditional pattern. The first of these changes has been an increasing specialization of function and the second the increasing use of time charters.

Specialization occurred first in the carriage of oil. At first oil for shipment was cased and transported by dry-cargo ships. Before the first world war, however, tank ships capable of carrying oil in bulk were developed. They were owned by the oil companies and used only in their own trades and so the carriage of oil was removed from the sphere of true tramp operations until a fleet of independently-owned tankers grew up. Apart from tankers, the chief development of specialized dry-cargo carriers occurred after 1950, with two periods of marked growth in the tonnage of such vessels.

The first period was in 1956–7 when specialized tonnage was developed from T2 tankers for the carriage of coal from Hampton Roads to Europe. Tankers are eminently suited for conversion into dry-cargo bulk carriers because of their longitudinal framing. The rash of conversions in 1956–7 was the result of the high level of coal rates ruling at the time and the desire of owners to put more general tramp ships on the trade than were, in fact, available. Rates of nearly £6 per ton were paid, which may be compared with average rates for other years as follows:[1]

1949	50s.	1954	35s. 6d.
1950	51s. 6d.	1955	58s.
1951	81s. 6d.	1956	82s. 6d.
1952	39s. 6d.	1957	55s.
1953	32s. 6d.	1958	23s.

Source: Daily Freight Register.

The second period started in 1958–9 and was, paradoxically, the result of the low level of freight rates. The freight index of the Norwegian Shipping News (1947 = 100) fell from 152·7 in 1956 to 78 in 1958; the Chamber of Shipping index (1952 = 100) fell

[1] All rates are Hampton Roads to Holland and near European ports.

from 157·0 to 67·1 and the Italian International Freight Index (1938 = 100) fell from 537 to 240. At these low rates properly converted bulk carriers could make a living while conventional tramp ships could not. Practically unconverted tankers were used in grain trades and because of their large deadweight capacity could survive at freight rates below the variable costs of conventional tramp ships while their entry to the market served to maintain the low level of rates.

The bulk carrier fleet at the beginning of 1961 is shown in Table 38. It can be seen that nearly one-half of all bulk carriers are ore carriers which have been built in response to the increase in the world demand for metals and the exhaustion of deposits in manufacturing countries. Of the 471 bulk carriers noted, 58 were converted tankers, while the others have been built specially, or converted from other types of vessel. Sixty per cent of the total tonnage was registered under the flags of Liberia, Norway, Britain and Sweden, the British share being 11·7 per cent and the Norwegian share 14·6 per cent. The Liberian registered tonnage was owned in either Greece or America, but mostly in America.

TABLE 38. World bulk carriers, 1 January 1961

	Ore carriers		Others	
	Number	*000's tons deadweight*	*Number*	*000's tons deadweight*
Converted tankers	29	402	21	329
Ore/Oil carriers[a]	57	1,502		
Coastal carriers			23	262
Others	144	3,090	197	3,126
Total	230	4,994	241	3,717

[a] Includes eight converted tankers of 122,000 tons deadweight.

Source: Reproduced from *World Bulk Carriers, 1961,* by courtesy of Fearnley & Egers Chartering Co. Ltd., Oslo.

Although speculators have entered the market and the building of bulk carriers has probably been carried too far, at least in the early 1960s, there is no doubt that their development represents a break from the traditional pattern which will continue. This is particularly the case in the growing ore trade;

shipments of ore from Spain have more than trebled since 1949, from Brazil increased over five times and from Marmagoa have increased over thirty times; total ore shipments in 1960 were over 100 million tons, that is, about one-fifth of the world's sea-borne dry-cargo trade, including the Great Lakes traffic. Ore shipments are now of about the same size as coal shipments before 1913, but British shipping carries a significantly smaller proportion of the world's ore cargoes in the 1960s than of the world's coal exports in the pre-1914 period. This cannot be attributed to the shipping policies of other countries as the bulk carriers are owned largely in countries which either do not produce or import ore or which do not assist their national shipping fleets. Bulk carriers are not restricted to ore and ships have been designed or converted for the bulk carriage of '. . . phosphate rock, liquid gases, cars, wine—even orange juice. Development is continuous and the possibilities are endless'.[1]

The change in the character of tramp shipping is not a single development, but a compound of two factors. On the one hand is the increase in size and speed of tramp ships in general, the economic causes of which were explained when discussing liners. The result has been a movement away from the 6,000 gross ton, 9- to 11-knot tramp towards the 10,000 gross ton 14-knot tramp. Even within the short period 1956 to 1961, the average size of the world tramp fleet increased from 9,427 deadweight tons to 10,722 deadweight tons and the average speed from 10·8 knots to 12·0 knots.[2] As the tramp fleet is still dominated by the Liberty ship, the increases in the average size and speed of new tramps are significantly greater than the increase in the averages for all tramps. On the other hand is the movement towards specialized functions for tramp ships: apart from ore carriers, specialized tramp ships probably now represent some 20–25 per cent of the world tramp fleet.[3]

[1] 'More Specialisation in Cargo Vessels,' *Financial Times* (29 March 1960).
[2] Westinform Shipping Report No. 184, 'The World's Tramp Fleet' (March 1961).
[3] The American Bureau of Shipping suggests that 7 per cent of the world fleet, that is, about 8 million gross tons or 12 million deadweight tons is made up of bulk carriers. This figure exceeds considerably the figure given in Table 38. The world general purpose tramp fleet is about 17 million gross tons, giving a total fleet (including bulk carriers) of 25 million tons on the basis of American figures or 22 million tons on the basis of the figures in Table 38.

The second change is partly tied up with the first. It is the increasing tendency for tramp ships to be hired on long term rather than voyage charters. The more specialized the ship, the narrower is the field within which it can seek employment. In these circumstances the long-term charter becomes attractive as it provides an assured income for a ship which, because of its specialization, is largely at the mercy of one or a few shippers. The shippers themselves, wanting to be assured of their shipping capacity and to know its price in advance, have welcomed the time charter as an alternative to building up their own fleets. The time-chartered vessel has not proved attractive to most British shipowners and in 1960 only 10–15 per cent of the dry-cargo fleet (40–45 per cent of the non-liner dry-cargo tonnage) was on time charter. In Norway, on the other hand, 35 per cent of the dry-cargo fleet (55 per cent of the non-liner dry-cargo tonnage) was on time charter in 1958.[1]

The advantages of the time charter are several. First, a charter obtained before a ship is built can be used as security for a construction loan. Second, a charter executed in a period of profitable rates remains profitable when voyage charter rates fall; as an offset to this, subsequent rises in voyage rates cannot be enjoyed. The ideal situation for the shipowner is to time charter his ships at the peak and in the early stages of a falling market, but to voyage charter them on a rising market. Third, the employment of the vessel being secured, managerial capacity is freed to attend to other vessels, thus increasing the tonnage one management can handle. In fact, time charters have in the past been widely regarded in Britain as the sign of a lazy shipowner and apparently have been resisted for this reason.[2] However, the shipowner who felt that time charters would not give sufficient worries to justify his existence always had the possibility of expanding his fleet. Fourth, time charters once executed involve few risks for the shipowner and provide a cushion for earnings in bad periods. A judicious mixture of ships on voyage charter and ships on time charter enables a tramp owner to

[1] British figures by courtesy of Chamber of Shipping, Norwegian figures from *Shipping World* (18 March 1959).
[2] The British liner companies which built tankers after 1956 generally held pre-construction time charters.

enjoy greater stability of earnings than if all his ships are on voyage charter. He can then borrow with impunity as a more highly-geared capital can be used than is safe for a company engaged only in operations in the voyage-charter market.

The international aspects of resource allocation in relation to the ownership of tramps are considered in Chapter XI. Here it may be noted that the cost structure for tramp ships can be regarded as two-tiered, not three-tiered as in the case of liners. Overhead costs are made up mainly of interest and depreciation as office and general administration expenses are relatively small. For a tramp company using no borrowed capital, depreciation dominates the overhead costs and capital charges become a residual. Variable costs consist of the commissions paid to chartering brokers, wage and victualling costs for crews, fuel, repairs and maintenance and ships' stores. Insurance, which is only insurance of the ship as the insurance of the cargo is the charterer's responsibility, is probably best treated as an overhead cost, although insurance can be avoided, in part at least, on a laid-up vessel.

The actual relation between the two groups of costs depends chiefly on the age and speed of the vessel concerned. For a new vessel, overhead costs, excluding interest, may be about one-third of the total costs. Once the vessel has been depreciated to zero, overhead costs become negligible, but because of the rise in repair costs as a ship gets older, the total costs for an older ship are likely to be little different from the total costs of a newer vessel, provided that the comparison is made between tramp ships owned in the same country. The result of the change in the structure of costs over the life of the vessel is that in slack markets the variable costs (paid-out variable costs less cost of lay up) for a new ship are lower than for an older ship. The older ship must then either lay up or be sold to an owner with lower wage costs. The lower wage costs then offset the high repair costs and make the variable costs of the old ship in the low-wage country near to those of the new ship in the high-wage country. This characteristic of the cost structure shifts the problem of tramp ownership to a problem of international resource allocation.

Another aspect of the cost structure is that wage cost is a more important part both of total costs and of variable costs for tramps than they are for liners. For two tramps of equal size, speed and age, the one with lower wage costs can always undercut the one with higher wage costs. The effect of higher wage costs can be eliminated if the owner paying higher wage-rates always owns bigger, faster and younger vessels than the owner paying low wage-rates. Some aspects of this question are best left to Chapter XI. Here, however, the problem facing the individual owner in securing such a result can be discussed.

What is required is for the high-wage owner always to be in the vanguard of progress and continually to face the possibility that a shorter life span than twenty to twenty-five years must be expected from ships in his ownership. It seems, therefore, that in high-wage countries tramp ships should be depreciated over a period of not more than ten years, any surplus over scrap value obtained at the end of ten years by the sale of the vessel for further operations being treated either as a windfall profit or as an offset to the higher price of the new ship than of that which has been sold.[1] Norwegian owners now appear to be working on the basis of a ten-year write-off period; the investment allowance in Britain enables British owners to do the same thing. The possibility of operating a ten-year write off, however, depends on the level of the freight market; few owners, for example, could have achieved this in the 1930s. This points to another advantage of the time charter; a preconstruction time charter can be refused excepting when rates are at a level to provide the necessary surplus for depreciation. At times of high rates it may pay an owner to sacrifice some of the short-term gains in the voyage market in order to secure a long-term charter which will enable him to write off his vessel over ten years. Certainly the only operational technique which offers any hope of enabling tramp operation in a high-wage country to remain viable is one which deliberately provides a short write-off period, with the explicit acceptance that the vessel will be sold when written off and replaced with a superior ship.

Overriding the short-term limitation imposed by the level of freight rates on achieving the aim discussed above is a long-term

---

[1] This price increase occurs because presumably the newer ship is larger and faster than the old ship; it is concerned with quality changes not with changes in the price level.

limitation set by the upper limits of economical size and speed of tramp ships. Many ports of the world cannot handle bigger vessels and already the large bulk carriers (and tankers) are restricted to certain trades. More ports capable of accommodating such ships are being built, but in the foreseeable future it is unlikely that the bigger ships will be freed of the limitations imposed by port facilities. A second limitation is at present provided by the increase in costs as speed increases. This limitation is not crucial, however, for the size/speed relation is partly of an either/or kind, that is, either 16,000 deadweight tons and 17 knots, or 35,000 deadweight tons (or larger) and 14 knots.

The limitation provided by ports is more important in particular trades than overall. Many British ports are unable to handle large ships and so long as British shipowners see their primary function as the servicing of British trades, they will find that the small ships suitable for those trades cannot compete with similar ships owned in lower-wage countries. In other words, until British ports can be improved to handle the largest bulk carriers, general tramps and tankers, a tendency towards an increasing proportion of bulk cargoes arriving in foreign tonage is to be expected. British tramp types must fail in the long run in any attempt to compete in these trades and need to seek employment in the big-ship trades and acquire big ships for the purpose. It is worth observing that the failure to provide ports capable of handling the most modern ships may damage the general economy of a country by denying it access to the cheapest forms of transport. British steelmakers, for example, may suffer in this way.

The economic analysis points to the necessity for substantial changes in the structure of the British non-liner dry-cargo fleet if it is to operate economically and profitably and possess the capacity even to remain at its present size. In 1961 the world deep-sea tramp fleet consisted of 2,447 vessels of over 4,000 deadweight tons of which 15 per cent by number were over 13,000 tons; the British fleet at the same time consisted of 373 vessels with only 7 per cent of over 13,000 deadweight tons in size. Such a relationship is the very reverse of what is needed and any future change which runs counter to the aim of increasing the proportion of the larger tramps will render growth impossible and jeopardize the maintenance of the present fleet.[1]

TANKERS

The post-war years have seen a remarkable expansion of the world tanker fleet, from 11 million tons in 1939 to 38 million tons at the beginning of 1960. This increase in the tanker fleet has been matched by a four-fold increase in oil shipments since prior to the war. Increases in the speed and size of tankers have meant that each ton of the present tonnage is more effective than each ton of the pre-war fleet and a surplus of tankers appeared in 1953. In 1956 as a result of the Suez crisis all available tankers were pressed into service, but since that time the surplus has reappeared; at the end of 1959, 5·6 million deadweight tons were idle, that is, 9 per cent of the total fleet. The idle tonnage consisted of two distinct classes of vessel. First, the older smaller tankers which could not compete with the newer ships and which were not held on time charter. Second, new ships which had been built speculatively and for which satisfactory charters could not be obtained. The future of the smaller tankers is highly uncertain and barring another international emergency it is doubtful if the ships laid up will ever re-enter service as tankers. The future of the larger vessels is less assured than the owners hoped when ordering them, usually in 1956–7, but the trend is in their favour.

The world's commercial tanker fleet is owned partly, about two-fifths, by the oil companies and their subsidiaries, with the balance owned by independent shipping enterprises and government agencies. Throughout the history of tanker operations, the share owned by the oil companies has declined and that owned by independent operators has increased. Although the picture varies from company to company, a generalized pattern of oil company tanker usage can be discerned. The companies supply about one-third of their normal transport requirements from their own fleets, a further one-third by vessels held on time charter, making up the remainder of their requirements by taking vessels on voyage charter. At this juncture it is not necessary to

---

[1] The argument is not that there is no room for smaller tramps in British ownership but that the bias should be towards the larger vessels.

inquire why the oil companies charter up to two-thirds of their tanker requirements; it is sufficient to notice that this is the way in which they operate. In their chartering the companies are internationally minded and, apart from the entry of some of the Cold War tensions, will normally charter the most suitable tankers, irrespective of nationality.

For the independent shipowner tanker ownership entails some special risks in that he is completely dependent for his livelihood on a few large oil companies whose residual requirements only he satisfies. It might appear reasonable to assume that in a slump the oil companies would first dispense with vessels on voyage charter, then reduce the time-chartered tonnage employed, replacing some of it by tonnage on voyage charter if that is cheaper, and only in the last resort laying up or scrapping their own vessels. In practice, however, the oil companies have tended to get rid of the vessels with the highest running costs, so that when rates fall they have as often withdrawn their own older tankers and retained tankers on voyage charter, provided the costs of taking a vessel on voyage charter are less than the costs of running their own older vessels. This means that, by and large, the owners of the most economical tankers have been able to find employment for them at rates above variable costs (the cost classification developed for tramps applies also to tankers) while the older tankers of the oil companies have been sold for scrap. Further, the oil companies showed by their support for the tanker pool (see Chapter VI, p. 81) that they were unwilling recklessly to wreck the prospects of the independent owner for the sake of short-term economies. In these ways the apparent riskiness of tanker ownership has been reduced in practice.

The most important change in tanker operation since the war has been the increase in the size of vessels. Before 1939 the typical tanker was about 12,000 deadweight tons. Ten years later the typical size had risen to about 16,000 deadweight tons, but since then has increased rapidly so that the vessel of 45,000 deadweight tons is common and ships of 100,000 deadweight tons have been put into service. This development was made possible by the post-war policy of the oil industry of refining at the marketing, rather than the producing, end of the tanker haul. Large vessels can be used for transporting crude oil, whereas much smaller vessels are, on the whole, necessary when refined products are carried. Although the policy of the oil companies with regard to refining made the large tanker possible, it was initially independent owners, not the oil companies, who built large tankers.

Alongside the change in the location of refineries went the huge increase in the world demand for oil which, by providing greater volume shipments, enabled large vessels to find regular employment. The part played by the closure of the Suez Canal in 1956–7 in the development of the large tanker must not be overlooked. The need for vessels travelling from the Middle East to Europe to use the Long Cape route created a shortage of tanker tonnage, while the limitation on the size of tankers which the Canal had imposed was removed. When the Canal was re-opened, it was found that a tanker of 65,000 deadweight tons could travel out in ballast using the Canal and return loaded via the Cape and compete with a smaller tanker using the Suez route both ways.

The economy of the larger vessel can be seen by comparing the cost of transport per ton of oil for ships of various sizes; the figures are given in Table 39. It can be seen that the cost per ton decreases rapidly until a vessel of about 70,000 deadweight tons is reached after which further increases in size produce relatively small changes in unit cost. In view of the restricted number of trades on which a tanker of over 65,000 tons can find employment, this size appears to represent an optimum for most purposes.

The economy of the big ship does not mean the end of the small ship as many oil ports cannot handle the larger vessels: this is true of most British oil terminals. The limitation imposed by British ports should not, however, inhibit the building of big tankers by British independent owners.

The increase in the size of tankers makes it more difficult for small shipowners to enter the tanker business using their own resources. The cost of ships, both to build and to buy second-hand fluctuates widely over time; a new tanker of 35,000 deadweight tons, which is probably the absolute minimum economic size for a new tanker in British ownership, is likely to cost about £2 million. The small owner, that is, the owner of two or three tramps, at least one of which is a Liberty or other wartime type, cannot solve the financial problem involved in becoming a tanker owner by borrowing and putting a tanker on to the voyage charter market. Such a course would clearly give him a highly-geared capital which would be vulnerable with unstable earnings. Recourse to the pre-construction time charter and loan gets over the problem of the highly-geared capital with

TABLE 39. Unit cost of transportation
by tankers of various sizes as percentages of cost by T2 tanker

Vessel size	Percentage of cost by T2
(tons dwt.)	%
16,600 (T2)	100
19,000	90
30,000	63
45,000	51
70,000	43
85,000	40
100,000	38

Source: Figures presented at Fifth World Petroleum
Congress, New York, June 1959.

unstable earnings, but such charters are less likely to be available today, or in the near future, to a small owner with no experience of tankers than to a well-known shipowner, whether experienced in tankers or not, or a smaller owner with tanker experience. Entry to the tanker business for a British shipowner appears, therefore, to be restricted to enterprises with adequate resources to build such vessels, to bigger companies for which the acquisition of an unfixed tanker through the use of loan capital would not represent an undue raising of the gearing of their capitals, or to the owner with a sufficient reputation to obtain a pre-construction time charter. These considerations do not restrict tanker ownership to liner companies; they do mean, however, that the small shipowner is unlikely to find his economic salvation in the ownership of tankers and will succeed only in producing his own economic damnation if he tries to purchase and operate smaller, secondhand tankers. They must be left strictly for owners with low wage-rates.

XI

Ship Owning and Resource Allocation

THE object of this chapter is to consider the second condition for expansion, namely, the ability to sell in international competition, where the ability to sell is based on the respective costs of providing the service. As in the preceding chapter, the argument is concerned with both the explanation of the past and the prospects for the future.

It is convenient for the present to assume that shipowners, capital and labour are all drawn from the same economy, but that the capital equipment, the ships, can be bought in the cheapest market. When all, or a substantial proportion, of the shipowners, the capital and the labour are drawn from outside the country in which the ships are registered there is no sense in which the shipping can be regarded as 'national'. This, for example, is the position of the flags of convenience fleets.

CLASSIFICATION OF COSTS

Some items of cost are internationally variable while others may be regarded either as constant for all nations or, if variable, to be variable in a random fashion. Thus, for example, if labour is always national, the wage costs in shipping will vary between nations; fuel prices, on the other hand, vary somewhat throughout the world but as ocean-going ships have considerable freedom to bunker in the cheapest markets, the variation is random. To avoid confusion with the categories of enterprise costs developed in the previous chapter, those costs which may be regarded as non-variable between nations will be described as international, while those which are variable between nations will be described as national. In Table 40 the classification in this way is given, together with the enterprise classification of each item from Chapter X. The main difference between the classification of Table 40 and that of Chapter X is that capital charges are included in the table. These could be excluded from the classification previously used because the return on capital, loan capital always excepted, is a residual of the operations of a single enterprise. For a nation, however, any industry must consider the return on capital because in the long run it can only continue to employ the existing capital and attract new capital if the return to that capital is no less than could be secured in alternative uses. It is assumed in drawing up the table that maintenance is carried out by crew members paid on nationally determined wage scales but that repairs are carried out in dockyards and that the shipowner will seek the lowest cost repairer.

TABLE 40. Classification of shipping costs

| Cost Item | Classification for ship types: | |
	Liners	*Tramps and tankers*
National		
Crew costs (including victualling)	v.o.	v.
Maintenance	v.o.	v.
Capital charges	o.o.	o.o.
Agency and office expenses	o.o.	o.o.
International		
Depreciation	o.o.	o.o.
Insurance	v.o.	o.o.
Cargo handling	v.	
Passenger costs	v.	
Stores (excluding victuals)	v.o.	v.
Port charges	v.o.	v.
Repairs	v.o.	v.

o.o. = organization overhead costs
v.o. = voyage overhead costs
v. = variable costs

The costs which are international, that is, which are, or can be, invariant with respect to the nationality of shipowners can be ignored when considering problems of international resource allocation. If some shipowners are forced by national laws to buy their ships, carry out their repairs, buy stores or to insure their ships in one country rather than in another, then for those shipowners depreciation,[1] repairs, stores and insurance become national rather than international costs. However, where such restrictions are imposed, they are usually accompanied by subsidies or other assistance and may, therefore, be ignored here.

A slightly more difficult question is that of port charges and cargo handling costs. All ships trading to a particular port are charged at the same rate in the absence of discriminatory practices. From the point of view of British shipping it is irrelevant whether British port costs are higher or lower than those in other countries. However, higher port charges or cargo costs in one country than in another may kill an entrepôt trade, or may make it more economical for shippers to dispatch goods to the cheaper port to continue their journey by rail or road. Either of these things will harm both the trade of the higher cost port and the shipping established in the trade of that port. However, there is no reason why the shipping should not change its trade route to the now cheaper port, for if more trade is moving to that port opportunities for more shipping exist. These opportunities may be missed because they are not seen until the lines already using the cheaper port have increased their services to match the expanding trade or because the shipowners trading to the dearer port lack the flexibility to seek other trades. These things are failures of enterprise and cannot be regarded as conferring an element of national variability on port charges.

National costs consist, basically, of capital charges and labour costs and it will, therefore, be on these two items that the international allocation of resources to shipping will depend. The consideration of the part of total costs of different shipping enterprises made up of labour and capital charges will then show the economic conditions for success in a maritime rôle.

---

[1] Does depreciation become a national cost when rates of write off for taxation differ between nations? Clearly, the answer is no, because the rate of write off does not condition the actual depreciation taking place each year. To recognize the differences would produce the paradoxical result that costs for a ship subject to a 40 per cent Investment Allowance would be higher in the first year than in subsequent years and it would obviously not pay ever to build a new ship!

Ship Owning and Resource Allocation

LINERS AND NATIONAL COSTS

It can be seen from the table that for liners all national costs are either organization overheads or voyage overheads so that short-period variations in these items have no effect on the employment of shipping. In the long period, however, all costs must be covered and within each nation shipping must yield returns on capital and pay wages no less than other enterprises if it is to attract and retain capital and labour. The returns to the liner operator are determined by the rates set by conferences and the volume of cargo available. The volume of cargo lies outside the control of shipowners, although a country may, by discriminatory measures, take steps to secure an adequate volume of cargo for its nationally owned tonnage.

Within any individual conference there may be lines from many countries or from only a few countries so that a picture of internationally determined rates and nationally determined costs, with the operator in the high wage/high profit economy being squeezed is an over-simplification. Where lines owned in only one or two countries dominate a conference,[1] the fixing of rates is reduced to a unilateral or a bilateral basis and the levels of costs in those countries become the main determinants of rates. So long as the dominant countries are high cost, the shipping owned in those countries will continue to secure returns sufficient to attract the necessary capital and labour, while the lower-cost operators will make higher profits than they regard as 'normal' which they will then use for putting superior ships on the trades or for expanding their fleets. In the long run, the economically predictable result, the extinction of the high-cost operator, will occur but that run may be very long indeed.

Liner owners operating within conferences can seek to increase their profits in either of two ways, namely, by lowering costs or by raising freight rates and passenger fares. It is always

---

[1] Of the forty-eight outward freight conferences from Britain in 1960, two had no British members, eight had British plus three or more foreign members, and seventeen had British plus one or two foreign members, the presence of Scindia Line in most Far Eastern conferences accounting for many of the non-British recordings. Twenty-one conferences had only British members and for thirty-eight conferences lines from less than three countries determined the freight rates, with British lines usually in the majority.

269

administratively easier to raise prices than to lower costs, so that high-cost liner owners operating within tightly-knit conferences and lacking non-conference competition have a considerable incentive to think of profits in terms of the level of rates rather than the level of costs and to lose the cost consciousness which is essential to a vigorous and expanding enterprise.

The existence of the shipping of several nations in a conference which is often cited as proof that rates are internationally determined, does not necessarily mean that rates are the lowest necessary to secure the service. If all the countries in the conference have similar costs, or if shipowners with varying levels of costs agree to pool receipts so that all make profits at a pre-determined rate, rates may be above the minimum without any shipowners making excessive profits. As the majority of conferences include the ships of only one or a few nations and the rates are fixed by agreement between the members of the conference, the profits of liner operations are no guide to the economic use of resources. A high rate of profit coupled with a free labour market is not a sufficient condition to establish that liner operations are an economic use of resources.

The existence of the conference limitations on competition means for shipowners in a high-wage country that, so long as they can prevent the ships of countries with greater advantages from joining conferences, they can maintain liner services even though these represent an uneconomic use of resources.[1] Complaints regarding excessive rates can be met by showing that profits are modest, although this is to dodge the issue. A country which has ceased to have any advantages, even in the provision of liner services can, if its shipowners are careful, maintain existing conference trades when it cannot expand into new trades. Traders using the ships concerned are then made to pay for the uneconomic use of resources in shipping through higher rates than are necessary and, often, than are being paid by their competitors in other countries.

---

[1] An idea of this possibility was probably implicit in the British opposition to the entry of Indian lines to conference services in the immediate post-war period. Even if the necessary analysis of the situation was not made, opposition based on a fear that the entry of a low cost operator to the conference would lead to British costs ceasing to dominate the determination of freight rates was more rational than opposition based on a fear of over-tonnaging the route.

Where, however, competition in liner services is truly international, that is, conference rates are just sufficient to allow the lowest-cost operator to earn normal profits, then differences between operators in the national cost items determine the economic allocation of resources in the long run. Where this is so, high-cost operators must either reduce their costs or receive subsidies if they are to continue liner services. If the wage rates paid in a country and the price of capital in that country are high relatively to international standards then, unless the liner operators can secure increases in productivity denied to owners in countries where wage rates and the price of capital are lower, there is no alternative to a subsidy if the shipping services are to continue.

In the previous chapter the only capital cost shown for liners was depreciation. It was estimated that depreciation comprises about 25 per cent of total costs for a liner operator with modern passenger ships and about 30–35 per cent for modern cargo liners. If interest on capital is also allowed, it is apparent that capital absorbs about 40 per cent of passenger liner receipts and about 50 per cent of cargo liner receipts, receipts in each case being considered as covering only interest on loans and 'normal' profits on equity capital. The same thing may be put another way by saying that the degree of capital intensity is high in liner operations.

The conclusion from the above analysis is that the operation of liner services with modern, elaborately-fitted vessels, is a capital intensive enterprise in which countries where capital is plentiful will have an advantage over those in which capital is less plentiful. Countries where capital is scarce are usually countries in which wage rates are relatively low. The use of aged ships involving the outlay of little capital, but the use of a considerable *amount* of labour in repair and maintenance work is then an economic proposition.

There is a situation midway between the new ship and the old ship positions which is based on the fact that different parts of ships date and/or wear out at different rates. The possibility then exists of retaining parts of the ship and reconstructing the remainder, a process which costs a lot less than the price of a new liner minus the sale price of the older vessel and may fit the ship

271

for many years of additional service. There are few examples in the British fleet of ships given such thorough-going reconstructions, nor has the course often been adopted in the past.[1] However, the German, French, Italian, American and, to a lesser extent, the Dutch passenger fleets show many examples of vessels given a lifespan beyond the normal by extensive reconstruction. Clearly, the reconstruction of old ships is not practicable in all circumstances, but whatever doubts may exist regarding the process in individual cases, it is a fact that cost-conscious liner operators do find that the method works. On a purely pragmatic basis, it deserves consideration, even if it could not be shown that by reducing one of the largest single items of liner costs, depreciation, it opens the possibility of lowering the total costs of a liner fleet.

TRAMPS AND NATIONAL COSTS

The term tramp is used here to include the whole range of tramps, bulk carriers and tankers which operate by being chartered on a time or voyage charter basis to shippers or to other shipping enterprises. The types may be grouped together in this way because the economic aspects of their operations, as considered here, are similar.

Tramp shipping is an industry in which competition is on an international basis, there are a large number of suppliers and the product, ton miles, possesses a high degree of homogeneity. The level of tramp rates is determined by supply and demand in the world markets with a minimum set by the zero supply rate of the lowest-cost operator. The minimum level to which tramp rates can fall is then that at which the lowest-cost owner just prefers to lay up his ship rather than continue to offer it for charter; that is, the minimum is the paid-out variable costs of the lowest-cost operator minus the costs of lay up for such an operator. In the long term, however, rates must be sufficient to prevent such an owner from scrapping his tonnage without replacement. Rates above this long-term minimum will then

---

[1] But note the reconstruction of the Union-Castle fleet in the 1930's. The modernization of the 28 years old *Queen of Bermuda* in 1961 is an encouraging contemporary example.

induce low-cost operators to expand their fleets even though the rates may be below the short term minimum for higher-cost operators. Every addition to the tramp tonnage of low-cost operators, obtained either by fleet expansion or by new entries, shifts the supply curve of tonnage to the right and makes a greater volume of tonnage available at all rates. There is, in this way, a downward pressure on rates and although the trend may be temporarily interrupted by booms, it is an interruption arising from the short period inelasticity of the supply of tonnage, not a reversal of the trend. The returns to labour and capital in tramp shipping are determined by the need only to attract labour and capital in countries in which productivity in shore-based industries is relatively low. Historically this has meant that for countries in which wages and profits in shore-based industries are high, both on average and at the margin, tramping has become increasingly uneconomic unless shipowners always offset the wage rate disadvantage by adopting ship types with a minimum labour input per ton mile.

If labour is free to accept employment either on sea or on land without restriction, the level of long-term profits on the capital actually employed in unsubsidized tramp shipping provides a reliable guide to the economic pattern of resource allocation. This does not dispose of all problems. Although the product of tramp shipping, ton miles, is homogeneous, the manner in which that product is supplied can differ. Tramps may be old, small and slow, or modern, large and fast. The operation of one type may be economic for an economy in which the attempt to operate the other would represent an uneconomic use of resources. Where capital is absolutely scarce and, hence, expensive and labour is absolutely plentiful and, hence, cheap, the secondhand, slow tramp is more likely to be economic than the fast new ship. As capital becomes less scarce and labour relatively less plentiful, economic allocation can be secured by moving to greater sizes and higher speeds. If the development of the economy continues, a point may be reached when even the best and most labour economical type of tramp is no longer an economic proposition, although the ownership of such vessels may be profitable during periods when freight rates are above their long-term level. The existence of this limitation was noted

T   273

in Chapter X, but apart from America there is at present no important maritime country the crew and capital costs of which are so high that the only type of tramp which can be economic is impracticable for other reasons.

For tramp ships the variable costs which have to be covered before a voyage is made include wage costs. Given equivalent ships, an owner in a low-wage country will continue to operate his vessels at freight rates at which the high-wage operator has to lay up. The important thing for the tramp operator in a high-wage country is, therefore, to keep his variable costs below those of an operator in a low-wage country and this usually means larger ships and faster ships. Larger ships because crew numbers do not increase in direct proportion to the size of ships; faster ships because extra speed enables voyage times to be shortened.

If the low-wage operator always has access to the big, fast ships then the situation is hopeless for the high-cost operator. However, it would be an unusual set of economic circumstances in which one operator had access to plentiful capital enabling him always to operate the most modern tonnage and at the same time enjoyed a cheap labour supply. If, however, the assumption regarding the identity of nationality of shipowners, crew and capital is relaxed and the employment of foreign labour is permitted, then a shipowner may enjoy this double advantage. The examples which spring to mind are American shipping, before the passing of the La Follette Act of 1915, the employment of low-cost Scandinavian, German and Greek labour in the period of unquestioned supremacy of British shipping and the use, currently, of coloured seamen, usually under long-term agreements.

In a sense the tramp ship owner has two problems to solve, whereas the liner owner has only one. The tramp owner has to keep both his variable costs and his total costs as low as possible; the liner owner has to be concerned only with total costs. The tramp operator has to be cost conscious because he cannot fix, or even influence, his freight rates unless he can agree with his fellow owners to form a pool as was done in the 1930s (see Chapter V). An apparently paradoxical result is produced, but it is paradoxical only so long as the conventional concept of the tramp as inferior to the liner is preserved. Because he has to keep his variable costs as low as possible, the tramp ship operator in a high-wage country cannot afford to operate inferior or old vessels or to use propulsive machinery which, although cheaper in first cost, is dearer in running cost than the most economical available. The liner owner in such a country can, however, afford the older ship or the reconditioned ship because such a ship can have lower overhead costs.

The conclusion which is usually reached is that tramp shipping is something in which low-wage countries excel. This conclusion is valid so long as low-wage countries can obtain the most modern and economical tonnage. It ceases to be valid, however, when differences in the operative efficiency of different ships under different flags are considered. The merchant marines of Norway and Japan before 1914 operated on the basis of second-hand ships, inferior to those operated by British owners. The cost advantage of lower wage rates in those countries was offset, however, by the higher repair costs and slower speeds of the vessels so that British tramps were able to compete. In the inter-war years the Greek and Yugoslavian[1] fleets operated the old, slow ships with high labour and repair requirements. The wage cost advantage which these ships enjoyed was offset by Norwegian owners by the use of diesel ships with low variable costs. The British tramp, although generally younger than the Greek and Yugoslavian tramp, did not have the same superiority and with its higher variable costs found it difficult to compete.

GENERAL CONSIDERATIONS

The preceding analysis makes it clear that labour is the most important element in determining the international competitiveness of ships owned in different countries.

The importance of wages as an item of cost and of low wage costs in conferring an advantage on one country differ for

---

[1] The willingness of tramp shipowners in the low wage countries to join an international agreement with British owners to limit competition instead of using their cost advantage to compete the British tramps out of existence strongly suggests that the cost advantage was less marked than generally supposed. The general assessment of the cost advantage was concentrated entirely on wage *rates* and ignored voyage times and repair costs.

Ship Owning and Resource Allocation

different classes of ships. Information on this point is difficult to obtain, particularly anything reliable in the way of international comparisons (see Chapter XII). The variations between wage costs in different types of ships in Britain are shown by the figures in Table 41. These figures should not be treated as being more than indicative as each group applies only to ships in a single trade and the cost items are shown as percentages of their total, not as percentages of total voyage costs. What is important is the relation between the different types rather than the generality of the proportion of the various costs for each type.

TABLE 41. Distribution of some voyage cost items for four British ship types, 1958

Cost Item	Passenger liner 30,000 tons 21½ knots steam turbine	Cargo liner 8,800 tons 18 knots steam turbine	Tramp 9,300 dwt. 12½ knots diesel	Tanker 19,000 dwt. 14½ knots steam turbine
	%	%	%	%
Crew costs	40·5	25·3	36·8	25·7
Repairs, stores, etc.	21·6	26·6	38·4	24·7
Fuel	37·8	48·1	24·8	49·6
	100·0	100·0	100·0	100·0

Source: Adapted from table given in a paper 'The Economics of Ship Time', read to the North East Coast Institution of Engineers and Shipbuilders by Mr. R. M. Thwaites; reported in *Syren and Shipping* (31 December 1958), p. 553.

Crew costs are shown as ranging between 25 per cent and 40 per cent of the cost items shown, although a definition of voyage costs which included port charges and cargo handling costs would change the relative proportions for the different ship types. Despite this inadequacy of the data, certain conclusions can be drawn from the figures. The proportion of crew costs to total costs is high when crew numbers are high, as in passenger ships, or when fuel costs are relatively low, as in slow tramp ships. In the case of passenger ships providing a given standard of service to passengers, the faster the vessel the less

276

important are crew costs relatively to fuel costs. This implies that relatively high-wage countries, if they do operate passenger liners, must operate fast ships. The increase in the speed of ships built for the service between Britain and Australia, from 18 knots pre-war to 21 knots in 1950 and 27 knots in 1960, illustrates the point exactly. Such countries can also operate economically fast cargo liners and big tankers, the bigger the better as relative crew costs fall sharply as tanker size increases; for example the manning on a British tanker of 32,000 deadweight tons is the same as that for a vessel of 47,000 deadweight tons. A realization of the economic case for fast cargo liner services is illustrated by the decision of the Ben Line and the Blue Funnel group to operate 19 to 20 knot services to the Far East in place of the service formerly maintained by slower ships. The analysis also helps to explain why owners of Liberian-registered tankers, the crew costs of which tend to be high despite the low manning scales, have been attracted to big tankers, going up to over 100,000 deadweight tons.

For a high-wage economy the operation of slow passenger liners providing a good deal of service to passengers, slow tramp ships and small tankers is not an economic use of resources and can be profitable only in booms or if the operators are protected from the full effects of international competition. Owners in such countries may continue to operate these types of ships in fully competitive services in the short term but in the long term will only do so if they are prepared to accept a low rate of return on the capital invested, a situation in which new capital for expansion is unlikely to be obtainable. This situation is commonplace in industries in which ploughed-back profits as a source of capital are high in relation to original share subscriptions. With such enterprises a satisfactory dividend rate on the original share capital hides the low rate of return on the whole capital actually being used. In such a situation expansion of shipping would be an uneconomic use of resources, but if the capital already in use cannot be removed from shipping for use in other enterprises without heavy loss then, provided the industry is paying wages at the level necessary to attract the required labour supply, the continuation of services may be economic. In other words, given the existing investment of resources the least uneconomic pattern of allocation may be obtained by maintaining a situation which would not be created if the opportunity to start again existed. Within this situation resources which cannot be removed from shipping should, when being re-invested in replacement tonnage, always be used in the most economic way possible, even if this means that some shipping enterprises change their natures over time.

It might also be observed that unless there are non-economic reasons for maintaining a shipping fleet, low profit rates are not a justification for a subsidy as this would simply serve to immobilize the already sticky resources in the industry. If, on the other hand, capital was mobile a temporary subsidy might be justified to prevent the industry running down and releasing its labour supply at a faster rate than those workers could be absorbed in other occupations.

External Economies

The discussion so far has concerned the allocation of resources in shipping solely in terms of economic situations which are uninfluenced by the actions of shipowners themselves. There are, however, external economies available for an established industry which enable it to survive in competition with shipping which lacks these economies. The difference between these external economies and the questions of wage and profit rates discussed earlier is that, although they may be available only to shipowners in a certain country at a particular time, they are generally capable of being matched by other shipowners in other countries in time.

First, there are the advantages to liner operators of the establishment of offices, agencies and berthing facilities throughout the world to handle passengers and cargo. Some of these advantages can quickly be matched by a new entrant, for example, the entry of Norwegian shipping to American trades in the inter-war period. The advantage of privately owned wharves and other facilities can less easily be matched by a new entrant. However, widespread municipal or state control of ports has lessened the advantage an established owner can derive in this way.

Second, an established shipowner can enjoy a reputation built up over the preceding years which helps him in securing passengers, cargoes and charters. The reputation of British shipping for fair treatment, safe and well-found ships and disciplined crews aids all British shipping enterprises. The reputation in tanker operation built up by some Norwegian owners in the inter-war years helped other owners when they sought time charters. The reputation which Greek and Panamanian ships acquired in the inter-war years because some ships under each flag were unsafe has, on the other hand, hindered shipowners with ships under those flags and made their ships often suspect without any real justification.

Third, although shipbuilding and repairing have been treated as international costs because all shipowners can have access to the cheapest yards, it is an advantage to the shipping of a country if it is backed by an adequate shipbuilding and repairing industry. The lack of such an industry on a sufficient scale created difficulties in the expansion of the Norwegian fleet in the post-1945 period. On the other hand, an inefficient industry can be a positive disadvantage unless shipowners are able to remain unresponsive to the various pressures put on them to patronize the home industry. The disadvantage will be at its greatest if the shipowners are not sufficiently outward looking to realize that the service industry is relatively inefficient.

Fourth, a country with an extensive fishing industry or coastwise shipping has a source of efficient maritime labour. A good deal of maritime labour is casual in the sense that a man may make two or three trips in an overseas ship and then seek either a shore job or a job on a coaster or a fishing boat for a period before making further ocean trips. If the labour switches between deep-sea maritime employment and shore jobs it will tend to be less efficient for maritime purposes than if it is employed in fishing or coastal trades when not undertaking ocean voyages.

Fifth, an established maritime nation usually has nautical colleges in which young men can be trained as officers and/or seamen, so that shipowners are not put to the expense of completely training their own workers. Such school training can never produce fully qualified officers and men and periods of further training on ships are necessary. In some countries, special training ships are maintained for this purpose, Britain being a notable exception. Shipowners are rarely completely freed from the costs of such training, and training centres are normally financed, in part at least, by contributions from the shipowners themselves. However, the cost to the individual shipowner is less when the training is carried out as a specialized function than when each has to do his own training. The advantage which the existence of labour trained in this way gives may be partly offset by the advantage which shipowners in countries not providing such facilities have in being able to engage the trained labour without making any contribution to the cost of training. Too much should not be made of this, however, as such shipowners usually have to pay higher wages in order to attract the labour: on the other hand, the rapid development of Japanese shipping around the turn of the century would not have been possible without the employment of trained European deck and engine-room officers.

Overseas Trade

A country with an extensive volume of sea-borne trade is often thought to have an advantage in ship owning. If a country's trade is to give an important advantage to the shipowners of that country it is necessary, first, that the trade be of the right nature and, second, that national shipowners have means of securing a share of that trade greater than their share in world shipping as a whole.

On the question of the nature of the trade, a high-value, low-volume trade (for example, the exports of a manufacturing nation) is not a strong basis for a large fleet. What is needed is a large trade in quantum terms, irrespective of its value. Given the large quantum trade, it makes a difference whether that trade is an export trade or an import trade, the difference depending ultimately on whether the exporter or the importer nominates the carrying vessels. If the exporter nominates the vessels then it can only be the volume of exports of the country which is important in determining the demand for its shipping. If the importer nominates the ships then the volume of imports is important.

If the right kind of trade is available, can national shipowners expect to gain from this? A country can expect that either its importers or its exporters will have the right to nominate the ships which are to carry the goods concerned, but it cannot reasonably expect to have it both ways. The possession of the right to nominate the carrying vessel does not mean that a national ship will always be nominated. All that can be said is that where a national-flag ship offers the same service at the same price as any other, then it may be expected that the national, rather than the foreign, ship will be chosen. If the price or the service are not the same then favourable shipping rules, flag discrimination, or moral pressure on traders will be needed to secure the selection of a national-flag ship.

In practice, shipowners try to ensure that goods shipped from their own country are carried c.i.f., that is, the exporter pays the freight and insures the goods before departure. There are administrative reasons for this preference in that it saves the shipowner having to collect his freight from the foreign importer and arranging himself to insure the goods in transit. It also protects the shipowners from the risks of variations in foreign exchange rates. With imports to their own country, shipowners are generally willing to accept f.o.b. shipments, for, although they leave the insurance question open the payment of freight in the home currency is secured. In the case of indirect trades, the shipowner will usually be indifferent between c.i.f. and f.o.b. shipment, unless it is markedly easier to collect freight payments from one country than from the other.

Initially, these preferences of shipowners were based on prudence and administrative convenience. In most export trades from Britain, except coal, liners have always predominated and under c.i.f. arrangements British ships secured the bulk of the traffic as the exporters nominated the carrying vessels. Most British imports, other than refrigerated goods, are bulk cargoes in the carriage of which tramps predominate and the f.o.b. arrangements applying to these cargoes also gave a preference to British ships because the importer nominated the carrying ships. In this way arrangements adopted for administrative reasons when British shipping faced little foreign competition served to create preferences for British ships when foreign competition became important.

Although a large quantum trade may be an advantage to the shipping of the country concerned, it is neither a necessary nor a sufficient basis for a shipping fleet unless official or unofficial action can secure that national ships are given a preferred position in the carriage of that trade. The separate experiences of American and Norwegian shipping illustrate these points. Over the post-war period the foreign sea-borne trade of the United States has been between one-quarter and one-third of the world's sea-borne trade, yet American liners are heavily subsidized, American tramps have declined in numbers since 1948, despite the formal preferences and the bonus freight rates on protected cargoes which they enjoy, and most American-owned tankers are registered under the Liberian and Panamanian flags. In the case of America the large trade has not been a sufficient condition for success because of the disadvantages, in the form of high wage costs, from which America suffers as a ship-owning nation. The Norwegian overseas trade is only about one-fortieth of the world's sea-borne trade, yet the Norwegian fleet is over one-tenth of the world's fleet and is unsubsidized, which makes it clear that a large trade is not a necessary condition for success as a ship-owning nation.

The conclusion reached is that a substantial national trade is a useful, but neither a necessary nor a sufficient, condition for success as a shipowner. It follows that a national trade which is growing more slowly than world trade cannot be regarded as a causal factor in the explanation of the slower growth of shipping owned in that country. Certainly a slow growing trade limits the growth of shipping enterprises engaged in that trade, but the growth of British shipping before 1914, and of Norwegian and Greek shipping in both the inter-war years and the post-1945 period shows that shipping lines faced with a national trade inadequate to satisfy their expansive desires can turn successfully to extra-national trades for employment.

XII

Labour Relations and Labour Costs
by
BASIL MOGRIDGE

I N the preceding chapters the effects of differences in wage costs on the economics of operating different types of ships were considered theoretically; the purpose of this chapter is to examine the relevant data with a view to discovering, in so far as it is possible to do so, what their effect has in fact been. The chapter is concerned throughout with sea-going labour only. First, the labour relations system is reviewed and then its working is examined in terms of a single, albeit major, criterion: the strike record. Labour supply and labour costs, the latter with particular reference to the differences between costs under different flags, are then considered. Finally, there is a brief summing-up and overall assessment.

Where international comparisons are made in this chapter the most frequent example taken is that between Britain and Norway. As has been pointed out in earlier chapters, the comparison with Norway is of particular interest since the shipping of that country has not enjoyed subsidies or flag discrimination in its own favour, and has been subject to very much the same external vicissitudes and disabilities as the British fleet.

THE LABOUR RELATIONS SYSTEM

(a) *Its Origins*

For years British shipping was plagued by an unceasing and bitter struggle between the principal organizations on the two sides—the Sailors' and Firemen's Union (founded in 1887) and the Shipping Federation (1890). The years 1888–90 saw the upswing of the trade cycle, and the new union prospered beyond

283

all expectations. In consequence owners representing a majority of the country's merchant tonnage came together in 1890 to form a Federation with the express purpose of combating the union and in particular of preventing it from holding a monopoly of the labour supply. The first few months of the Federation's existence coincided with a turning of the economic tide. In the depression which followed the Federation developed a highly efficient strike-breaking apparatus and in port after port managed to secure a monopoly of the labour supply for itself. By the end of 1893 the union's power was broken; indeed, in the three years from 1891 to 1894 its membership (as affiliated to the T.U.C.) fell by over 93 per cent. The union made some recovery in the next two or three years, but it was short-lived, and right up to 1911 the union was, in terms of membership, a mere shadow of its former self. But it remained what it had become within two years of its foundation, a body characterized by aggressive militancy.

There were frequent localized stoppages in these years, but it was not until 1911 that the union attempted a national strike. In the event favourable economic conditions, together with a remarkable solidarity among transport workers in general, resulted in substantial concessions in a number of ports. In some these concessions included the establishment of local 'joint boards'—negotiating machinery. Even the Shipping Federation came to 'recognize' the union; this was one step in the direction of a more harmonious relationship, but only a small one. 'Recognition' did not involve the closed shop, or even national negotiating machinery. Indeed, at the outbreak of war in August 1914 both the Federation and the union were building up fighting funds in preparation for a showdown.

The onset of war put hostilities within the industry in a new light, and the national interest became a major consideration. In the summer of 1917 the combination of submarine menace, acute labour shortage and growing rank-and-file unrest made labour relations in this vital industry a matter of immediate and grave concern to the Government, which consequently sought to bring the parties together. It invited the Federation and the union to meet to discuss labour supply, Chinese labour, and the possibility of national standard wages; and a joint committee of representatives of the two bodies—unimaginable only a few years before—was set up under the chairmanship of an official of the Ministry of Shipping.

The first problem which came before the new committee was the vexed question of control of the labour supply. The union demanded sole control; the owners had always fiercely opposed that, and continued to do so. Deadlock was averted by the suggestion that there should be a single source of supply, *jointly* controlled. This proposal, made by the union's founder and then leader, Havelock Wilson, was immediately accepted by the Federation. That hurdle over, the committee went on to discuss a national joint board to deal in detail with these questions of wages and supply. By the end of November the proposed new body had been set up, under the title 'National Maritime Board', and had already fixed the first national wage rates.

Thus it was that in 1917 the long-standing claim of the union for national bargaining—national wages and conditions, and a national joint board to negotiate them—was at last conceded, together with an equal share in the control of the labour supply. The latter meant that the union could, over wide areas, enforce membership as a condition of employment. The former— national bargaining—meant that the national labour market was now effectively unified; members of the Federation would not pay rates above those agreed by the Board, and members of the union would not accept rates below.

(b) *The National Maritime Board*

The National Maritime Board which came into existence in November 1917 was based on the principle of equal representation of both sides of the industry, with a chairman provided by the Ministry of Shipping. The Board worked so well, in spite of the long record of bitter struggle before 1914, that it survived the dissolution of the Ministry after the war. In 1919 a revised constitution was drawn up, and in January 1920 a new National Maritime Board came into being, one in which there was no Government participation. Instead of a chairman provided by the Ministry of Shipping, there were henceforth joint chairmen provided by the two sides. At the same time both sides were slightly enlarged: the Liverpool shipowners' association came in alongside the Shipping Federation, and the masters' union came in alongside those representing navigating officers, engineers, sailors and firemen, and cooks and stewards.[1]

Apart from these changes in composition the new Board was essentially the same as the old; indeed the present constitution is still virtually that drawn up in 1917. The objects of the Board, now as then, are threefold: 'the prevention and adjustment of differences' between shipowners and their seafaring employees; 'the establishment, revision and maintenance' of national wage rates and conditions; and 'the establishment of a single source of supply of Sailors and Firemen jointly controlled by employers and employed'.[2] These three topics—disputes, wages and conditions, and supply—are treated in subsequent sections of this chapter; here it will suffice to emphasize the comprehensive nature of the Board's competence. The fact that it does not confine itself to wages and hours but deals with a host of other matters as well is considered to be one of the main causes of the Board's success in promoting harmonious relations between employers and unions; as the historian of the Federation puts it, 'the members of the Board have formed the habit of solving their problems because the scope of the Board covers so many subjects which are not essentially controversial at all. And that habit of agreement has in due course spread to controversial subjects'.[3]

There is another way too in which the wide scope of the Board has fostered the 'habit of agreement'. The prevention of disputes, the fixing of wages, and the joint control of supply appear together in Article 1 of its constitution; and this juxtaposition there reflects their close connection in reality. Joint control of the supply of sailors and firemen turned out to mean the closed shop for those groups; without it the membership of the union would have been much smaller, especially during the inter-war years when unemployment among seamen was heavy. Fear of losing joint control seems, particularly in the 1920s but even in more recent years, to have been a major factor restraining the

---

[1] The radio operators did not join the Board till 1941.

[2] National Maritime Board, *Year Book 1960*, p. 130; and Charles P. Hopkins, '*National Service*' *of British Seamen, 1914–1919* (London, 1920), pp. 155–8.

[3] L. H. Powell, 'Industrial Relations in the British Shipping Industry', in *International Labour Review* (June 1952), p. 701.

seamen's union from militancy either in negotiations or in taking
strike action.

(c) *The Legal Framework*

There are other factors too which encourage restraint. One
such is the principle of discipline. The concept of discipline is a
pervasive one in industrial relations, and especially so in merchant shipping with its special dangers to life and limb—not to
mention property. Interpretations of this concept have under-
gone considerable changes over the years, and most shipowners
have moved with the times; but it must be said that certain
sections of the merchant fleet still retain a near-military
approach. No less important in favouring restraint is the fact
that the legal framework of labour relations in British shipping is
redolent of attitudes which in shore industry are virtually
extinct. The instrument governing labour relations in the
British shipping industry is the Merchant Shipping Act of 1894
(as slightly amended by that of 1906); it has been said, with
truth, that this Act in certain respects belongs to the age of the
windjammer.

This is not the place to go into the legal complexities of the
position, but a few points will serve to indicate the situation. A
'seaman lawfully engaged' who 'neglects, or refuses without
reasonable cause, to join his ship, or to proceed to sea in his
ship, or is absent without leave at any time within twenty-four
hours of the ship's sailing from a port, . . . or is absent at any
time without leave and without sufficient reason from his ship or
from his duty' is liable to forfeit up to two days' pay and for
every twenty-four hours of absence either up to six days' pay or
the expense of hiring a substitute; and, except in the U.K., is
liable to imprisonment for up to ten weeks with or without hard
labour.[1] Again, if he is guilty of 'wilful disobedience to any lawful command'—irrespective of whether the offence is committed
when the ship is safe in port or on the high seas—he is liable to
up to four weeks' imprisonment, with or without hard labour,
and fines;[2] above all, if he 'combines with any member of the
crew to disobey lawful commands, or to neglect duty, or to
impede the navigation of the ship or the progress of the voyage'

[1] 57 & 58 Vict., c. 60, s. 221 (b).   [2] Ibid., s. 225 (b).

he is liable up to twelve weeks' imprisonment, with or without hard labour.[1] The Merchant Shipping Acts make no provision for relaxation of these disciplinary provisions in the case of trade disputes, even when the ship is in port.[2]

Few would advocate that strike action be legally permissible when a ship is at sea. But the fact that seamen who strike when their ship is safely in port can be jailed for so doing places ship-owners in a peculiarly favoured position. Thus, not only do the existence of the National Maritime Board and the by now traditional attitude of the union make an official strike most unlikely, but in addition the legislation relating to the industry makes *any* strike action extremely hazardous for those who do come out. Large-scale participation cannot be prevented, and mass arrests as a counter-measure have not been attempted since the 1920s; but a determined company can easily concentrate on the national or local strike leaders, real or presumed, and this is what happened in the 1955 and 1960 strikes, when a number of striking seamen were imprisoned.

(d) *The Parties*

This summary account of the labour relations system would not be complete without a word more on the parties. Throughout the last fifty years the two principal ones have been the Shipping Federation and the seamen's union, originally called the National Sailors' and Firemen's Union (N.S.F.U.) and since the mid-1920s entitled the National Union of Seamen (N.U.S.).

On the owners' side, the Employers' Association of the Port of Liverpool joined the second National Maritime Board (1920), but the Shipping Federation had and has a membership some three times that of the Liverpool association, and in fact runs the day-to-day business of labour supply, in Liverpool as elsewhere. What transpires in the policy-making inner councils of the employers' side, when the Liverpool association and the

---

[1] Ibid., s. 225 (e).

[2] Merchant seamen, like workers in gas, water, or electricity supply, are not covered by the Conspiracy and Protection of Property Act of 1875, which laid down that an agreement or combination to strike or incite is not a criminal conspiracy, nor by the Trade Disputes Act of 1906, which laid down that such an agreement or combination is not a civil wrong for which damages are recoverable.

Federation confer together, remains undisclosed, but it would be surprising if the Federation were not the dominant partner offstage as well as on.

Before the 1914–18 war the Shipping Federation was as immoderate as the N.S.F.U. Indeed, 'there was . . . no other employers' organization quite as aggressive and as unscrupulous as the Shipping Federation'.[1] Both the Federation and the union underwent a fundamental change in the decade 1910–20, and more especially during the war years. After 1917 each pursued a moderate policy towards the other; both thenceforward reserved their aggressiveness for those who threatened to disturb the new-found harmony.

On the employees' side the major body is the N.U.S., which is by far the biggest union among Britain's merchant seafarers. In its own field—notably sailors and firemen, and cooks and stewards—the N.U.S. has virtually 100 per cent membership in consequence of the closed shop.[2] But its position was not always so strong. N.U.S. membership among cooks and stewards was negligible until the 1940s, and even among sailors and firemen numbers belonged to a rival union up to the mid-1920s.

The N.S.F.U./N.U.S. has always suffered from an unusually high degree of internal dissension, sometimes resulting in outright breakaways. In the early days the shipowners themselves promoted and supported rival unions; but they appear to have ceased to do so by 1914. The actions of owners were in any case by no means the only factors making for local unrest; to the difficulties inherent in the unionization of seamen[3] were added the problems of financial and administrative mismanagement, and of dictatorial right-wing leadership.[4] In 1911 and 1912 two important, though localized, breakaways occurred, quite

---

[1] John Saville, 'Trade Unions and Free Labour', in A. Briggs and Saville (eds.), *Essays in Labour History* (London, 1960), pp. 329–30.

[2] A tiny handful manage to dodge the column; a larger number fall behind with their contributions.

[3] Once the closed shop was secured the recruitment problem was solved; but 'communications' between rank-and-file and union leaders have remained a major difficulty.

[4] Havelock Wilson's political position, starting as Lib-Lab and moving to the right during the 1914–18 war and after, facilitated good relations with the Shipping Federation but created difficulties with some members of his union and with other unions.

independently of shipowners. These two splinter groups joined forces in 1912, and at the end of 1921 merged with a union of cooks and stewards to form the Amalgamated Marine Workers' Union (A.M.W.U.). For the next five years the A.M.W.U. was a substantial disruptive force *vis-à-vis* the system which the N.S.F.U. and the shipowners had built up. But the system did not break down. The N.S.F.U., by pursuing a very conciliatory policy towards the owners, managed to secure and extend the closed shop among sailors and firemen; to the power conferred by the closed shop the N.S.F.U. added other measures, notably strike-breaking and litigation, with the result that the A.M.W.U. collapsed early in 1927.[1]

The other major disruptive force in the inter-war years was the Communist party, notably through its trade union front organization, the Minority Movement (the British section of the Red International of Labour Unions). In the 1920s Communist policy was action within existing unions; in the early 1930s, policy having changed, an abortive attempt was made to form a separate seamen's union to rival the N.U.S.—the new union, set up at a very unpropitious time as far as economic conditions were concerned, had a brief and insignificant career. Communist influence was again prominent in such unrest as there was in 1947 and 1948, but since then has been of only minor importance.

A third body antagonistic to the present N.U.S. and to some features of the labour relations system came into being in 1960, being launched at the time of the strike of that summer; it is still in existence at present (September 1961). This 'National Seamen's Reform Movement', as it is called, is a 'ginger' movement concerned not with replacing the N.U.S. but with changing its policy and operation in the direction of greater militancy and increased democratic control.

Neither the A.M.W.U. (1922–7) nor the Communists achieved any modification of the system. Nor has the National Seamen's Reform Movement, though its existence and activity were undoubtedly one of the factors impelling the N.U.S. to

[1] For a fuller account, see B. Mogridge, 'Militancy and inter-union rivalries in British shipping, 1911–1929', in *International Review of Social History*, no. 3 (1961), pp. 375–412.

take a more militant line since mid-1960, and one of the reasons for the wage increase and cut in hours conceded at that time.

Of the seafarers' unions other than the N.U.S. and still in operation, little need be said here. The N.U.S. itself organizes ratings in deck, engine-room and catering departments, and the only other seafarers' unions are those organizing officers (engineers and radio operators have been considered as officers for some decades now). On the whole the officers' unions have pursued a moderate policy; the few strikes of navigating and engineer officers that did take place in the years 1912–27 did not affect ocean shipping, and none have occurred since. In the early 1920s the radio officers' union[1] undertook three major strikes, but has not gone on strike since then.

LABOUR DISPUTES

How has the labour relations system as outlined above worked out in terms of industrial peace? In the years before the 1914–18 war conflict was endemic in the British shipping industry, and local stoppages were frequent. Even the national strike of 1911 assumed the character of a wave of local strikes, since in some ports men came out before the national strike was declared, in a number they came out some while after, and all the settlements were local. But the stoppage, if ragged, was certainly national in scope as well as intent; tens of thousands of seaman came out on strike, and hundreds of thousands of working days were lost. The following year the union called a strike in London; and, though it can hardly have seemed likely at the time, this strike of 1912 was the last strike ever called by the N.S.F.U./N.U.S.[2]

Minor strikes were called by other seafarers' unions in the years 1913–14 but ocean shipping was not involved. With the exception of a very short strike, confined to some four ships in Liverpool, in the autumn of 1917, the war years were similarly free of strikes in ocean shipping; but in the early 1920s there was

---

[1] Then the Association of Wireless and Cable Telegraphists, later renamed the Radio Officers' Union.

[2] The last official strike called by any union in the ocean shipping industry was in 1926.

a recrudescence of strike activity. For the upheaval of this latter period three major causes may be cited. Firstly, there was severe depression following hard on a freight boom, and falling money wages understandably caused unrest; furthermore, the total annual income of seafarers fell sharply owing to the widespread unemployment.

Secondly, there was bitter inter- and intra-union strife, for reasons only partly economic. It was in this period, the early 1920s, that unofficial strikes became an important phenomenon in the shipping industry; their most prominent aspect was protest against the policy of the leadership of the union, the N.S.F.U./N.U.S. In the 1920s the top priority of the union's president, Havelock Wilson, was harmony with the shipowners; this he regarded as essential, in the deflationary situation of the time, to the maintenance of the National Maritime Board and the closed shop for sailors and firemen. To this end, harmony with the owners, the N.S.F.U./N.U.S. under Wilson sacrificed all else. It is not surprising that the rank-and-file, encouraged by the A.M.W.U. and by the Communists, rebelled. That revolt was not more frequent, or more widespread when it did take place, is attributable to the necessity of being in favour with the union in order to get a berth.

Thirdly, another cause of industrial unrest was that important groups of seafarers were outside the National Maritime Board system. Radio operators, generally employed by shipowners only at one remove,[1] did not gain representation on the Board until 1941. In the early 1920s their union was active in resisting wage cuts and dilution of labour; it called three major strikes in this period, one of them lasting twelve weeks. The other group excluded from the Board was much larger; this was the catering department of the liners. The union which organized liner cooks and stewards withdrew from the Board in the summer of 1921 and was not allowed back; after some months the N.S.F.U. was recognized as 'representing' cooks and stewards on the Board, as it already did represent sailors and firemen; but it was not in fact able to recruit any appreciable number of liner cooks

---

[1] Most operators were employed by the wireless companies, and only indirectly by the shipowners, inasmuch as the latter hired both equipment and operators from the wireless companies.

and stewards until the 1940s. Liner cooks and stewards, like the radio operators, remained outside the National Maritime Board, and, having no commitment to it, were yet another volatile element in the labour relations of the industry.

Thus the period 1920–6 witnessed a number of important strikes. Then things began to change. Early in 1927 the A.M.W.U., the great rival to the N.U.S., finally faded out, and two years later Havelock Wilson died. He was replaced by W. R. Spence, a more tactful man, and relations with other unions and with the rank-and-file of the N.U.S. improved. Within a few months the Great Depression came, and the worsening of economic conditions made strike action seem pointless. When business livened up again the new leader of the N.U.S. pursued an energetic policy which, with the forceful support of Ernest Bevin, secured substantial gains without strike action being taken.

No strikes took place during the 1939–45 war. In 1947 a cut in the basic wage was made as the price of a degree of stabilization of employment (see pp. 305 and 309), and there was considerable unrest; but it did not blossom into strikes of any duration. In that same year the leader who in 1942 had taken over the leadership of the N.U.S. from Spence, died, and was replaced by T. Yates. Sir Thomas, as he later became, appears to have exercised during his term of office (1947–60) a particularly tight control over the union; that, combined with modest advances in wages and conditions, kept the industry strike-free until May 1955. The strike which took place then brought twenty-nine years of industrial peace to an end.[1]

The strike which occurred in May–June 1955 was confined to two ports and liner shipping. Only 1,700 seamen were involved; but it lasted nearly four weeks and the number of working days lost was officially estimated at 25,000.[2] Only one strike has taken place since—that of 1960—but it was a much larger affair; both liner and tramp shipping were involved, and no port in the country remained unaffected. This strike took place in July–

---

[1] In the General Strike of May 1926 the A.M.W.U. participated officially and some N.U.S. members joined in unofficially. Strikes in 1927, 1929 and 1933 affected only the China coast (that of 1927) and the short-sea trades across to Ireland.

[2] *Ministry of Labour Gazette* (May 1956), p. 172.

September 1960, in two separate phases whose duration was, together, over nine weeks. The number of seamen involved was 5,000 in the first phase, 4,000 in the second; the total of working days lost has been officially estimated as 123,000.[1]

These two strikes of 1955 and 1960 originated in different ways, the former in a protest against working condition, the latter in a protest against a disciplinary action. But both blew up into something much bigger, as other more deep-lying discontents found outlet. Common to all the complaints about pay, hours, accommodation, discipline, the lack of union representation on board,[2] the Merchant Shipping Acts and so on, was a fierce resentment directed against the union. The N.U.S. was criticized for the distance between national and local officials on the one hand, and rank-and-file members on the other; for undemocratic methods; for complacency and half-heartedness in pursuing the interests of its members. The formulations of these criticisms of the union were many and various, and sometimes lurid; but, shorn of the element of exaggeration, they appear to have had some substance. Most fundamental of all was the widespread feeling that the union was unduly concerned about retaining the goodwill of shipowners: 'Sir Thomas Yates and his colleagues have sided with the angels for so long that they have sacrificed the trust of many of their followers.'[3]

To sum up then, from mid-1926 to mid-1955 the ocean shipping industry was strike-free; from 1920 to mid-1926 and from mid-1955 to 1960 the incidence of strike action was grave, but the owners did at least have the advantage that their major 'opponent' on the opposite side of the bargaining table was far from militant.

LABOUR SUPPLY

(a) *The Labour Force*

On the eve of the 1914–18 war the British merchant fleet, totalling some 19 million tons gross, employed about 260,000

---

[1] Ibid., May 1961, p. 187.

[2] Many foreign merchant fleets have 'ship's delegates' (the equivalent of shop stewards in shore industry) to take care of any union matters that may arise while the ship is at sea or in a port where there is no representative of the union; the British merchant fleet has no such ship's delegates.

[3] Industrial correspondent of the *Daily Telegraph* (15 August 1960).

seamen;[1] today the fleet is roughly two millions tons larger, but the number employed is only some 200,000. This large decline in manpower requirements reflects the more economical manning associated with bigger ships and with oil-firing.

Owing to the nature of the industry, with varying numbers of ships in commission, some at sea, some in port, and with men signing on and off in different places, returning to shore work, and coming back to sea, the measurement of the labour force involved is a matter of considerable complexity. One approach is to take all those who follow the sea service; another, all those actually employed on a given date. The difference between the magnitudes resulting from these different methods is clearly very considerable in a period of unemployment; a more satisfactory indication of the labour requirements of the fleet is given by a third method, which adds together the crews of all ships in service during the year.[2] The figures used in Table 42 for the years up to 1938, are those compiled by this third method. Unfortunately such figures are not available for the post-war period; for these years therefore recourse has been had to figures of the 'effective strength' of the Merchant Navy (i.e., those currently on the effective section of the Central Register of Seamen). Since these do not include Asians serving under Asian agreements, official estimates for such Asians have been added. The resultant totals for the post-war period are not strictly comparable with those for the years up to 1938, but for practical purposes the differences may be ignored.

In the 1880s and 1890s the proportion of foreigners, other than Asians under Asian agreements, rose substantially, reaching a peak in 1903. But, together with that increase, resistance to their employment grew, and the Merchant Shipping Act of 1906 introduced a linguistic test designed to limit the numbers of foreigners in the British merchant fleet. The disparity with pay and conditions ashore lessened in these years, particularly during the shipping boom of 1911–13, and the merchant service

---

[1] 1913, 256,000; 1914, 262,000.

[2] To 1925 the first crews of all vessels in service at some time during the year; thereafter the crews of vessels employed on a censal date, plus the first crews of other vessels in service at some time during the year. These methods may involve some double counting of individual seamen, but the result will not be significantly affected.

consequently became more attractive to British labour than it had been. At the same time the countries of continental Europe were expanding their own merchant fleets, and their navies, and the demand for seamen was consequently growing there. Thus, in the decade preceding the 1914–18 war the proportion of such foreign seamen in the British fleet declined to some 12 per cent.[1]

TABLE 42. Labour force of the British merchant fleet

| | Total Labour Force | Percentage of Labour Force which was non-British | | |
		Under Asian agreements	Other foreigners	Total
1913	256,000	18	12	30
1919	234,000	20	7	27
1920	245,000	20	6	26
1925	237,000	23	5	28
1930	236,000	23	8	31
1935	182,000	26	5	31
1938	192,000	27	5	32
1955	200,000	25	n.a.	n.a.
1960	184,000	23	n.a.	n.a.

Source: Calculated from: *Statistical Abstract of the United Kingdom*, various years; O.E.E.C. *Maritime Transport*, 1955 and 1960.

The war hastened the process. About one-fifth of that 12 per cent consisted of Germans, and these left the labour force, either voluntarily or by internment. After the war—a watershed in this as in many other respects—the labour market in shipping was no longer the international free-for-all it had been only a few years earlier. The wages of seamen serving on British ships (except for those on Asian agreements) had been standardized, and that of itself reduced the interest in recruiting foreigners. The N.S.F.U., which had recently acquired joint control of supply, was fiercely nationalistic particularly towards the Germans. In 1919 the proportion of foreign seamen (other than those on Asian agreements) was down to about 7 per cent. In the remainder of the inter-war period it fluctuated between 5 and 8 or 9 per cent; since then it has probably been smaller still.

[1] Quantitative data for earlier years are unfortunately not comparable with those in the table.

Labour Relations and Labour Costs

Much more important is the rôle played by Asian labour recruited in Asia. In contrast to the decline after 1903 in the proportion of other foreigners, the proportion of such Asian seamen continued to grow through the 1914–18 war and up to 1938, when it was about 26 per cent. Thereafter figures are sparse, but in recent years at least the figure has been slightly lower, around 25 per cent. If one takes only shipping engaged in foreign trade, the proportion is of course somewhat higher, probably 27 or 28 per cent. Unlike other foreign labour, which at least since the 1914–18 war has been paid British rates, these Asian seamen are paid much lower rates; a considerable part of the economy on rates is however mopped up by heavier manning.

The Norwegian fleet also employs some Asian seamen under Asian agreements, again on lower pay per man; but this cheap Asian labour has never played the important rôle in Norwegian shipping that it has in British. The proportion of such Asians on Norwegian foreign-going ships has varied in recent years between 1 and 3 per cent; the corresponding figure for Britain, as mentioned above, is some 27 or 28 per cent. Much more important for Norwegian shipping than such Asians is other foreign labour. Before the 1914–18 war the proportion in Norway's foreign-going shipping was about a third; it was nearer a quarter in 1924, and by 1937–8 had fallen to below 10 per cent (about twice the British figure at this time). In the post-war period Norwegian shipping has, however, been faced with a serious shortfall in the domestic supply of labour; this shortfall has been met by drawing heavily on female and foreign labour. In the 1950s the proportion of women in the foreign-going fleet —they had been a negligible quantity before the war—rose from 2–3 per cent to over 6 per cent, while that of foreign seamen (other than Asians on Asian agreements) fluctuated between 12 and 19 per cent.[1] No saving in wages is made in this way, since both women and such foreigners are paid Norwegian men's rates; but in the case of foreigners there is some saving on social security contributions.

[1] An eighth of these foreign seamen serving on Norwegian ships are in fact from the U.K. The remainder are drawn mainly from Denmark (a quarter), Spain (an eighth), Italy, Germany, the Netherlands, and Sweden, in that order. As this short list shows, there are high-wage as well as low-wage countries among the sources of labour used.

(b) *Control of Supply*

Control of the labour supply was long a key issue in the British shipping industry, and one most often expressed in the union's struggle for, and the owners' fight against, the closed shop. The special difficulties inherent in the unionization of seafarers made the union particularly eager to secure the closed shop; but prior to 1917 the closed shop in shipping had been obtainable only rarely, in boom periods and in response to local labour market conditions.[1] During the twenty years ending in mid-1911 the shipowners generally had the whiphand. But in the three years preceding the 1914–18 war the struggle was a much more even one, and the lively economic conditions that so greatly helped the union to win its strike in the summer of 1911 obtained for much of that period.

Then in August 1914 war broke out. The war itself, with the resultant shortage of seamen, further strengthened the union's position *vis-à-vis* the employers, at the same time increasing the latter's ability to pay. Not surprisingly, the main concessions made in the first three years of the war were on the wages front. But in the last few months of 1917 the labour relations system itself was subjected to radical change, which put the unions on an entirely new footing, as partners with the owners on a national joint board. The constitution of this new National Maritime Board enshrined a new principle, that of joint control of supply. The N.S.F.U.'s new power in this respect was reflected in the institution of a formal closed shop for sailors and firemen, and this appears to have lasted for the remainder of the war, lapsing some time in 1919.

Then in 1922 the N.S.F.U. secured its reintroduction. That it managed to do so, in spite of the poor and deteriorating economic position of the industry at the time, is remarkable; but it is worth noting that this reintroduction of the closed shop for sailors and firemen was not wrung from the owners against their will, but agreed to by them, or at least by the Shipping Federation, in order to help the N.S.F.U. crush its nascent rival, the A.M.W.U. Both the Shipping Federation and the N.S.F.U. saw the

[1] The closed shop appears to have operated widely in the boom years 1889–90. Earlier instances are rare, but include the 1850's and, in the north-east, the mid-1820's.

A.M.W.U. as a threat to the established order, and to the harmony that had been achieved; to re-establish a closed shop in favour of the N.S.F.U. seemed an excellent way to hasten the A.M.W.U.'s demise.

In one or two ports the closed shop was long in being implemented, but by the end of 1926 it was more or less fully operative in all ports; after that it was virtually impossible to get a job as sailor or fireman without being a member of the N.S.F.U. The Great Depression made the closed shop difficult to maintain, but by the mid-1930s it appears to have been in full swing again, and has remained so.

In the catering department things were different. From the mid-1920s until 1942 the catering department was largely non-unionized; but during the latter year the union secured compulsory membership of catering department ratings on the majority of the liners, and by the end of the war could claim 90 per cent of the catering department on all vessels together.

As a rough summing-up we may say that the N.S.F.U./N.U.S. has had the closed shop in the deck and engine-room departments since 1922–6, and in the catering department since 1942–1945. (It must be pointed out that the closed shop has never been operative for officers.)[1] Norway provides a striking contrast in this matter of the closed shop. There the closed shop is illegal, but this has not prevented the seamen's union from recruiting well over 90 per cent of those eligible for membership. While not having the closed shop the Norwegian union has nonetheless taken full advantage, it would appear, of the tight labour market position prevailing there since the war; the British seamen's union has long enjoyed the closed shop but in recent years has hardly made the most of its bargaining strength.

(c) *Supply in Relation to Demand*

The depression in shipping which set in towards the end of 1907 brought serious unemployment in its train, and it was not until 1910 that a real improvement began. In most of the period 1911–14 business was good, and labour supply and demand appear to have been tolerably well equated. Then came the

---

[1] More precisely, not since 1889–90, when for a few months joint action by an officers' union and the seamen's union enforced it in some ports.

war, which brought serious labour shortage. On the one hand, transfers of merchant seamen to the Royal Navy, together with ship losses and some desertions, cut back the labour force of the shipping industry, which could find replacements ashore only with great difficulty; on the other hand, freights were high, and shipping both a highly profitable business and a national necessity. Consequently the demand for labour was far in excess of the supply.

The rapid demobilization at the end of the 1914–18 war flooded the labour market. Throughout 1919 the number of unemployed seamen remained above 17,000, but by the summer of 1920 much of the surplus labour has been absorbed. The improvement was shortlived; as 1919 had witnessed a swollen labour supply, so 1920 saw a contraction of demand, for in that year the freight boom collapsed. By the end of the year the slackening activity in shipping was being reflected in the growing number of jobless seamen; by the early summer of 1921 a third of Britain's seamen were out of work. Thereafter the number fell; but the average unemployed in each of the years 1922–6 was still around 20 per cent. In 1927–9 it was between 17 and 18 per cent. But by the end of 1929 it was rising again, and by the end of 1930 it was over 30 per cent. It remained over 30 per cent throughout 1931, 1932 and 1933. Then it slowly came down; but as late as July 1939 it was still 20 per cent.[1]

It is clear that British shipowners suffered from no general shortage of labour at least until the mid-1930s; large numbers of officers and other skilled men were among the unemployed until about that time. But then an important change took place; shipping recovered from the Great Depression more slowly than many shore industries, and lost a number of skilled ratings and officers to those industries as a result. When shipping business did liven up, the improvement was accompanied by the rapid expansion of the Royal Navy and Air Force. So for varying periods in the years 1936–9 the merchant fleet experienced serious shortages of navigating, engineer and radio officers, and at times there were also insufficient able seamen. Thus in the

---

[1] These figures, which relate to insured employees in the shipping service, are based on data in the *Ministry of Labour Gazette* for those years, and express the number recorded as unemployed as a percentage of the estimated total insured.

last part of the inter-war period, despite the high unemployment figures, owners sometimes had difficulty in finding qualified crews.

Apart from these features of the years 1936–9 the inter-war period was characterized by a prolonged and general surplus of labour so far as the British shipping industry was concerned. The war intensified and generalized the labour shortages of 1936–9. By the end of 1940 the position was critical, and in May 1941, after discussions initiated by the Shipping Federation and the N.U.S., the Ministry of Labour issued an Essential Work Order to prevent seamen from leaving the industry. At the same time a pool system was introduced, whose 'primary purpose . . . was to minimize delay to ships through shortage of crew supply'.[1] It also stabilized employment. All officers and ratings not specifically retained by a particular company were transferred to a pool, and owners wishing to engage men had to do so through the pool. When the Essential Work Order expired in March 1947 compulsion disappeared with it, though some other features of the pooling system were retained in the Established Service Scheme (see p. 315) which was brought in in the same month.

Though compulsion was removed in 1947, shipowners have since been benefitting from another governmental provision, namely that young men otherwise liable under the National Service Act for compulsory military service, were exempt so long as they were employed in the Merchant Navy. By comparison with the pay of a private on 'National Service', the remuneration of a merchant navy rating was handsome, and a number of young seamen were recruited in this way. It is impossible to say how many seamen in the age group affected by the liability to compulsory military service chose to spend some years in the Merchant Navy for that reason; the official view of the shipping industry seems to be that the number was not large. But it is clear that the possibility of avoiding military service by joining the Merchant Navy has been a factor considerably alleviating the labour market position for shipowners, who have thus been spared some of the consequences of full employment.

Norwegian owners have not enjoyed the benefit of a similar

---

[1] L. H. Powell, *The Shipping Federation. A History* (London, 1950), p. 86.

Labour Relations and Labour Costs

exemption, and have had to face full employment as best they could. The result has been twofold; increased recruitment of foreigners and women; and high wages.

LABOUR COSTS

(a) Composition of Crew Costs

Crew costs consist of three main components: wages, social security contributions, and victualling. The relative importance of each component varies appreciably from flag to flag, along with differences in the social system. In Italy, for example, wage payments account for less than one-half the owners' crew costs.[1] It is a curious fact that published figures of crew cost, or total operating cost, often either leave out one of the three components (usually social security contributions) completely, or bracket two of them together, so that there seem to be hardly any figures indicating the relative importance of each one under different flags. Table 43 is an attempt to combine various sources so as to arrive at such figures; it should not be taken as much more than an illustration of the diversity which evidently exists.

TABLE 43. Crew cost components on a representative ship in the 1950s

Cost component	U.K.	Norway	Nether-lands	France	U.S.A.
	%	%	%	%	%
Wages	75	71	69·5	68	88
Social security contributions	2·5	4·5	14·5	20	4·5
Victualling	22·5	20·5	16	12	7·5
Repatriation	—	4	—	—	—
Total crew costs	100	100	100	100	100

Source: Calculated from: Jean Latty, Traité d'économie maritime, vol. 2 (Paris, 1954), p. 439; Study of the Operations of the Maritime Administration and the Federal Maritime Board, Hearings before the House Committee on Merchant Marine and Fisheries (Washington, 1955), p. 281; Motor Ship (October 1958), p. 295.

[1] Review of Maritime Subsidy Policy, report by a joint working committee, House Committee on Merchant Marine and Fisheries (Washington, 1954), p. 44.

Labour Relations and Labour Costs

Clearly, international comparisons of crew cost which take only wages into account are inadequate. The matter is further complicated by the fact that these proportions vary not only from flag to flag but also over time. Figures for Norwegian foreign-going shipping given in Table 44 indicate that appreciable shifts in the relative importance of these components can occur even within the short space of a decade.

TABLE 44. Crew cost components in the Norwegian foreign trade fleet, 1949 and 1958 (total of all owners' crew expenses)

Cost component	1949	1958	1958, taking 1949 as 100
Wages	66·8	72·9	258
Social security and welfare contributions, and crew travelling expenses	10·2	9·6	224
Victualling	23·0	17·5	180
Total crew costs	100·0	100·0	237

Source: Calculated from *Mannskapsstatistikk* (Skibsfartens Arbeidsgiver-forening, Oslo, 1960), pp. 75, 80, 83.

In this case, as the third column indicates, the cause of the shift was that wages rose much faster than the other components of crew cost, victualling showing the lowest rate of increase.

(b) Accommodation

Before passing on to consider in turn the three components of crew costs, crew accommodation must be mentioned. Though not part of operating costs, and thus not part of crew costs as here defined, it is nonetheless an important cost item arising out of the ship's manning needs.

The more ship space devoted to crew accommodation, the less is available as earning capacity for the carriage of passengers or cargo. Unfortunately, quantitative measurement, even in straightforward terms of cubic or square feet of space per man, is not undertaken except for ships considered as individual cases; it is thus difficult to compare one national fleet with another. Statutory minima (for decades higher in Norway than in Britain) for volume and floor space are laid down in a number of

303

countries, but this does not tell one what standards are actually operative: a given national fleet may well include numbers of ships better than the national minimum, or—when that minimum has not been long enough in force for conversion and new building to ensure compliance throughout the fleet—worse.

One is left therefore with qualitative assessments. On the basis of that evidence, then, it seems that the general standard of crew accommodation aboard British ships was lower than under several flags in the inter-war period. Until the late 1930s at any rate the general standard aboard British ships lagged behind that achieved in the German, Dutch, and Scandinavian fleets.[1] Since then the general standard of crew accommodation in the British fleet has improved greatly, and British owners have probably not continued in recent years to possess the advantage of relatively low standards of crew accommodation.

(c) *Social Security*[2]

Shipowners' social security costs under different flags vary according to both the scope of the insurance provided and the method of financing it; social security may be organized principally by individual companies (with substantial variations in consequence under one and the same national flag) or, as in western Europe generally, under national schemes financed partly or wholly by employers' contributions. Employers' contributions are often high where wages are relatively low, as for example in Italy; and sometimes low where wages are high. The matter is one of considerable complexity.

In Britain industrial accident insurance, to take one example, included seamen long before the 1914–18 war; but the financing is on a tripartite basis (employers, employees, and the State), whereas in some countries, Norway among them, employers bear the whole burden of industrial accident insurance. In respect of health insurance costs, on the other hand, Norwegian

---

[1] See Capt. H. Taprell Dorling in *Brassey* (1939), p. 156.

[2] The main foreign sources used in this section are: Hans-Gerhard Voigt, *Die soziale Lage der Seeleute in der Handelsschiffahrt - ein internationaler Vergleich* (Schroedter, Hamburg, 1956); *International Survey of Social Security, Comparative Analysis* (I.L.O., Geneva, 1950); *Unemployment Insurance Schemes* (I.L.O., Geneva, 1955); D. B. Skårdal, *Social Insurance in Norway* (Committee for International Social Policy, Oslo, 1955).

shipowners may have had an easier time of it than British owners until the mid-1930s, and in old age pension insurance perhaps up to 1948.

In unemployment insurance another difference emerges. Norwegian seamen have been insured against unemployment only since the war, whereas British seamen have been so insured since 1920. Furthermore, Norway has nothing corresponding to the Established Service Scheme, operative in Britain since 1947.[1] This Scheme, which replaced the wartime Merchant Navy Pool (see p. 301), introduced a notable degree of stabilization of peacetime employment. Two types of service are distinguished, 'established' and 'unestablished'. Established seafarers accept a two-year contract; when not actually on articles (or employed off articles, as when doing ship work in port) they hold themselves available for employment and receive in addition to national unemployment benefit, 'Establishment Benefit'. Established men are given preference for work over unestablished men; not all are eligible for establishment (officers must be certificated, ratings must have at least twelve months' sea service), and not all seafarers wish to tie themselves down in this way. Under the terms of the scheme, the shipowners virtually guaranteed to offer establishment to 70 per cent of those eligible;[2] this proportion does not seem ever to have been reached, though it is probably now nearer 65 than 60 per cent. Whatever the exact figure, and it is not published, it is certainly somewhere between 60 and 70 per cent, which is still a remarkable achievement. The Scheme, which is operated by the shipowners' organizations, is financed by a levy on the owners' wage bill. The size of this addition to crew costs is

---

[1] A similar scheme was introduced in France a few months later.

[2] 'The number ... who can be brought within the scheme must depend upon the employment of ships. ... The intention, however, is that as many as possible should be within the Established Service Scheme having regard to reasonable fluctuations of trade and in any event not less than 70 per cent of the Seafarers eligible under the Scheme.' (Para. 1 of the Agreement, as in National Maritime Board, *Year Book 1960*, p. 13.)

Eligibility is confined to those 'of proved character and ability', physically fit, and having either a navigating or engineer certificate or twelve months' sea service. Asian and African crews are excluded, as are those serving in various specialist capacities found on passenger liners (hairdresser, butcher, swimming instructor, etc.) unless promoted from a post where already established.

apparently not a large one; an official U.S. publication gives figures which make the cost of the levy about 2 per cent of wages,[1] and that would be a smaller proportion still of total crew costs—something like 1·5 per cent.

Comparing Britain with Norway the overall picture on social security costs seems to be that Norwegian owners enjoyed some advantage in the inter-war years. They may still have had a small one in the post-war period, but even if they did it was probably more than counterbalanced by the disadvantage in crew travelling expenses—an additional cost which bulks large in the Norwegian fleet owing to the high proportion of cargo vessels plying cross trades and consequently touching Norwegian ports only very infrequently.

(d) *Victualling*

Victualling costs are generally high where wages are high, low where wages are low. But there are many more variations than that bald statement would imply. For one thing, even in those countries which have victualling scales laid down by law or collective agreement, these are only minima, and there will be substantial differences between different companies all operating above those minima. Nevertheless some comparisons have been attempted from time to time, and one or two of the more interesting and reliable are worth citing.

As one would expect, Japanese victualling costs are low. But in the mid-1930s British shipowners managed to feed their Asian ratings at a cost of 18s. per month per man compared with the cost to Japanese owners of 21s.[2] No similar information relating to the position since the war is available.

A victualling cost advantage that British owners have enjoyed in the post-war period, and possibly in the inter-war years as well, is that over Norwegian owners. The size of the difference cannot be ascertained with any certainty, but according to estimates prepared by the U.S. Maritime Administration,

---

[1] *Merchant Marine Study and Investigation*, Hearings before a subcommittee of the Senate Committee on Interstate and Foreign Commerce, Part 7 (Washington, 1950). The percentage is calculated from the figures on pp. 1751, 1758 and 1765.

[2] Calculated from the Imperial Shipping Committee, *British Shipping in the Orient* (1939), p. 123.

Norwegian victualling costs may be as much as a third higher than British.[1] Other countries with victualling costs per man higher than Britain, according to the same source, include Denmark and France.

(e) *Wages and Hours*

As Tables 43 and 44 suggest, the proportion of crew costs accounted for by wages may be taken as falling typically within the range 65 and 75 per cent. But wages are themselves made up in a complex way: there is firstly the basic wage, secondly overtime pay, and thirdly a host of bonuses, allowances and supplements—for service in particular areas, on particular types of ship, for particular lengths of time, and so on. Furthermore, the relative importance of these three elements varies considerably.

The basic wage can be as little as 52 per cent of the total wage, though that is an extreme case taken from the U.S.A.[2] Unfortunately, in consequence of the fact that no figures of British seamen's earnings are published—apparently none are collected —the proportions obtaining in the U.K. fleet cannot be quoted. Very full statistics are however available for the Norwegian fleet, and Table 45 gives the average proportions for a few grades in foreign-going shipping.

The above gives some indication of the variety within the merchant fleet of a single country; but it reflects only variations over time and variations between grades. A breakdown by trading areas and by types of vessel would show further variation—all still within the ships of one flag. Between different flags there would presumably also be variations, even comparing ships of the same type, plying the same route at the same time, though unfortunately comparative figures of such a kind do not exist.

These manifold variations in the importance of the three components of wages, and still more the lack of information on flag-

[1] *Study of the Operations of the Maritime Administration* (op. cit.), p. 281. The figures relate to 1953, and the British crew is one without any Asians. The ship is apparently a 'representative' cargo liner.

[2] *Proposed Amendments to the 1936 Merchant Marine Act*, Hearings before House Committee on Merchant Marine and Fisheries, Part 1 (Washington, 1953), p. 459.

Labour Relations and Labour Costs

to-flag differences in this respect, limit the value of international comparisons of any one of the components. Nonetheless, such comparisons are not otiose, provided their limitations are kept in mind.

TABLE 45. Wage components in the Norwegian foreign trade fleet, 1948 and 1958 (Percentage of total earnings)

Grade	1948 (November)		1958 (March)	
	Basic wage	Overtime	Basic wage	Overtime
	%	%	%	%
Chief mates	80	12	64	19
Second engineers	72	20	57	27
Able seamen	81	14	70	16
Stewards	91	1	61	18
All seamen	n.a.	n.a.	70	14

Source: Calculated from *Statistisk Årbok 1949* (Oslo), pp. 260–1, and ibid., *1959*, p. 222.

(i) *Allowances*

An international comparison of the provisions regulating the various bonuses, allowances and supplements could well fill the pages of a book, and would probably be confusing rather than enlightening. In the case of Britain and Norway there is probably not a great difference in the effect of these allowances on total wage costs.   The more important of the three components of wages are the basic wage and overtime, and here a comparison, if confined to those two countries, is a little more manageable.

(ii) *Basic Wage*

The historical development, under the two flags, of the basic wage of able seamen is of considerable interest. In the years before the 1914–18 war, the Norwegian seamen received a much lower wage than his British counterpart—often as much as 30 per cent less—and Norwegian owners clearly had a very substantial advantage in wage costs. The effect of the war was radical; sharp though the rise in British pay was, that which took place in

308

Norwegian pay was sharper, and in 1919 the basic wage of an A.B. aboard a Norwegian ship was 11 per cent higher than the corresponding wage on board a British ship. This novel state of affairs did not last. When the boom collapsed money wages fell in Norway as elsewhere, but in addition the kroner suffered a rapid decline in value relative to other currencies, and the consequence was to restore Norway's competitive advantage in wage costs. From 1920 to 1924 the depreciation of the Norwegian currency transformed the drop in the A.B.'s basic wage from one of 41 per cent in terms of kroner to one of 76 per cent in terms of sterling.

Then in the mid-1920s the kroner began to gain in value again, but the A.B.'s basic wage in kroner continued to fall, so that when both the kroner and the basic wage stabilized in 1928 there was still an appreciable differential between the Norwegian A.B.'s basic wage and the British. This gap remained throughout the 1930s.

The picture since the 1939–45 war is very different. 1947 saw a reduction in the basic wage in Britain—in the case of an able seaman from £24 to £20, a cut of one-sixth. This put the British A.B.'s basic wage below the Norwegian for the first time since 1919; it has remained below. But one must also take account of the effect of British 'efficient service pay', whose introduction in 1947 accompanied the reduction in the basic wage. Efficient service pay is graduated in one-year steps up to four years' 'efficient service',[1] when the maximum is payable. Statistics on British seamen's earnings are non-existent, making it impossible to say how many A.B.'s receive how many years' efficient service pay; but in any case, even if one includes the maximum efficient service pay with the basic wage, the resultant rate is still below the Norwegian A.B.'s basic wage alone, right from 1947 to August 1960.[2]

Though the A.B. is generally regarded as the key grade in international comparisons of seamen's wages, his basic rate is

---

[1] The definition is of some detail, but its main effect is to exclude the least experienced, such as deck boys, and any whose conduct has been unsatisfactory.

[2] There is a supplement according to length of service in the Norwegian merchant navy also, but this so-called 'age supplement' is payable only after a number of years' service with the same company, and does not affect wage costs to anything like the same extent as British efficient service pay.

only a very rough-and-ready guide to basic rates in general.[1] Differentials vary greatly from flag to flag. If the A.B.'s rate in country A is appreciably higher than in country B, it is highly likely that the rates of most other non-officer grades will be higher and probable that most officers' rates too will be higher in country A than in country B, though the margins in each case may be very different from that existing between A.B.s' rates. The smaller the difference between A.B.s' rates in the two countries, the less can be said with confidence of the relative positions of other seamen's rates. Furthermore, the compilation of comparative figures for officers and some grades in the catering department is complicated by the fact that the basic rate varies, within the ships of one flag, according to tonnage, size of crew and so on; and different countries organize their systems of gradation differently. But it would appear, without making a detailed study of the development of the basic wages of other grades, that for most of the interwar period the basic wages of merchant seamen generally were higher in Britain than in Norway, and that in most of the post-war period they have been at least as high in Norway as in Britain.

(iii) *Overtime*

The third component of wages is overtime pay. Overtime provisions are partly a question of the form and amount of compensation for work beyond a stipulated norm, partly a question of the level of that norm. The first question is complicated by the fact that some compensation for overtime is in money, some in unpaid leave ashore. The following comparison is confined to the second question—of the level of the norm beyond which compensation is provided.

The system in the deck and engine-room departments is (except for a few 'day-men' whose work can generally be

---

[1] Sometimes comparisons of basic wages alone—or worse still of an A.B.'s basic wage alone—are presented as if they give a sufficient indication of *overall crew costs*. That that is not so will be evident from the last three tables. In 1958, taking the Norwegian fleet in foreign trade as a whole, basic wages were 70·0 per cent of total wages, which in turn were 72·9 per cent of total crew cost; that is, basic wages were just over 51 per cent of total crew cost. In some other years the figure might be lower still; and certainly it would be lower in certain trades taken separately. Under some other flags too the percentage might be lower.

Labour Relations and Labour Costs

confined to the sort of working hours customary ashore) one of 'watches'. There is a two-watch system and a three-watch system. Under the former a man works 12 hours out of each 24, and 84 a week. The three-watch system, on the other hand, means working 8 hours in the 24, and a 56-hour week; it also requires three men where the two-watch system requires only two. Britain abandoned the full two-watch system in 1936, but did not replace it by the full three-watch system until 1943; in the interim there was a transitional arrangement whereby 64 hours per week were worked. In Norway the three-watch system was introduced in 1919, but limited to the engine-room and only partially implemented even there. In 1939 it became compulsory on deck for vessels of over 2,500 tons, and in 1947 on deck and in the engine-rooms for vessels of over 1,200 tons.

Continuing with the deck and engine-room comparison, the other aspect of the matter is the number of hours per day or per week beyond which extra compensation is provided. An I.L.O. study carried out in the mid-1950s[1] shows that in the deck department ratings on Norwegian ships were compensated after eight hours a day as early as 1939, while in 1955 the corresponding figure for British ships was still twelve hours. For engine-room ratings there was no difference in the hours per day (eight) after which compensation was made, but in Norwegian ships there was, as early as 1939, also compensation after 48 hours in any week, whereas in 1955 the British figure was 56. (The latter was reduced to 48 in 1960, but from January 1961 the Norwegian figure was also reduced—to 45.)

Provisions for day-men show a lesser disparity than those for watch-keepers, but still one in which Norwegian hours were the lower. Turning finally to the catering department, there too British seamen were working longer hours than their Norwegian counterparts: in 1939 the maximum hours worked in the catering department of Norwegian vessels, whether passenger-carrying or not, was 63 hours a week, whereas in 1955 the corresponding figures for British ships were 63 on cargo vessels, 70 on passenger vessels.

[1] (A) Conditions of Seafarers in Smaller Ships and (B) Changes in Hours or Work on Board Ship since 1946, PTMC 1/2 (I.L.O., Geneva, 1956). The data on hours used above refer to foreign-going vessels, not 'smaller ships'.

(f) *Manning*

Thus far the comparison has left manning out of account. It is high time to bring it in. One country will, by reason of custom or collective agreement or legislation, man a given ship with a larger crew than will another; and even if the number of crew is the same, the composition of that crew may be very different. Comparisons of manning are of extreme difficulty. In some countries the scales are not comprehensive; and there is no information regarding the extent to which actual manning in any country normally exceeds the minimum, nor whether the difference between actual and minimum manning is constant. Comparisons of manning practice are few and far between; the following is a summary of the limited evidence of this kind which is available.

The earliest comparative evidence to hand refers to the 1930s. Then, apparently, Norwegian manning of both dry-cargo boats and tankers was lighter than British. According to a partial British source the deck department on Norwegian freighters had a more diluted skill structure than that of comparable British vessels; that is to say, had fewer A.B.s, but more ordinary seamen and boys. Certainly Norwegian ships, in common with several other countries at this period, generally carried no radio officer, his duties being carried out by navigating officers or deck ratings; they received an additional payment for the extra service, but the shipowner did effect a net saving of some pounds a month on a ship with this 'mate-operator' system. (Since the war to have 'mate-operators' instead of radio officers has been rare.)

For the post-war period the only published comparison of manning which is at all comprehensive relates to January 1949.[1] Of the three cargo-vessel types taken, all show Norwegian and Dutch manning to be heavier than British, and Brazilian to be much heavier; Italian manning appears as heavier than British in one case and lighter in two, and Greek manning as lighter in all three cases. Panholib manning is not included in the table, but is probably lighter.

Since 1949, however, minimum manning scales have been revised in some countries; in Norway for example in 1950. A numerical assessment of present international manning practice,

[1] *Merchant Marine Study and Investigation* (op. cit.), pp. 1750–70.

based on such information as is available, suggests that British manning requirements for tankers and cargo liners are among the heaviest in the world; but to an unknown extent the apparent British disadvantage here arises from the inclusion of Asian seamen in the figures, despite the fact that one Asian contributes less to the wage bill than one European. The competitive disadvantage of British tankers and cargo liners, due to their generally heavier manning, may therefore be a small one or even non-existent. In the case of tramps and bulk carriers there does not seem to be the same apparent general disadvantage, and indeed the size of the crews of British-flag ships is sometimes lower than on ships owned in the main competitor countries.

(g) *International Comparisons of Crew Costs*

What does all this add up to? A partial answer is provided by Table 46, which presents in summary form a number of cost comparisons from various sources. All but one of the comparisons refer to dry-cargo vessels (number x relates to a tanker). Some of them refer only to wage costs, some to wages and social security, some to wages and victualling, and some to all three components of crew cost; these latter are of course the most useful, but in the earlier years the omission of social security is not too serious. One of the inter-war comparisons (number vi) explicitly disregards differences in manning.

A word on the reliability of the information is needed. It will be apparent from the preceding parts of this section that the comparison of crew costs under different flags is an extremely hazardous operation. One important dilemma has not yet been mentioned: that is, whether, in making such comparisons of total crew costs, to take actual cases or hypothetical cases. If actual ships are taken, it is hard to find ones that are fully comparable, and still harder to gain access to the cost figures. If hypothetical ships are taken then the problem is to know just what victualling, overtime, manning and so on to apply, since information on the actuality is so fragmentary. The comparisons given in the table below vary in the method of compilation used; sometimes even the method is not explicitly stated in the source.

The official U.S. comparisons in Table 46—those numbered

TABLE 46. Comparative crew costs on various ship types, 1901–60
(Index, U.K. in each case = 100)

No.	Year	Items covered	U.K.	Norway	Denmark	Netherlands	Germany	France	Italy	Greece	Yugoslavia	Japan	U.S.A.
i	1901	w	100	69									175
ii	1925	w	100	50			50						
iii	1931	w	100			90	75	76	59	69	44–50		
iv	1931	w	100										154
v	1936	w	100									54	
		wv										53	
vi	1936	wv	100	95		131	122	109	90	79		37	163
	1937	wv	100	95		112	122	64	60	79		37	163
vii	1949	ws	100	98		122			85	130			288
		ws	100	96		112			81	124			304
		ws	100	96		114			81	124			312
viii	1949	ws	100	108		120		104					317
		wvs	100	110		114		109					272
ix	1949	w	100	90	140			121	96	125			412
x	1949	ws	100	91	100	74		106	97				286
xi	1951	ws	100	111									425
		ws	100	106		152							360
xii	1953	wvs	100	110	121	111		145	107			86	381
		wvs	100	125	131	126		164	122			97	433
xiii	1958	w	100	120		122							436
		ws	100	124		142							443
xiv	1960	wvs	100	104–111	120–130	100–108							

w: wages only
wv: wages and victualling
ws: wages and social security contributions
wvs: wages, victualling, and social security contributions; i.e. total crew costs

Labour Relations and Labour Costs

Notes and sources:

i. Small freighters. *Annual Report of U.S. Commissioners of Navigation* (1901), p. 107, quoted in John G. B. Hutchins, *American Maritime Industries and Public Policy* (Harvard U.P., Cambridge, Mass., 1941), p. 520.

ii. Size or other details not specified; presented as typical. *The Times* (11 September 1925).

iii. 7,500-ton. *Fairplay* (31 December 1931); figures relate to a time before the devaluation of the pound.

iv. 8–9,000 deadweight tons. Saugstad, op. cit., p. 25.

v. Cargo liner on Eastern trade routes. Imperial Shipping Committee, op. cit., pp. 123–5.

vi. 2–5,000 ton freighters, ocean-going. Standard manning assumed. The figures for '1937' are the 1936 figures revised to take account of new exchange rates but not of any changes in wages. Urs Geymüller, *Staatlicher Protektionismus zur See zwischen den beiden Weltkriegen* (Schahl, Lorrach-Stetten, Switzerland, 1953), p. 59.

vii. The three vessels, all sailing the North Atlantic, are an EC-2 Liberty, a C2-S-B1, and a C3-S-A2. *Merchant Marine Study and Investigation*, op. cit., pp. 1750–70. Figures for January 1949.

viii. Liberty vessel. Ibid., p. 1385. January 1949.

ix. Size not specified. In coal trade, U.S.A. to France. *Merchant Marine Study (Transfers to Foreign Flag)*, Hearings before a sub-committee of the Senate Committee on Interstate and Foreign Commerce, Part 1 (Washington, 1954), p. 66.

x. T2 tanker (about 16,600 deadweight tons). *Merchant Marine Study and Investigation*, op. cit., Part 1 (Washington, 1949), p. 16.

xi. A representative vessel on two different routes. *Review of Maritime Subsidy Policy*, op. cit., p. 43.

xii. A representative vessel. The two sets of figures take the British ship (= 100) as having a white crew and a mixed crew respectively. *Study of the operations of the Maritime Administration*, op. cit., p. 281.

xiii. A C2 class vessel (about 9,000 tons). U.S. Department of Commerce, *Manual of General Procedures for Determining Operating-Differential Subsidy Rates*, quoted in *Motor Ship* (October 1958), p. 295.

xiv. Size and other details not specified; presented as typical. Statement by a Danish shipowner, quoted in *Shipping World* (20 July 1960), p. 44. It is clear from the date that these estimates do not take into account the large wage increase granted to British seamen in August 1960.

---

vii, viii, and x to xiii—appear to combine the two methods of actual cases and hypothetical cases. These official U.S. comparisons emanate from the U.S. Maritime Administration, which attempts to carry out a continuing study of operating costs (including crew costs) and shipbuilding costs in a number of competitor countries; the purpose of this study is to discover the size of the discrepancy between U.S. and foreign costs, so as to determine the level of countervailing subsidy payable.[1] The relative levels of the costs of the foreign fleets among themselves is something which is discovered in the course of the enquiry, but is not its object. It is precisely this disinterestedness with regard to the relative level of non-U.S. costs which, together with the scope of the undertaking, makes these U.S. comparisons valuable.

Lastly, the question of representativeness of sample must be mentioned. In the case of the comparison numbered ii the round figures indicate that this is an informed impression rather than a sample, representative or otherwise; but in the other comparisons, and in the table as a whole, the question of representativeness of sample is a major one. It lies in the nature of the source material, fragmentary as it is, that the table should be open to criticism on this score. The only answer is that it is a compilation of such reasonably reliable data as are available.

In the commentary on the table which follows, it must be remembered that, except where the contrary is explicitly stated, the discussion is confined to dry-cargo vessels.

One of the facts most strikingly brought out by the table is the high level of U.S. costs at all dates for which quantitative information is available.[2] This cost disadvantage is, of course, at the root of U.S. subsidy policy (see Chapters V and VIII) and the operating subsidies are designed to compensate American liner owners for their high crew costs.

Clearly Japanese costs, even allowing for social security costs (not included in any of the comparisons in the table before 1949), were far below British in the 1930s, and, though the table does not show it, doubtless they were in earlier decades also.

---

[1] The collection of data on ship operating costs was made more difficult by the unwillingness of shipowners to furnish the information needed. As one senior civil servant in the State Department told a Congressional committee: 'The shipbuilders co-operated to a surprising extent, much better than the foreign operators did. In fact, we didn't have much trouble on the building side, but we had a lot of trouble on the operating side. In fact, we have had a terrible time on the operating side.' (*Merchant Marine Studies*, Hearings before a subcommittee of the Senate Committee on Interstate and Foreign Commerce, Part 1, Washington, 1953, p. 45.)

[2] It would be tempting to conclude that U.S. crew costs have been higher than British throughout the period. But the gap between the first two dates—1901 and 1931—is too long for such a conclusion to be warranted. Indeed there is some evidence to suggest that for at least a part of the early 1920s U.S. *wage* costs at least may have been as low as British.

Since the war however that disparity has evidently shrunk. If Japanese crew costs (all three components included) on a Japanese ship are compared with those of a British vessel with mixed (British and Asian)[1] crew such as is typical in Eastern trades, then the Japanese cost advantage dwindles, according to the 1953 comparison in the table, to a mere 3 per cent; and in statistics of this kind 3 per cent must be considered to be within the margin of error. What is clear from this comparison is that if there was a crew cost advantage either way in 1953 it was only a very small one.

The table also sheds some light on competition from eastern Europe. In the inter-war years Britain experienced severe competition from the low-wage tramps of Greece, Yugoslavia, Finland, Latvia, and the U.S.S.R., all of whom enjoyed a large crew cost advantage. Post-war data for these countries are sparse in the extreme. It is particularly regrettable that the post-war figures for Greece refer only to 1949; if any were available for the 1950s they would probably show a drastic reduction in Greece's cost advantage over Britain since 1949.

The position with regard to crew costs on Panamanian ships is interesting. In the Panholib fleets social security provisions are generally minimal,[2] and labour has to be attracted primarily by the wage levels offered. These vary not only from company to company but also from ship to ship according to the nationality —or nationalities— of the crew. Officers and skilled ratings can often command high wages, and those paid have in fact attracted considerable numbers from western Europe, including Britain.[3] The overall picture for the Panholib fleets appears to be one of great variety, both in the composition of crews and the rates paid; authoritative general statistics on the personnel of

[1] More precisely, seamen (whether British or not) on British rates of pay, and seamen on Asian rates.

[2] State social security schemes are virtually non-existent, but some of the large U.S. tanker companies operating ships under Panholib flags do have pension schemes for officers for example.

[3] According to one estimate in 1959 the number of seamen of all nationalities working aboard ships of Panamanian, Liberian and Honduran registry was about 70,000 (*Syren and Shipping*, 16 December 1959). Other sources suggest that the main nationalities represented in the 1950s were German, British, Norwegian, Dutch, Italian, Greek, Indian, and Chinese; these are not listed in order of magnitude since that is not known.

these fleets appear to be non-existent, so that the figures for Panama must be treated with particular reserve. Table 47 gives the available information, that for 1957 having been given to a Congressional committee by representatives of U.S. tanker companies actually operating under Panholib flags. Since these figures do not include Britain in the comparison, the table is presented on a base *U.S.A.* in each year = 100.

TABLE 47. Comparative crew costs on two ship types, 1949 and 1957 (Index, U.S.A. in each case = 100)

No.	Year	Ship type	Items covered	U.S.A.	Country Panama	U.K.
1.	1949	Liberty	ws	100	51	32
			wvs	100	56	37
2.	1949	T2 tankers	ws	100	n.a.	35
3.	1957	T2 tankers	ws	100	23	n.a.
4.	1957	T2 tankers	wvs	100	72	n.a.
5.	1957	T2 tankers	w	100	75–82	n.a.

Note: w, v, s, as in Table 46.

Sources: 1. Table 46, no. viii.
2. Table 46, no. x.
3. *Ship Transfers to Foreign Flag*, Hearings before the Merchant Marine and Fisheries Subcommittee of the Senate Committee on Interstate and Foreign Commerce (Washington, 1957), p. 57.
4. Ibid., pp. 64–65.
5. Ibid., p. 101.

For the last decade or more Panholib ships have probably on the whole had crew costs in the same range as ships sailing under the major western European flags.[1]

What, finally, can be said on costs under the flags of western Europe? Before the 1914–18 war British costs were probably as high as any in Europe most of the time. The inter-war years were a time of upheaval: first, the freight boom, then depression

---

[1] Prior to the early 1950's a number of Panholib owners took advantage of the possibility that flag-of-convenience registration offered to use ships that in one way or another were unsuitable, often because of bad accommodation, sometimes because of unseaworthiness. But since then a great improvement has occurred, and the number of inferior ships has greatly diminished, and may now be of negligible proportions.

in the 1920s with round after round of wage cuts, then the Great Depression; latterly this was in turn accompanied by a round of currency devaluation which overlapped with gradual recovery, which in turn made possible a series of wage increases. The relative cost positions of different flags in this supremely international industry are often modified, and in the inter-war years important changes were frequent. Table 46 does no more than pinpoint a few salient facts. With Italy for example Britain seems to have remained at a disadvantage on crew costs in the inter-war period and into the late 1940s; but then Italian costs seem to have caught up and perhaps overtaken British. French costs rose above British as early as the 1930s, but then after devaluation fell back; around the late 1940s French costs once again overtook, and by 1953 far exceeded, British costs. These statements on France and Italy, however, assume that the omission of social security in the comparisons before 1949 does not make the relative overall crew cost positions any different from that implicit in the figures for wages alone or for wages and victualling. In view of the importance of social security costs in total crew costs under the French and Italian flags that assumption is dangerous, even for the inter-war years. French and Italian total crew costs may have levelled up to and overtaken British total crew costs earlier than the table suggests.

Dutch and German costs seem to have climbed above British as a result of the currency changes in 1931. Dutch costs on dry-cargo ships have apparently been higher than British again at least from 1949 to 1958. But Dutch tanker costs, comparison x suggests, may have followed a quite different course; a similar discrepancy between dry-cargo and tanker cost comparisons is suggested by the figures for Denmark.[1]

The crew cost comparison with Norway is of especial interest. On dry-cargo vessels, Table 46 suggests that before the 1914–18 war, and for some years after, wage costs were very substantially lower than Britain, but that by the later 1930s there was very little between them. Until the 1930s certainly the inclusion of victualling and social security costs would not greatly affect the

[1] The main factor making relative cost positions for tankers differ widely from those for dry-cargo vessels is manning. The lack of reliable comparative information on tanker manning is greatly to be regretted.

relative position of the two flags on crew costs. The comparison numbered vi, as already mentioned, takes no account of manning, so that the 5 per cent difference between Norwegian and British wage costs may be an underestimate; the inclusion of victualling and social security costs would alter the picture somewhat again. The Norwegian advantage in overall crew costs in the later 1930s then was probably less than 10 per cent. In the Orient, however, the position was that 'Norwegian wages are generally on the same level as British, and there does not appear to be any sound reason for Norwegian success in competition except efficiency'.[1] Since the late 1940s or early 1950s Norwegian crew costs have been generally at least as high as British, and at times probably substantially higher.

The last of the comparisons in Table 46 refers to July 1960. The unofficial strike of British seamen which began in that same month came at a time when National Service was beginning to run down and the Shipping Federation was doubtless apprehensive about the future effect on labour supply to the British shipping industry; the result was that a large wage increase was granted, together with a reduction in hours. This rise in wage costs is not reflected in comparison number xiv, which was made before the increase occurred.

The ending of National Service has not been slow in making its effect on labour supply to the industry felt. Moreover, since January 1961 the National Union of Seamen has had a new General Secretary, and one who seems likely to take advantage of the increasing labour shortage. It seems that a period of change has begun, and that the crew costs of British shipowners will rise not only absolutely but relatively to those of owners operating under other flags.[2]

LABOUR AND THE GROWTH OF BRITISH SHIPPING

In labour relations in British shipping a factor which stands out is the attitude of the principal trade union. Except in open company unionism, few employers can ever have enjoyed the

[1] Imperial Shipping Committee, op. cit., p. 45.
[2] This new General Secretary died after a year in office, and has been replaced; but the argument still seems valid (September 1962).

partnership of a union leader so powerful in his own union and so accommodating to employers as the Havelock Wilson of the 1920s. Though the union recovered its dynamism under Wilson's successor, and was particularly energetic in the mid-1930s, by the 1950s it was once again in quiescent mood. It certainly cannot be said to have been bellicose (towards shipowners) since the outbreak of the 1914–18 war. The other striking fact about labour relations in the industry in the past fifty years is that ocean shipping was strike-free from May 1926 to May 1955 —well nigh half the period. If British ocean shipping has grown so slightly since 1910 this can hardly be blamed on inharmonious labour relations or on irresponsible unions.

As to labour costs, the disadvantage on this score which the industry clearly suffered in the first thirty or so years of this century has progressively dwindled since. In the 1950s British owners had crew costs appreciably lower than a number of foreign merchant fleets, and in comparison with Norway were certainly at no disadvantage on crew costs. Though labour costs may help to explain the slow growth of British ocean shipping in the inter-war years,[1] they appear to be of little importance in accounting for the same phenomenon in the post-war period.

[1] Even then the importance of crew costs must not be overemphasized. As indicated in Table 41, crew costs are only some 25 to 40 per cent of operating costs narowly defined. On a broader definition of operating costs, crew costs would be a smaller proportion.

XIII

The Conference System

As an almost classic example of cartellization, the confer- ence system has always attracted attention. The intention of this chapter is, first, to provide sufficient information about conferences to place them in their context as an element in liner operations and, second, to answer the question, 'What effect, if any, have conferences had on the development of British shipping?' For these purposes it is not necessary to present a complete account of the operations of conferences, nor to examine fully the cases for and against them.

CONFERENCE ORGANIZATION

A conference is an association of competing liner owners engaged in a particular trade who have agreed to limit the com- petition existing among themselves. As a minimum, they will have agreed to charge freight rates or passenger fares for each class of traffic according to an agreed schedule of charges and to show no discrimination between shippers. To the agreement foreswearing all forms of price competition may be, and usually is, added an agreement to regulate sailings according to a pre- determined pattern and to recognize the berth rights of other members. A further step may be to add a full pooling agreement under which profits and losses on the trade covered by the con- ference are shared between the member lines. When this stage is reached competition between the conference lines has ceased completely. In addition to these internal arrangements, each conference may have an agreement with the shippers, that is, with its customers. This is known as a loyalty contract and is designed to secure the continued custom of the shipper and to prevent the entry of outside competition. When such a contract has been completed the conference usually agrees to provide a regular service, either by each member acting independently or by collective action. The conference does not agree to, although members usually will, provide additional sailings when trade is at a peak, while shippers have no sanctions under the contract against shipowners who fail to provide the contract sailings.

The need for a conference system arises from the economics of liner operations. Once a liner has been put on berth in a trade practically all costs become overhead costs and the additional cost of carrying an extra ton of cargo is only the cost of loading and discharging that cargo. This means that if a liner operator can secure a rate of freight above the costs of handling the cargo, that makes a contribution to his overheads and, rather than sail with empty space, it is worth taking the extra cargo. Clearly, if all the cargo is at that rate the liner operator cannot survive, but so long as he is free to vary rates it will always pay him to accept such a rate rather than refuse cargo. With free competition, all rates would be forced to this level whenever any surplus of shipping space appeared and operations would become unprofitable for all concerned. The shippers, who would gain initially from the rate reductions, would eventually suffer if regular services ceased to operate.

An agreement among competing lines to charge the same freights, with sanctions against undercutting in the form of forfeiture of the deposit made with the conference, overcomes the situation outlined above, but it does not prevent shippers deserting the regular lines for other ships at times when the owners of those ships are prepared to undercut the conference rates or to offer a better service. Further, it cannot prevent shippers despatching by non-conference ships valuable cargoes, on which the conference lines usually charge high rates, and leaving only low value cargoes, which are rated cheaply, to the conference ships. In other words, an agreement among competing lines can lead to them not competing for the skim while the cream has gone to non-conference ships. The loyalty contract was instituted to prevent this situation.

The first conference was formed in August 1875, when the lines engaged in the United Kingdom–Calcutta trades agreed to charge similar rates and to grant no preferences or concessions to any shippers. The need for an arrangement arose from the overtonnaging of the Far Eastern trades as a result of the opening of the Suez Canal and the consequent lowering of freight rates to the level of direct voyage costs. The shippers, particularly the big ones who had been able to extract concessional rates from the shipowners, did not welcome the conference agreement and turned to ships outside the conference which would offer them lower rates. In 1877, the deferred rebate system (see below) was introduced and shippers who patronized only conference ships became entitled to a rebate of 10 per cent of the freights paid. Once the loyalty contract was adopted, the conference succeeded in its aim of maintaining rates at a profitable level.

The rapid improvements in steamships in the period meant that the situation which had existed in the Calcutta trade was experienced also in other trades, and the solution to the problem adopted by the shipowners in that trade became a prototype which was copied in other trades. Conferences have never attempted to cover all trades or all commodities in any trade. They apply particularly to the outward trades of manufacturing countries which import raw materials heavily so that the tonnage available for the outward trade exceeds the volume required to lift the trade.

Conferences were of British origin because Britain, with one minor exception,[1] pioneered the idea of liner services. Today, conferences are international organizations. As an association each conference applies only to a single trade and the members of that conference are only associates in so far as that trade is concerned. Links between conferences are provided by lines which are members of several conferences, and by agreements between conferences to consult before taking decisions which may impinge on the other's sphere of operations. On the whole, however, each conference may be regarded as a separate entity covering the trade of a certain route and pursuing its business in that trade without more than the minimum necessary regard for what is happening in other trades.

---

[1] On the North Atlantic the American-owned Black Ball line of sailing ships was running a scheduled liner service from about 1820. However, it was only the departures which could be scheduled as trip times could not be calculated in advance.

The Conference System

The affairs of each conference are controlled by the votes of its members, with varying requirements as to the constitution of a quorum and the size of majority required to carry a proposal.[1] Voting rights are usually on the basis of one member one vote, irrespective of the volume of tonnage possessed by that member; associated members may not be entitled to vote. The voting arrangements are important as they mean that the vote of the largest member in the conference counts for no more than that of the smallest. The picture of a conference as a democracy with equality of voting is an over-simplified one as the larger members carry more weight in discussion than the smaller members. This is because the consequences for the conference if a large member decides to withdraw following a majority vote unacceptable to him are more serious than if a small member makes such a decision. Membership is on the basis of lines, not on the ownership of those lines, so that two lines owned by a single group have two votes. Voting does not appear to be nationally determined, save in infrequent cases, such as that of some German lines in the 1930s.

The votes of members determine the freight rates and fares which all charge. The members control the operation of any supplementary service or pooling agreements which have been signed. New lines can only be admitted to the conference on a vote of existing members. The meetings of conferences are private and the conference decisions are usually stated either without explanation or with a stereotyped explanation without detail. There is no form of public control over the operations of conferences in any country outside the United States and even there the regulating activities have been *ad hoc* rather than continuous.

As stated earlier, conference arrangements frequently include pooling agreements under which services and/or earnings on the trades covered are pooled between the member lines. Conferences are reticent about the extent to which pooling agreements are operated, the only information on the subject being contained in two documents submitted by the Federal Maritime

[1] For information regarding quorum and voting requirements in the conferences covering American trades, see Celler Committee, evidence of C. G. Morse, Part 1, vol. 1, pp. 690-1.

Board at the Celler Committee Hearings. The first of these documents relates to joint service agreements effective in September 1958 which had been filed with, and approved by, the Board. Such agreements provided for joint services between two or more nominally competing lines. In all, sixty-one such agreements were listed, of which fifty-eight provided for joint services and the other three provided in addition for the apportionment of receipts or profits. The second document relates to effective pooling agreements at the same date and lists twenty-three such agreements.[1] Under these agreements either freight receipts or profits and losses were apportioned between the member lines in agreed proportions.

Under the service agreements, the parties to each agreement contract to co-ordinate their activities and limit their sailings in accordance with the agreement. There is no information as to how frequently such agreements break down when the limitations imposed become intolerable to the member lines. However, twenty-two of the agreements listed had been current for ten years or more in September 1958, and some of these replaced agreements which had been cancelled during the war. The only inference is that such agreements have proved reasonably effective. Under these agreements each line can compete in service to shippers, but only within the limits of its capacity as provided under the agreement, unless it can secure the berth rights of another member of the agreement or can obtain a larger share of the sailings when a new agreement is negotiated.

Where pooling agreements exist all competition among member lines ceases, except for that which is directed to securing a greater share of the pool when the agreement is renewed. Such an agreement also deadens the incentive a line may have to improve its tonnage, its service to shippers or passengers or the frequency of its sailings. In other words, competition in all forms is almost completely stifled and is replaced by a cartel agreement while deferred rebates and contracts with shippers provide a check to the entry of non-cartel competition. Again, information on the longevity of these agreements is lacking. However, of the twenty-three pooling arrangements effective in American trades in 1958, four were over twenty years old and a

[1] See Celler Committee Hearings, part I, vol. I, pp. 774–9.

further nine were between thirteen years and eight years old, again suggestive that such agreements have a considerable life expectation.

These agreements must be considered as an undesirable aspect of conference organization and the limitation on internal competition which they provide as dangerous to the maintenance of efficient shipping services. The object of conference arrangements is to eliminate competition on price because such competition would force all rates to the level of direct costs whenever a surplus of tonnage appeared. The limitation of price competition might be acceptable, given the consequences of such competition, if competition in other ways were possible, and efficient lines were not precluded from expanding at the expense of their less efficient rivals. However, where joint service or pooling agreements are in force, all forms of competition are so heavily restricted that there can exist little incentive or opportunity within the conference for any line to expand.

LIMITATIONS ON MONOPOLY POWER

Within the trade covered, the conference has a monopoly. The existence of this monopoly has led to a great deal of criticism of conferences and to several investigations as to their effects.[1] The earlier investigations concentrated on the external effects of conferences rather than on their internal arrangements and accepted the necessity for such organizations. The Royal Commission of 1909 believed that ties between shippers and conferences were justified and that the abuses of the deferred rebate system should be tolerated in the interests of achieving a strong conference system. The Imperial Shipping Committee supported this view. The Alexander Committee considered that conferences were necessary, but that Government control was

---

[1] The most important reports are: Report of Royal Commission on Shipping Rings, 1909, Cmd. 4668; Report of Imperial Shipping Committee on the Deferred Rebate System, Cmd. 1802, 1923; U.S. Congress, House of Representatives Committee on Merchant Marine and Fisheries, Investigation of Shipping Combinations (Alexander Committee), Washington, 1913 and 1914; Report from the Committee on Merchant Marine and Fisheries (Bonner Committee), Providing for the Operation of Steamship Conferences, Report No. 498, House of Representatives, 87th Congress, 1961.

essential to secure the advantages without the corresponding disadvantages and recommended that the deferred rebate system and the use of fighting ships be outlawed in American trades.

Much of the recurrent criticism of conferences is based on a misunderstanding of the monopoly power which they possess. This monopoly power is, in fact, limited in four ways.

(a) *Tramp Competition*

First, there is the competition from tramp ships in the case of bulk cargoes or of cargoes which can be bulked, for example, by a number of shippers co-operating for that purpose. Although the loyalty contract is intended to prevent such competition, these contracts are not universal (see below) and a shipper is able to put on another hat, as it were, before shipping by a non-conference ship. In this way he technically satisfies the conference rules and collects the rebate on liner shipments while obtaining the advantage of lower rates when these are available in the trip charter market. Two checks exist against this. The first is that conference rules cover both f.o.b. and c.i.f. shipments, so if either the importer or the exporter has a shipping agreement with the conference the goods should travel by a conference ship: this rule is designed to cover the case of a contracting exporter who transfers the ownership of goods to a non-contracting importer before shipment. The second check is that the agreement with the shipper covers all goods in which he has an interest: this rule covers goods which a contracting exporter has transferred to a non-contracting agent for shipment.

(b) *Shipper's Retaliation*

Second, if a conference tries to press its monopoly advantage beyond the limit of its strength it may pay a big shipper to start his own shipping organization, for example, the Unilever Palm Line in the West African trade, the Vestey Blue Star Line in the South American meat trade, and the West Australian Farmers Line in the Australian wheat trade in 1936. Although the reasons why producers started their own shipping ventures have been a compound of many factors, behind those factors often lay the feeling of the shippers concerned that their trades were being hampered by the monopoly positions established by the conference lines. The lessons learned from the consequences of trying to press too far the monopoly advantages should exercise a powerful restraining influence on shipping conferences. However the lessons are not always taken to heart; for example, the Gran Colombiana line was started because the conference lines charged freight rates on the exports of Colombia, Ecuador and Venezuela which were considered to be hampering the trade of those countries, while in the New Zealand trade it took the entry of Italian and Dutch passenger ships to persuade the conference lines to provide facilities which they had previously stated could not be provided.

(c) Commodity Competition

A third check arises because few commodities can be obtained only from one part of the world so that for most commodities two or more conferences will be quoting rates. The competitive power in a third market of similar products from different countries is partly determined by the respective freight rates from the two producing countries to the third country, including conference and tramp rates and, in some cases, land freight rates. A conference which attempts to use its monopoly position to levy excessive freight rates can easily find that the trade disappears. If all conferences presented a tightly-knit association this form of check would be much reduced in effectiveness; it is the lack of a central conference organization which maintains this check. The possibility exists, however, that although an excessive freight rate may lead to a trade being killed with eventual loss to the conference lines themselves, they will not realize the causal relationship and amend their rates accordingly, so that a serious and avoidable loss is imposed on traders. According to some sources this happened in certain British trades in the inter-war years. The secrecy with which conferences surround their operations prevent any assessment of the extent to which this may have happened. The existence of differential rates of tariff or import quota arrangements may provide protection for shipowners in particular trades rather than give advantages to exporters and a closely knit conference, such as exists in the export trade from New Zealand to Britain, may continue to absorb the benefits of preferential tariff arrangements until either the trade is harmed or a rival shipping organization is started by the exporters.

The existence of different freight rates on cargo of the same type for different journeys of about the same length is no proof that one rate is excessive. The distance travelled is only one element in the cost of carriage, the remainder being the costs of loading and discharging the cargo and the ship time occupied in these operations. When port facilities are good and handling charges low, ships operating from that port can charge lower rates than ships operating from less well-equipped or more costly ports; the difference between the handling charges at Continental and British ports in the inter-war years was one reason why rates from the Continent to overseas destinations were often lower than rates from British ports. In so far as port costs accounted for the difference in rates it was not the conference lines operating from British ports which damaged British trade but the ports themselves. Where full cargoes can be lifted from one port, rates can be lower than where several ports must be visited in order to assemble full cargoes; it was the need to visit numerous small ports to obtain complete cargoes which caused rates in the New Zealand trade to be higher than those in the Argentine trade in terms of pence per ton mile.[1] The liner operator has to consider the voyage as a whole and if there is little cargo from A to B but plenty from A to C he can charge lower rates for similar items of cargo travelling from C to A than from B to A because the costs of the whole round voyage to C can be spread over more items.

(d) *Non-conference Lines*

A fourth check is provided by the activities of non-conference lines, together with the ability of a line to leave the conference without penalty on giving ninety days' notice. Shippers accept the restrictions on their activities imposed by the conference tie in return for the regular and assured services provided by conference operators. However, non-conference lines may also provide regular services. Although these services may be relatively

[1] See Imperial Shipping Committee, *Rates of Freight in the New Zealand Trade,* Cmd. 1564, 1922 and *Rates of Freight in the Trade from the United Kingdom to New Zealand,* 1935.

infrequent, they give to a shipper the opportunity of holding his cargo for the non-conference ship: he will take this course if the saving in rates is greater than the cost of holding the goods for the less frequent service. Here the ability of a shipper to change his hat is important. A check on the freedom of shippers is provided by the possible refusal of the conference lines to handle any urgent shipments from a shipper who normally uses non-conference ships, even if he agrees to pay full rates. This countervailing power of the conference to protect its position in this way is limited in the case of conferences trading to the United States by the activities of the regulatory authority which would cancel the registration of a conference taking such action. In the case of other conferences, such reprisals are officially frowned upon and when they take place are usually explained as being the unauthorized actions of subordinates in shipping offices.

Where conference arrangements break up and rate wars start, a common cause is that the claim of one line for a larger share of the trade and consequently more frequent departures has not been recognized by the other members of the conference, that is, rate wars are frequently internecine squabbles not connected with the overall exercise of the monopoly but arising from the terms of the service agreements within the conferences. The check on the monopoly power of conferences through the secession of member lines is, therefore, largely a check on their ability to raise rates by creating or maintaining a shortage of tonnage. Against this, however, must be set the raising of rates which occurs when a trade is over-tonnaged and ships are used at less than full capacity instead of some ships being laid up. The situation of an over-tonnaged trade is, however, unstable and the conference arrangements are susceptible to rate cutting by seceders or outsiders. The main exception to an endemic tendency to over-tonnaging occurs in trades which are dominated by one line or by the several lines of one group. In such a situation far from the trade being over-tonnaged it is likely to suffer from a shortage of shipping space at peak periods, high charges and inferior ships. Such a conference is then particularly vulnerable to outside competition from better ships; the encroachment of foreign lines into some traditionally British trades undoubtedly arose from this situation. A similar position may also occur when the several lines in a conference are completely loyal to their service or pooling arrangements within the conference in which case there is no internal force impelling the member lines to seek continuous improvements in their services and the possibility that outside competition will be attracted by the opportunities presented by a stagnant situation is strong.

DETERMINATION OF FREIGHT RATES

That limitations to the monopoly power of conferences exist does not remove all grounds for concern regarding the methods of operation of conferences and the effects of those methods on trade, shipping and the allocation of resources in general. The existence of service and pooling agreements within conferences, the methods by which freight rates are determined, the secrecy with which conferences surround their operations and the lack of any public control over their operations in most maritime countries other than the United States, are perhaps the main reasons why such concern is felt. Even in the United States, where the Federal Maritime Board[1] was supposed to be a watchdog over the activities of conferences, the Celler inquiry unearthed considerable evidence of undesirable practices which had escaped the notice of the appointed guardians. The internal agreements of conferences were considered above; the questions of secrecy and public control lie outside the scope of this work; the way in which conferences determine freight rates and passenger rates, but mainly freight rates, is discussed here.

The liner operator is interested in making a profit overall, on the whole trip, or on a related series of trips. A typical liner cargo may consist of hundreds of consignments of widely different categories of goods. On no two trips is an identical assortment carried. The costs of carrying these goods are partly directly identifiable, that is, handling costs, but mainly unidentifiable, that is, the whole cost of making the voyage which has to be spread over the cargo and the passengers (if any)

[1] The Board has since been reconstituted as the Federal Maritime Commission and its regulatory powers extended. In certain respects these powers may now be excessive although much depends upon the way in which they are administered.

carried. Further, liners are not always fully loaded, so that the costs, which are largely fixed, have to be allocated in terms of average capacity utilization. The result is that the cost incurred in carrying any consignment cannot be discovered except as to the part which is handling charges. As to the remainder, the shipowner has simply to hope that at the rates established, taking good trips with bad, and with a reasonable share of highly rated freight, he will find himself with a profit on his operations.

It is conceivable that each type of cargo could be charged on a two-part tariff with a general rate for all cargo to cover overhead costs and a variable rate depending on loadability. This would mean increases in rates on cheap commodities and decreases in rates on valuable commodities and would have the virtue of relating freight rates to the actual costs incurred in carrying that freight. At the same time, such a tariff would drive away some low-value cargo, perhaps killing the sea movement of it completely, while scarcely increasing the quantity of high-value cargo carried. Such an outcome would imply that the previous pattern of international resource allocation was not optimal and was being maintained only by means of shipping charges below the real costs of the services provided.

In practice, the conference operators divide goods into several classes, taking into account what the traffic will bear, that is, the value of the goods, loadability, bulk in relation to weight, and so on, and charge each class separately; of these items, value is the most important in rate determination. Rates for each class from each of a number of ports are then compiled, taking account of the amount of cargo from the port, the handling facilities available, the balance of the inward and the outward trade and the distance to be steamed with the cargo. Permanent changes in costs, for example, an increase in wages, are met by overall percentage changes in all rates in the schedule, while temporary cost changes, such as extra costs arising from congestion in particular ports leading to delays, are generally met by temporary surcharges which are removed when the cause of the rise in costs disappears. A complaint from an individual shipper about his place in the schedule may be met by shifting the commodity concerned to another class or bracket of the schedule or by starting a new class. The schedules themselves have grown up over time, depending upon what it was once thought the traffic would bear, subject to non-discriminatory amendments[1] in response to pressures from shippers and to the addition of new items. Any rate in the schedule could be changed because even the lowest rates exceed the extra costs incurred by the operator in carrying that cargo. The operator, however, has to look at his operations as a whole and short-period (that is trip by trip) marginal cost pricing would leave uncovered a substantial part of the costs incurred.

The consequences of the system of freight rate determination are several.

First, there is a certain inflexibility to the changing needs of trades, particularly with regard to the relative rates from different ports and a high rate (as distinct from a temporary surcharge) based on inconvenient facilities, or wasted ship time to lift a limited volume of cargo, may continue after facilities have improved and the cargo volume increased. Promotional rates to enable a trade to be built up are rare;[2] one reason for countries desiring shipping fleets of their own is the feeling that conference rates and shipping allocations, being based on existing, or past, trade volumes, prevent those trades from growing.

Second, non-discrimination between shippers allied with the system of charging individual classes of cargo according to their relative values means that the rate schedules involve cross-subsidization. Large shippers, whose bulk shipments are cheaper to handle than numerous small parcels, expect, but rarely receive, rates which take account of this cost saving and may decide to buy or charter vessels to handle their own shipments, probably competing with exclusively shipping enterprises in filling any space remaining in their vessels. They are particularly likely to do this if the goods have a high value per ton or are markedly easy to load. The existing rate structure means that shippers of large consignments, of valuable goods and of easily loaded goods, are subsidizing shippers of small

---

[1] Non-discriminatory in the sense that all shippers of that commodity get the same rate, but discrimination may exist because, for example, gas stoves and electric stoves are charged at different rates although having similar weight and bulk.

[2] For example, the Indian claim that '. . . India lost the lucrative trade in yarn with China because the P. & O. Company did not want that channel of trade for this country'. *Indian Shipping*, III, no. 2 (February 1951), p. 18.

consignments, of low-valued goods and of goods which are awkward to load or stow. If the shippers who have been forced to subsidize the others decide to carry their own cargoes this reduces the cargo available to the conference lines and so necessitates rate increases on the other classes of goods. Although the rates may subsequently fall when the volume of shipping space offered by the conference has been adjusted to the loss of cargo, the new long-period rate will be above the old cross-subsidized rate. In so far as the relative positions of big shippers and small shippers are concerned, the small are in a less favourable position. It must be said that in practice where industrial concerns have entered shipowning on their own accounts it has more often been to avoid the uncertainties of the tramp market than to escape the impact of liner rate structures.

Third, the system of rate adjustment at meetings of the conferences is not one suited to the rapid alteration of rates to meet changing conditions of trade. Much depends here on the organization of the individual conference. Sometimes the chairman has the power to give an immediate decision on a rate which binds the whole conference. In other cases it is possible to contact the conference members by telephone and get their views. Telephoning can produce quick action where the required proportion of shipowners agree, but if such agreement cannot be secured in this way, the matter has to await a full meeting of the conference where the problem can be properly discussed. In this case, action might be very slow. In one important outward-freight conference from the United Kingdom, a permanent rate sub-committee is maintained which meets fortnightly, and more frequently if necessary, to consider requests from shippers for variations in rates.

The schedule of freight rates is regarded as confidential and a shipper can only determine the rate he will have to pay on any particular consignment by applying to a conference line or to the agent of such a line. The non-publication of the rate schedule is justified by the conference lines on the ground that publication would make it too easy for outsiders to undercut the conference rates. In theory, a non-conference operator can only obtain the schedule by patient inquiry from the conference lines by a co-operative shipper obtaining one or two rates at a time.

A schedule built up in this way, however, would have to be constantly checked because, although overall changes in the scheduled rates are published, individual changes, such as moving an item from a higher to a lower bracket of the schedule, are not published but are simply notified to all conference lines and their agents. In practice, however, a non-conference operator can obtain the desired information by buying the conference schedule from an agent, although the agent commits a serious breach of confidence by selling the schedule in this way. Secrecy regarding the structure of rates appears, therefore, to serve little purpose and some shippers believe that the publication of rates would enable them to arrange their transport operations more economically.[1] Further, secrecy appears to make rate wars more, not less, likely as in conditions of secrecy such a war can start either deliberately or accidentally, whereas where rates are known only deliberate rate wars are possible. A non-conference operator determined to start a rate war can always do so, but if he has to guess at the conference rates he is more likely to cut rates further than necessary than not to cut them enough. In this way the rate war becomes more damaging for all shipowners concerned. Certainly, the American requirement that all rates be filed with the Federal Maritime Board within thirty days of any change did not appear to hinder the operations of the conferences concerned.[2] This is a requirement which might well be copied in other countries.

The uneasiness which is often felt about the rate policies of Conferences led the New Zealand Government in 1956 to enter an agreement with the conference lines regarding the procedure for negotiating freight rates. Under this agreement there are four steps in the negotiation of rates. First, the determination of the nature and frequency of the services required; unless any change is desired this is a once-for-all decision and is not reconsidered every time a rate change is negotiated. Second, the shipowners supply to a firm of chartered accountants, nominated

---

[1] See memorandum from Dutch and Belgium sources to the Users' Committee of the Transport and Communications Section of the International Chamber of Commerce, 1958.

[2] The newly constituted commission must receive notification of all rate changes and has the additional power of being able to object to any rate. Shipowners outside America are justifiably aggrieved about the latter provision.

by the shippers, full information as to the trading and operating results of the tonnage engaged in the New Zealand trade. This information is strictly confidential to the accountants. Third, the accountants prepare for the information of the shippers, a short report on the situation and this report forms the actual basis on which rate negotiations are entered. Fourth, the shippers and shipowners agree a schedule of rates.[1] This method can only work when the shippers, or a large proportion of them, can present a single front through, for example, a Producers' Association. The method then represents the minimum degree of control which needs to be exercised over the actions of any monopolist if the public interest is to be preserved. Within the method, difficulties must arise concerning the allocation of all costs other than the direct costs of carrying New Zealand exports; these other costs include, for example, the voyage to New Zealand the costs of which will be different at every level of outward freights. Despite the agreed procedure for rate negotiations with the conference lines and its safeguards against excessive freight rates, New Zealanders have not felt entirely easy about the shipping services provided, and generally welcomed the entry of competition from the Dutch round-the-world services established after the exclusion of Dutch lines from the Indonesian trades.

THE LOYALTY CONTRACTS

Conferences claim that they make possible the running of regular shipping services offering non-discriminatory freight and passenger facilities at stable and foreseeable rates, thereby catering for the needs of trade for stability and the assurance of fair treatment, both in the sense that no preference is exercised between shippers and that a trader knows that if he has shipped at a certain rate today his rival will not be able to ship at another rate tomorrow. Conference rates are usually guaranteed for two months or more ahead and in particular cases, for example, where a shipper is tendering for an overseas contract requiring heavy shipments, guaranteed rates up to a year in advance may be quoted. In order to justify the investment of capital in

[1] Information supplied by courtesy of the New Zealand Treasury.

providing a regular service at stable rates the conferences claim that some form of tying arrangement between shipper and shipowner is necessary. There are two forms of such tie.

The older of the two tying systems is the deferred rebate. Under this system a shipper who has not employed a nonconference ship for twelve months receives a refund at the end of the period of part, usually 10 per cent, of his freight payments in the first six months of that period. The price of sending a shipment by a non-conference ship is the loss of any rebate earned to date in the current half year, plus any rebate due from the previous half year. The strength of this tie varies with the level of freight rates and the volume of business. A shipper wishing to make a single abnormally large shipment at a time when tramp rates are low may easily save enough to compensate for the lost rebates. A non-conference operator desiring to break into a trade may pay shippers who ship with him their lost rebates,[1] although only a state-owned company can usually afford such payments. In most cases, however, the deferred rebate constitutes a substantial tie, perhaps more substantial than is desirable because the deferment of the rebate makes the entry of new lines extremely difficult.

The system has been widely attacked. In the United States it was outlawed by the 1916 Act following the recommendation of the Alexander Committee. In the Australian outward trade, rebates were declared illegal under the Australian Industries Preservation Acts, the prohibition lasting from 1910 until an amendment to the Acts was made in 1930. In the South African trade an Act of 1911 prevents liner companies who operate a deferred rebate system from holding mail contracts. Opposition to the system was particularly strong in India in the inter-war years. In other countries at different times there have been limitations placed on the use of deferred rebates, the most recent being the Japanese prohibition between 1949 and 1958. Sometimes objections have been directed to the whole system as such, sometimes to the time for which rebates are deferred and sometimes to the unilateral nature of a contract which does not place shipowners under any compulsion with regard to services or stability of freight rates. It is significant that, except in the

---

[1] See, for example, Cmd. 1802, 1923.

case of America where the prohibition of deferred rebates has been maintained, in most cases the strongest objections have come from countries without large ocean shipping fleets. The neat way in which the Japanese case appears to illustrate this statement should not be misunderstood for, while it is possible to argue that Japan accepted deferred rebates when the Japanese fleet was large, prohibited them when the fleet had been destroyed and then restored them when the fleet had been largely rebuilt, it is more significant that the prohibition in 1949 stemmed from American direction and was in line with policy in the United States whereas the restoration in 1958 came after the Americans had withdrawn from Japan and was part of the Japanese 'reverse course' policy.

The second type of tie is the contract, or dual rate, system which is generally used by those conferences which are debarred from using deferred rebates and is offered by many conferences as an alternative to deferred rebates. Under this system the shipper and the shipowners enter a contract under which the former agrees to send all his shipments by the conference lines for the contract period. Such contracts may be concluded between individual shippers and a conference or between an association of shippers and a conference, for example, as in the South African trade. Breach of the contract by the shipper entails the immediate cancellation of the present and future contract benefits, perhaps for a specified time, and sometimes entails a penalty related to the past shipments by the shipper or the payment to the conference lines of the freight lost on the shipment sent in a non-conference ship. The difference between the contract and the non-contract rates in American trades is usually 10 or 20 per cent, somewhat higher than the usual rate of deferred rebate in other trades. British outward conferences which operate the dual system offer a lower rate of discount under the contracts than under the deferred rebate system (see below).

The dual rate system was accepted in the United States because it was not specifically condemned by the Alexander Committee. However, in 1958 the Supreme Court[1] cast doubts on the legality of the system and in the same year interim legislation was enacted specifically legalizing the dual rate

[1] *Federal Maritime Board* v. *Isbrandtsen Company*, 356 U.S. 481.

system for two years; this period expired in 1961 but was extended temporarily. Two investigations into the dual rate system and the operations of conferences generally were launched. One was a series of hearings before the Special Sub-committee on Steamship Conferences (Bonner Committee) and the other a series of hearings before the Antitrust Committee of the Committee on the Judiciary (Celler Committee). The report of the Bonner Committee was made public in 1961 together with a Bill to amend the Shipping Act, 1916, to provide greater control over the operations of conferences. This Bill was not passed into law because of its many objectionable provisions. Another Bill, which has become law, legalized the dual rate system and strengthened the supervision exercised over conferences. The possibility of further legislation cannot be dismissed.

A third method of preventing the encroachment of outsiders is the use of fighting ships. When a non-conference ship enters a trade, the conference lines may pool their resources to provide a ship on berth to match the sailing time of the interloper and to cut rates below those quoted by the non-conference operator. In this way, the collective resources of the conference are used to break the non-conference operator. As a device to prevent new entry to trades this is particularly powerful because of the disparity in strength of the forces ranged on either side, while shippers have every incentive to take the rates offered by the fighting ship rather than those offered by the non-conference vessel. Fighting ships were outlawed in the United States by the 1916 legislation; fighting ships and deferred rebates were thought of as two great predatory weapons. The American enactment in this connection might well be copied in other countries, as the use of fighting ships in conjunction with tying arrangements weights the scales against new entrants to an extent which can easily ossify the structure of trades; indeed, this is their purpose.

The question must be asked whether tying arrangements and fighting ships are necessary for the survival of conferences and of regular liner services? If some tie is necessary, is the contract system generally sufficient, or must shipowners have recourse to the more objectionable deferred rebates?

The Conference System

In April 1960 the forty-eight freight conferences outward from the United Kingdom offered the following terms:

Deferred rebate (net rates, usually less 10 per cent, four to six months deferred)	11
Contract (typical terms are net rates less 9½ per cent immediate)	10
Contract and Deferred Rebate (terms as for contract and deferred rebates alone)	21
No Ties (net rates)	6

Source: Compiled from R. K. Bridges, *Freight Conferences and Rebate Terms*, 2nd ed. (Kingston, 1960).

Of these forty-eight conferences six dispensed with all forms of tie. Two of these six conferences cover short sea trades and are not directly comparable with the other conferences in the list. The four deep-sea conferences each cover outward trades in which the character of the return cargoes is such that the danger of outsiders entering the trade is slight. The absence of tying arrangements in one-eighth of the outward conferences from the United Kingdom therefore proves nothing about the necessity for loyalty contracts in general, although it perhaps suggests that the freedom from ties could be extended to other trades without danger. Of the forty-two conferences with tying arrangements, one-half offered shippers the choice of deferred rebates or contracts.[1] Little information is available respecting the relative popularity of each tie; in the only conference which was prepared to give information on the point practically all shippers selected the contract system which was alternative to the deferred rebate system.

In the other conferences, the contract system alone and the deferred rebate alone were about equally represented. It is clear, therefore, that although most of the conferences concerned believe that some tie is necessary, there is every reason to suppose that it would be possible to outlaw deferred rebates without serious consequences to either shipowners or shippers.

Of the 110 active conferences in the foreign trade of the

[1] The offer of this alternative was recommended by the Imperial Shipping Committee in Cmd. 1802.

United States in 1958, sixty-two used the dual rate system and forty-eight had no form of protection. The *prima facie* conclusion from these figures is that if over 40 per cent of conferences in the American trade find they can dispense with the tie, then presumably the others could also. This was the view taken by a number of witnesses at the Bonner enquiry. This conclusion ignores the uncertain legal position of the contract system before 1958 and the positions in individual trades with regard to non-conference competition. For example, of the forty-eight conferences without a tying system, nineteen had no non-conference competition to worry about. The high percentage of American conferences without a tying system can lead to no conclusions regarding the necessity or otherwise of loyalty ties. However, the viability of the conferences restricted to the use of the dual rate system shows clearly that deferred rebates are not necessary to preserve liner operations. Where a tie is necessary, American experience shows that the contract system is quite adequate for the purpose.

The existence of a tying arrangement is not, in itself, sufficient to prevent a rate war from breaking out. The highly damaging rate war of 1949 in the Indian trade occurred despite the existence of a tying system. It arose from the dissatisfaction of a Dutch member of the conference with its share of the trade under the service agreement after a Danish line had been admitted to conference membership in order to prevent the rate war which would have occurred had the Dane remained outside the conference. A recent freight war, that in the Pacific in 1959–60, occurred despite the use of the contract system and its causes were outside competition, dissatisfaction of the Barber-Wilhelmsen Line with conference arrangements, and allegations concerning malpractices by conference ships. The withdrawal of Barber-Wilhemsen from the conference was prevented, but the full use of contracts and fighting ships did not succeed in breaking the rate war, nor solve the problem arising from the overtonnaging of the routes concerned. On the other hand, a rate war in the North Atlantic trades in the inter-war years was broken by the solidarity of the conference lines and the loyalty of shippers in the face of rate cutting by a non-conference British shipowner.

The Conference System

A rate war is, in fact, a symptom of an overtonnaged route, not a necessary consequence of the absence of tying arrangements between shippers and shipowners. The conference system attempts, by regulation of entry, to prevent over-tonnaging within the individual conferences, although over-tonnaging often has to be accepted as the lesser of two evils. Here is the real dilemma: if the conference admits new members freely it is likely to promote a rate war within the conference due to over-tonnaging, whereas if it refuses to admit new members it is likely to promote a rate war between conference and non-conference lines. There is no easy way out of this dilemma and deferred rebates, the contract system and fighting ships are necessarily palliatives rather than solutions. What is certain is that so long as any form of freedom of the seas survives, differences of opinion between those in possession of particular trades and those outside those trades regarding the capacity of those trades to absorb tonnage will continue and periodic rate wars will occur whether conference tying arrangements exist or not. It would be an unhealthy situation if conferences were able to prevent rate wars because in all economic activities the possibility of new entrants is ultimately the strongest and most certain force making for efficiency. However, without any tying arrangement between shippers and shipowners, rates on many trade routes would vary from day to day depending on the daily relation between the volume of trade and the volume of available shipping. Such instability of rates is, on balance, undesirable because of the additional uncertainty which it would impose on traders. On the other hand in the North Atlantic passenger trade where both conference and non-conference lines operate rates are quite stable although at different levels.

RATE STABILITY

Do conferences, in fact, give rate stability? The importance of rate stability in facilitating trade constitutes an essential part of the justification for the limitations on competition imposed by the conference arrangements.

A survey of 6,869 basic liner rates applicable to the main items of trade between Latin America and the United States,

1947 to 1953 inclusive, showed that 3,867, or 56·3 per cent, of the rates had been stable for two years or more. Of these stable rates, 23 per cent had been stable for two consecutive years, 53 per cent for three years or more, and the balance for four years and over, all during a period of rapidly rising prices.[1] This evidence is indicative, but not conclusive. No information is available regarding the nature of the commodities for which rates were stable and unstable respectively, the extent of other competition in the carriage of these commodities, nor the volume of trade taking place at these rates.

A comparison between the conference rates on raw cotton from American Gulf ports to Europe and the Norwegian Shipping News Freight Index for the period 1947 to 1958 inclusive reveals the following situation:

	Highest rate	Lowest rate	Number of rate changes
	July–Dec. 1947 = 100		
Trip charter index	192·0	73·3	
Time charter index	249·5	57·8	
Conference rates. Gulf to:	*in dollars*		
U.K. ports	1·85	1·40	8
Scandinavian ports	2·00	1·55	11
French Atlantic and German ports	1·85	1·40	10
Mediterranean ports	1·85	1·40	10

Source: Bonner Committee, pp. 282–3.

The greater stability of the conference rates is obvious. While this stability is clearly desirable and helpful to trade, the number of changes of the conference rates within the narrow limits of 45 cents in each case is quite large. An examination of the timing of these changes reveals that in most cases the free market and the conference rates were out of phase. Thus, at the end of 1948 the conference rate to Scandinavia was moved up when the free market rates were falling, was reduced in 1949 as free market rates fell, and again early in 1950 when free market rates began to climb as a result of Korea. The rate reached its peak early in 1953, three months after free market rates had begun

[1] Bonner Committee, p. 284.

to fall, then fell to match the fall in those rates. A new rise began with the Suez crisis, the conference rate reaching a peak after the free market rates had turned down. None of the other three conference rates were quite so badly out of phase as this one, although the general pattern was similar.

Information regarding rates charged by United States–Europe conferences exhibits a different pattern. This information is available for the general cargo rates of five separate conferences over the period 1940 to the end of 1958. Four of the five conferences maintained their rate schedules unchanged from 1940 to 1951, the fifth from 1940 to 1946; variations in rates on individual items by moving them within the schedule are not recorded. Since rates first moved, there were two increases in each of four conferences in 1951 but only one increase in that year for the conference which raised rates in 1946, a further increase in each conference in 1955, following reductions in 1952/3, and either one or two increases in each conference in 1956/7.[1] These rates exhibit much more the pattern expected from conference rates except for the reductions in 1952/3 which, not being a consequence of cost reductions, suggest that rates had been pushed further in the preceding boom than cost increases justified.

Although not strictly applicable to the present study, the pattern of rates charged by the conference lines on the short-sea routes between Britain and Ireland is worth considering. Rates were raised twice in 1940 and not again until 1946. Between 1946 and 1957 the port-to-port rates were increased eight times. These rates display the stepped pattern which should be expected from conference rates, although the frequency and magnitude of the increases, 88 per cent from May 1946 to October 1957, hardly accord with conference claims. These rates cannot be compared directly with tramp rates as the tramp rates in the Irish Sea trades have been based on a schedule since 1936. The scheduled tramp rates, which were under the control of the Ministry of Transport from 1940 until 1952, were changed on five occasions, including an increase of 10 per cent in June 1952 which was authorized by the Ministry in the period of transition from control to (scheduled) freedom, the fifth change

[1] Ibid., evidence of Charles R. Andrews, pp. 746–7.

345

being a reduction of 1 per cent. The total increase in the scheduled rates between the beginning of 1952 and mid-1958 amounted to 32·5 per cent at the maximum and in some sections increases were lower because of competition. The increase in the conference rates in the same period was 47 per cent.[1]

Some information is also available from rate indices. There is no shortage of indices of tramp rates, but indices of liner rates are uncommon. The best known liner rate index is German and relates to cargoes carried to north European ports on German account but not necessarily in German ships. The movements of the tramp and liner indices in this trade for the period 1950–9 are shown in Figure 3. The greater stability of liner than of tramp rates is clear, but there is some evidence of lagged phasing, the lag being between two and three months, which corresponds reasonably well with the period for which a conference rate is fixed in advance. The rise in liner rates in 1954, however, lagged six months, that is, two to three rate periods behind the tramp rate.

A lesser known, but extremely valuable, index relates to British trade for the period 1946 to 1957 inclusive. The figures are not reproduced here.[2] The index shows clearly the greater stability of liner rates than of tramp rates. The movements which occurred in the liner rates index were generally upwards, the rise being the result of cost increases in the period. There were fluctuations about the rising trend, however, and these were related to, but lagged four to five months behind, similar changes in the tramp rate index.

For earlier periods little information could be obtained. Table 48 shows liner and tramp rates in the German trade for the period 1927–1938. The liner rate shows somewhat greater stability than the tramp rate, although the correspondence between their movements is close. There is, however, clear evidence that the liner rate tended to lag behind the tramp rate in adjusting to falls in demand, particularly in responding to the depression.

[1] *Report of Tribunal of Inquiry into Cross Channel Freights, Rates* (Dublin, 1959), pp. 84, 130–3.
[2] See D. L. McLachlan, 'Index Numbers of Liner Freight Rates in United Kingdom Trades 1946–1957', *Yorkshire Bulletin of Economic and Social Research*, X, No. 1 (June 1958), pp. 50–62.

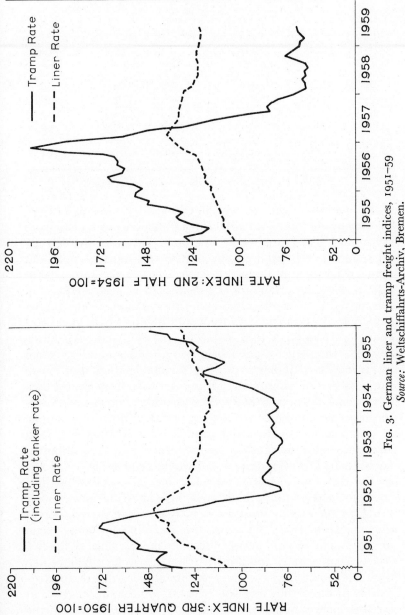

FIG. 3: German liner and tramp freight indices, 1951–59
Source: Weltschiffahrts-Archiv, Bremen.

TABLE 48. Tramp and liner rate indices, 1927 to 1938
(Base 1913 = 100)

Year	Liner index	Tramp index	Year	Liner index	Tramp index
1927	120	99	1933	66	49
1928	113	96	1934	62	48
1929	114	100	1935	63	50
1930	112	77	1936	66	62
1931	95	73	1937	73	86
1932	69	60	1938	77	64

Source: Der Wettbewerb in der Seeschiffahrt, p. 130.

Although the evidence is inconclusive, it is difficult to resist the conclusion that there exists at least a tendency for changes in conference rates as a whole not to be determined solely by reference to costs per ton mile, but to respond to supply and demand forces in a damped fashion, which gives stability, but also in a lagged fashion for which there is no justification. On the conventional assumptions about the method of determining conference rates, their stability would be upset only when cost changes occurred, or in response to long run changes in trade volume, rising when trade falls off on a route and falling when trade increases. If both costs and available trade per ton of shipping are moving in the same direction, rates would then have a bias towards stability. The theoretical determination of the expected course of rates over a period of time is not simple as that course would be determined by a compound of cost changes, trade changes and changes in the volume of shipping. In general, however, liner rates would tend to move in the *opposite* direction to tramp rates if conferences behave as they claim to behave, unless both liner rates and tramp rates were being dragged up by similar cost increases. In a period such as that between 1947 and 1958 the trend should have been upwards achieved in a series of discrete moves; three of the five North Atlantic rates and the Irish rate did, in fact, behave like this. The Gulf rates, however, went up and down with approximately the same time intervals between peaks and troughs as in the free market rates, but lagged up to six months behind the free market rates. The less conclusive pattern yielded by the indices is of the same type. If conferences wish to respond to changes in the supply of and demand for tonnage, they can do so effectively only if rates are moved in phase with free market rates. If the conferences ignore market forces, except in so far as market changes alter the cost per ton mile of carriage, then rates would tend to move in the opposite direction to free market rates which rise when cargo is plentiful in relation to shipping space and fall when shipping space is plentiful in relation to cargo. It is clear that the conference claim that the system promotes a greater stability of rates than is the case with free market rates is well founded. It is apparent, however, that while conferences do restrict their rate fluctuations to within narrow limits, they sometimes end up with a compromise between free market rates and rates which respond only to changes in the cost per ton of carriage. To chase the market and exhibit a damped, out-of-phase, fluctuation is to give to both shippers and shipowners the worst of both worlds, to place a severe strain on the loyalty of shippers and to provide a direct incentive to the entrance of non-conference competition.

One consequence of the pattern of liner rates established by conferences is that liner companies do not profit from booms as tramp shipping is able to. In theory this is offset by the higher profits in times of slump of liners than of tramps. In practice, the offset is limited; in slumps liner rates are well maintained but the degree of capacity utilization of liners falls. The overall utilization pattern (somewhat simplified) is that in slumps some tramps lay up while liners continue to operate with part cargoes and in booms both liners and tramps are used to full capacity. The result is that although in theory liners and tramps should do about equally well over a long period, in practice this is not so. Each boom period provides both the trading opportunities and the profits for an expansion of tramp tonnage which is able to secure entry to those liner trades in which the volume of cargo available exceeds the regular carrying capacity. Such entry may be secured by obtaining time charters for vessels, either from large shippers or from liner companies short of tonnage. The more rigidly structured is the shipping of any country and the more clear-cut is the division between liner owners and non-liner owners, the less will that country profit from booms.

The above argument helps to explain some part of the divergent growth experiences of British and Norwegian shipping. British shipping tends to be much more clearly divided between liner companies, tramp companies and tanker companies than is Norwegian shipping. Most large Norwegian shipowners own tonnage of all three classes so that they can profit whenever one branch of shipping is doing well. Each owner can move dry-cargo tonnage freely between his liner and his tramp trades while he has an opportunity equal to that of the British tramp owner to profit from the demands of British liner companies for additional tonnage in times of boom. This explanation refers only to part, perhaps a small part, of the discrepancy between the respective growth rates and does nothing to explain why British shipping has largely retained its particular structure.

Effects of Conferences on British Shipping

The second task of this chapter is to answer the question, 'What effects, if any, have conferences had on the development of British shipping?'

Had conferences remained as organizations with the minimum limitations on competition and had all members always observed the conference rules to the same extent, there is no reason, in theory, why conferences should have affected the development of British shipping, either favourably or adversely. However, the minimum limitations on competition have been generally exceeded and conference rules have neither been observed at all times by all members, nor broken by all members to the same extent. Also, as pointed out above, theory and practice have diverged in the effects of conference rate policies on the expansion of shipping; this question will not be considered further in this section.

Where competition within conferences has been limited by joint service or pooling agreements, any incentive to be enterprising which the member lines might otherwise have had was stifled. In the period before 1914 this did not matter particularly for British shipping. This was partly because service and pooling agreements were less common than in later years, partly because competition within the British industry as a whole was strong and partly because the only serious rival in the provision of liner services was Germany, with the shipping companies of which the conference lines had concluded territory sharing agreements. As has been shown earlier, these arrangements, by restricting the British participation in the growing European trade, restricted the opportunities for expansion; however, the expansion of world trade as a whole in the period was large enough to enable British shipping to maintain an average rate of growth over the period 1890–1913, which was satisfactory given the size of the British fleet in 1890 in relation to the total of world shipping. In the inter-war years the position was very different. As a result of amalgamations within the British industry, internal competition had become less strong. Many nations, such as America, Italy, Japan, the Netherlands and Norway had emerged as important shipowners with ambitions towards liner trades. Further, Britain no longer held the technological lead in shipbuilding and marine engineering which had been hers before 1914.

During much of the inter-war period, the restrictions on competition within conferences meant that the agreed services continued to be provided by ships of traditional types, offering traditional facilities, including speed. There was little drive to investigate the economics of faster ships or ways in which service to shippers and passengers could be improved. All British liner companies were operating within the framework of conference arrangements so that the depressive effects of the service and pooling arrangements impinged on most British liner tonnage. As a result of the stagnation in many conference services, ships operating outside conferences had clear opportunities to provide either cheaper services or better services in competition; conference arrangements are designed to meet outside competition in price, but not outside competition on quality. The result was inevitable: the lines which observed their agreements fully continued to provide, say, 14-knot passenger services while lines outside the conferences provided 16-knot or 18-knot services and skimmed the cream of the trade. Eventually those outside lines were accepted into the conferences and were allocated a share of the trade which they could never have won had competition existed within the conferences. The British industry, as the major liner owner, was the chief sufferer from such competition. At the same time as this outside competition occurred, some non-British lines broke their agreements within the conferences and, while generally, but not always, abiding by the conference pricing arrangements, provided faster or more frequent sailings and generally superior facilities.

The disadvantage which British shipping suffered in questions of speed in the period is brought out in Table 49. The most important part of this table is the middle, which is squared off. It can be seen that in each of the size groups shown, British ships were proportionally under-represented at the higher speeds and over-represented at the lower speeds within the groups. The possible explanations for the inferior British position include the subsidies which non-British lines enjoyed, a genuine belief that slower ships would provide a superior economic performance and a failure to break from conventional modes of thought induced by the cartel arrangements of conferences with service or pooling agreements. The subsidy policies certainly had some effect and 94 per cent of the ships included in the table were owned either in Britain or in countries which were granting subsidies. However, as argued in Chapter V, the subsidies given by Germany, Italy and Japan before 1930, when most of the ships concerned were built, were relatively small. Further, if the analysis of Table 49 could be extended to include cargo liners down to, say, 5,000 tons, the pattern of the table would be little changed but the proportion of ships owned by non-subsidizing, non-British countries was very much higher. The existence of a belief in the value of slower ships is possible; however, such a belief, if it existed, was more an act of faith than a reasoned conclusion. This itself can be attributed largely to the manner in which the competitive spirit of liner owners was stifled by conference rules, that is, it was chiefly the insulation of the cartel arrangements which led to the fall in efficiency, not a lack of efficiency, which led to the cartel arrangements. This explanation fully accounts for the position in the Far Eastern trades

The Conference System

as noted by the Chairman of the Imperial Shipping Committee (see page 127).

TABLE 49. Speeds of ships in size classes, 1934

	Percentages of ships in size classes:								
Speeds of ships in knots	30,000 tons and over		20,000–29,999 tons		15,000–19,999 tons		12,500–14,999 tons		10,000–12,499 tons	
	U.K. %	For. %	U.K. %	For. %	U.K. %	For. %	U.K. %	For. %	U.K. %	For. %
25 and over	33	66	—	—	—	—	—	—	—	—
22 to 24	66	33	0	100	0	100	0	100	—	—
19 to 21	20	80	30	70	30	70	0	100	33	66
16 to 18	—	—	76	24	65	35	54	46	37	63
13 to 15	—	—	—	—	70	30	68	32	49	51
10 to 12	—	—	—	—	—	—	100	0	30	70
All speeds	41	59	53	47	58	42	57	43	43	57

Note: *Normandie* excluded from largest size class.
Source: Compiled from Brassey (1935), pp. 327–33.

The second point initially raised in this section was the question of conformity to conference agreements. On the whole, British shipowners appear to 'play the game' according to the rules in most circumstances. In business, however, this is not always an advantage so far as growth is concerned, particularly when the rules are devised to preserve a *status quo*. Few rate wars since 1920 have been inspired from British sources while the settlement of rate wars has usually been at least a partial defeat for those who obeyed the rule: the famous Indian rate war in 1949 is an excellent example. The breach of service or pooling agreements gives the shipowner who commits the breach an advantage over his rivals as he is the one supplying the quicker, more frequent or generally better service. It was frequently complained between the wars, and also before 1914, that German lines honoured conference agreements only when it suited them to do so. Malpractices, such as rate cutting, the use of unfiled rates, secret rebates, erroneous measurement or classification of cargo and special privileges for shippers, such as free passages, divert cargo to the lines adopting such practices from those obeying the rules. It would be naïve to pretend that no British shipowner ever indulges, or has ever indulged, in such practices. It is true, nevertheless, that the accepted code of commercial morality differs in different parts of the world and practices which are regarded as normal behaviour within the code in some countries are outside the code in others. Conferences, being basically British inventions, have rules which accord by and large with British business mores; the pursuit of what is considered to be normal business conduct in many parts of the world consequently constitutes a breach of conference rules and often assists those shipowners and the shippers in their countries compared with British shipowners and shippers.

Theoretically, there is no reason why conferences should have adversely affected British shipping, but in practice because the minimum limitations on competition have generally been exceeded and because shipowners outside Britain have more frequently broken the rules when it suited their interests to do so than have British owners, conferences had a generally adverse effect on the development of British liner services in the inter-war years.

Another adverse effect which, while not inherent in the cartel organization, yet occurred, is a decline in intra-British competition as a result of the co-operation of lines in conferences, but irrespective of that cessation of competition required by service agreements. It will be shown in Chapter XIV that British lines are organized into large groups, each with interests in many trades. Two lines, Alpha and Beta, one owned by group A and the other by Group B may participate in a certain trade, co-operating in the conference, rationalizing their sailings, perhaps pooling their receipts and competing only in the intangibles of service and reputation. In another trade, line Gamma, also owned by group B may be in operation, but no matter how inefficiently it conducts its operations, no line of group A will normally enter into direct competition. If A can buy the line, or another line, Delta, already operating alongside of Gamma, it may do so, but because line Beta of group B operates in a conference with line Alpha of group A, group A will not directly challenge line Gamma for fear of inviting reprisals in that conference. In practice the extent of the inhibition of competition is greater than in the example, for each of the liner groups has several lines, each engaged in different trades so that somewhere within its whole operations, and probably at more than one point, each group is in ostensible competition with each other group. The result is a highly complex interlocking oligopoly with an almost overwhelming tendency not to take action which might invite reprisals. Foreign operators, not restricted by these fears, will rarely hesitate to seize the opportunity presented by this situation and to win trade from inefficient lines.

For a relatively high-wage country such as Britain, the provision of liner services may be both more economical and more profitable in the long run than the provision of tramp services although this difference can be removed if large, high-speed, tramps are owned. Conferences do not determine whether or not a particular pattern of resource allocation is economic, but they are an important factor in determining profitability and hence influencing the actual, as opposed to the ideal, pattern of resource allocation. It is not possible to determine how far the provision of liner services by Britain was, and is, economic and how far such provision was, and is, profitable as a result of conference arrangements while being uneconomic with regard to resource allocation. It is clear, however, that conferences by discriminating against newcomers and by maintaining freight rates at above the levels which would exist in their absence, helped, and are helping, to preserve the position of high-cost operators against the encroachments of lower-cost operators. On a *ceteris paribus* basis[1] it is probable that the existence of the conference system has been an important element in the maintenance of British liner tonnage and further that any increase in British wage costs relative to those in other countries increases the importance of conferences. In other words, rising levels of British maritime wage rates will increase the extent to which liner shipping relies for its maintenance on monopoly advantages. The long-run vulnerability of such a position must not be overlooked.

The point above regarding discrimination against newcomers may be taken further. Conferences deny that such discrimination

---

[1] In particular, assuming that conferences had no adverse effects on efficiency.

occurs. 'At their September meeting in 1960 the attention of the [Maritime Transport] Committee was drawn to a specific instance of liner conference practices. The effects of such practices, in the opinion of some members, were comparable with the effects of flag discrimination. In this connection, it was established that some governments outside the O.E.E.C. have pleaded that the growth of their national fleets is hindered by the practices of liner conferences.'[1] The immediate effect of this discrimination is to favour established liner owners, including British owners, and if retaliation can be avoided the final effect is that the fleets of the conference members can be maintained, or even expanded, in a manner which would not otherwise be possible. If retaliation occurs, the ultimate result is less certain and may, indeed, be unfavourable. The effects of discrimination by conferences on the attainment of the optimum resource allocation are as serious as the effects of any governmental discrimination while being less easy to prevent because many governments '. . . have no powers . . . to intervene in matters relating to liner conference activities'.[2]

In summary, it may be said that conferences have had both favourable and unfavourable effects on British shipping.

The favourable effects arose from the limitation on price competition and the monopoly advantages, including the barrier to free entry which conferences present. The result of these factors has been the maintenance of British liner tonnage at a greater level than would otherwise be the case. In so far as the conference arrangements helped to protect the unsubsidized operator against the recipient of subsidies, they helped to prevent a worsening of world patterns of resource allocation. Where, however, they went further than this, as before 1930 and since 1945 if not between those years, the preservation of British shipping services which are uneconomic in nature has worsened the pattern of resource allocation. Whether this is regarded as good or bad for Britain depends upon the economic valuation of the contribution of British shipping to defence, the balance of payments and the general prestige and trade of this country. The conclusion that any overall favourable effect

[1] *Maritime Transport 1960*, Report by O.E.E.C., Paris, 1961, para. 88, p. 36.
[2] Ibid., para. 89, p. 36.

exists to be considered in this way depends on the assumption that retaliation, either direct or indirect, to conferences has not countered the favourable effects. That this assumption may be valid in the present, or was valid in the past, is no *a priori* reason for anticipating its continuing validity.

There is an attractive argument which can be used to demonstrate further favourable effects of conferences and which was hinted at above. The argument is thus: conferences, or something very much like them, are essential for the maintenance of liner services, Britain retains advantages in the provision of fast liner services, therefore, conferences are essential to the maintenance of British shipping. The argument is, however, fallacious because it wrongly equates liner services and liner-type ships. A liner service is a regular scheduled service which may be maintained by a ship of any quality. The ships in the running of which Britain possesses advantages are large, fast ships, often refrigerated or with other special equipment. Such ships are generally liners, but need not be; they may, for example, be 'super' tankers or large bulk carriers. Liners, on the other hand, are not necessarily faster or otherwise superior to ships engaged in non-liner services. Therefore, although it has been convenient to regard the types of ships in which Britain's advantage lays as including liners, this is not the same as saying that the advantage lays in the provision of liner services.

The unfavourable effects of conferences have arisen from the retaliation of other countries, from the dampening of profit earning capacity and opportunities for expansion in times of boom, and from the existence of agreements within the primary rate agreements. Such agreements have removed much of the competitive incentive to efficiency and cost-consciousness and have emphasized the maintenance of the *status quo* at the expense of the urge to expansion; the growth, indeed the continuance, of British liner services has been hindered and jeopardized in this way. These internal service and pooling agreements still exist and although British lines do not appear, today, to be as withdrawn behind the protection of their cartel arrangements as in the inter-war period, this changed attitude is largely a consequence of the almost continuous prosperity since 1939 and a

357

reversal of attitude is possible if the international liner situation again becomes seriously depressed.

Liner owners generally regard conferences as essential for the maintenance of British shipping. Conferences cannot, however, make economic an uneconomic use of resources. Where the use of resources in shipping is uneconomic, conferences may be a necessary, but need not be a sufficient, condition for profitability; this consideration has particular relevance in the present context of rising maritime wages in Britain. The large tankers, bulk carriers, fast refrigerated vessels, and express passenger vessels on routes on which air competition is not yet overwhelming, that is, the types of vessels the operation of which is more likely than any other to constitute an economic use of resources for Britain, are all vessels which can quite easily operate outside conferences. It appears, therefore, that whatever the position in the past, conferences in the present largely serve to maintain the profitability of uneconomic patterns of resource allocation; further, they tend to preserve ship types which are most affected by subsidized competition and by flag discrimination. The necessity for conferences for the preservation of the British mercantile marine is, therefore, highly questionable, unless that mercantile marine is considered as wedded indissolubly to its present structure. If conferences are to continue, legislation to make it illegal for British lines to be parties to supplementary agreements, which agreements would fall foul of the Registrar of Restrictive Practices if they existed in a domestic industry, would be a valuable stimulus to British shipping.

XIV

The Structure of the British Industry

T<small>HE</small> structure of the British industry in 1960 is set out in Table 50. As the table shows, eight large liner groups[1] between them owned over 80 per cent of all British liner tonnage, in addition to some tramp and tanker tonnage. The ownership of the tramp fleet is well dispersed, with a few large fleets and many small ones. The tanker fleet is owned mainly by the oil companies, the remainder being owned independently by shipowners as such. In this chapter it will be most convenient, first, to comment briefly on the ownership of tramps and tankers and then to discuss at greater length the ownership of liner tonnage.

Ownership of Tankers and Tramps

Of the British tanker fleet, nearly four million tons is owned by the oil companies themselves. The oil companies were originally forced into shipowning because of the unwillingness of shipowners at the end of the nineteenth century to invest in such revolutionary craft as tankers. Indeed, it was not until after the first world war that the world independent tanker fleet became significant and not until after the second world war that the British independent fleet became important.

Independent shipowners own just over 1·25 million tons of the British tanker tonnage. The largest tanker owners are Mavroleon and Kulukundis, and Hunting and Son; both also own tramp ships and bulk carriers.

Mr. Mavroleon has been a shipowner in Britain for a number of years in the well-established pattern of what are usually

---

[1] A group, as the term is used here, consists of two or more lines with a common ownership or control. It is not the exercise of control, but the possession of control which is important.

TABLE 50. Ownership of British merchant vessels, 1960

Owners	Liners	Ship Types: Tramps[a]	Tankers	Total tonnage owned
	000's tons	000's tons	000's tons	000's tons
P. and O. group	2,007	205[b]	157	2,369
Shell Co.			1,506	1,506
Furness group	1,291	63	66	1,420
British Petroleum[c]			1,383	1,383
Blue Funnel group[d]	971			971
Cunard group	947			947
British and Commonwealth	769	57	46	872
Ellerman group	631			631
Esso			491	491
Vestey group	466			466
Caltex			368	368
United Molasses group[e]	60	301		361
Inverforth	336			336
Mavroleon and Kulukundis[f]		114	190	304
T. and J. Harrison	268			268
Thomson S.S. Co. (Ben)	208			208
Hunting group		21	172	193
Watts, Watts and Co.		60	127	187
Denholm Co.[g]		134	26	160
Canadian Pacific	121			121
Ropner companies		88	25	113
Palm Line[h]	111			111
Hogarth companies		108		108
Stanhope Shipping Co.		81	24	105
Lyle S.S. Co.		103		103
Other liner companies[i]	448	38	29	515
Other oil companies[j]			173	173
Other tanker owners[k]		205	467	672
Large tramp owners[l]		644		644
Other tramp owners[m]		728		728
Total[n]	8,634	2,950	5,250	16,834

ᵃ Including dry-cargo bulk carriers.

ᵇ Classed as general traders, these ships may be employed as either liners or as tramps.

ᶜ Includes tonnage of Warwick and Lowland Tanker companies, in which B.P. have 50 per cent interests.

ᵈ Includes Elder Dempster by virtue of Holt's holding a controlling interest in the holding company which owns Elder Dempster.

ᵉ For convenience the Runciman tonnage is included with United Molasses since Runciman's manage the United Molasses tonnage.

ᶠ Messrs. Mavroleon and Kulukundis (U.S. Resident) are directors of the companies grouped here.

ᵍ Includes tonnage with which the Denholm Company is associated, for example, that owned by E. D. Naess.

ʰ Owned by Unilever.

ⁱ A number of unrelated companies, of which the most important are China Navigation, Bibby, Elders and Fyffes (owned by United Fruit of America) and Common Bros.

j Three oil companies each owning small quantities of tonnage.

k Includes sixteen companies of which ten also own tramps or bulk carriers. The most important are John I. Jacobs, Bowring S.S. Co., Silver Line and two related Anglo-Dutch companies.

ˡ Eleven tramp owners each with over 40,000 tons. The most important are Reardon Smith, Buries Mark, Bolton S.S. Co., and France Fenwick.

ᵐ A group of fifty companies owning between 2,000 tons and 40,000 tons of tramp shipping, excluding fleets made up of small vessels of under 2,000 tons each.

ⁿ The equivalent totals shown by the Chamber of Shipping for 30 June 1960 are:

Liners	8,764,000 tons
Tramps	3,304,000 tons
Tankers	5,457,000 tons
Total	17,525,000 tons

The discrepancies arise from:

   i. the different dates adopted;

   ii. the exclusion of smaller vessels from the table;

   iii. the exclusion of tonnage owned by the Ministry of Transport but managed by shipping companies.

Source: Compiled from List of U.K. Ship owners given in *Shipping World Year Book* (1960), with tonnage figures from *Lloyd's Register of Shipping*, vol. III (1960–1).

known as the London-Greeks. These people, resident in London and often British subjects when of the second generation, begin as ship brokers and ship managers. Many then acquire one or two tramp ships on their own account, or own a share in each of the ships which they manage. The Messrs. Kulukundis are Greeks, resident in New York. The two companies which are included in Table 50 are Counties Ship Management and London and Overseas Freighters. The first of these is a management company formed in 1936 and managing ships owned by a large number of mainly single ship companies. These companies, in their turn, are owned mainly by Greek interests, resident either in Greece or in London. Mavroleon, after the war, saw the opportunity to build up a fleet of independently-owned tankers and in 1947 placed orders for two 16,000 deadweight ton tankers. In 1948, with Messrs. Kulukundis, London and Overseas Freighters was set up; this company owns tankers which are let mainly on time charters. The companies have not relied exclusively on their own resources to finance expansion, but have frequently borrowed for the purpose.

Hunting and Son were the first British shipowners to own tankers. In 1893 the Northern Petroleum Tank Steamship Co. Ltd. was formed and later that year the tanker *Duffield* was launched. In the inter-war years the tanker fleet was expanded and eleven tankers were built in the 1920s alone. The fleet in 1960 was about 20 per cent larger than in 1939. The company has financed much of its activity from borrowed money and has its ships let out on time charters.

A company, the name of which does not appear in the table but which deserves separate comment, is the Anglo-American Shipping Co. This company was formed by Erling D. Naess in association with British interests as a subsidiary of the Norness Shipping Co. The companies are registered in Bermuda but the ships are registered in Britain. The only ships owned by Naess interests which appear in the table are those owned jointly with, or managed by, the Denholm Co. The Anglo-American is another company which works with a great deal of borrowed money and in 1960 had outstanding nearly £6 million in 5½ per cent notes issued to Mitsubishi Shipbuilding and Engineering Co. Ltd., being 70 per cent of the cost of two large tankers, in addition to £5 million in 7 per cent redeemable loan stock.[1] The company owns large tankers and bulk carriers.

The ownership of British tramp ships is well diffused. There are a few substantial fleets, of which the most interesting is that of the Bolton S.S. Co. This company which owns high-class tramp ships, some of which are time chartered to liner companies, in 1960 put into service the first British ship to be specially designed for free-piston/gas-turbine propulsion. Such adventurousness is sufficiently rare to be worthy of special note.

Nearly one-quarter of British tramp tonnage is owned by fifty small companies which cannot be classified into larger units. However, these are not necessarily all independent companies as it is common practice, particularly among non-British owners, for single ship companies to be formed and for one interest to control a number of these companies. This ownership structure is based on the traditional form of regarding each ship as a separate venture: its ownership, divided into sixty-four shares, is spread among different individuals each of whom takes up one or more shares in each of a number of ships rather than owning some shares in a company which, in its turn, owns all the ships. Many of the tramp companies in Britain owning one or two ships have been formed since 1945; indeed about 15 per cent of all British tramps are owned by companies formed since 1945. Non-British interests are heavily represented in these small companies.

The position of these non-British interests in British shipping may be noted. Up until about 1956 the bulk of the British independently-owned tanker fleet was owned by companies which although technically British, were themselves owned by, and received their driving force from, non-British interests. The same is true of bulk carriers today and these companies are providing a drive in British shipping which many of the older established companies lack. It may be remarked in this connection that when a non-British subject registers ships in Panama or Liberia he is considered, by the British industry, to be acting in a wholly anti-social manner and contributing to the growth of the 'phony' fleets; when, however, he sets up a company and registers ships in Britain, the British industry claims credit for the vessels put on the British register as evidence of the health of the

[1] Information from *Stock Exchange Year Book*, 1960.

industry. The contrast in attitudes seems paradoxical and reflects a deep-seated confusion between British-registered ships and ships owned by British owners. When the total of British-registered ships is discussed, and the growing fleet of large independently-owned tankers is noted, it needs to be recalled that many of these ships are not owned by British owners and that much of the initiative for building up the British independent tanker fleet came from non-British sources. The British shipping industry as such may be regarded as made up of all the companies owning British-registered tonnage, but this is not the same as the tonnage owned by British shipowners.

Another point to be noted is that the entry of new companies since 1945 and their demonstrated ability to raise money in Britain shows quite clearly that British lines, had they wished, could have raised capital for expansion. In fact, no British shipping company quoted on the Stock Exchange has issued new shares for cash since 1945. Only five British liner companies had any debenture or loan capital in 1960 while only a further four had liabilities to creditors, including bank overdrafts, which exceeded the *book values* of their investments, debtors, stores and cash, excluding the value of their fleets. A few of the tramp companies made greater use of borrowed money, but these were mainly new companies.

A third point is that if non-British owners voluntarily chose to register their ships in Britain, which involves setting up a British company to own the ships, then Britain cannot have been such an unfavourable country in which to own ships as many British shipowners would have the world believe.

OWNERSHIP OF LINER TONNAGE

The present group structure of British liner ownership is largely a twentieth-century development. Two distinct phases in the combination movement, which has resulted in the group structure, can be discerned. The first of these was a series of mergers each of which produced larger lines from the merging of several competing lines. The second was a series of amalgamations of lines into groups under common ownership, but without necessarily altering the apparent line structure.

The Structure of the British Industry

The first part of the development of the group structure occurred when competing lines agreed to merge in order to limit competition. Competition reached the point where combination was considered when the volume of tonnage in a trade became excessive in relation to the available cargo. This occurred in a number of trades in the nineteenth century, for example, the North Atlantic trade, but became widespread only in the depression of 1904–11. With combinations to limit competition, it was common practice for the several lines to lose their separate identities and either to take a completely new name or to continue under the name of the most powerful of the original competitors. This part of the combination movement was practically ended by 1914; the numerous mergers of this kind in the years 1912–14 were really the lagged responses to the depression which ended in 1911.

The second part of the development overlapped this first part, although its main period was after 1914. This second part consisted of the amalgamation of lines, not necessarily competing lines, into a common ownership, usually with each line retaining its identity. This process started with the American-owned International Mercantile Marine which grew up by combinations to limit competition, but changed its character after 1901. The first identifiable British group was the Ellerman; Ellerman had bought up a number of lines in the nineteenth century, but the group did not emerge as such until a reorganization in 1901. The next step in the group structure was with Royal Mail which, as Table 51 shows, was active in adding lines from 1909 onwards. In this way, the second part of the grouping movement occurred while combinations to limit competition were still occurring.

As a generalization, it may be said that combinations were a consequence of intense competition whereas amalgamations were the outcome of prosperity. Both parts of the combination movement occurred before 1921 and in subsequent periods of prosperity and depression there was little scope for further amalgamation or combination. The apparent exception, the amalgamations during the 1930s, is the result of the breakdown of the Royal Mail group.

The largest group is that formed around the Peninsular and

365

TABLE 51. Some amalgamations among British shipping lines, 1900 to 1960 (The list is not complete)

Year	*Line amalgamated*	*Group absorbing*
1902	China Mutual	Blue Funnel
1903	Beaver	Canadian Pacific
1906	Shire (half interest)	Royal Mail
1909	Elder Dempster	Royal Mail
1910	Pacific S.N.	Royal Mail
	Blue Anchor	P. and O.
1911	Shire (half interest)	Royal Mail
	Glen	Royal Mail
	Union Castle	Royal Mail
	Houlder Bros.	Furness Withy
	Anchor	Cunard
1912	Warren	Furness Withy
1913	Nelson	Royal Mail
	Archibald Currie	British India
1914	British India	P. and O.
1915	Indra	Blue Funnel
	Allan	Canadian Pacific
1916	Prince	Furness Withy
	New Zealand Shipping	P. and O.
	Commonwealth and Dominion	Cunard
	Royal	Cunard
	Donaldson	Anchor (Cunard)
	Wilson	Ellerman
1917	Knight	Blue Funnel
	Union S.S. Co.	P. and O.
	Hain S.S. Co.	P. and O.
	Nourse	P. and O.
1919	Quebec S.S. Co.	Furness
	Orient S.N. Co. (half interest)	P. and O.
	Bullard King	Royal Mail
	Khedivial Mail	P. and O.
1920	General Steam	P. and O.
1921	Brocklebank	Cunard
1926	Shaw, Savill and Albion (with White Star)	Royal Mail
1926	White Star (from International Mercantile Marine)	Royal Mail
1928	Cairn	Furness
1934	White Star (from Royal Mail)	Cunard
1935	Shaw, Savill and Albion (from Royal Mail)	Furness
1936	Anchor (from Cunard)	Runciman
	Glen (from Royal Mail)	Blue Funnel

Year	Line amalgamated	Group absorbing
1937	Royal Mail ⎫ Pacific S.N. ⎬ from Royal Mail	Furness
1944	Lamport and Holt (*ex* Royal Mail)	Blue Star
1947	King	Union Castle
1952	Henderson	Elder Dempster
1956	Union Castle	British and Commonwealth
1960	Orient (half interest)	P. and O.

Oriental Steam Navigation Company (always known as P. and O.). The company was incorporated by Royal Charter in 1840 for the transport of mail and passengers to Iberia and the East. With the opening of the Suez Canal, its interests were extended to Australia. In 1910 the company acquired Lund's Blue Anchor Line and its services to Australia via South Africa. The Blue Anchor Line has lost its identity, although the service lived on under the name of P. and O. Branch service in the inter-war years. The biggest acquisition by P. and O. was in 1914 when the British India Steam Navigation Co., with its extensive shipping and trading interests in India and the Far East was acquired. With this line, P. and O. also acquired the Australasian United Steam Navigation Company which British India had acquired in 1886. Further amalgamations followed quickly. The New Zealand Shipping Co., was acquired in 1916, the opening of the Panama Canal having created new opportunities in the New Zealand trade. Further, when the Furness Withy group had obtained control of Houlders in 1911 (see below) the Australian interests of Houlders had been sold to the New Zealand Shipping Co., and so, together with the Federal Steam Navigation Company which was owned by the New Zealand Shipping Co., passed into P. and O. ownership. In 1917 a further three lines were acquired. Chief among these was the Union Steam Ship Co. of New Zealand with extensive coastal, trans-Tasman and trans-Pacific interests. The Hain S.S. Co. with a large tramp fleet and the Nourse Line, another tramp fleet, were also acquired. These two fleets were acquired for the sake of their tonnage and the profits tramps were earning at the time, but at the prices ruling were scarcely prudent purchases. In 1919, P. and O. acquired a 50 per cent interest in the Orient

Steam Navigation Co. which had been formed in 1878 and had formerly operated its Australian service in conjunction with the Pacific Steam Navigation and later with the Royal Mail Line. The Orient Line maintained a passenger service to Australia and so with this purchase P. and O. obtained a virtual monopoly of the Australian passenger service as the Royal Mail service was not continued after the 1914–18 war. It was to counter this monopoly that the Australian Government started its own passenger line which was afterwards grouped with the Aberdeen Line as the Aberdeen and Commonwealth and was associated with Shaw, Savill and Albion as part of the White Star Line, all eventually passing through the Royal Mail group to the Furness Withy group. In 1919, P. and O. also acquired the Egyptian Khedivial Mail Co. Then in 1920 General Steam Navigation, a company running excursion and coastal ships was acquired, while later the General Steam acquired from the disbanded Royal Mail group the Moss Hutchison Line with connections in the Mediterranean trades. The next acquisition by P. and O. was the Strick Line. Finally, in 1960 in connection with joint P. and O. and Orient services to Australia and across the Pacific, full ownership of the Orient Line was acquired.

With a total tonnage of 2·4 million tons in 1960 the P. and O. group is the largest shipping group in the world. This powerful group was not, until the last few years, marked by great enterprise. 'Gorgeous it was, no doubt, with a string of jewels embedded in the east, but getting heavy and sluggish with age.'[1] It was heir to the traditions of the East India Company, proud, autocratic and intolerant, resistant to change. It shows very clearly the danger which arises when one policy embraces a large segment of the industry; when the author of that policy is a man of strong personality, firmly entrenched in his position, then a large part of the industry is subject to his *Diktat*. P. and O. have, however, come to life dramatically. It is probably true to say that although P. and O. have taken over Orient financially, Orient have taken over P. and O. in operational terms and the willingness to experiment, to adopt new ideas, for which that company were known have now affected the senior partner. The venture in the Pacific, which the shackled Union S.S. Co. was

[1] *The Times* (22 May 1961).

unable to undertake after the loss of the *Niagara* during the war and the scrapping of the *Aorangi*, is a portent of the new régime. A further sign is the recent purchase by P. and O. of two Belgian liners no longer wanted for the owner's Congo trade, and the later purchase by the New Zealand Shipping Co. of a Cunard liner.

As a digression it may be noted that it is most unusual for a British liner company to buy a vessel, either from another British owner or from overseas, although inter-group transfers sometimes occur. Before the three purchases mentioned above and the purchase of another Belgian liner by Booth Line (part of the Vestey group) there were only five passenger liners in the entire British fleet which were not then owned by the company for which they had been built. Because of the limited market for secondhand passenger tonnage, vessels usually change hands for relatively low prices. The annual depreciation charges on a secondhand ship over its anticipated remaining life are, therefore, considerably smaller than the annual depreciation on a newly built vessel over a full life span. The willingness to purchase tonnage from other owners and to convert it, if necessary, to suit a different trade is a sign of cost-consciousness which British liner owners too infrequently display.

The second of the larger liner groups is that owned by Furness Withy. In 1898 Furness Withy established Manchester Liners as a subsidiary company to take advantage of the opportunities created by the opening of the Manchester Ship Canal. The first important amalgamation occurred in 1911 when Houlder Brothers and Company was acquired, a line chiefly engaged in the South American meat trade. Houlders themselves are now a small group of lines, including companies owning ore carriers and tankers. In 1912 Furness Withy acquired a controlling interest in the Warren Line and in 1934 the existing name of Johnston Warren Lines was given to a company formed within the group from the Johnston, Warren and Neptune lines. In 1916 the Prince Line was acquired and in 1919 the Quebec Steamship Company. The latter is now fully integrated into the Furness Withy Line and has lost its separate identity. Then in 1928 the Cairn Line entered the group. In 1935 the Shaw, Savill and Albion Line was acquired from the wreckage of Lord

Kylsant's Royal Mail group. Shaw, Savill and Albion was the result of a late-nineteenth century combination between two competing lines in the Australasian trade. It had passed subsequently into the ownership of the White Star Line, then in 1926 had become part of the Royal Mail group when White Star was purchased by that group. Two years after the acquisition of Shaw, Savill and Albion, the Royal Mail Line and Pacific Steam Navigation passed into the Furness group, again as a result of the break up of the Royal Mail group. These acquisitions made the Furness group the second largest in the world. The group was the first among British liner groups to own tankers and bulk carriers; it also conducted the notable, and conspicuously successful, experiment with the passenger liner *Southern Cross* which was built with engines aft in tanker fashion and without any cargo space. The present tonnage of the group, 1·4 million tons, includes passenger liners, meat carriers, general cargo liners, ore carriers, tankers and tramps. Its main interests are in the American trades, particularly in those to South America, although it is also strongly represented in Mediterranean and Australasian trades.

The third group shown in the table is the Blue Funnel group. It is usual to regard Blue Funnel and Elder Dempster as separate undertakings.[1] However, although the operations of the two companies appear to be independent, Blue Funnel owns a controlling interest in Liner Holdings which owns all the capital in the Elder Dempster Line and they therefore constitute a single group as defined here. In the discussion the Blue Funnel side of the group will be discussed first, then Elder Dempster.

The Blue Funnel part of the group is one of the most personal and most individual of all the large shipping lines. Alfred Holt formed the Ocean Steam Ship Company in 1865 to own ships trading to the Far East. In subsequent years mainly by his own expansion, Holt built up a network of feeder services in the Far East to collect cargo for his ships and also started a service to Australia. Two companies were purchased during the 1914–1918 war in order to secure entry to the trades between North America and the Far East. Of the lines which have been

---

[1] See, for example, P.E.P., 'The British Shipping Industry', *Planning*, xxv, no. 437 (November 1959), p. 207.

absorbed by Blue Funnel, none retains its separate identity, save the Glen Line which was purchased in 1936. Even the Glen Line ships bear the distinctive Blue Funnel characteristics although they preserve the Glen funnel markings. The characteristics of Blue Funnel ships are their great strength and plain workmanlike appearance. The advantages of these attributes are seen in the number of ships built to Blue Funnel specifications which have achieved a notable longevity. Currently, the group is building a class of 20-knot freighters for Far Eastern services, a commendable recognition of the needs of the situation.

The other part of the Blue Funnel group is the Elder Dempster Line and its subsidiaries. Although owned by the Blue Funnel group, Elder Dempster has not been absorbed into the Blue Funnel Line in the same way as the Glen Line. In 1869 the British and African Steam Navigation Company was formed with Elder, Dempster and Co. as managing agents. In 1890 it merged with another company and the name Elder Dempster was applied to the shipping company. In 1891 the company became associated with Harland and Wolff through a common directorship which paved the way for its integration into the Royal Mail group in 1909. In 1911 the Glen Line was absorbed and within the group was merged with the Shire Line which Royal Mail had acquired in two stages. After the break up of the Royal Mail group, Elder Dempster was set up as an independent line owned by Elder Dempster Lines Holdings. The name of the holding company, which is controlled by Ocean Steam Ship Company (Blue Funnel) was changed to Liner Holdings in 1953. The Glen Line passed directly from the Royal Mail group to Blue Funnel. In 1952 Elder Dempster acquired the Henderson Line largely in order to use its tonnage in West African services. This rather surprising purchase becomes explicable when the connection with Blue Funnel is realized. The purchase enabled the Henderson cargo tonnage to supplement the West African fleet, while Blue Funnel, with its extensive connections in the Far East, could take over the former Henderson services.

The fourth liner group is Cunard. Cunard is one of the senior British shipping companies and has maintained a transatlantic service since 1840. Early in the century the company agreed to resist the wooing of J. P. Morgan, who had secured the White

Star Line, provided the Government assisted it to build two record-breaking vessels, known as *Lusitania* and *Mauretania*; the special position which the line occupies today is largely the consequence of the decision taken regarding the construction of these two ships. In its time, the company has absorbed a number of its rivals, including the enforced marriage with the White Star Line as it emerged from the Royal Mail combine. There are only two extant lines in the Cunard group, apart from the name line. First is the Port Line, formerly known as the Commonwealth and Dominion Line[1] which was acquired in 1916. This line is engaged in the Australasian trades. The other is T. and J. Brocklebank which was acquired in 1921; the Brocklebank fleet consists of cargo liners engaged mainly in Far Eastern services.

Cunard takes itself seriously by virtue of its ownership of the largest British liners and its senior position in the prestige North Atlantic service, but its post-war construction has been uninspiring. As with so many other shipping groups during the past five years, there have been significant changes in the control of the Cunard group, but the present management is apparently more excited by aeroplanes than by ships. The extraordinary history of the proposal to replace the ageing *Queen Mary*, and the manner in which the company withdrew from the proposal after obtaining the promise of a subsidy from the Government, do not shed a favourable light on the company's foresight. In 1961 two relatively modern cargo/passenger liners were sold and replaced in the fleet by chartered Swedish cargo tonnage, Cunard's own capital, apparently, being required for its air venture. In 1962 a number of important changes were made in the operations of Cunard. First, it was decided that the express passenger liners should not be withdrawn for overhaul during the peak passenger season; the former arrangement was, to say the least, remarkable. Second, plans were made for improving the four passenger liners built between 1954 and 1957 for the Canadian service; the improvements will make the ships suitable for cruising. Third, the *Mauretania* is to seek a share of the lucrative trade between New

[1] The line was formed in 1913 by the combination of four lines engaged in the Australian trade.

York and Southern Europe. Fourth, tenders were sought for the construction of four fast cargo liners. These things suggest that Cunard has found a new vigour which augurs well for the future.

The fifth liner group is the British and Commonwealth formed in 1956 by amalgamating the Clan Line and Union-Castle. The Clan Line had been formed in Glasgow in 1890 by the Cayzer family which now controls the group. It brought into the group its own extensive fleet of modern cargo liners, the Houston Line, the Scottish Shire Line (not to be confused with the Shire Line which was merged with the Glen Line) and the Thompson Steamshipping Co. Union-Castle had been formed in 1900 by a combination of the competing Union and Castle Lines in the South African trade. In 1911 it passed into the Royal Mail group.

After the disintegration of the Royal Mail group, the Union-Castle Line reverted to independent ownership and struggled to find its feet. From 1929 to 1940 no dividends were paid. The fleet was modernized and expanded during the later 1930s, higher-speed ships being placed in service to satisfy the requirements of the new mail contract and to meet the developing German and Dutch competition. In 1919, while in the Royal Mail group, the line had purchased the Natal Direct Line (Bullard, King and Co.) and it retained this on leaving the group. The recuperative powers shown by the line in the 1930s were remarkable and by 1939 it had a modern, well-equipped fleet and given a period of peaceful prosperity would almost certainly have placed itself in a sound position. In 1947 the company felt the need to have at its disposal additional trading vessels and considered that tramp tonnage would usefully supplement the liner tonnage owned.[1] Accordingly, the King Line with a substantial tramp fleet was acquired. The King Line had also been part of the Royal Mail group and after the break up of the Kylsant empire was closely connected with Union-Castle, with a common chairman.[2] By the 1950s Union-Castle was in difficulties, having a number of ageing ships and insufficient resources for their replacement. New money could have been

[1] See M. Murray, *Union-Castle Chronicle* (London, 1953), p. 34.
[2] See R. M. Wilson, *The Big Ships* (London, 1956), p. 165.

raised, but the will was lacking and in 1956 the line was taken over by the Clan Line. The extent to which the drive of Union-Castle had run down is shown in the design of the new mail ship which was on the stocks in 1956; she was a virtual repeat of ships built in 1949 which themselves were repeats of ships built before the war, which in turn were based on the *Carnarvon Castle* of 1926.[1] After the amalgamation the ship on the stocks was altered during construction to give a higher speed and to incorporate stabilizers thereby matching contemporary standards. Ships built subsequently mark a radical break with Union-Castle tradition.

The next big liner group is that built up by the late Sir John Ellerman. In 1901 Ellerman sold the North Atlantic interests of F. Leyland to the International Mercantile Marine and then formed the Ellerman Lines from the City Line, Hall Line, Wescott and Laurence, Palgrave, Murphy and Co. and the Ellerman-Harrison Line. Subsequently the Papayanni Line and Bucknall's were absorbed. Control of the Wilson Line of Hull was also obtained, although not until 1959 was this fully owned by the Ellerman group. The ships of Ellerman's Wilson Line retain their distinctive colouring, but the ships of the other lines now all use common funnel markings, while only the Ellerman and Papayanni ships are distinguishable by their nomenclature. The services covered by the group are world wide, mainly cargo services. All the capital is privately held by the Ellerman family and the lines are managed by executives. It is neither an expansive nor a particularly exciting group, the total tonnage being now some 8 per cent smaller than in 1939. When the present Sir John Ellerman, who is without issue, dies, a reconstruction of the companies is inevitable as the payment of death duties by the estate of the principal shareholder will entail serious problems for the companies.

The other groups are smaller. The Vestey group started with the Blue Star Line formed in 1920 to carry meat from the Argentine because the Royal Mail would not grant Vestey's suitable carriage rates. The line entered the Australian trade in the 1930s and became famous in the inter-war years for its

---

[1] The *Carnarvon Castle* and her sister ships were refitted in 1936 to bring them into line with newer vessels.

enterprise in cruising. In 1944 the Lamport and Holt Line, which had been part of the Royal Mail group, was acquired and then the Booth Line, both companies with South American interests. The United Molasses group as shown in Table 50 is hardly a group at all. It consists of the ships owned by United Molasses for their own trade and the Anchor Line purchased from the Runciman family. The tramping fleet of the Moor Line is still apparently owned by the Runciman family, but has been associated with the United Molasses ships in the table because of the close chain of connection between that line and the Anchor Line, which Runciman's continue to manage. The final group, as such, is the Inverforth group comprising the Bank Line, MacAndrews and Co. obtained from the break up of the Royal Mail group, Inver Tankers, and the United Baltic Corporation.

The eight large liner groups, namely, P. and O., Furness, Blue Funnel, Cunard, British and Commonwealth, Ellerman, Vestey and Inverforth, between them own over 80 per cent of all British liner tonnage. Only three of them own tramp types, including bulk carriers, or tankers, the P. and O. group being the largest tanker owner. Most of the interest in tankers among the liner groups is recent, having arisen since the Suez crisis. Under present conditions, an expansively minded group must either own a fleet of oil tankers or bulk carriers, or make a frontal assault on liner trades in which the group is not at present engaged, particularly indirect trades. British liner owners generally do not favour the latter course (see p. 379) while it is in the liner trades of the world that the impact of discrimination and subsidy policies is greatest. The latter are not prohibitive as the expansion of the Norwegian and Dutch liner fleets since 1945 shows conclusively. The former inhibition is more important, particularly as such an assault would often mean an attack on the trades of British liner owners who are not expansively minded. From the point of view of British shipping as a whole it is desirable that such attacks should occur as, if opportunities exist in the trades concerned which the British lines serving those trades do not seize, foreign lines are certain to enter. Many opportunities which were available during the 1950s have now been taken by foreign lines, particularly in the

Pacific where Norwegian lines are important and in South African and Australian trades in which Dutch liners have found many openings. That past openings have been missed does not debar the taking of future opportunities which present themselves.

Outside the eight large groups there are a number of smaller liner companies. Of these, T. and J. Harrison and the Ben Line are the most important. These are both cargo liner companies. The Harrison Line trades to Central America and South and East Africa, its ships tend to be somewhat slow, between 11 and 14 knots, and the tonnage owned in 1960 was about the same as in 1939. The Ben Line, trading to the Far East has realized the importance of speed as a competitive factor and while the older ships in the fleet have speeds of 15 knots the newest vessels have speeds of 18 knots, with something in hand for a further speeding up of the service. The tonnage owned increased by 80 per cent between 1939 and 1960 and with the increase in speed the effectiveness of the present fleet must be about 120 per cent greater than that of the pre-war fleet. The company is entirely owned by the Thomson family of Scotland. Its expansive policy shows, first, that a family line need not necessarily stagnate when the founder dies and, second, that expansion since the war in the Far Eastern trades has been possible for British lines, despite the poor showing of some of the lines engaged in the area.[1]

The other liner companies are smaller. Canadian Pacific is owned in Canada by the railway company and operates a passenger and cargo service from Britain to Canada. The services date from 1903 when the Canadian interests of Elder Dempster were acquired, including the Beaver Line which Elder Dempster had bought in 1899; Canadian Pacific continue the Beaver system of nomenclature with its cargo liners. The 1903 purchase gave Canadian Pacific a through route from England to the East via the railway system in Canada and the passenger service in the Pacific for which a mail contract had been awarded in 1889. The competing Allan Line[2] was absorbed in

---

[1] Brocklebank is the other main British line with extensive Far Eastern interests which has expanded since 1939.

[2] Although the lines competed, they were closely allied. Sir Hugh Allan was the first president of the Railway Company, and the Allan Line often chartered Canadian Pacific tonnage to maintain its mail contract.

1915 and in the inter-war years the Canadian Pacific fleet reached its peak with four large passenger ships in the Pacific and nine in the Atlantic. During the war, three of the four ships formerly engaged in the Pacific were sunk and the service has not been re-opened. The Atlantic service is now reduced to three new ships. The surviving ship of the trans-Pacific fleet was used on the Atlantic service until 1958 when she was sold to the Hamburg-Atlantic Line and after an extensive refit re-entered the Atlantic service under the German flag. The Palm Line has already been mentioned (see p. 328). The only other liner company which calls for special mention is the Bibby Line of Liverpool engaged in Far Eastern passenger and cargo services. The mainstay of the Bibby services was the transport of Army personnel mainly between India and Britain. With the great reduction in this traffic since the war, the line has curtailed its activities and is now smaller than in 1939.

THE CAUSES OF THE GROUP STRUCTURE

Why has British liner shipping become dominated by large concerns each embracing a number of formerly separate companies? There are parallels to this pattern in several other countries, notably, France, Italy, Japan and, to a lesser extent, the Netherlands, while German shipping at one time seemed set on a similar course. In fact, German shipowners were influential in the formation of J. P. Morgan's International Mercantile Marine in America at the end of the nineteenth century. There was also a strong Germanic influence in Harland and Wolff, the Belfast shipbuilders, who were closely associated with Sir Owen Philips (later Lord Kylsant) in the formation of the Royal Mail group. The basic difference between the structure in Britain and that in other countries, except Germany, is that in Britain amalgamations were only partly intended to lessen competition by the combination of lines serving the same trades, whereas this was the dominant factor in other countries. In the course of the growth of the British groups, the main pattern after 1900 has not been the elimination of competition but the extension of services without the creation of competition: there are, however, exceptions to this generalization.

377

If a generalization can be made it is that each British shipping group started when a powerful company, wishing to enter a trade in which it did not already participate, bought out a line in that trade instead of making a direct entry. It is doubtful if it will ever be known why the pattern was the one rather than the other. It is rational, however, for a line wanting to enter a trade to secure entry by purchase if it calculates that the cost of doing so is smaller than the cost of breaking in by competition. In the nineteenth century the break into the trade was apparently almost invariably thought to be cheaper; in the twentieth century the purchase of a line was presumably thought to be cheaper. The only significant institutional change which can be recognized between the two periods is the development of the conference system.

Once conferences had been extended to cover the majority of liner trades and had allocated the berth rights in those trades, a line wishing to expand in liner trades faced three choices. First, it could look for a trade not covered by a strong conference in which it could develop; this, for example, seems to have been the choice made by Norwegian shipowners in the inter-war period. Second, it could put its ships on the trade, risk a rate war if not accepted into the conference and, after the rate war, either retire or take its place in the conference with a share of the berth rights. Many foreign lines have selected this choice at different times and as rate wars have probably more often ended with victory for the aggressors than for the defenders,[1] the aggressive competitors were, by these means, enabled to increase their shares of many trades. Third, the line could buy another line with its berth rights and hope at a future conference meeting to secure a bigger share of the trade.

It is not easy to see why the third choice was that made by British lines before they were integrated into groups, although

[1] Conferences have always had to take account of the views of the governments of other countries and British dominated conferences, which originally were virtually all conferences, probably defended their trades more strongly against the entry of another British line than against a foreign line, fearing that the government of the country owning the line or that of the country at the other end of the trade route the subject of the conference agreement would take retaliatory action against the attempts to preserve an all-British monopoly. This is pure speculation because conferences are even more unwilling to say why they do things than they are to say what they do.

it became an obvious choice (see Chapter XIII) once the groups had been formed. One point is that by buying an existing line its goodwill was also obtained, whereas a new entrant would have no established good will; on the other hand, the greater the goodwill being acquired, the greater the purchase price. As most countries are unwilling to see their shipping controlled by foreigners, non-British owners wanting to establish liner services did not have the choice of buying a British line and very often there was no other nationally-owned line they could buy. The fact that liner services were a British invention and up until after the 1914–18 war, world liner services were dominated by British ships made the positions of British lines and foreign lines trying to secure entry to established services different.

On the question of 'why?' the only conclusion which can be reached is that for some unknown reason after 1900 the custom grew up whereby one established British line did not enter into a trade held by another established British line. An argument can be made out that the 'unknown reason' was simply that this method was considered by prudent shipping men to be cheaper. This, however, is only a partial answer and leaves unanswered the question, 'Why was it cheaper?' The answer to that question is two-fold. First, entry to a new liner trade means setting up an organization of cargo and passenger agents. Second, the cartel arrangements of conferences with the allocation of berth rights were designed to prevent new entrants and, as between British lines, they succeeded in this aim. However, they did not succeed in the aim as between British and foreign lines. This was partly because British lines have always shown a reluctance to employ foreign firms as cargo and passenger agents, whereas foreign firms have not been similarly inhibited. The other factor is that non-British firms did not have the choice of purchasing existing lines and had either to face the probable costs of a rate war or to remain excluded from the trades.

The group structure can be explained by the foregoing argument provided that all liner trades were in fact in the hands of conferences and that no free trades, or no newly developing trades, existed in which an expansive liner company could find an outlet for its energies. Put another way, the second and third choices discussed above were not exclusive alternatives as the first choice existed. If a short explanation could be produced to show why British lines largely ignored the first choice and, concentrating on the second and third, built up the group structure which is seen today, then the problem to which this whole book is directed would be answered.

CONSEQUENCES OF THE GROUP STRUCTURE

Whatever the cause of the emergence of the group structure in British shipping, several consequences of that structure are clear.

First, the existence of expansive shipping lines has had little effect on the total of British tonnage. Such lines did not push more British tonnage into world trades, but simply altered the house flags under which a given total of British tonnage operated. In this connection it is significant that the period of the amalgamations corresponded exactly with the period in which the expansion of British shipping ceased.[1] As Table 51 shows, the main period for combinations was from 1911 to 1919, when shipping was highly prosperous and there were opportunities for expansion by new tonnage. Perhaps combination became a habit or a matter of emulation as ambitious shipowners sought to build up bigger empires than their fellows by the quickest means possible, namely, combination. The consequence, a turning away from expansion by building extra tonnage, is undeniable.

A second consequence of the grouping is that a situation has developed in which the decisions of a single man, or a single group of men, affect a large number of lines. The decision of Lord Kylsant to buy White Star was the main factor leading to the collapse of the Royal Mail group with substantial damage to a number of other leading lines. This was a spectacular example, but just as serious for the competitive spirit and growth of

---

[1] This timing of amalgamations is not, of course, unique. However, in other industries it has generally been the case that stagnant markets have stopped expansion so that the individual firm could expand only at the expense of its rivals. This was probably true of shipping in the period 1904–11 when the amalgamation movement started, but in subsequent years when the market was growing, the expansion of individual enterprises continued to take the form of amalgamation rather than direct growth.

British shipping has been the caution and reverence for historic cost with all its inhibitions against risk-taking which the heads of some groups displayed during critical periods in the industry's history.

A third consequence arises from the nature of the competition between the groups. A vital difference between large groups in shipping and in most other industries is that a newcomer has great difficulty in securing entry to liner services. In most industries if a large group is built up and then gradually succumbs to the inertia of tradition and the glory of the *status quo*, a small firm or another group can usually step into its markets. In liner services the conference system makes this very difficult indeed, and, given the way in which the groups are each associated with the other groups in a number of conferences, makes it impossible for one group actively to compete with any other without inviting repercussions at another point. These are not necessary conditions for the cessation of real competition and expansion but they seem to have proved sufficient.

A fourth consequence of the concentration of British shipping companies is that the task of management is increased. It is impossible to say what size of shipping enterprise is optimal, whether technically, financially or managerially. However, apart from enterprises which have let out their tonnage on time charter, the operation of ships requires continuous decision-taking by the management. Although delegation is possible, because each trade is a separate undertaking with a separate set of problems calling for decisions, the maximum size of enterprise which can be effectively managed is probably smaller in shipping than in most other industries. A great deal depends, of course, on the calibre of the man or men taking the ultimate decisions and the maximum economic size of an enterprise with first-class people at the top is a great deal bigger than if second-class people are running the company. As a basically stagnant industry,[1] shipping has probably not been able to attract its share of able young men, while the strong family connections in most companies limit the opportunities outsiders have of reaching top positions. There are undoubtedly some very able people

---

[1] The average compound growth rate, 1910 to 1959 was 0·53 per cent.

in shipping, but at some time or other each of the main groups has been managed by people whose management potential was below that required. It would be better for the industry as a whole if the larger groups could be broken down a little; a fleet of about 0·5 million tons[1] is probably the economic maximum for a liner company. The manner in which Blue Funnel and Elder Dempster are managed separately, even though Elder Dempster is owned by a company which is, itself, controlled by the same people as control Blue Funnel, points to an acceptable ownership structure. If the rather cumbrous groups are maintained, they can only be continuously effectively managed if each makes appropriate provision for management succession, including the recruitment of young men, particularly graduates, who can reasonably aspire to seats on the Board by the age of 45.

There are welcome signs of change in the upper strata of the industry. But until the leaders of the industry, from whom others take their cues, cease blaming their troubles on the environment in which shipping has to operate and begin accepting that environment and seeking ways of expanding within it, British shipping is unlikely to be expansive or even to retain its present position in the world.

[1] The largest Norwegian ship owner operated about 450,000 tons in 1961, made up of liners, tankers and bulk carriers, and has doubled in size since 1939. The expansion continues but not at the same rate as smaller companies are expanding and a levelling off at about 600,000 tons is not improbable. This will not be caused by capital shortage as the company is quite ready to borrow for expansion. The structure of the highly efficient and expansive Norwegian fleet, in which each line is independent and there are no groups as in the British fleet, suggests that 750,000 tons is probably the outside limit for efficiency of management and even that may prove too large if inefficient managers secure control, as Norwegian experience again shows.

XV

The Question Answered

'THE primary object of this book is to answer a single question, namely, why has the tonnage of ships registered in the United Kingdom declined from over 45 per cent of the world total in 1900 to about 16 per cent of that total in 1960?'[1] In the preceding pages the factors which have, or might have, contributed to this relative decline were examined. Here the threads can be drawn together and the four possible answers to the question, which were outlined in the first chapter, considered. In doing this, all qualifications and subtleties are excluded: the judgments of this chapter cannot be considered apart from the longer discussions in the earlier chapters of the book.

CHANGES IN ECONOMIC FACTORS

The first possible answer to the question is that changes in cost conditions since 1900 have created a situation in which British shipping could not grow in competition with more favourably placed fleets.

Crew costs are the main internationally variable cost item. Differences in crew costs, whether arising from variations in wage rates, social security payments or in manning scales, affect the economic operation of shipping. International crew cost comparisons are difficult to make because the necessary information is not collected in some leading countries, notably Britain. Most of the available information relates only to wage rates or wage costs. Wage rate comparisons ignore variations in both manning and in the non-wage elements of crew costs; wage cost comparisons ignore the non-wage elements. The proportion of crew costs made up of non-wage elements varies significantly from country to country.

[1] The opening sentence of Chapter I.

383

For the above reasons, most cost comparisons need treating with suspicion and small variations in wage rates or wage costs, although they *may* be significant, cannot be so regarded in the absence of additional information. This being so, the information available provides insufficient ground for attributing to British crew costs a major rôle in an explanation of the slow growth. Norwegian tramps before 1913 and Greek and Yugo-slavian tramps in the inter-war period, were assisted by their lower wage costs compared with British tramps although this was partly offset by the higher repair costs of old ships. Japanese ships of all kinds enjoyed lower wage costs for much of the period since 1890 although the advantage may now have disappeared. However, Norwegian crew costs for part of the inter-war period and since 1949, Dutch crew costs for much of the period 1920 to 1960, Danish, French and Swedish crew costs for varying periods have all been higher than, or not significantly different from, British crew costs, without preventing the growth of those fleets. As an answer to the question, therefore, British crew costs do not appear to have been of great importance.

The above should perhaps be qualified by saying that British crew costs need not have been of great importance if shipowners had always adopted the ship types appropriate to the British level of costs. This was not always done and so crew costs have at times appeared to be causal factors.[1]

INTERFERENCES WITH THE COMPETITIVE PROCESS

The second possible answer is that the assistance given to the shipping of other nations created a situation in which British shipping, even when operating with lower costs, has been unable to compete.

In the inter-war period the shipping policies of countries other than America had a relatively minor effect on British shipping. They certainly created difficulties for British liners and some-times for tramps, but these were never crucial although they often appeared to be greater because much post-war British

---

[1] It might be added that if sterling should be devalued in relation to the currencies of other maritime countries the whole position with regard to crew costs would be altered and ship types which are unprofitable at the existing exchange rate would become viable.

tonnage was too slow for current conditions. Further, there was plenty of room for expansion in trades not affected by the shipping policies of others: for example, the Norwegian expansion in the period occurred within such trades.

Since the second world war a good deal of discrimination has been introduced into shipping. This affects only a small proportion of world trade, although some of the trades most affected are those in which British ships have traditionally engaged, many of them trades which British shipowners developed. To be suddenly thrust out of such a trade is, of course, unfair, but lamentations do not help. Other shipping has suffered with British shipping; in particular, Dutch shipping suffered additionally the loss of the Indonesian trades. As in the inter-war years, despite the subsidies and preferences, there have been free trades in which expansion was possible.

For both periods the conclusion is that had shipping policies not existed, some awkward problems for British shipping would have been avoided and life, therefore, made easier. The environment in which shipping has had to operate has never been easy, however, but this did not stop British shipping growing before 1914, nor Norwegian and Greek shipping in the inter-war years, nor Norwegian, Swedish and Dutch shipping in the post-1945 period.

The impact of unfair competition since 1900 has limited the expansion of British shipping in traditional trades and helped to create a situation in which considerable flexibility was a necessary condition of success. To argue that this competition has had *an* effect on the growth of British shipping is not, however, to say that the adverse effect on growth was a necessary consequence of such competition nor that the original question can be answered in terms of the shipping policies of other countries.[1]

---

[1] In the 1950s British shipping tonnage grew by 19 per cent, while that of the Netherlands, Norway and Sweden, all paying about equal wage rates and operating without state assistance, grew by 48 per cent, 116 per cent and 77 per cent respectively. If these figures are standardized for value to take account of the higher construction costs of passenger tonnage the British figure is raised to 31 per cent, the Dutch figure to 70 per cent, while the Norwegian and Swedish figures are virtually unchanged. The differences in these growth rates cannot be explained in terms of either cost differences or unfair competition.

The Question Answered

RANDOM FACTORS

The third possible answer to question is that random factors, that is, factors which have affected shipping without having been directly related to shipping, may have prevented British shipping from maintaining its position in the world. The random factors are a mixed 'bag' and each item must be considered separately.

(a) *British Trade*

Since before 1914 British trade has grown more slowly than world trade and this was very apparent in the years of recovery from the depression in the 1930s. However, a large trade is neither a necessary nor a sufficient condition for success as a shipowner, and the slow growth of British trade simply meant that those shipowners who depended on that trade had to seek other outlets for their energies if they wished to expand. Had British trade grown as fast as that of the remainder of the world, shipowners servicing that trade could have expanded without the need to open new routes, provided always that they maintained their share of the British trade, which they have not done. The most that can be concluded is that if British trade had grown faster, this might have induced a greater expansion of British shipping; that British trade did not expand in this way meant that shipping had to find its own impetus for growth.

(b) *War*

It is quite clear that the first world war produced a situation in which some decline in the relative position of British shipping was inevitable. It is not true, as is often alleged, that the wartime profits of Norwegian shipping, which next to Greek shipping had the highest growth rate in the inter-war period, permitted a post-war expansion which British shipping could not match. Nor is it true that British shipping was starved of profits or crippled by taxation. The most important consequence of the war was the growth of the American fleet which, after the war, retained trades which had formerly been serviced by British ships. The American participation in these trades subsequently

386

declined, although it never returned to the 1913 level. However, it was Norwegian and Japanese ships, not British, which profited from the opportunities created by the decline in the size of the active American fleet and by the opening of new trade routes through the Panama Canal. The purchase of war-built tonnage at inflated prices, following the inability of British owners to build during the last eighteen months of the war, did not help the industry. It was suggested in Chapter IV that a decline in the British proportion of world tonnage from 40 per cent in 1913 to 34·5 per cent in 1939 could reasonably be regarded as the direct consequence of the war.

The second world war was directly less important as British shipping suffered less than most of its rivals in terms of net (but not gross) losses. Norwegian shipping perhaps had a marginally better financial experience than British shipping but not enough to account for the disparities in growth since 1945. There was another huge increase in American tonnage, much of which was put into reserve after foreign shipowners had been given an opportunity to buy what they wanted. Financially, British shipping did not gain from the war; although the war years as a whole were more profitable than any period of comparable length in the preceding generation, the sharp rise in shipbuilding prices meant that the profits had to be used to maintain the real capital.

(c) *Taxation*

Nowhere in the preceding chapters has taxation as a factor inhibiting the growth of British shipping specifically been considered.

International tax comparisons are extremely difficult to make. In Table 52 two sets of estimates of tax on companies in the 1930s are given. In each case the comparisons are made by constructing model companies with certain capitals, turnover, profit and so on and applying to these the fiscal legislation of the different countries. The figures relate to companies generally, not specifically to shipping companies, and so take no account of special tax advantages enjoyed by maritime enterprises. Clearly, also, they do not take account of the different levels of profits earned nor of the tax actually paid; they are, in fact, estimates

The Question Answered

TABLE 52. International comparisons of taxation

| | First Model[a] | | Second Model—1935–6[b] | | |
| | Feb. | April | Small | Medium | Large |
Country	1932	1934	company	company	company
	%	%	%	%	%
Belgium			32·6	33·6	43·9
Denmark			18·9	27·2	56·9
Finland			33·3	39·9	54·0
France	39·24	43·13	49·0	49·6	62·5
Germany	62·67	60·55	67·2	69·7	81·5
Italy	28·91	28·75			
Netherlands			23·5	31·1	60·6
Norway			45·8	48·2	74·3
Sweden			21·9	29·6	60·5
United Kingdom	20·00	18·59	8·6	21·9	59·3
United States	26·51		46·0	46·0	72·7

Taxation as percentage of earnings:

[a] Taxation within a 12½ year economic period on a capital intensive company as a percentage of accounting profit. Social charges included with taxes proper. Method described in *Internationaler Steuerbelastungsvergleich*, Einzelschriften zur Statistik des Deutschen Reichs, Nr 23 (Berlin, 1933); figures from p. 613.

[b] Similar basis. Small company with income up to 3,000 kroner, medium company 6,750–10,000 kroner, large company 200,000–500,000 kroner. Calculated by Lindahl, *Undersökningar rörande det Samlande Skattetrycket i Sverige och Utlandet* (Stockholm, 1936), p. 121.

Source: Derived from *Der Wettbewerb in der Seeschiffahrt*, pp. 204–5. Original sources not available.

of the tax which would have been paid in each country shown had companies made the profits estimated.

Subject to the necessary reservations, the figures suggest that in the 1930s British taxation rates were such that the burden of taxation on British companies was relatively low. Among important ship-owning nations, apparently only in Denmark were company profits more lightly taxed than in Britain. It seems impossible, therefore, to make anything of taxation as a factor contributing to the stagnation of British shipping in the inter-war period.

For the post-war period a comparison of the relative burden

of taxation on the shipping of different countries has proved impossible to make[1] because of the very frequent changes in tax rates in different countries. British shipping clearly has been more heavily taxed than that in the tax-free Panholib countries, but differences between tax burdens in western European countries have not been extreme. In particular, British and Norwegian shipping have been about equally taxed and shipowners in both countries agree on this. Any attempt to explain the poor British performance since the war in terms of taxation must imply, therefore, that the Norwegian growth was also retarded for this same reason. Table 53 shows that the Norwegian growth rate for the period 1954 to 1960 averaged 9·3 per cent per annum, scarcely indicative of substantial retardation.

Although freedom from taxation would have left British shipowners with more of their earnings available for expansion, if they had wanted to expand they could have borrowed the money or raised new share capital. Further, there is no evidence that British shipping as a whole has been short of money or realizable assets since 1945, so that there can be no certainty that lower taxation would have resulted in a greater expansion of shipping.

(d) *Government Restrictions*

The British Government is frequently blamed for the ills of British shipping. A particular cause of complaint is the restriction imposed on the transfer of British ships to foreign registry after 1939. It is difficult to see how the removal of these restrictions would have caused a greater growth rate to be achieved. Existing businesses have not been permitted to transfer to Bermuda to enjoy tax-free operation; however, Norwegian shipping companies have also been prevented from avoiding taxation by adopting flags of convenience.

Shipowners frequently complain that the Government has neither opposed discriminatory measures by retaliation, nor imposed such measures as direct assistance to the industry. However, such discrimination would only help British shipping provided no other country indulged in further retaliatory

[1] Because of its complexity, the task was given to a professional body specializing in fiscal work and studies; they had to admit defeat.

action. The size of British trade in relation to the British fleet makes it clear that if a round of discrimination occurred so that British shipping was restricted to British trade, the fleet would be both smaller than at present and its future growth possibilities limited to the growth of British trade. In the long run, which in this case might not be very far in time from the initial act of discrimination by Britain, British shipping would be harmed, not helped, by such action. This question is discussed more fully in the Epilogue.

A more legitimate complaint is that since the war the Ministry of Transport has been more interested in rail and road, than in sea, transport and has, therefore, not employed a specialist staff to look after the industry and provide it with information or to assess and meet its complaints.[1]

As to the first point, the industry itself has done little in this direction and there is nothing in the two main shipowners' associations to correspond with the economics section of Norges Rederforbund. There is no collection of data on costs and results; no studies are made of the economics of shipping operations to assist shipowners in planning their business; there is no output, either published or private, of papers with any analytical pretensions. Certain privately operated organizations make regular studies of the industry, but the scope of these is restricted by a lack of information. Further, these organizations live by selling reports to their subscribers, and the pressure to maintain a constant and regular output of material and to cover their costs means that studies of a long-term nature cannot be made. Despite these limitations, much of the work done is excellent in quality and no criticism of it is intended; the point is that by its very nature it needs supplementing by longer-term studies based on full information about the operations of shipowners which at present is not available.

On the second point, the published material from the industry can rarely stand up to critical study, and unless the submissions

---

[1] The position of coastal shipping, which is not directly considered in this work, has been irreparably damaged by the subsidies to railways which have taken traffic away from sea routes. But this also occurred before the railways were nationalized because of the system of charging freights which involved the cross-subsidization of cheap and bulky commodities by high value, low bulk items, thus preventing coastal shipping attracting the type of traffic in which it had a real advantage.

to the Ministry are more cogent there can be little wonder that
they are not met more sympathetically. The point cannot be
overlooked, also, that the industry does not itself collect and
make available the information which is necessary for an assessment, instead of mere acceptance, of the validity of the complaints made in the published material.[1]

(e) *Summary*

The random factors obviously have some part to play in
answering the question. Of these, the effects of the 1914–18 war
on growth were necessary effects in the sense that the industry
by its own actions could scarcely have countered them. The
effects of the slow growth of British trade on the expansion of
British shipping could have been avoided by increased participation in non-British trades. Norwegian experience, particularly
since 1945, shows clearly that although taxation may have
limited the expansion of British shipping, it cannot account for
the low growth rate experienced. The policies of the British
Government, except for a short period in the 1930s, have not
helped British shipping; on the other hand, they have not been a
major hindrance.

Growth Rates, 1890 to 1960

It is now clear that the first three of the four possible answers
cannot be sustained; neither separately, nor together, can these
answers be regarded as more than partial. Before turning to the
fourth answer, it is worth examining in some detail the growth
rates of the tonnage owned in different countries, both for the
whole period 1890 to 1960 and for shorter periods within that
long period. This is done in Table 53.

From the first column in the table it can be seen that the
average annual growth of the British fleet was significantly
lower over the whole period than that of any other country in
the table and that of the world fleet as a whole. The impossibility of explaining this as being due to any of the causes which
have been discussed above is apparent when the other columns

---

[1] These points have not been discussed with the Ministry of Transport which is
in no way responsible for the opinions expressed.

are examined, or when the countries above Britain in the table are considered.

It can be seen that for only two of the periods shown, 1890 to 1909 and 1954 to 1960, did the British fleet succeed in maintaining an annual compound growth rate of more than 2 per cent.

TABLE 53. Average annual compound growth rates of twelve leading maritime fleets, 1890 to 1960

Country	*Average percentage growth per annum:*								
	1890 to 1960 %	1890 to 1909 %	1904 to 1913 %	1913 to 1920 %	1920 to 1929 %	1929 to 1939 %	1939 to 1949 %	1949 to 1954 %	1954 to 1960 %
Japan	5·6	11·2	8·4	12·2	3·4	3·0	−16·3	22·8	11·6
Greece[a]	5·2	—	7·2	−6·0	9·8	3·5	−2·8	−1·2	25·5
Netherlands	3·5	4·7	6·7	5·4	5·1	0·1	0·0	2·2	6·3
Denmark	2·9	5·0	2·4	0·8	2·8	1·0	0·3	5·4	6·4
Sweden	2·8	3·4	3·4	0·4	3·5	0·5	3·0	5·2	5·9
Norway	2·7	1·2	3·6	−1·7	3·8	4·1	0·3	5·6	9·3
Italy	2·5	2·4	2·5	6·7	3·9	0·5	−3·4	9·3	4·5
U.S.A.[b]	2·4	2·1	1·5	28·9	−1·5	−2·4	2·5	−0·3	−1·7
France	2·1	3·0	2·6	6·7	0·4	−1·4	−0·2	5·8	4·4
Spain	1·4	1·4	1·1	2·9	1·5	−2·4	0·4	2·0	6·1
Germany[c]	1·4	5·1	4·2	−40·1	19·8	0·9	−46·3	85·5	13·3
U.K.	0·6	2·7	1·9	−0·3	1·0	−1·1	−0·3	1·2	2·4
World	2·3	3·4	3·2	3·4	3·6	0·2	−0·2	4·8	6·3

a Figures in first column relate to period 1901–60.

b U.S. Reserve Fleet excluded in all post-1945 figures; Great Lakes tonnage excluded throughout.

c Since 1945 only West Germany included.

In the earlier of the periods the British growth, in relation to that of the world, was satisfactory; in the later of the periods, however, the apparently favourable British growth needs to be compared with a world growth rate over twice as high and the higher rates in all other countries in the table other than the United States. It is clear that the impetus of British shipping was lost in the decade 1900 to 1910, since which time the industry has lagged, although the better growth rate in the period 1954 to 1960 perhaps indicates that a new impetus has been discovered: the future alone will show whether this is so or not.

The Question Answered

The eleven countries above Britain in the table are mixed. Some apparently can be dismissed, the growth of their fleets being due to operations of national shipping policies. This, for example, seems to apply to Italy, Spain and the United States. Both Japanese and French shipping have also been subsidized. In the case of Japan, however, the destruction of the fleet between 1939 and 1949 removed the effects of prior subsidies. For France, subsidies were important for all periods up until 1949; since that time French shipping has enjoyed only limited assistance and the growth rate achieved in the period 1949–60 has not been a consequence of that assistance. German shipping was subsidized in the 1930s, its only period of very low growth, but for the remainder of the period was practically free from assistance; despite the destruction of the fleet twice in the period, the overall growth rate exceeds that of the British fleet. Subsidies cannot even begin to explain the places of the other five countries in the list.

Shipping of the Netherlands was highly profitable during the 1914–18 war, but not during the 1939–45 war. The Netherlands expansion from 1913 to 1929 can perhaps be explained in terms of wartime profits, but not that between 1890 and 1913, nor that between 1939 and 1960. As a predominantly liner fleet, Dutch shipping has been affected by the subsidy and preferential policies of others, with the particular disadvantage of being completely excluded from the Indonesian trades. Further, Dutch shipping suffered severely from the maintenance of the gold value of the currency after 1931.

The growth of Danish shipping can be explained in terms of wartime profits in the period 1920–9, but as the growth in this period was lower than in the 1890–1909 and 1949–60 periods, such an explanation is clearly inadequate to account for the overall growth rate. Very much the same applies to Swedish shipping, except that some of the post-1949 expansion may also be a consequence of wartime profits. These do not help with the explanation of the growth in the period 1890 to 1913.

For Greek shipping, an explanation relying on low labour costs may be valid for the periods 1904–13 and 1920–39, while a good part of the growth in the period 1954–60 represented the transfer of tonnage from flags of convenience, the owners of which had gained substantially from tax free operation. However, the low wage rates in the earlier periods were associated with the high repair costs of old ships. In the later period, the Greek-owned Panholib fleet grew up to meet the demands of the world for extra tonnage, which needs the shipowners in some of the older countries were neglecting. The ships were registered under the 'phony' flags because of the political situation in Greece and while tax-free operation undoubtedly helped, if this had not been available those same owners would have established their fleets in other countries. Had that country been Britain, as it probably would have been (the amount of British registered tonnage owned by Greek interests is a sign of this), the British fleet would have expanded, but that expansion would not have arisen from the activities of native British shipowners.

Finally, there is Norway. The expansion of the Norwegian fleet started in the twentieth century, the fleet suffered heavy losses in two world wars and has never enjoyed any significant government assistance. The profits from the first world war were largely lost in the inflation after the war and the depreciation of the currency, while profits in the second war were only a little greater than those enjoyed by British shipping. In the earliest periods, up until 1913, Norwegian shipowners enjoyed a crew cost advantage, although this was partly offset by high repair costs and slow voyages. In the post-1949 period, Norwegian crew costs were no lower, and may have been higher, than those on British ships.

This brief analysis supports the conclusion that differences in costs, the effects of subsidies and discrimination and the impact of random factors cannot provide more than a partial explanation of the slow growth of British shipping since 1900. It is clear that the answer to the question posed at the beginning of this book must be sought in internal constraints on growth.

INTERNAL CONSTRAINTS ON GROWTH

If internal constraints on growth existed, they can only have arisen from the attitudes of shipowners to changing circumstances; the genesis of such attitudes must be sought in the history of the industry and its place in the British economy.

The Question Answered

British shipping achieved supremacy when iron and steam replaced wood and sail in the construction and propulsion of ships. The circumstances of Britain's industrial and colonial experiences favoured a rapid growth of the industry, while the traditionalist attitude of American shipowners, who refused to acknowledge the superiority of the steamship, removed Britain's chief international rival. From about the middle of the nineteenth century British shipping was a vigorous and expansive industry. The early pattern was of relatively small companies, financed initially from the savings of the shipowners and their friends and then from ploughed-back profits. Competition between companies was intense and the shipowners themselves were usually hard-driving business men, rarely associated with the 'gentry' or the ruling classes of the country. The growth of the industry showed British business at its most competitive, aggressive towards rivals but, unfortunately, equally ruthless and disregarding in its attitude to its employees.

However, after about 1875 changes appeared in the industry. During the last quarter of the century the extent of internal competition in the industry began to decline as competing shipowners realized that they could each increase their profits by co-operating with their competitors. This was effected in two ways. First, competing lines frequently amalgamated, usually by the stronger taking over the weaker, but often enough by an equal merging of interests. Lines such as Union-Castle, Shaw, Savill and Albion, and Elders and Fyffe date from this period. Second, where lines did not merge in this way they agreed to limit the competition between them by forming conferences. These two approaches to a less competitive atmosphere, which did not touch the tramping side of the industry, were both the result, and the cause, of other changes. Clearly, the older generation of shipowners with their individualistic outlook and ferocious independence could not settle down to work together in mergers. The possibility of shipowners associating with their rivals depended upon the replacement of the older type of owners by people with skills in negotiating and a smaller personal pride in the achievements of the ships of the lines bearing their names. A result of the reduction in competition was that shipowners became more remote from ships and the smell of salt than were their predecessors. Coincident with these changes, shipowners became more socially important figures, the purchasers of land and the recipients of titles. It would be an exaggeration to say that in fifty years shipowners had changed from bearded salts to courtiers, but the change had differed from this only in degree.

The leading shipowners at the end of the nineteenth century were men accustomed to co-operation rather than aggressive competition. Further, the shift of their interests from the ships themselves to the offices running their ships meant that operations were increasingly seen through the balance sheets. They were disposed to further amalgamation, to the creation of large units by financial means rather than by building new ships and fighting their competitors to win new trades. When faced with international competition from the emergent German liner fleet co-operation and the sharing of territories was a natural outcome.

Until the German competition occurred, British shipowners had been able to regard the oceans of the world as virtually a British lake with the only problem that of determining the sphere of each within this lake. By the time that international competition became serious, which roughly coincided with the depression of 1904–11, the idea of paramountcy was firmly embedded. The crumbling of the basis of this belief occurred almost unnoticed, apparently for two reasons. World trade was expanding up until 1904 so that the outside competitive pressures were not strong. Alongside this, the emergence of the new type of shipowner and the larger organizations isolated the owner from his most valuable source of commercial intelligence, his ship masters. This source has never been replaced by any formalized system for collecting information on world trades.

It has been shown that the period between the 1904–11 depression and the end of the war was one of great activity in amalgamations as expansively-minded owners increased the fleets under their control.[1] By carrying out these amalgamations at a period of peak freight rates, inflated values had to be paid

[1] Strictly, the amalgamations between 1911 and 1914 were usually to limit competition, while those between 1914 and 1919 were to build up larger organizations.

for the lines acquired, this causing unwarranted increases in capitalizations which hampered the industry in its attempts to meet the competition of the inter-war years. Within each group many different trades were represented, each with its own problems, needs and possibilities, increasing the tasks of managements. In short, by the end of the 1914–18 war the combination of a group structure and the conference system had resulted in an industry heavily biased towards maintaining the *status quo* and ill-adapted to showing flexibility to meet the enormous changes of the inter-war period.

When the lines were merged the family interests of each of the member lines in each group were recognized by the enlargement of boards of directors to include members of all the families. This increased the area from which the top management could be drawn. At the same time, however, it made the shipping industry less attractive to people who had the ability and ambition to reach senior positions. Although this is impossible to document, it is suggested that shipping, like other industries in which family connections have been strong in the main firms, has been unable to recruit or retain sufficient new management blood of high quality.

The tramping side of the industry followed a slightly different pattern. Some tramp companies were taken over by liner groups in the period of extensive amalgamation, but, by and large, the tramping industry has retained its structure and still consists of many small companies. These owners might, therefore, have been expected to continue to show vigour and adaptability. It is not clear why they did not, although difficulties in raising finance may have been a primary reason. Again, detailed documentation is impossible. Nevertheless, it may be suggested that some of these difficulties may be accounted for by the long-term decline of local banks and, even more tentatively, by the links, through common directorships, between some of the national banks and the larger shipping groups.

It will be recalled that the early growth of steamship companies was financed from the resources of shipowners plus the money they could raise from their friends. The lines which survived into the twentieth century were mainly those which had a good profit record and had been able to expand from these profits. Outside capital was sometimes obtained, but the tradition was one of self financing. Indeed, one general characteristic of family concerns is that, if possible, recourse to outside capital is avoided in order to retain the undisputed control of the concern within the family. However, in the nineteenth century borrowing was common and remained so until the depression of 1904–11. In this period heavily indebted lines failed and the financially conservative men who then controlled the major shipping lines observed the failures and took the lesson to heart. Borrowing became anathema. In this way, a double tradition, no new capital and no borrowing, grew up which has limited the rate of expansion to that which can be achieved from profits. This may not be a serious limitation in time of prosperity, but when existing activities are unprofitable it means that the resources are not available for undertaking other activities which promise to be profitable. The situation has become one in which past performance and the availability of ready cash have determined the willingness of owners to build new ships, whereas in the nineteenth century it was predominantly the profits to be expected from the new ship on which the decision to build was based.

The critical period for British shipping was that between 1920 and about 1958. In this period tremendous changes in trading patterns, in competition, in ships, in cargoes, and in the movement of passengers occurred, to which the industry was slow in adapting itself. The shipping industry by 1920 was one geared to the maintenance of supremacy, not to the meeting of changes. Practically all liner owners were members of conferences and while stagnation was not a necessary consequence of this, the lack of competition within the conferences, together with the group structure of the industry, appeared to be sufficient to produce a situation completely lacking dynamism.

The change within the liner industry from competition on rates to competition on service or even full pooling, had an effect on the cost consciousness of liners. Where price is competitively determined, the prize goes to the man with the lowest costs, while any increase in cost items must be followed by a search for cost-reducing methods if the enterprise is to survive. Where, however, price is not determined in this way but is

The Question Answered

based on costs, the incentive to reduce costs is lacking. This has two effects. First, overheads can be increased and loaded on to prices. Second, there is no drive to seek lower cost production functions, either in ship operating or in cargo handling.

Finally, the effects of over one-half century of almost unchallenged supremacy must be noted. Complacency is an all-pervading legacy of Victorian Britain and affected most industries which reached positions of strength and importance in that period. The apparently tremendous security of Britain and all things British in the pre-1914 era made anything less than absolute leadership practically unthinkable. The 1914–18 war came at an unfortunate time in this regard for it distracted attention from the cracks which before the war had begun to appear in the foundations of that security. After the war these cracks were treated as the effects of the war and the general expectation was that they would be sealed with a return to normality. But normality and 1913 never returned and the British shipping industry was called upon to face problems to the solution of which its whole structure and attitude was not adapted.

Earlier, it was stated that the critical period for British shipping was that between 1920 and 1958. The earliest of these dates represents that at which the group structure of the liner companies was completed: the subsequent changes consequent upon the collapse of the Royal Mail group changed the ownership of a number of lines, but not the group structure itself. During the 1920s the industry maintained a considerable momentum despite the difficulties of an over-valued exchange rate. The real testing time was the turn down in world trade after 1929. Throughout the previous depression, that of 1904–11, the industry expanded by seeking new trades.[1] In the depression after 1929 there was little such activity and the industry gave every impression of sitting back and waiting for the world to concede it the living which it felt its self-assumed crown justified. It was here that the consequences of the past were seen. The shipping enterprises which best weathered the depression were those, such as the Norwegian companies, which, holding nothing and

[1] This search gave rise to vigorous competition which was followed by numerous amalgamations between competing lines.

399

so having nothing to lose, had explored new trades and new cargoes in the 1920s. By 1939 there were many signs that the British industry had grasped the situation, when another war again distracted attention and caused a reversion to older attitudes in the face of all the threats to existence which the war entailed. After the war the tremendous prosperity of the industry seemed to endorse the rightness of its policies, while the constant expectations of a slump provided grounds for prophesying doom to the reckless foreigners who had expanded their fleets. However, thirteen years of prosperity, during which the British industry expanded only so far as its own resources allowed, pointed the contrast between the British and other shipping industries. In character with the retained grandeur from the pre-1914 days, the expansion of others was explained by unfair methods and Government assistance, and while this has been the core of hundreds of speeches and of the industry's policy document of 1960, yet it has begun to be seen to have worn thin. There are signs of change in the industry, most of which have emerged since 1958 and which point to the possibility that the long period of relative decline may be ending. The signs cannot be discussed here, although they are taken up in the Epilogue.

The attitudes of the industry affected its reaction to changing circumstances in many different and frequently subtle ways. It has proved possible to formulate six specific directions in which the British industry reacted in a growth inhibiting manner, and these are given below. The list represents the effects of the inhibitions of the industry as a whole, not those of each individual shipowner. For practically every item on the list it is possible to produce an exception in the shape of an owner who reacted differently to the majority of his colleagues. Because the industry is not monolithic, but a collection of companies each with its separate identity, character, problems, and approach to solving those problems, almost any generalization is unfair to someone.

First, independent British shipowners, with a few notable exceptions, neglected the tanker practically until 1956.

Second, although British shipowners led the world in switching from sail to steam, the diesel engine was less enthusiastically adopted in Britain than in any other country paying comparable wage rates in the inter-war years, despite the clear economies in running costs.

Third, speed as a competitive factor and as a source of economy in labour and total fleet costs was largely neglected by British shipowners, except on the North Atlantic, from 1914 virtually until after 1956.

Fourth, British owners continued to build tonnage in Britain when better ships or cheaper ships could have been obtained from overseas. In the 1930s, for example, the knowledge that tankers could be built more cheaply on the Continent than in Britain was regarded by shipowners as a reason for not building tankers rather than for building them abroad. For about the last ten years British shipowners have been as free to build overseas as they were before 1939, but the majority contented themselves with complaining about British prices and relatively few orders were placed abroad.

Fifth, standardization of tramps, bulk carriers and tankers has been largely neglected by British shipowners and shipbuilders, despite the knowledge that such standardization could cut costs.

Sixth, the industry has tended to blame others for its misfortunes. In doing this it has usually failed to discriminate between troubles arising from the greater enterprise of other shipowners and those caused by unfair competition. This lack of self-criticism is a marked feature of the *Survey of British Shipping* (1960) and also of the earlier unpublished reports.

There can be no reason to doubt that the attitudes discussed above and the consequences listed have had an adverse effect on the growth of the British industry. Saying that they have had *an* effect, however, is a long way from saying that they are the cause of the relative decline and that, therefore, the introductory question can now be answered in terms of internal constraints. It has been argued that the first three possible answers to the question are inadequate, either singly or together to answer the question and the rejection of these answers was bolstered by an examination of the growth rates of shipping in a number of countries. Nevertheless, it is true that the factors outside the British industry, on which these rejected answers depended, have not been constant over the period considered. The final step in the argument, therefore, is to ask whether had all the external factors been constant could a relative decline such as that noted have occurred. This question can be answered in the affirmative by means of an analogy drawn from Norwegian experience.

Bergen is one of Norway's leading sea ports and before 1925 more tonnage was registered there than in any other Norwegian port. Wage rates have been the same as in other ports, the owners in each port have remained independent of those in other ports, and the shipping of all ports has always expected to find its employment mainly in non-Norwegian trades. The economy of the town of Bergen has for many years been heavily dependent on shipping so, if anything, shipowners have found capital relatively easier to obtain there than in other ports, such as Oslo, where competition from other industries is greater. In this situation, differences between the growth rates of Bergen's shipping and Norwegian shipping as a whole can only arise from the differences between Bergen shipowners and other Norwegian shipowners. The differences which have occurred in growth rates produced the following position:[1]

	Bergen's share of total Norwegian tonnage:			
	1929	*1939*	*1957*	*1960*
	%	%	%	%
Tankers	25	11	10	
Dry-cargo vessels	24	23	15	
Passenger vessels	36	35	30	
Total	23	18	13	12
Index of percentage share, 1929 = 100	100	78	56	52

This relative decline occurred mainly because shipowners in Bergen were slower in switching from steam to diesel propulsion than were most Norwegian shipowners and did not expand their tanker fleets as fast as other shipowners.

[1] Norwegian data from A. S. Svendsen, 'Bergen's Shipping', Paper no. 8 of the Norwegian School of Economics and Business Administration, Bergen, January 1958. 1960 figures calculated from *Årbok over Skandinaviske Skipsrederier* (Oslo, 1961), pp. 115–45.

The Question Answered

If Britain and the world are now written for Bergen and Norway, an almost identical pattern results.

| | British share of total world tonnage: | | | |
	1929	1939	1957	1960
	%	%	%	%
All vessels	30	26	17	16
Index of percentage share, 1929 = 100	100	87	57	53

By analogy with the Bergen experience this is clearly a pattern which could result entirely from internal constraints. If the concept of the trend tonnage extrapolated from 1919 as developed in Chapter IV is used, it is found that the British fleet in 1929 was very slightly larger than the trend for that year. The calculation of the trend tonnage took into account the effects of the first world war. This means that it is possible to make the following statement: random factors provide a valid answer to the introductory question for the period 1913 to 1929; for the period since 1929 the question can be answered solely in terms of internal constraints. This statement may be expanded by saying that in the 1930s British shipowners reacted somewhat better than Bergen shipowners to changing conditions, whereas since 1939 their reactions have been more constraining. In neither period have their reactions been such as to prevent a relative decline in British shipping.

Epilogue: The Future

I T is implicit in the preceding pages that British shipping has excellent prospects for the future. The internal constraints on growth which have been noted are inimical to the realization of these prospects. There are, however, signs that a new spirit is showing in the industry which will remove some or all of these constraints. It is because this new spirit has been detected that in Chapter XV the critical period for the industry was stated to have lasted from 1920 to 1958: since 1958 there are signs that the traditional responses to competitive pressures are disappearing.

Eight signs of the new spirit have been discerned in the industry. First, there has been a recognition of the need for more research into all aspects of ship operating, including that necessary to determine trade trends and predict changes. Second, some owners of cargo liners have built or ordered freighters with speeds of 20 knots instead of the more common 15 knots. Third, tanker owners have swung over to the large tanker; whereas the typical tankers built for liner companies only two or three years ago were of about 20,000 deadweight tons, 45,000 tons is now usual. Fourth, owners of passenger vessels have bought secondhand ships from other owners and have begun to follow foreign practice in reconstructing ageing liners for further service. Fifth, tramp owners have overcome their pre-occupation with the 9 to 12 knot, 10,000 deadweight ton vessel and are building faster and larger ships. Sixth, some ship owners have noted that possibilities for expansion exist by opening new trades. Seventh, some liner owners give the impression of having begun to examine critically that traditional institution, the conference system. Eighth, and perhaps most important, influential sections of the industry seem to have rejected the view that all the troubles of British shipping can be attributed to people and forces outside the industry and to be coming to the view that the industry's salvation lies largely in its own hands.

It would be too much to say that the industry has been revolutionized or that all shipowners have become infected with the new spirit. Yet, unless these straws in the wind are figments of an imagination which wants to see British shipping as a vigorous and enterprising industry, there is ample ground for optimism. Although there is ground for optimism, there is none for complacency or for the view that the cheering signs are, in themselves, enough. In particular, too few shipowners are as yet touched by the new spirit. Further, some of the signs have not yet been translated into action; for example, very little research has been started, few new trades have been opened, the conference system has not been thoroughly examined.

ASSISTANCE FOR THE INDUSTRY

The possibility must be faced that the signs of a new spirit which have been detected are delusive or, if real, that the new spirit will be killed off by the cold winds of a few years in which profits are difficult to make. If that happens, the alternatives of allowing the industry to run down or preserving it, although uneconomic, must be considered. Assistance directed to producing a new structure and composition of the industry can be justified on economic grounds, whereas assistance towards the preservation of an unchanged industry can only be justified on non-economic grounds. What are these grounds?

(a) The Needs of Trade

It might be argued that British trade would be hampered if the shipping industry was to decline greatly in size. The needs of trade have been cited to justify subsidies to American shipping, but the argument is fallacious. Trade would be hampered, not helped, if the industry was protected by preferential arrangements enabling it to charge freight rates above internationally determined minima; assistance by subsidy would impose an equivalent burden, although differently distributed. A strong, economic shipping industry helps British trade, but a protected industry would simply impose new burdens and so be a hindrance.

Epilogue: The Future

(b) Defence

The mercantile marine has proved vital to the defence of the country in two world wars and it is generally assumed that it would be necessary in any future conflict. The economist is in no position to assess the validity of this assumption, although some observations may be made.

First, there is no necessary relation between the optimum sized fleet considered economically, the fleet which shipowners choose to own and the fleet required for defence purposes. Second, if the defence requirement is for a larger fleet than that which unsubsidized shipowners provide, the gap can be filled by means of a reserve fleet without subsidizing shipowners. The size of the reserve fleet required in relation to the active fleet can be calculated as described in Chapter IX. Third, the total of shipping tonnage in the world is not determined by the flags under which that tonnage operates, so that in a war the shipping of other countries would be available if British ships were not. Naturally, a high price would have to be paid to charter the ships, just as in previous wars when foreign-owned tonnage was chartered. However, there is no *a priori* reason to suppose that the cost of chartering foreign tonnage in war must exceed the total cost over years of peace of protecting an uneconomic industry. As a counter to this, however, it needs to be borne in mind that the cost during peace is an internal cost, whereas the cost during war would be an external one. Therefore, although the former cost may exceed the latter, a consideration of the foreign exchange situation in wartime may indicate that the more expensive course is desirable. This, in itself, is only a partial argument as the possibility always exists of stock-piling foreign exchange rather than of maintaining an uneconomic mercantile marine. Finally, the nature of future possible wars must be considered. In an all-out nuclear war shipping is unlikely to be of much value because the war would be short. In a limited non-nuclear war there would, by definition, be neutral nations from which ships could be chartered.

(c) Balance of Payments

A consideration of the need for external balance may suggest that a less than optimum distribution of resources is necessary in order to secure a contribution to the financing of the import bill. Put another way, it is not enough to show that resources used in shipping earn less than if used in alternative occupations if those resources when used in shipping produce, or save, more foreign exchange than if otherwise used, provided always that saving foreign exchange is an important aim. In a world where free trade is the exception, the trade pattern does not follow closely that which strict adherence to the law of comparative advantage would dictate. It, therefore, does not follow that for Britain to divert resources from relatively uneconomic uses in shipping to more economic uses in other industries would increase national welfare. The product of those resources used in their most economical fashion would not necessarily be saleable overseas to yield the foreign exchange required to sustain the import bill arising from the present level of national income, let alone that arising when a higher proportion of shipping freights was payable in other currencies and imports had risen as a result of a higher level of national income caused by the transfer of resources from shipping to more productive uses.

It was shown in Chapter VII that between 1952 and 1960 the contribution of British shipping to the balance of payments fell from 12·2 per cent to 6·1 per cent of the import bill. The question of whether the fleet is worth preserving must take account of this trend. It is clear that to increase exports by 6·1 per cent in order to cover, by other means, the payments for shipping services would not be easy, and might be impossible. For this reason, therefore, there is apparently a strong case for subsidizing British shipping if that course is necessary in order to preserve its contribution to the balance of payments. However, there is a paradox here. If the trend is extrapolated it is clear that in the not too distant future shipping will be making a negligible contribution to the balance of payments and, in the long run, is clearly not worth preserving for the sake of its contribution. How soon this situation would arise is dependent partly on the level of freight rates. It will occur earlier if rates fall below the level of 1960, but later if rates rise substantially above the level of that year. The other element in the paradox is that if the right type of ships are owned, the question of the preservation of the industry would not arise as it would be both profitable and economic, and would increase its contribution to the balance of payments.

In the previous paragraph it is implicitly assumed that the choice is between a subsidized industry of about its present size and the complete disappearance of the fleet. Even on pessimistic assumptions about the future of the industry, its disappearance is most unlikely in the foreseeable future. On such a pessimistic assumption a decline in the size of the industry by ten, twenty or even fifty per cent is conceivable. The question to be asked, then, is whether the net loss to the balance of payments (that is, the loss after taking account of the exports produced, or the imports replaced, by the resources freed from shipping) is sufficiently serious to warrant a subsidy. Looked at in this way, the case for a subsidy is even weaker.

The conclusion is that despite the value of shipping's contribution to the balance of payments, the present trend is for that contribution to fall and the industry, as it stands, is scarcely worth subsidizing in the long run to preserve the contribution. If the industry, by its own actions reversed the trend in the balance of payments, it would also be in a position where no question of subsidy arose.

(d) *Prestige*

The prestige which is presumed to attach to the possession of a national fleet is something which many newly independent nations suppose to be important. While regretting the check on economic growth which the use of resources in this way might occasion, it is possible to sympathize with the aspirations involved. For a mature country, such as Britain, such sympathy cannot be extended to the pursuit of a basically irrational aim.

(e) *Conclusion*

The case for subdizing British shipping is, apart from defence arguments which cannot be assessed here, weak. If the industry will study, and adapt itself to, the conditions of the 1960s it will need no subsidy.

Epilogue: The Future

MEETING STATE-AIDED COMPETITION

The existence of state-aided competition, particularly that arising through discriminatory legislation, poses special problems for British shipping and is resulting in pressure on the Government to take steps to counter the effects of such competition. The four main ways of countering such competition are diplomatic, retaliatory, compensatory and evasion.

(a) Diplomatic

The rôle of diplomatic action is limited by the obvious suspicion which attaches to any party who is making propositions which, whatever their status in respect to eternal verity, are coincident with the self-interest of the party. This limits the value of diplomatic activity by countries advocating free trade principles in shipping, particularly when those countries are themselves protecting other sectors of their economies or have assisted their own shipping in the past.

(b) Retaliatory

Retaliatory action is a matter of tit-for-tat; as considered here it relates only to discrimination. Retaliation is a game which countries such as Britain, Norway, Liberia, Panama and Greece are in a particularly poor position to play. This is brought out by the figures in Table 54.

In considering the effects of increased discrimination, including retaliation by Britain, it is assumed that most countries, either initially, or in retaliation, demand that 50 per cent of their imports travel in national flag ships. What would be the position of British shipping in such circumstances?

Approximately two-fifths of British imports by weight are from, and one-third of British exports by weight are to, Commonwealth countries. Some members of the Commonwealth, such as India and Pakistan would, in an extension of discrimination such as is postulated, probably insist on their full share of the trade, whereas other countries, such as Australia and Canada, would be unlikely to do so. Further, over one-half of British imports by weight are of oil and petroleum products, chiefly from Middle Eastern countries which, although

Epilogue: The Future

TABLE 54. World trade and shipping, 1959

| Country | Share of world trade by weight: | | Share of world shipping by tonnage, U.S.R.F.[a]: | |
	Exports	Imports	Included	Excluded
	%	%	%	%
United Kingdom	4·0	11·2	16·4	18·7
Liberia	0·2	0·2	9·7	11·0
Norway	0·7	1·0	8·8	10·0
United States	14·8	17·0	20·5	9·6
Japan	1·0	5·1	4·9	5·6
Italy	0·8	4·6	4·0	4·6
Panama	0·0	0·0	3·8	4·3
France	2·7	6·1	3·6	4·1
West Germany	1·7	4·5	3·6	4·1
Netherlands	2·4	7·4	3·5	4·0
Sweden	1·8	2·3	2·8	3·2
Greece	0·1	0·4	2·4	2·7
Denmark	0·3	1·6	1·7	1·9
	30·5	61·4	85·7	83·8

a U.S.R.F. = United States Reserve Fleet, that is, ships laid up in American ports on Government account which are brought into service only in exceptional circumstances.

Source: Calculated from U.N.O., O.E.E.C., trade figures; Lloyds tonnage figures.

developing chauvinistic tendencies, could not quickly build up a tanker fleet to carry 50 per cent of their exports, although they could easily time-charter tankers of Liberian registry. Finally, discrimination, except occasionally in the case of migrants, has not been applied to the carriage of passengers. Taking these factors into account, it would appear that under the operation of a universal 50/50 rule applied to imports, Britain could raise the share of imports (at present just over 50 per cent) carried in British vessels, to perhaps 75 per cent while the employment of predominantly passenger liners would not be affected. What this means in terms of employment for the British fleet is difficult to say; probably about one-half of the British ships now engaged in cross trades would fail to find employment under the conditions postulated and the fleet be reduced by some 20 per cent.

410

Epilogue: The Future

Overall, therefore, even on the basis of optimistic assumptions, retaliation by adopting flag discrimination is not a policy which would commend itself to the whole British industry. To parts of the industry, for example, those lines engaged in direct trades with discriminating countries, retaliation appears attractive as a possible policy. The danger is that if Britain was to start on this path it would be taken as a signal for other countries, at present not discriminating, to adopt similar measures.

(c) *Compensatory*

Compensation applies principally to trades affected by subsidized competition and would itself take the form of subsidies. True compensatory subsidies require accurate calculation, if they are to do no more, and no less, than provide compensation. If properly calculated they should offset the effects on shipping of the subsidy policies of other countries so that shipping services which would have been uneconomic, whether other countries paid subsidies or not, would remain uneconomic. Such subsidies would then have two effects only. First, they would prevent the subsidy policies of other countries from speeding up the process of removing uneconomic sections of the industry. Second, they would prevent those other subsidy policies from killing those sections of the industry which lay between the margin of profitability in a free trade world and that in a world in which subsidized competition was being faced. The first of these effects may be worth achieving in some circumstances, for example, if labour is being released from the industry more quickly than it can be absorbed in other parts of the economy, but generally it is hardly worth adopting a subsidy policy simply to secure a change in the rate of decline. Only the second effect is always worth seeking.

At the time of writing it does not appear that the shipping types which represent an economic use of British resources have, by and large, been rendered non-competitive by the subsidy policies of others. The situation, however, is one which needs watching as a continuation of the shipping recession may lead to an increase in the number of countries giving subsidies and to increases in subsidies in countries which already have adopted subsidies. If this does not happen, the position will remain that with a few exceptions the British ships which are adversely affected by the subsidy policies of other countries are uneconomic. Compensating subsidies to British shipping would, therefore, preserve the uneconomic sections of the industry and retard, or prevent, the change to more competitive ship types.

(d) *Evasion*

Evasion means taking action to avoid the effects of subsidies and discrimination by concentrating upon those trades and ship types which are the least affected. In a world in which disturbances to the free competitive pattern are increasing rapidly, evasion may be little more than an ordered retreat and need supplementing by other means if a mercantile marine is to be preserved. Without under-estimating in any way the seriousness of the situation, either in the 1930s or in the 1950s, it is yet true that evasive action was possible and fleets which took such action were able to grow in the face of both subsidies and discrimination.

Evasion is somewhat more difficult for the British fleet as a whole than for any other. This is partly because of the greater size of the British fleet and its participation in most branches of world shipping. The main reason, however, is that in most cases for a single British line to avoid the consequences of the shipping policies of other countries in one trade means competing directly with British shipping in another trade; there are certain inhibitions among British shipowners regarding such a course. Apart from these inhibitions, if one British line preserves its position in total only at the expense of another line, that has not necessarily benefited British shipping as a whole. On the other hand, the general trend of world trade is upwards, providing opportunities for expansion, while if the line taking the evasive action does come into competition with another British line it will usually also compete with the shipping of other countries and so has the possibility of securing a net benefit for British shipping. It must be recorded as a matter for regret that British shipping companies have not more frequently taken evasive action in the past. For the immediate future the opportunities for evasive action seem great enough that there is no necessary reason why the shipping policies of other countries should prevent the growth of British shipping as a whole.

Epilogue: The Future

SHIPPING AND THE COMMON MARKET

How will the future prospects of British shipping be affected if Britain joins the European Common Market? The question is unanswerable in concrete terms, although some observations may be made.

First, if shipping freights to British ports are higher than rates to Continental ports it may well become cheaper to route either or both British imports and exports through Continental ports. Such a difference in rates could arise either because British ports were less efficient than Continental ports or because conferences covering trades to British ports insisted on higher rates. If the reason why goods are transhipped in Europe is the level of British port costs, British ocean shipping will be directly damaged unless it can participate fully in the trades to Continental ports, that is, can start services from those ports before the Continental shipping lines expand to match the expanded trade. If the reason for the change in routing is higher freight charges by conferences covering British trades the diversion itself can be avoided if the shipowners recognize the position.

Second, changes in world trading patterns resulting from the Common Market will alter the demand for shipping on trade routes in different ways. The external trade of the Common Market as a whole will increase if the increment to the imports of each country within the Market resulting from rising incomes exceeds the decline in imports from countries outside the Market from diversion of trade caused by tariff reductions within the area. If this happens, there will be a greater trade in which British shipping can participate provided it can secure a share of the trade to Continental ports. If the increment in the external trade of the area due to rising incomes falls short of the decrement due to changing tariffs, British shipping will find competition keener for the smaller trade volume. British trade as a whole is likely to increase with its Common Market partners but to decrease with other countries. This will provide new opportunities for short-sea shipping and the ports on the east coast of England, but will entail difficulties for ocean shipping, particularly for liners, unless more services to Continental ports can be started.

Epilogue: The Future

Third, on almost any assumption about trade trends it is probable that British liners will have increased competition from European-owned vessels and that the conference umbrella will become less effective as a protective device. The main competition is likely to come from Dutch shipping which has expanded since the war much more rapidly than has British (see Table 53). Italian shipping will also provide keen competition.

Fourth, the Common Market as a whole will be in a stronger position than is Britain alone to bargain with other countries which are paying subsidies or operating discriminatory practices. However, the extent to which the shipping policies of countries other than America have created problems for British shipping is limited and any gain from a reversal of those policies would be similarly limited. Further, the gains will not be reserved for British shipping, but will have to be fought for in competition with the shipping of other non-subsidizing nations.

Clearly the points above do not constitute a full survey of the possibilities and the slight discussion provides no basis for a firm forecast. Nevertheless, certain conclusions are possible. First, the Common Market is unlikely to provide any great new opportunities for British *ocean* shipping. Second, British shipping will probably have to fight to retain what it holds at present. Third, if the signs of change listed at the beginning of this Epilogue are delusive British entry to the Common Market may provide the *coup de grâce* to much of British shipping, particularly liners. In short, the Common Market is more of a challenge than an opportunity for British shipowners, but not a challenge which should overwhelm them unless they decide that it shall.

The Contribution of British Shipping to the Balance of Payments

THE method used in calculating the contribution of British shipping to the balance of payments is set out in Table 55. The credit items consist of the expenditures in foreign currency which would have to be made if all British trade was handled by foreign ships and the losses of foreign exchange at present earned by British ships. The debit items are in two parts. In Part A are the foreign exchange expenditures now made which would be saved, and the foreign exchange which it is estimated would be earned from foreign ship-owners, if all British trade was handled by foreign ships. The differ-ence between the credit items and debit items of Part A is the amount by which net foreign exchange receipts would have been lower or payments higher in the absence of a British fleet. The debit items in Part B consist of the payments at present made to foreigners for British shipping services less the foreign exchange receipts from foreigners at present. The difference between the total of the credit items and the sum of debit items A and B is the additional cost to the balance of payments which would have arisen in any year had the British fleet not existed, that is, it is the contribution of the fleet to the balance of payments.

Most of the items shown in the table do not require further com-ment and figures are available for them for the three years 1952, 1958 and 1960, for which the calculation is made in Table 56. Items 10 and 13, however, require further comment. If all British trade was carried in foreign ships, as an offset to the foreign exchange used in freight payments would be the purchase by those ships of stores in British ports. A figure is available for actual purchases, item 13, and also for the percentage of tonnage entered and cleared at British ports which was foreign owned. Item 10 is then calculated by dividing the actual expenditure by the percentage of entrances and clearances which was foreign owned and multiplying by 100. The actual expenditure is shown as a deduction from debit items B instead of a credit because doing so preserves the significance of the difference between the credit items and the debit items A.

The main items for which information is not available are 1 and 9. Gross freight payments on imports are not recorded in British statistics. A direct estimate of the amount for 1952 is available,[1] but it is apparently calculated by grossing up on the basis of the freights

TABLE 55. Method of calculating shipping's foreign exchange contribution

---

Credits

1. Total freight disbursements on imports.
2. Earnings of British ships in carrying British exports.
3. Earnings of British ships in cross trades.
4. Fares paid by British passengers to British and foreign ships.
5. Fares received from foreign passengers on British ships.
6. Charter hire received from abroad for British ships.

Debits

   A
7. Disbursements abroad of British ships.
8. Charter hire paid to foreign shipowners.
9. Consumption of imported goods by British and foreign ships in British ports.
10. Disbursements by foreign shipowners in British ports if all British trade handled by foreign ships.

   B
11. Freight on imports paid to foreign ships.
12. Fares paid to foreign shipowners by British passengers.
13. *Less* disbursements by foreign shipowners in British ports.

---

earned by foreign ships and the tonnage of such ships entered at British ports. This method does not take account of the greater British participation in the trades in which freight receipts per ton of shipping entered are high, for example, liner trades, than in those in which freight per ton of shipping (not per ton of cargo) is low. If the same method is used for 1958, it produces a figure 10 per cent lower than is given for that year by the addition of the payments to foreign shipowners and the receipts of British shipowners, for carrying British imports. These figures are available from the Treasury and the Chamber of Shipping respectively and their sum is presumably

[1] See H. F. Karreman, *Methods for Improving World Transportation Accounts, Applied to 1950–1953*, National Bureau of Economic Research (New York, 1961), table 28, p. 72.

Appendix

TABLE 56. Contribution of British shipping to the balance of payments, 1952, 1958, 1960

Item	1952 £m.	1958 £m.	1960 £m.
Credits			
1. Freight on imports	345	408	453
2. Export freights of British ships	145	150	148
3. Cross-trades freight earnings	305	339	345
4. Fares from British passengers	32	34	32
5. Fares from foreign passengers	43	51	53
6. Charter hire of British ships	17	23	26
Total credits	887	1,005	1,057
Debits			
A			
7. Disbursements abroad	234	291	308
8. Charter hire of foreign ships	54	137	195
9. Consumption of imports	56	38	40
10. Disbursements by foreign shipowners	115	145	140
Total debits A	459	611	683
Total cost to balance of payments if all shipping services had been provided by foreign ships	428	394	374
B			
11. Import freights paid to foreigners	132	172	193
12. Fares paid to foreign shipowners	6	6	6
13. *Less* actual disbursements by foreign shipowners	− 70	− 72	− 74
Total debits B	68	106	125
Additional cost to the balance of payments if shipping disappeared, i.e. contribution of British shipping to the balance of payments	360	288	249

Sources: *United Kingdom Balance of Payments: 1958 to 1960*, Cmnd. 1329; 1959 to 1961, Cmnd. 1671: Chamber of Shipping, *Annual Report* (1961–2). Supplemented by own estimates.

very close to the freight cost of British imports. For this reason, the figure for 1952 has been lifted by 10 per cent to bring it into line with the 1958 result. For item 9 the only information available is of oil bunkers shipped at British ports and although this is only a part of the total import cost of maintaining a shipping fleet, it has had to be treated as the whole.

The interpretation of these results is given in Chapter VII, pp. 185–7.

Bibliography

THE following is a list of some important books and reports on shipping, most of which were consulted in writing this book. Those publications which are marked with an asterisk are not readily available in this country, but all are available from either the publishers or foreign libraries.

BOOKS

BEHRENS, C. B. A., *Merchant Shipping and the Demands of War* (London, 1955). This is the volume on merchant shipping in the British war history series.

EVERSHEIM, F., *Auswirkungen der Schiffahrts-Subventionierung* (Bremen, 1958). English and German text. English title, 'Effects of Shipping Subsidisation'.

FAYLE, C. E., *The War and the Shipping Industry* (London, 1927).

FISSER, F. M., *Trampschiffahrt* (Bremen, 1957). English and German text. English title, 'Tramp Shipping'.

GORTER, WYTZE, *United States Shipping Policy* (New York, 1956).

GRIPAIOS, H., *Tramp Shipping* (London, 1959).

*INSTITUT FÜR KONJUNKTURFORSCHUNG, *Der Wettbewerb in der Seeschiffahrt* (Jena, 1940). This German book is an indispensable source of material on shipping before 1939.

KEILHAM, W., *Norway and the World War* (Oslo, 1927).

KOOPMANS, T., *Tanker Freight Rates and Tankship Building* (Haarlem, 1939).

*LATTY, JEAN, *Traité d'économie maritime* (Paris, 1954). French text.

MANCE, SIR OSBORNE, *International Sea Transport* (London, 1945). This is an important, but apparently neglected, volume.

NIELSEN, R. E., *Oil Tanker Economics* (Bremen, 1959). English text.

*NORTH WESTERN UNIVERSITY, *The Economic Value of the United States Merchant Marine* (Evanston, 1961). A symposium. Appeared after this book was finished.

419

Bibliography

POWELL, L. H., *The Shipping Federation. A History* (London, 1950).

*RADIUS, W. A., *United States Shipping in Trans-Pacific Trade, 1922–1938* (Stanford U.P., 1944).

RICARDO, J., *The Anatomy of the Navigation Laws* (London, 1847).

SAUGSTAD, JESSE E., *Shipping and Shipbuilding Subsidies* (U.S. Department of Commerce, 1932). This is the standard work on the subject.

SMITH, J. RUSSELL, *Influence of the Great War upon Shipping* (New York, 1919).

SVENDSEN, A. S., *Seeverkehr und Schiffahrtswirtschaft* (Bremen, 1958). English and German text. English title, 'Sea Transport and Shipping Economics'.

—, *Skipsfartspolitiken i Norge etter krigen* (Bergen, 1957). Norwegian text.

Professor Svendsen is Norway's leading academic shipping economist. His textbook is necessary reading for all students of shipping economics.

THORBURN, T., *Supply and Demand of Water Transport*, Stockholm School of Economics (Stockholm, 1960). English text. This is also a standard text.

THORNTON, R. H., *British Shipping* (London, 1959). This is the second edition of Mr. Thornton's famous book which first appeared in 1939. It contains a brief history of shipping and an excellent account of the working of a liner organization.

OFFICIAL REPORTS AND HEARINGS

British:

Imperial Shipping Committee, 'Report on the Deferred Rebate System', Cmd. 1802, 1923.

—, 'British Shipping in the Orient' (London, 1939).

Report of the Royal Commission on Shipping Rings, Cmd. 4668, 1909.

Report of the Departmental Committee on Shipping and Shipbuilding, Cd. 9092, 1918.

American:

'Merchant Marine Study and Investigation'. Hearings before a subcommittee of the Senate Committee on Interstate and Foreign Commerce (Washington, 1949–50).

Bibliography

'Merchant Marine Studies'. As above (Washington, 1953).

'Study of the Operations of the Maritime Administration and the Federal Maritime Board'. Hearings before the House Committee on Merchant Marine and Fisheries (Washington, 1955).

'Monopoly Problems in Regulated Industries'. Hearings before the Antitrust Subcommittee of the Committee on the Judiciary, 'Ocean Freight Industry' (Washington, 1959–60). Celler Committee.

'Steamship Conference Study'. Hearings before the Committee on Merchant Marine and Fisheries (Washington, 1959). Bonner Committee.

Report from the Committee on Merchant Marine and Fisheries (Bonner Committee), 'Providing for the Operation of Steamship Conferences', Report No. 498 House of Representatives, 87th Congress (Washington, 1961).

Other Reports:

Chamber of Shipping of the United Kingdom, Reports of Fact Finding Committee (London, 1939). These reports, each of which deals with a separate aspect of shipping, have not been published.

General Council of British Shipping, 'Survey of British Shipping' (London, 1960).

O.E.E.C., 'Report to the Council on the Present Situation of International Maritime Transport' (Paris, 1956). This report was not published by O.E.E.C. and the circulation of the duplicated report was restricted.

—, 'Study on the expansion of the Flags of Convenience fleets and on various aspects thereof' (Paris, 1958).

P.E.P., 'The British Shipping Industry', *Planning*, xxv, no. 437 (November, 1959).

Index

Index

Index

426

Index

Index

Index

75, 79, 377; raising capital, 19, 40, 190; scrapping, 121; shipbuilding industry, 39–40; size and speed, 121, 125; state aid, 19–20, 27, 31–2, 33, 40, 100, 101, 120–2, 125, 135, 188–90, 191, 194, 195, 352, 393; tankers, 75, 79; trade, 19, 23, 32, 39, 92, 117, 128, 194, 202–3, 410; tramps, 88, 109, 275; 1914–18 war, 36–7, 54; 1939–45 war, 139–40, 151, 157, 393
Johnston Warren Lines, 366, 369
Jute, 195

Khedivial Mail Co., 366, 368
King Line, 367, 373
Knight Line, 366
Korea, *see* War
Kulukundis, Messrs., 359–62
Kylsant group, *see* Royal Mail

Labour costs, 266–8, 275–8, 302–21, 383–4, 393–4; availability and quality of data, 2, 3, 302–9 *passim*, 313–16, 383–4; and capital costs, 268–78; composition of, 302–3; and conferences, 269–71, 355; diesel and steam, 81, 83–4, 275, 400–1; and flags of convenience, 142, 210, 215–20, 226, 228, 230–2, 266, 317–18; and growth rates, 321, 383–4, 385 n., 393–4; other international comparisons, 13–14, 19, 22, 35, 42, 73, 84, 88, 95, 100, 102, 104–5, 114, 119–20, 166, 275, 302–3, 313–20, 321; and repair costs, 88, 251–252, 259, 271, 275, 395; sailing and steam, 14, 15–16; and size and speed, 81, 89, 100, 113, 120, 166, 169, 181, 186, 240, 260, 273–7, 358, 401; and subsidies, 72, 104–5, 114, 115, 119–20, 216, 220, 271; per ton-mile, 14, 273; *see also* Cost structure, Crew accommodation, Crew travelling expenses, Hours of work, Liners, Manning, Social charges, Strikes, Tankers, Tramps, Victualling, Wages, *and individual countries*
Labour force, composition of: of British shipping, 13–14, 232, 274, 294–7, 306; of Japanese shipping, 19, 280; of Norwegian shipping, 297, 301–2; of Panholib shipping, 219, 317–18; of U.S. shipping, 19, 216, 274; use of Asian

and other coloured labour, 14, 19, 274, 284, 295–7, 305 n., 306; use of female labour, 297
Labour relations: in ports, 10–11, 237; in shipping, 283–94, 298–9, 320–1; *see also* Labour supply, Strikes
Labour supply: cheap, from abroad, 13–14, 19, 20, 274, 284, 295–7; and compulsory military service, 89, 301–2, 320; control of, and closed shop, 284–287, 289, 292, 298–9; Established Service Scheme, 293, 301, 305–6, 309; fishing and coastwise shipping, 279; hiring, 237 n., 301; Merchant Navy Pool, 301; and mobility of capital, 277–8; shortage, 88–9, 297, 300–1; surplus, 91, 220, 226, 286, 292, 299–301, 411; training, 33, 226–8, 279–80
Lamport and Holt Line, 367, 375
Latvia, 317
Lay-up, 43, 64–7, 80, 83, 91, 93, 107, 115, 160, 186, 220, 251–2, 262, 349; minimum supply price, 64, 251–2, 259, 272; *see also* U.S.A., Reserve Fleet
Lebanon, 194, 210, 214
Liberia, 5, 191, 202, 208, 210, 212, 217, 228, 230–1, 256, 277, 409–10; *see also* Flags of convenience
Liberty ships, 138, 155, 216, 221, 257
Libya, 194
Liechtenstein, 214
Lifespan, *see* Age
Liner Holdings, 370, 371
Liners, 235–50, 269–72, 275–7, 322–58; British, 14–15, 34, 47–8, 54–5, 85–8, 90–1, 106–8, 163–4, 166–7, 250, 359, 360–1, 364–82; building costs, 249–50; cargo, 67–8, 166, 235–6, 240–7, 249–250, 404; chartering of, 231; combined passenger and cargo, 235–7; cost structure, 238–9, 244–7, 267, 269–72, 274–277, 332–4; definition, 235; establishment advantage, 14–15, 34, 278–9, 379; labour costs, 100, 237, 245, 270–271, 274–7, 313, 314–15, 355; operation of, by tramp owners, 68, 88, 157; operation of, as tramps, 181; owners and specialized ships, 243–4, 375; owners and tankers, 77–8, 168, 258 n., 375; owners and tramps, 53, 186–7, 350, 367, 373; ownership, 359, 360–1, 364–82; passenger, 47, 90–1, 100–2,

429

Index

Newsprint, 243
Niarchos companies, 213
Nigerian National Line, and conference, 195
Nitrates, 22
Norddeutscher Lloyd, 115
Norges Rederforbund, 390
Norness Shipping Co., 362
North Atlantic, 1, 16–17, 24, 30, 34, 87, 92, 93, 102, 108, 111, 113–15, 116, 125, 163, 164, 191, 238, 240, 324 n., 342, 343, 365, 371–3, 376–7, 401
Northern Petroleum Tank Steamship Co., 362
Nortraship, 152–4
Norway: Bergen owners, 402–3; bulk carriers, 256; c.i.f. and f.o.b., 34, 204; depreciation, 177, 178, 260; diesel, 80–4, 94, 109, 275, 402; employment of fleet, 34, 41, 61, 64, 93–4, 208, 258, 282, 306, 350, 402, 409–10; exchange rate, 43, 64 n., 66, 84 n., 88, 394; as flag of convenience, 210, 231–2; foreign exchange shortage, 174–5, 222; growth, and share of world tonnage, 5–7, 16, 37, 41, 43, 44, 79–81, 94, 139–140, 156, 158, 165, 167, 176, 195, 208, 221–3, 233, 375, 385, 392, 394, 399–400, 410; labour, 14, 22, 35, 42, 73, 80, 84, 88, 210, 275, 297, 299, 301–12, 314, 317 n., 319–20, 321, 384, 385 n., 394; lay up in various years, 93; liners, 130–1, 167, 258, 278, 375–6; ownership, 350, 382 n.; and Panholib tonnage, 214, 223, 233, 317 n., 389; participation in various trades, 41, 87, 92–3, 128–30, 202–4, 376, 387; profits, 41–3, 76–7, 93–4, 153, 154, 394; raising capital, 43, 76, 80, 94, 130, 171–2, 174–6, 222–3, 402; refrigerated capacity, 165; shipbuilding industry, 175, 279; shipowners' association, 390; state aid, 100, 101, 104, 105, 394, 409; tankers, 75–81, 155 n., 175, 177, 222–3, 402; taxation, 42, 153, 177, 178, 388–389, 391; trade, 92, 117, 178, 202–4, 282, 410; tramps, 22, 34–5, 41, 73, 88, 167, 258, 260, 275, 384; 1914–18 war, 37, 41–3, 44, 386, 394; 1939–45 war, 139–40, 143, 151–4, 158, 387, 394; *see also* Scandinavia
Nourse Line, 366, 367

Ocean S.S. Co., 370–1
Officers, 19, 279–80, 286, 291, 292, 299, 300–1, 308, 310, 312, 317 n.
Oil: British imports of, 70–1, 161–2, 169–70, 409; companies, 47, 75–6, 161, 165, 169, 187, 222–3, 225, 230–2, 255, 262–4, 359–61; countries producing, 226, 409–10; terminals, 169, 261, 264; world trade in, 73, 74, 90, 160–1, 262; *see also* Tankers
Oligopoly, 355
Ore, 162, 198, 243, 256–7, 369
Onassis companies, 213, 220
Operating costs: sail and steam, 13–14, 15–16, 28, 30, 35; steam and diesel, 82–4; in 1914–18 war, 42–3, 48; inter-war, 64, 76; *see also* Cost structure, Size and speed
Organization costs, 238–9, 245, 251, 267, 268
Orient Line, 366–9
Overhead costs (organization and voyage), 238–9, 245–6, 259–60, 267, 269, 275, 323, 399
Over-tonnaging, *see* Tonnage

Pacific, 19, 34, 40, 54, 87, 92, 122, 131–134, 190, 342, 367–70, 376–7, 387; *see also* Far East trades *and individual countries*
Pacific S.N. Co., 103, 124, 366–7, 368, 370
Pakistan, 189,194, 195–6, 199, 200, 205 n.
Palgrave, Murphy and Co., 374
Palm Line, 328, 360–1
Panama, 5, 124, 139, 151, 156, 210, 212, 216, 217, 221, 279, 317–18, 409–10; *see also* Flags of convenience
Panama Canal, 133–4, 367, 387
'Panholib', 211 n.; *see* Flags of convenience
Papayanni Line, 374
Passenger costs, 237–9
Passenger fares, 102, 120, 237–8, 269–270, 332
Passenger traffic: volume of, 47, 91, 163–4; *see also* Air travel, Emigration, Liners
Patris, 201
Pendennis Castle, 240, 374
Peninsular and Oriental S.N. Co., *see* P. and O.

431

Index

payments, 186–7; ballast voyages, 25, 67–8, 112–13; British, 25, 34–5, 47, 70, 73–4, 81, 85–8, 108–13, 134, 166–7, 181, 258, 261, 359–61, 363, 367, 373; building costs, 249–50; charter, 187, 258–9; cost index, 179–81; cost structure, 251, 259–61, 267, 272–7; and decline in coal trade, 70, 73–4, 81, 95; definition, 251; diesel and steam, 83, 109, 113, 275; labour costs, 22, 35, 73, 87–8, 95, 102, 113, 119–20, 166, 252, 272–7, 313, 314–15, 317, 355, 384; and liner owners, 53, 186–7, 350, 367, 373; market, perfection of, 251; operation of liners as, 181; operation of liner services by tramp owners, 68, 88, 157; owners and tankers, 78; ownership, 254, 359–61, 363; Panholib, 167, 221–222; size and speed, 57, 94, 96, 113, 166–7, 173, 181, 186–7, 240–1, 257, 261–2, 274–5, 355, 357–8, 384–5, 404; standardization, 401; world tonnage, 34, 166, 257, 261; *see also* Book values, Bulk carriers, Cargo, Flag discrimination, Freight rates, Lay-up, Profits, Specialization, Subsidies, *and individual countries and trades*

Transfer of registry: to avoid flag discrimination, 200; restrictions on, 155, 171–4, 216, 223, 224, 229–30; *see also* Flags of convenience

Transshipment, *see* Entrepôt trades

Trend lines, 62–3, 72, 94–5, 136, 402

Turkey, 45–6, 99–102, 189, 194, 199, 214

Unemployment, *see* Employment (labour)

Unilever, 328, 361

Union Castle, 200, 240, 272 n., 366–7, 373–4, 395

Union S.S. Co., 131, 366–7, 368–9

United Baltic Corp., 375

United Fruit Co., 211, 230, 231–2, 361

United Molasses group, 360–1, 375

U.S.A.: aid funds and reconstruction of foreign fleets, 151, 189, 190, 193, 225 n.; and conferences, 325–6, 327–8, 331, 332, 336, 338–40; defence requirements, 39, 190, 224, 226–8, 231; growth, and share of world tonnage, 5, 6, 15, 37–9, 62, 122, 129, 134–6,

139–42, 386–7, 392–3, 410; labour, 19, 40, 72, 88, 160, 216–17, 220, 223, 226–228, 245, 274, 282, 314, 316, 318; liners, 124, 130, 244–5, 272, 282; oil companies, 213, 223, 228, 231–2, 360; ownership, 38–9, 79; and Panholib tonnage, 124, 151, 155–6, 211, 213, 214–17, 221, 223–8; participation in various trades, 19, 38, 40, 54, 96, 125, 128, 131–4, 190; profits, 151, 154; raising capital, 39, 101, 123–4, 130–1, 223–4, 225; Reserve Fleet, 5, 62, 155, 157, 158, 387, 410 n.; ship sales, 38–9, 142, 149, 150, 155–6, 216, 222; shipbuilding industry, 38, 124, 224; size and speed, 123, 125; state aid, 39, 54, 62, 72, 96, 100, 101, 122–4, 125, 128–136, 151, 188–91, 194, 197–9, 202, 224, 225, 282, 393; tankers, 79, 80, 123–4, 225, 282; taxation, 223, 388; trade, 23, 27, 37, 92, 101, 117, 125, 129–35, 194, 197–8, 202–4, 282, 410; tramps, 88, 123–4, 151, 282; 1914–18 war, 36–9, 54, 122, 128, 135, 386; 1939–45 war, 139–42, 151, 154, 387; *see also* Emigration

U.S.S.R., *see* Russia

Variable costs (as distinct from overhead costs), 238–9, 245–6, 259–60

Variable costs, internationally ('national costs'), 266 ff.

Vestey interests, *see* Blue Star

Venezuela, 194, 207, 329

Victualling, 14, 302, 306–7

Voyage charter, *see* Charter

Voyage costs: and cruising, 91; diesel and steam, 83; and freight rates, 67–8, 83; sailing and steam, 35; *and see* Cost structure

Voyage profits: definition, 181; distinguished from total earnings, 183; *and see* Profits

Wages: composition of, 307–8; of foreign and coloured labour, 14, 274, 295–7, 313; and hours, 307–8, 310–11; increases, 14, 42, 220, 291, 293, 308–9, 320, 355, 358; national and port rates, 14, 285, 296, 402; reductions, 85, 220, 226, 292, 293, 309; and social charges, Italian, 119–20, 302, 304; and total